Take a Look

Fifth Edition Observation and Portfolio Assessment in Early Childhood

Sue Martin
Centennial College

Pearson Canada
Toronto

To
Pauline Brown
Nursery Class
Wanstead Church School
London E.11
England

because she practises what I preach.

Library and Archives Canada Cataloguing in Publication

Martin, Sue, 1951–
   Take a look : observation and portfolio assessment in early
childhood / Sue Martin.—5th ed.

Includes bibliographical references and index.
ISBN 978-0-321-53825-3

   1. Child development—Evaluation—Textbooks. 2. Observation (Psychology)—Methodology—
Textbooks. 3. Behavioural assessment of children—Textbooks. I. Title.

BF722.M37 2010   305.231   C2008-906274-4

ISBN-13: 978-0-321-53825-3
ISBN-10: 0-321-53825-0

Vice-President, Editorial Director: Gary Bennett
Editor-in-Chief: Ky Pruesse
Editor, Humanities and Social Sciences: Joel Gladstone
Marketing Manager: Loula March
Associate Editor: Brian Simons
Production Editor: Melissa Hajek
Copy Editor: Maryan Gibson
Proofreader: Lisa LaFramboise
Production Coordinator: Avinash Chandra
Composition: Macmillan Publishing Solutions
Permissions Research: Sandy Cooke
Art Director: Julia Hall
Cover Design: Anthony Leung
Cover Image: Veer Inc.

For permission to reproduce copyrighted material, the publisher gratefully acknowledges the copyright holders listed on page 470, which is considered an extension of this copyright page.

1 2 3 4 5   13 12 11 10 09

Printed and bound in the United States of America.

Contents

Preface

Take a Look: Observation and Portfolio Assessment in Early Childhood is intended for people who seek a deep and reflective approach to working and living with young children. This will include readers from a variety of experiences and backgrounds: early childhood educators, student teachers, home childcare providers, early learning personnel kindergarten and elementary school teachers (K–3), parents of young children, resource teachers, early interventionists, educational psychologists, child and youth workers, and social workers.

The book provides a focused approach to authentic assessment in early childhood. This is consistent with current research and exemplary practice. Its detailed coverage of observation methods leads the reader to develop skills in seeing, recording, and understanding the development of young children. The book also reflects a sympathetic understanding of childhood and encourages adults to be responsive to the individual needs of each child.

Take a Look aims to help readers achieve the following general outcomes:

- Develop a philosophy of assessment of children in their early years.
- Compare and contrast a variety of different observation and recording methods, and select and use those that best meet their needs.
- Create a comprehensive portfolio record-keeping system suited to the needs of an early-childhood agency, parents and other stakeholders.
- Analyze observational and contextual data in order to create holistic and sympathetic assessments of individual children.
- Demonstrate the use of observation and portfolio documentation as a measure of program accountability.

In philosophy, *Take a Look* emphasizes the importance of taking the time to gather pertinent information about individual children so that we can understand them holistically and contextually. Armed with this knowledge, the adults in the children's lives can learn to respond more fully to those children.

Behind the development of this text is a belief that children are competent, that we should build on their emerging skills, that play is the central vehicle for the child's learning, that children's natural curiosity leads to meaningful inquiry, and that adults need to understand and be responsive to young children's needs. Facilitating, guiding, documenting behaviour and events, promoting higher cognitive functioning, providing children with a positive role model, designing optimal environments, and offering an emotionally and physically safe place to be are essential components of the educator's responsibilities.

While components of *Take a Look* are informational and skill-building, it also encourages educators to think critically about issues in early care and education. Not all content offers definitive answers to contentious issues; the reader must consider the issue and from their research and experience make their own decisions.

Educators today are presented with a number of challenges that require them to be current, skilled, and organized. Consequently, it is increasingly important to have observation and documentation systems that are effective and efficient while remaining sensitive and responsive. Such systems also help to improve programming, increase accountability, provide mechanisms for appropriate assessment, identify causes for concern, raise awareness of children's different needs, monitor developmental progress and support optimal environments for children.

While some standardized assessment tools are needed in some situations, the emphasis here is on a contextualized understanding of each child's competence. Observation and portfolio documentation provide full, meaningful, and authentic ways of assessing children's development. This approach also gives educators a clear idea of how to support a child's emerging skills, how to deliver a curriculum according to his or her individual styles, and when to plan to introduce meaningful learning experiences.

Children are most frequently found in groups and *Take a Look* endeavours to provide tools for the educator to observe both the individual child and the group. Watching group interactions provides the observer with the opportunity to understand play behaviours, communications, and group dynamics. *Take a Look* focuses on building on the positive; however, the reality of the educator's job requires that they observe signs, symptoms, and indicators that warrant careful documentation.

The *Take a Look* approach will help you to avoid hasty decisions that affect children negatively, judgments of behaviour based on insufficient evidence, and planning that is unresponsive to children's individual needs or developmental stages. Try to be thoughtful and reflective as an observer while honouring your intuitive responses to children.

Take a Look takes advantage of recent research in neuroscience, as well as up-to-date perspectives on children's development. You will find that the contents follow current trends in curriculum development and guidance strategies. *Take a Look* shows how authentic assessment process can be used as either the central approach to assessment or to complement system-wide formal assessments.

New features of the fifth edition

Hearing from people who have used this text, people from New Brunswick to New Zealand, from British Columbia to Britain, has been both exciting and challenging. Most of these people are in several different fields of work associated with young children; I have learned much from them and from new research, and my response to all lies in the following changes I've made to this edition:

- Content has been added to help the reader's observation and portfolio assessment skill-building.
- The potential for using technology for recording and analyzing observational data has been more clearly identified.
- There is greater scope in how to represent observational data in graphic formats.
- There is broader coverage of the evaluation of children's environments, with examples that challenge aspects of current practice.
- Functional assessments for children who have special needs are explained more fully.
- There is better response to educators who are experiencing stress in teaching a prescribed curriculum while at the same time having to document each child's achievement and demonstrate accountability.

- The running record (reading), as well as observable literacy skills, have been included.
- The copious lists of children's observable characteristics have been broken down into more manageable sub-lists.
- Many new photographs of children in action, in situations that might warrant making useful observations and recordings, have been included.
- The steps to take to develop a personal philosophy of assessment in early childhood have been included.
- We've considered the ethical challenges, as well as professional issues, related to recording, sharing, analyzing, and storing records.
- There is general improvement of the content, format, and presentation of the material.

General features of *Take a Look*

Every chapter begins with **Focus Questions** that enable readers to review their current understanding and skill level, followed by **Learning Outcomes** that summarize the knowledge readers will gain from the chapter.

Clear explanations of the methods of observation and information gathering are essential to understanding, choosing, and using each. **Definition boxes and Key Features boxes** help readers find basic information quickly and efficiently.

All data collection techniques are explained and are presented in their positive and negative aspects; concise **Advantages and Disadvantages lists** clearly indicate the strengths and weaknesses of each. The lists will help students select appropriate methods and avoid common pitfalls.

Child Development Focus boxes review standard methods of observing and recording data and **Taking a Special Look boxes** give information on how to observe children with special needs.

Observation Samples that demonstrate good practice for the core observational and recording methods are included in most chapters. As every observation is unique to the child, the situation, the observer, and the chosen methodology, an "ideal" is difficult to supply, but all the samples have identifiable strengths. Learners are asked pertinent questions to help them appreciate the strengths and challenges of each sample.

Weblinks to useful Internet sites are offered at the end of each chapter. They will reinforce and extend students' understanding of that chapter.

Instructor's Supplements

Take a Look is accompanied by an Instructor's Resource CD-ROM with documents for assisting observation and the following supplements:

Instructor's Manual   With history and teaching notes, information on assessment, and lists of additional resources, the Instructor's Manual provides answers to the chapter-opening Focus Questions.

The Instructor's Manual also offers bountiful material for power-point or overhead use. Examples of observations have been added to assist learners understand the potential of some of the methods. A whole chapter about measuring outcomes, which was included in earlier editions of *Take a Look*, is available here. This may help educators to demonstrate the achievement of standards or program outcomes.

Test Item File   In addition to test questions and an answer key for each chapter, the Test Item File includes rubrics for offering feedback for authentic assessment of the student educator's learning.

CourseSmart   CourseSmart is a new way for instructors and students to access textbooks online anytime from anywhere. With thousands of titles across hundreds of courses, CourseSmart helps instructors choose the best textbook for their class and give their students a new option for buying the assigned textbook as a lower cost eTextbook. For more information, visit www.coursesmart.com.

Acknowledgments

Much has changed since the first edition. Jacob has gone where all good dogs end up—dog heaven. Our older child, Simon, is saving lives as a flight paramedic and is now married to lovely Jennifer and they have a wonderful son, Thomas. Our daughter, Cassandra, has completed her masters in Justice Administration and lives happily with three cats she observes closely. Andrew, my husband, who has supported me through more than 30 years in education, has continued to provide administrative expertise and attention to detail with research and bibliographies. Thank you for all your help—there is little reward! My dad always supports my work, even if he disagrees with my opinions: thanks, I appreciate you so much!

These are the times when you find out who your real friends are. Mine function in different corners of education: university professors, government employees, students, and other folks starting out on their teaching careers. Some of the very best have been Esther Keys and Patricia Corson.

I am most grateful to the early childhood instructors who reviewed this edition of *Take a Look*, supplying useful ideas for improvement:

Cathy Coulthard; Leslie Kopf-Johnson; Charlotte Marcella, Vanier College; Heather Houston, Canadore College.

I also wish to express my thanks to the editorial team at Pearson Education Canada: Brian Simons, Melissa Hajek, Maryan Gibson, and Lisa LaFramboise, who worked very hard to complete the fifth edition.

Thanks also to Winnie the Pooh, who offered the insight, "It's best to know what you are looking for before you look for it." The greatest wisdom can come from where you least expect it.

1 Observation: An Introduction

Thomas explores the blocks and discovers what he can build. His imagination is growing and the pretend play that results allows for play partnerships.

The children's rights supersede your observer rights. Be respectful of the children.
University of Alberta, Faculty of Education, Child Study Centre (2008)

You well know that the teacher in our method is more of an observer than a teacher; therefore this is what the teacher must know, how to observe.
Maria Montessori (1913)

Skilled observers gather information in a systematic, detailed and precise way while recognizing their own inevitable subjectivity.
Mary Fawcett (1996)

People Watching

A mother gazes at her newborn infant. The baby looks at her. At first the baby's sight is unfocused, yet she is attracted by the configuration of her mother's face. The infant is, perhaps, "programmed" to have this interest. It encourages social interaction and leads to emotional bonding. Drawn to faces and signs of movement, the infant learns through watching as well as through her other senses. All babies are born to be people watchers. Mother and baby look at each other!

"Don't stare," says a mother to her young child, in the expectation that she can shape the child's instinctive **behaviour**. Socially acceptable behaviour requires that observation be subtle. Required behaviour is learned more by example than by verbal reinforcement; watching others is integral to the process of social learning.

Have you ever watched the hellos and goodbyes being said at an airport? If you were not too caught up in your own emotions, you might have wondered about the demonstrations of feeling, the honesty of expressions, or the social or cultural determination of particular behaviours. What are the stories behind all those faces? If you have ever done this kind of thing, then you too are an observer.

"I did not expect her to do that," "She must be frustrated to react that way," and "He is a very quiet person" are all informal but subjective interpretations of observations. We all observe, deduce, and respond in all our communications with other people. Most adults go through this process without really considering what is happening.

The same process occurs when we are more conscious of making observations. The significant difference is that, when we use observation as a method for collecting information, we must do it carefully, systematically, accurately, and as objectively as possible.

Why Observe?

We observe children because we are drawn to them; we want to protect, nurture, and teach them. Every adult involved with young children in any role or capacity will observe the children for somewhat different reasons.

Twelve core reasons for observing young children

1. to learn about children and their development
2. to understand each individual child and each child within a group
3. to track developmental patterns of progression and regression
4. to help create a developmental profile or portfolio about a child
5. to uncover the process of learning (combining observable actions and inferences about how a child is thinking)
6. to provide data for authentic assessments
7. to identify any cause for concern about one or more children
8. to recognize group dynamics
9. to provide protection, as well as appropriate environments
10. to refine our role with children and establish who we are in their lives
11. to offer data for the measurement of educational or other elements of progress that are interpreted at a group level (e.g., Early Development Instrument)
12. to assess the achievement of learning outcomes, benchmarks, curriculum expectations, and other standards required at the end of a program

Below we expand upon the list and further explain the importance of observing children. For ease of managing the ideas, we have created subcategories.

Why adults observe individual children

We may observe informally from a distance, or we may see what occurs when we are engaged with the child; and we

- are sentimental and have strong bonds with the child.
- are drawn to the child's face and behaviour.
- wish to understand the child as an individual.
- focus on the child's competence—what she can do, rather than what she cannot do.
- gaze with love (as a parent/grandparent, etc.).
- observe to know what interests the child.
- become more playful.
- wish to tune into the world of the child.
- find the complexity of the child's play both engaging and revealing.
- can engage within the child's own rhythm and flow of activity.
- acknowledge how special each child is.
- determine the child's concentration/attention levels.
- can appreciate the child's **holistic** development, as well as his development in each domain of development.
- wish to understand every part of the child's development, as well as the holistic picture of the child.
- want to determine the child's talents, individual style, and way of being smart.

- deduce how a child is feeling.
- gain insight into the child's temperament, personality, and individuality.
- have a deep desire to meet the needs of the child.
- may want to select a developmentally appropriate gift for the child.

(Later in this chapter, we will examine the importance of focusing on the individual in more detail.)

Why adults observe groups of children

We may participate with the group of children while we watch them, or we may take a step back and observe from a short distance. We

- find their activity fascinating.
- see that there are leaders and followers.
- notice the children's interactions in everyday situations, as well as in play, in learning, and at other times.
- enjoy seeing complex play sequences involving imagination, pretence, and different realities.
- may feel sentimental or invested in the group.
- can find that their behaviour reminds us of our own childhood.
- want to understand how they relate to each other.
- notice elements of competition.
- notice when children assist each other, and we can help **scaffold** their learning.
- have an understanding of the power dynamics of the group.
- want to determine if any children are being included or excluded.
- can address bullying.
- can develop strategies for "managing" the group.
- can enhance the children's play and the learning they gain through meaningful, spontaneous, child-directed activity.

(We mention a variety of recording strategies for children in groups in Chapters 4, 5, 6, and 7.)

How observation can assist the professional's work

There are many roles and a wide range of responsibilities that professionals have with children. Broadly, we

- learn by observing; the children themselves are our finest learning tool.
- build our observation and recording skills in order to improve the child's experience (possibly with an Individual Program Plan or an Individual Educational Plan for the child), meet the child's needs by making whatever accommodations are necessary, and support the child's learning (in practice, this is called program planning).

- appreciate the developmental sequences and patterns described in textbooks.
- appreciate the factors that shape the child's behaviour and understand every observation with awareness of culture and context.
- learn about what to look for by observing children and blending that information with class-based learning, print materials, and technologically assisted resources.
- examine the usefulness of theoretical models that explain observable development.
- test our own theories about children and their development.
- conduct action research using targeted observations.
- learn to use **normative profiles** carefully after observing a very wide range of behaviour.
- contribute to large-scale observational data collection in a **group level measure**.

How observation helps us to address health and safety

- ensuring the child's safety and preventing difficulties before they arise
- establishing a daily baseline for the child's health and condition
- helping us to check the child's health status and to establish individual growth patterns
- alerting us to how the child uses materials
- providing knowledge of what the child eats and drinks
- identifying risk-taking behaviour
- alerting us to safety concerns in the environment

(These issues will appear again at several points through the book.)

Why observation contributes to individual assessment

Whatever the backdrop—school or agency—there are several reasons to observe children as part of their own assessment process:

- Naturalistic observations ensure that observations are contextualized, not analyzed without that context being understood.
- Authentic and current assessment needs to be based on recent observations that capture meaningful developmental information. Everyday situations enable a child to play spontaneously and reveal the complexities of her thinking and feeling. These complexities can be captured by observing the child in natural situations more effectively than in formal testing scenarios.
- Both family and professional observations help round out our understanding of the child. Family information, photographs, the child's own work, and many other related artifacts provide much better understanding than a cold numerical test score.

- Ensuring both the validity and reliability of an assessment approach requires that all data is collected as objectively as possible and is seen within its natural context. Skilled observers can record the child acting in a way that is typical for him and record that data as objectively and meaningfully as possible. While many standardized tests are shaped around an understanding of developmental profiles, they often require a child to continue with the test until she fails one or more test item. Naturalistic observations focus on the level of a child's current success, rather than on what she cannot yet accomplish.

- We often need to determine the frequency, duration, severity, or appropriateness of one or more behaviours. We can do this using the correct observation method (event sampling).

- Evaluation of the child's behaviour with reference to valid and reliable norms may be part of an assessment process, but norms should not be used as benchmarks for success or to indicate what the child "should" be doing.

- When professionals record and analyze observations using appropriate methods, observation can complement standardized assessments.

- We may want to confirm or contradict the outcome of a standardized test.

(See portfolio assessment in Chapter 8. Standardized assessment is reviewed in Chapter 11.)

How observation helps adults guide children

Guiding children is about nurturing, caring, being there, supporting, and mentoring. Observing children can help us to better understand children and guide them appropriately, in these ways:

- We learn how to nurture the child by reading her body language, verbal utterances, and individual cues.

- We determine when the child needs help by his actions and other signals.

- We offer supports and mentoring when we observe that they are needed.

- We observe and support the building of children's self-esteem through personal achievement.

- We see how play can be promoted or extended for therapeutic purposes, as well as healthy development.

- We see when to establish rules and how to set boundaries by observing carefully.

- We observe communication skills as we see children talk, convey meaning through body language, and listen to others.

- We develop appropriate guidance strategies and formal policies based on many observations of children at different stages of development.

- We decide when we need to intervene or stand back.

- We see the child's moral understanding as we observe her interactions in play and "work."

- We ensure that consequences for behaviour are appropriate.

- Most importantly, we establish the best way of scaffolding the child's learning.

How observation can help us appreciate specific aspects of the child's behaviour, as well as the child's holistic development

Focusing on particular developmental domains can help us understand what is happening in that domain for a particular child, but it can also contribute to our understanding of that domain and lead us to internalize typical patterns of behaviour. These are the specific domains and features of development that we are looking for when we observe children:

- gross motor skills and mobility
- fine motor skills and hand–eye coordination
- self-help skills
- temperament and personality development
- behaviours connected with the child's thinking skills
- facial expressions, body language, and communication of meaning
- child's social skills, self-regulatory skills, social and emotional intelligence, and empathy and altruism
- communication skills, including language acquisition and stage of understanding and using words
- language and the understanding of grammar and social conventions in speech
- achievements and self-esteem
- sexual development
- place in family/group
- aesthetic appreciation, use of symbolism and representation
- spontaneous artwork
- guided craft skills
- ability to follow instructions, response to rules and requests
- reading skills, comprehension, and writing skills (decoding and encoding)
- ability in scientific discovery, from the most simple sensory level to the most complex abstract level of functioning
- ability to learn from mistakes, leading to insights about thinking and making decisions
- imagination and pretending
- mathematical thinking (such as shape, colour, mass, seriation, construction, sorting, matching, design, etc.)
- moral understanding and socially acceptable behaviour

(In Chapter 2, we will look at each of these behavioural domains as we explore the link between observation and development, and later when we summarize observational recordings.)

How observation can help determine our role

- Understanding who we are in the child's life is essential. We must ask ourselves, am I a sister, aunt, uncle, mother, father, babysitter, neighbour, grandparent, early childhood educator, assistant, program volunteer, nurse, special educator, resource teacher, camp counsellor, play therapist, early interventionist, mental health expert, teacher, mentor, after-school caregiver, swim instructor, psychologist, speech therapist, minister, religious instructor, vacation amusement facilitator, party clown, librarian, doctor, physical therapist, art teacher, family resource worker, dance teacher, coach, or occupational therapist? Our designated role is the starting point of establishing how we relate to the child.

- Our responsibilities may be shaped by the particular role we have and the professional basis for that role; however, observing how the child relates to other children, and to us, will help shape our role.

- When we understand our role and responsibilities, we can then determine how to carry out that role; observing other colleagues may also help.

- While constantly observing the child, we need to establish a leadership role with him. Observing him and reflecting on our own behaviour will lead to seeing how to guide the child, support his learning, keep him safe, or whatever else our role entails.

- Sometimes the child tries to shape our role too much, and this can lead us to cross professional boundaries.

(The observer's role is discussed a little later in this chapter.)

How observation can help to identify causes for concern

Having gained observation skill, we will refine our knowledge of child development and of what is "typical" behaviour. We may also notice when something isn't quite the way it should be. Our observations may lead to identifying a real concern or to checking out a hunch. Observations may

- be part of a screen for developmental concerns (leading to early intervention).
- help us notice behavioural challenges that are more persistent than is typical.
- be part of the recorded information about a child's challenging behaviour.
- help us understand possible causes or triggers of a behaviour.
- pinpoint changes in a child's demeanour that lead us to make further observations.
- help us check out our hunches about a child's needs or problems.
- take time, but they can help reveal details of a child's communication challenges.
- be part of an assessment process that determines a child's need of special education services.
- document behaviours or physical signs of potential abuse or neglect.
- help us see how traumatic or worrying events shape a child's behaviour.

(See Chapter 10 for details about identifying a range of concerns through observation.)

Why observation can support team communication about a child's development

In an ideal world, we would all have access to the human and practical resources we need to do an exemplary job. But that is not always the reality. We do, however, need to make maximum use of what we have to ensure that we do our best to meet the needs of children and their families. Observation can help us to achieve this, in many ways:

- Collaboration, by way of sharing observations and their meanings among a team of professionals, can assist assessment. Also, sharing information with parents can be useful.
- We can observe the child alone, children interacting, children and professionals interacting, children and their parents interacting, and family interactions. The observations themselves help us to refine our communication skills and assist us in working with parents.
- Observations can be recorded and shared with others for improved understanding. Technology can support the recording process and the potential for sharing information with team members, external professionals, and families.
- Parents may easily be encouraged to contribute to the assessment process if they feel that their observations are valid and can contribute to a complete understanding of their child.
- Using observations as the content material, we can share information about how the child is doing—generally, or in relation to an aspect of the program, the other children, etc.
- We can gain important data that contributes to legally required documentation.

(Each of the above items is discussed at numerous points throughout the text.)

Why observation supports effective program evaluation

Here again, observation is the basis of decision-making:

- In program evaluation, there is a heavy demand for an array of different observations. These might include observing individual children, seeing children interacting with each other, noticing children and professionals interacting, and seeing how children and their parents interact, as well as how children use, or are affected by, the physical space (narrative observation methods are useful for this; see Chapter 3).
- The program might be observed for its physical structure, safety practices, health promotion, inclusion or exclusion of children, aesthetics, use of space, and many other aspects. We might use rating scales to determine the degree to which an assessment category is present. (See Chapter 6 for a variety of ways of gathering and managing this information.)
- From time to time we need to make observations so that we can determine if the program has met required standards or outcomes (e.g., curriculum standards or program outcomes).
- We may wish to establish a program's general effectiveness, in which case we need to know what to look for to define "effectiveness" before seeking any evidence of it.
- We may need to observe and then evaluate the program's use of space for its safety and learning potential. Prepared checklists are available for this purpose, but they might not suit your particular purpose—select an observational tool carefully.
- We observe the patterns of the day so we can base routines on children's needs.

- We make observations in order to determine the effect of the environment on the child; we may also call in experts to measure toxins, moulds, and other contaminants.

- We must monitor the program's inclusion policies and practices regarding the accommodation of children of diverse backgrounds, abilities, and needs.

- Programs may establish their own criteria for program effectiveness based on the staff's understanding of children's developmental stages; these usually depend on the creation of an observational checklist. (See Chapter 5 for checklist methodology.)

- For a strong program, we need to establish the program's success using a set of benchmarks or standards. We gather the data by observing children's behaviour and then reviewing that behaviour in relation to specified program outcomes, such as kindergarten readiness.

- When we use a group/population level measure, we develop a group profile. This requires copious observations and questionnaires to be completed by educators. We can use the outcome of the process to demonstrate the program's effectiveness, the children's readiness for school, and comparisons to other programs or geographic areas. These observations are often dependent on the educator's close knowledge of the child.

(See Chapter 12 to explore program evaluation.)

Principles of Observation

Now that you have a good idea about why we need to observe, you may be wondering about how you should do that. To fulfill the purposes mentioned above, we need to know about a number of methods of recording. We discuss how to choose and use these methods in Chapters 3 to 8. But before that, we need to look at some principles of observation, and then, in Chapter 2, we will explore how we can look for developmental information and come to see that observation and development are intricately entwined.

How we make meaning from what we observe

Perception

Perception is the process of making meaning from sensory information. Observation is the process of gathering sensory information. We tend to rely on visual information, but other senses can offer a fuller observational account.

Observing is not the same as interpreting. We are very familiar with seeing and making inferences all at once; for example, we must do both at once as the basis of decisions as we drive around town. But for effective observation, we need to have discipline because our observation could become unfocused, time-wasting, and judgmental. Plan to observe and record regularly for your benefit and for the children.

Descriptive and analytical language

Our use of language—in particular, how well we articulate our ideas—supports the higher-order mental operations we need. Language and thought have been considered to be partners for centuries, with recent linguists and theorists being challenged to articulate their connection. Karl Kraus, who was a stickler for the use of correct language usage, is reported to have said, "Language is the mother of thought, not its handmaiden" (1909). Lev Vygotsky echoed a somewhat similar view, saying, "Thought development is determined by language, i.e. by the linguistic tools of thought and by socio-cultural experience . . ." (1986). Jean Piaget and many other key developmental theorists and linguists have also delved into this arena. Noam Chomsky claimed that "Language serves essentially for the expression of thought" (1979). More recently, based on his evolutionary studies, Chomsky takes the stance that language most probably precedes most thought. We need language to help us think, and having that language facility allows thought that would probably not otherwise occur—or if it did occur, we would have no language to articulate it. Consequently, we need language to help us both to observe and to record our observations; and we are dependent on our adult cognitive processes and our parallel language facility to think in the necessary higher realm and to make sense of what we recorded.

Constructivist approach

Constructivist theory explains that we make our own individual understanding from direct experience and how we process that experience. "[E]ach individual constructs knowledge rather than receives it from others" (McBrien and Brandt 1997, cited on Association for Supervision and Curriculum Development web site)

When we apply constructivist theory to children, it helps us to appreciate their learning processes and our role in their education. Jean Piaget helped us to understand that there are distinct stages in thinking. Now we have reached adulthood and the maturity and cognitive capacity that allows us to think in a higher realm—what Piaget called formal operations.

The dual processes of **assimilation** (taking in information) and **accommodation** (adjusting previously understood ideas to the new information) are occurring within us almost all the time. They resolve themselves in **equilibration**, a balance between ourselves and our environment. This is the core of our meaning-making ability. These mechanisms allow us to build an internalized version of what we perceive externally.

Thinking skills

We do not operate using higher-order skills all the time, even though we have that capacity. Much of our time, say, at home, we may think in mostly lower-order operations, as we make a cup of coffee, vacuum the floor, or watch television. At other times, such as solving a mystery in a book we are reading, we may use a variety of mental strategies in the middle and higher levels. Many practical activities do not require higher-level skills, but there are many street-smart activities that warrant either middle- or higher-level thought. Working with children, we are likely to use thinking operations of all levels during the day. As students, we may, hopefully, operate at the higher-order level when in class, doing assignments, observing children, analyzing our observations, studying from textbooks, discussing ideas, debating, or even accessing online resources (when we need to think critically about the reliability of the sources we access).

As you review the lists below, try to identify the thinking operations that you will rely on as you improve your observation and assessment skills.

Lower-order thinking involves mental actions such as defining, data collecting, enumerating, measuring, naming, recalling, recognizing, describing, labelling, using cause and effect for a purpose, comparing, sorting, using trial and error, differentiating, recording, and following practical instructions (each based on basic knowledge).

Middle-order thinking involves mental actions such as summarizing, converting, extending, operating, showing, using, articulating, translating, comprehending, applying, explaining, defending ideas, estimating, paraphrasing, organizing, creating systems, sequencing, remembering multiple ideas, data management, calculating, planning, computing, linking actions and reactions, applying standards to data, solving problems, following principles, selecting, inferring, contextualizing, distinguishing, discovering, constructing, demonstrating, manipulating (ideas), modifying, explaining, hypothesizing, generalizing, giving examples, paraphrasing, interpreting, predicting, rewriting, summarizing based on categorizing (each based on comprehension and application).

Higher-order thinking involves mental actions such as analyzing, debating, breaking down, making mental combinations, theorizing, appraising, assessing, formulating, presenting ideas visually, using creative processes, solving theoretical challenges, data analyzing, philosophizing, calculating complex numerical challenges, deconstructing, remembering complex ideas, illustrating (an idea), supporting, concluding, using convergent and divergent skills to solve abstract problems, categorizing, creating a new paradigm, compiling, composing, designing, developing, reorganizing, holding in mind multiple factors, reconstructing, deducing, critiquing, evaluating, explaining, assessing, interpreting, relating, contrasting, defending theories, explaining, diagnosing (each based on analysis, synthesis, or evaluation).

Making inferences about any child involves both understanding and explaining your observations.

> Inference is defined as the attempt to generalize on the basis of limited information. Information is always limited because it is impractical, in terms of time and cost, to obtain total knowledge about everything. If everything were known, there would be no need for inference. (O'Connor 2006)

Perspective

"The way we see things is affected by what we know or what we believe" (Berger 1972). How we approach any new experience is clearly shaped by prior experiences, and those experiences carry with them feelings and associations that are entirely personal. So these things may be brought with us when we observe something new. Our perceptual lens is not entirely objective, but it assists us in understanding what we see.

A challenge for us is that our personal perspectives tend to include biases, even if we are not conscious of them. To become a professional who uses observation as part of the job, it is essential to take time to identify and address any potential biases. Our perspective must be professional and as objective as possible.

Finding meaning through a body of knowledge

If we were to use our own knowledge to make meaning, based on our direct experience of children, we might have some meaningful insights to offer. However, there is a much bigger body of knowledge available to us. For many years, philosophers, linguists, pediatricians, development experts, scientists, researchers, theorists, educators, and others have contributed a broad body of learning that is applicable to our work with children. Using relevant aspects of this knowledge base can help us to see in a different light what we observe. We might explain a particular phenomenon, offer a context for behaviour, or provide a stage framework that we can apply to our observations. While none of the providers of knowledge can offer us an ultimate truth or perfect ideas, some theorists are more reliable or applicable than others.

Your job is to become a developmental expert yourself by reading and absorbing some of the knowledge, creating new knowledge, and finding out where information can be accessed when needed. You need to learn to discern what is a valid and reliable source, and gain skills in using contradictory ideas to debate alternative explanations. You can hold in mind some key theorists and their ideas, using those ideas as a filtering process to reach the understanding you require.

Practice

The more experience we have at observing, the better able we are to make sense of what we see. But we must challenge ourselves to be rigorous in our observation and recording; it is too easy to become sloppy and subjective, especially if we are not monitored either by others or by our own sense of duty.

We have an additional challenge in juggling the role of student and that of practising professional. Students may have time to observe (although they may not feel they have this luxury!), but the professional must often juggle hands-on responsibilities with the children and the need to observe and document what is seen. On the one hand, we need to record observations as objectively as possible; and on the other, we need to apply our higher-order thinking skills to the data we have recorded. There are two distinct steps:

1. observing objectively
2. interpreting and making meaning from the recordings

Early in the observation skills-development process, we need to concentrate on separating these steps. If we do not, then we are more likely to make biased or subjective comments, as well as inaccurate interpretations. Later in practice, in order to respond quickly to the children, we will need to combine observation and interpretation and make interpretations "on the go." Unfortunately, there is no shortcut to making quality observations and interpretations.

Focus on the individual

"Did they like the creative activity?" a teacher asked an ECE student who came into her office. As the student replied, the teacher realized that she hadn't asked a very useful question. Imagining that each child's response to a situation is identical can be a mistake. We must focus on the behaviours of an individual child far more frequently than we do on the group.

If you can see only the general flow of action, you will not have insight into the set of individuals in your care. Without singling out children to observe closely, you are very likely to miss the particular skills that they have acquired and fail to acknowledge the areas of development that you can support.

However, individuals do function within groups. Group dynamics can be better understood when the individuals in the group are first observed separately. For this reason, you must learn to work at observing individual children and avoid making assumptions or generalizations. In time your observations can centre on the interactions within the group; but first you will need to refine your skills by observing one child at a time.

DEFINITION: Authentic assessment

Authentic assessment is assessment that takes place naturally and without stress as part of everyday experience.

Observation as authentic assessment

The strengths of systematic observation as a form of **authentic assessment** are numerous. Observation

- enables adults to take responsibility for the process of the child's development.
- is the key to evaluating development.
- is important because adults can bring about changes in a child's behaviour.
- focuses on what a child can do.
- forms the foundation of effective individual program planning and group planning.
- allows for variation between and the individuality of children in their development and needs.
- presupposes no curriculum theory but can support almost all types of program planning.
- enables behaviour to be seen in context.
- can be more objective and tends to be less biased than standardized tests.
- allows for understanding of each interacting aspect of development.
- enables the observer to carry out evaluation in familiar surroundings.
- can be faster and more effective than other methods of gaining information about development.
- encourages parents' involvement and professional teamwork.

The Observer's Role

"Watching the kids" is a phrase sometimes used to mean looking after or caring for children. It is interesting that the nonprofessional phrase accentuates our responsibility for observation.

We face inevitable conflicts in our jobs as caregivers, teachers, and parents. Consider a parent who spends a lot of his time watching his children and pointing out to everyone how advanced they are. He does not take responsibility for interacting or even being with them; rather, he observes and expresses his pride in their accomplishments. Other parents and caregivers may be so busy doing practical, domestic jobs that they don't take time to "stand and stare"—to watch their children with any sense of wonder or intrigue. Some are so involved with their children's activities that they do not notice their changing behaviours and increasing skills.

All adults involved with children need to observe those children constantly. Only a small amount of the information observed can be recorded or analyzed. An adult's active involvement with the children can make more formal observations difficult. Some methods enable us to be interactive as we observe, but these require yet another skill.

Your professional or personal relationship with the child shapes how you relate to her. If you have a job description, that document might articulate the parameters of your job, but it is most likely that the role is not well described. Just because your role hasn't been stated with clarity does not mean that you should be idle. Your professionalism requires you to set about your work as though you understand the professional role, your everyday responsibilities, and whatever it is that you are accountable for. At the centre of any role with children is observing them. At the lowest level of caregiving, you need to "watch" them to ensure that they are safe and that you don't lose them. Without observing and understanding the children, you will not manage to engage with them, build trust, or facilitate their development.

Nonparticipant observation

Early attempts at the more formal types of observing and recording need to be done while the observer is detached from the children. Students and skill-building teachers need to remove themselves from the children for this **nonparticipant observation**. Through the practice of observation, student educators' perspectives will alter. They will gradually notice things that they missed before, become more objective about what they do see, and become more analytical about the information they record. This nonparticipant role is a necessary part of learning how to observe effectively.

Practising teachers should, from time to time, remove themselves from direct contact with the children. This helps the teachers watch more carefully what is happening and usually makes them more responsive to those children. Taking the time to be a nonparticipant in the program does not mean prolonged time away from the children, however, and should never be an excuse to ignore a child's needs.

With young children, you may find it useful to be a noninteracting observer from time to time. Sit on a small chair in a position that does not interfere with their activity and is not in a significant traffic area. Here are some suggestions:

- Avoid making the facial expressions and eye contact that initiate communication with the children.
- Wear comfortable, fairly plain clothes; avoid wearing anything that will attract a child's attention.
- Try to avoid obvious staring at a child, which could make the child feel uncomfortable.
- Distance yourself so that you can see and hear the child without being in their play area or personal space.
- Ensure that sufficient appropriate supervision is provided so that all the children's needs are met while you observe.
- If a child draws you into conversation, respond in simple sentences to explain what you are doing. Remember to follow through with any promises you make to her regarding later activities.
- Make regular times for your nonparticipant observation so that the children get used to your doing it. Older children may imitate you.

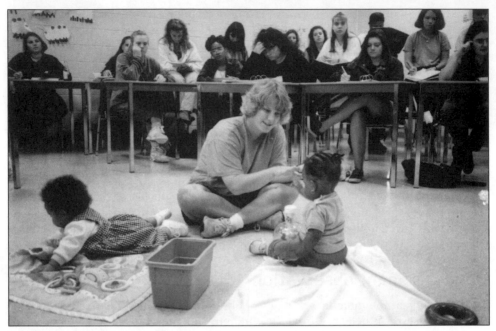

Early childhood education students use an in-class opportunity for nonparticipant observation of infants. Skill in objective recording needs to be gained from practice.

- Never use nonparticipant observation as an excuse for not involving yourself with the children when you should be responsible for their care.
- Remember this chapter's opening quotes, "The children's rights supersede your observer rights. Be respectful of the children."

Participant observation

Some teachers who have gained skill in observing children may make only brief notes as they work. They practise **participant observation** while they are involved with the children. Those teachers who have developed their skills may be more responsive to casually observed information.

For training purposes, there are more ways of improving your skills of observation. Visit childcare agencies and schools for opportunities. Use a college's onsite laboratory–school facilities as a particularly helpful setting. A lab–school can help students with their skill development in several ways:

- Children can be brought to class for a "set-up" observation opportunity. All the students will see the same behaviour at the same time and can learn to record and analyze appropriately.
- Observations in the lab–school can be recorded for later replay in class. Reviewing the material as a class can be good practice, as what is seen is the same for everyone.
- Students can go into the lab–school and observe as nonparticipants. Situations can be set up so that they can all focus on the same aspect of development.

- Observation booths can enable students, individually or in groups, to observe children. Ideally, a sound system would enable the students to hear language and other sounds. This is a nonintrusive way of observing, which does not influence the recording. Students can observe while others play the interactive role, setting up activities for the children.

- If the centre is large enough, students may be able to do a placement practicum or internship at the lab–school. As they get to know the children better than they would as visitors, students can try out different observational styles in nonparticipant and participant approaches.

The parents and teachers of the children to be observed may require some explanation of the purpose of focused observation by the students in a class situation. Of course, those students should gain their permission beforehand.

Observing groups of children

When educators have gained skill in observing individual children, they then need to increase their skills by observing children in groups. However, children must always be viewed as individuals; and *when they are in groups, we need to see them as a group of individuals.*

As well as all the developmental information that we can gain from each child, group observation allows us to see such things as

- how the children interact.
- the group's dynamics.
- the type of social play in which they are engaged.
- how groups are formed and then change into other groups.
- the cohesion of the group.
- what interests and motivates children's play and activity.
- the type and quality of the children's spontaneous play.
- how understanding new concepts emerges from group investigations.
- where the power sits within the group.

One challenge of doing group observations is to balance direct involvement with children and the need to document key information about them—and to do both at the same time.

Professionalism and Confidentiality

When you receive a psychological or medical report, it may arrive with a confidential sticker attached, making it clear that the report contains information to which access should be limited. An observation is also confidential material and should be treated as such. The circle of stakeholders involved in an observation, or those who require a degree of access to the information it contains, may be wider than you might at first imagine. This situation can present some challenges.

Who has, or should have, access to the formal records or informal notes that teachers and caregivers need to keep? While legal requirements vary, you must ensure that you interpret and practise **professionalism** and, when appropriate, **confidentiality** regarding all the information that is stored or shared. Follow the basic principle that information about a child is the concern of only that child, his or her custodial parent or guardian, and anyone with whom the parent consents to share it. In taking responsibility for the care or education of a child, you must ensure that any legal requirements regarding access to information and privacy are met. Your school or other agency must have a policy that determines who has access to what information and under what circumstances.

At enrolment, most agencies and schools enter into an agreement with parents and guardians that observations and information-gathering will be carried out. Student educators, however, must always request and gain parental permission before carrying out their observations, documentation, and record-keeping relating to a child. As a professional courtesy, students should provide parents with corrected copies of any such studies.

All written records need to be kept in secure, preferably locked, files. They should be labelled and dated. Files need to be updated regularly; the contributors should sign all their entries. Any significant content must be communicated to the parents in an appropriate manner with any necessary explanations. Parents should have open access to their children's files at any reasonable time. If you think that there is any reason to withhold information from a parent, that information is probably inappropriate and possibly **subjective**.

It is easier to accept the need for confidentiality with formal documents. Practising teachers find the challenge is to maintain the same level of confidential treatment with all pieces of information regarding a child. Parents' comfort level regarding privacy is very personal and may be culturally determined. Avoiding risks is essential and may require careful organization. While you may think that a posted chart recording the feeding, sleeping, and elimination pattern of the day is acceptable for infants, you will need to work out an appropriate practice for your setting with the parents.

In the days when children ran out of school clutching their readers of varying proficiency levels, it was quite clear to the parents—as well as to the children themselves—who was at the "top" or "bottom" of the reading class. You can avoid this kind of practice today.

Briefing parents about their children's challenging behaviour might be an excellent idea. While it is useful to share daily observations, you must be sensitive about timing. The end of the day might be the wrong time to deliver what could seem to be bad news; offering the comments when others might overhear them is also inconsiderate.

Students are in a difficult position with regard to confidential record-keeping. Their observations should not reveal the identity of a child to anyone who might accidentally come across the record. As student educators are learners themselves, their observations might not be as objective as they could be, and the inferences they contain might not be appropriate. The deductions the students make might be based on insufficient information or analyzed on the basis of an inaccurate explanation of a child's behaviour.

It is also important to remember this:

> Any information that is learned about a particular program or a child and his/her family should be discussed only with the staff of the program, the instructor, and other students in the context of class learning activities. Such information should be shared only for the purpose of enhancing your learning and that of your peers, not as "gossip." (Watson School of Education 2006)

Schools and agencies have different attitudes to student educators' access to children's records. In some cases, the students might be considered to be in a better position to appreciate a child's behaviour depending on the contextual information offered; however, to many in supervisory roles, this access presents an unnecessary intrusion into the family's privacy.

Centres working with students need to decide how to seek permissions regarding these observations (see the permission form on page 20) and the amount of information about the child that is made available. Certainly some information, and the observer's bias, may influence the objectivity of the person making the record. An agency might request that a staff member countersign students' observations to indicate that permission has been given to make the observation and that the observation is consistent with that staff member's knowledge. Feedback can be very useful for students; without breaching confidentiality, they may find that they contribute new insights to other professionals' knowledge of the child or children being observed.

Objective Observation

You may be relieved to hear that it is impossible to be completely objective when observing children. But it is a hard task to reach an acceptable level of **objectivity** in all your observation and recording. Cohen and Stern (1978) address this truth:

> For teachers observing the children with whom they work and live, absolute objectivity is impossible, and objectivity itself becomes a relative thing. As a matter of fact, it is to be hoped that no teacher would ever try for so much objectivity that she would cease to be a responsible and responsive adult to her group.

No two people will see the same child in identical ways. Two open and honest teachers can be asked to observe the same child. What they see and the interpretation they make will depend on what they decide to look for and on their own particular perspectives. According to these teachers, both tell the "truth," or their own version of it. To scientists, this might appear to be an unacceptable variation; however, observers of children need to decide what is an acceptable degree of objectivity.

How can you ensure that you keep to the truth when others see the child's behaviour in a different light? How you see depends on your skill in observing, what you are seeking, and your own perspective. If these are the variables, you can improve your reliability as an observer by increasing your skills, determining what you are looking for, and reviewing your personal perspective.

The Objectivity Continuum

Objectivity ◄─────────► Subjectivity

- There are no absolutes.
- All observations fall between the two opposites.
- Objectivity is usually desirable.
- Subjectivity is not always "wrong."
- Appreciation of the reasons for the degree of objectivity is always essential.

Permission Form

Child Observations, Case Studies, and Portfolios

Student and Parent Agreement

Without written permission I will not observe and record information about your child. Please sign in the space provided if you agree that I may make observations and study your child. It would be helpful if you could initial each of the boxes if you are willing for me to undertake any or all of the techniques of information gathering.

I _____ *(student name)* will not refer to the child in any written manner by his or her real name. Information recorded will be written objectively, treated professionally, and kept confidential.

_____   _____
(student's signature)   *(date)*

I _____
   (parent's name)

agree to have _____
          (child's name)

observed ☐   photographed ☐   audiotaped ☐   videotaped ☐

by _____
   (student's name above)

at _____
   (agency/home)

for the purpose of study in child development at _____

(school/college) for a period of _____ *(weeks/months)* on the consideration that copies are made available to me, the parent, if I so request.

_____   _____
(parent's signature)   *(date)*

Bias

Whatever stage we are at in our professional or adult lives, we have all had experiences that shape our perceptions. The way we take in information is determined by our previous experience and knowledge. We bring to situations previously acquired attitudes and beliefs. Some of these are well founded; others are born of some **bias** that derives from incorrectly understood information, negative experiences, or inappropriate generalizations. Most biases are subtle, and other people may not even recognize them. Some may be much more blatant and recognizable to others. Some may even be considered acceptable. Observers can eliminate or reduce many of their biases by acknowledging and confronting them.

> Regardless of our objective, having an open unbiased mind with no preconceptions . . . is a distinct advantage. (Rothchild 2007)

Eventually, observers will realize that there is more to observation than seeing. What separates human observation from a mechanical means of recording is how we perceive what we observe. The selection of how, when, and what to observe is a skill we must work on. **Perception** involves seeing and making meaning. The educators' task is to fine-tune their perceptions so they see, and process what they see, through experiences and well-informed sensory and mental functioning.

TAKING A SPECIAL LOOK: Observing exceptional children

How we see people may be shaped by our experience and our emotions. If we have little knowledge of **exceptional children** (children who have special needs), we could be fearful or negative about observing them. Recognizing this helps both you and the exceptional child speak positively about who he is and be clear about his abilities, rather than focusing on his disabilities. Getting to know the child and increasing your knowledge about his condition will usually reduce any fears and help you relate to him. Children with **atypical** skill levels in one or more domains may have abilities in other areas that you can see more easily if you observe with a positive outlook.

Teamwork

Many people have a role in caring for, nurturing, and educating each child.

> The first critical factor of teamwork success is that all the team efforts are directed towards the same clear goals. . . . This relies heavily on good communication in the team and the harmony in member relationships. (Dudiy 2005)

Where there is responsibility for a child, there is also a need for a combined effort toward the observation and assessment of that child.

Parents are the most important stakeholders in children's lives. They may be the adults who take the leading role in observing their children and responding appropriately to their needs. Quite naturally and spontaneously, a mother or father will watch a child; such observation may elicit a wide range of feelings and responses. This informal monitoring of the child's behaviour, and of changes in health or development, may well be the most significant assessment that is ever done. The professional involved in the child's care must never forget that the child is a member of a family and that the family may be able to offer closer insights than the trained caregiver. No assessment can ever be complete without including the parent's observations.

Front-line caregivers need to consider their observations in light of what is known about the child. This is done most usefully in discussion with co-workers and parents. Interested parties may be able to exchange observations in a relatively informal way—frequently at the start or end of the day, or perhaps at nap time, for a younger child.

Supervisors and others involved in the delivery of care and education may add their own observations or help make objective inferences about the child. When observed behaviour causes concern or is difficult to interpret, an "outside" professional, such as a psychologist, may be brought in. Legislation varies, but professional principles and good practice indicate that this should be done only after seeking parental permission, support, and involvement. Psychologists, occupational therapists, childcare consultants, and social workers will not be able to make a fair and appropriate assessment without input from the day-to-day caregiver or teacher and the parents.

The transdisciplinary play-based assessment (TPBA) model (Linder 1990) offers the idea of holistic assessment, with the involved professionals working with the parents in a way that enables all parties to observe simultaneously and take the time to discuss deductions that have been made. Linder states, "Team discussion is critical, and having the same foundation improves team communication" (1990, p. 17).

Not all observations are, or could be, conducted when all those involved with the child are present. Communication systems should be in place to share information in convenient ways.

The team approach increases the reliability of inferences made from observation. This model also encourages each adult to take responsibility in the process. An indicator of good-quality childcare is the practice of teamwork in observation and program planning.

The role of the parent

Within a home setting, it is always the responsibility of the parent(s) to care for and protect the child or children. Nieces, nephews, and/or children of neighbours in the home may increase that responsibility. This requires constant observation! The love and feelings of protection that parents have toward their children, along with their general sense of responsibility, are most important. These come quite naturally to most adults; to others, knowing how to observe and respond is more difficult. In their ideas of observational and nurturing responsibilities, adults who have experienced poor parenting in their own early years, or perhaps have experienced times of stress in their own lives, can be influenced by ingrained patterns in their own behaviour.

Most parents do a wonderful job of observing and responding to their children's needs. But however strong their observation skills, it is likely that they can improve their perceptions by becoming more knowledgeable about child development and by watching the development they see in their children. One of the best known educators and observers was Piaget, who used his own children as subjects. His intensive observation, documentation, and analysis of his own children's behaviour form a basis for our current understanding of developmental psychology today.

All parents will encounter a range of adults who play a role in the lives of their children. Some of these people will have advanced training in child development or in other professional fields. Others will have less formal preparation, but copious amounts of experience with children. Parents can find sharing the responsibility of the care of their children very difficult. It is easy to appreciate that the intense relationships between parents and children are forged in ways that, at first, exclude others. As families vary in their complexity, parents may perceive somewhat different boundaries of responsibility for their children.

Childcare centres, schools, home childcare, and all programs for children deliver quality service when teamwork is effective within the program.

> Through parental involvement we are better able to meet the developmental and personal needs of children. As early education professionals, we can serve as valuable resources for families concerning most areas of child development. Therefore, we believe that families and child care centres can and should work together to provide an environment that facilitates the growth of each child into a physically and emotionally healthy individual. (Seneca College, the King Campus Observation Laboratory Teaching School web site 2007)

Reaching beyond the program's delivery to parents is essential: parents must be considered key partners in the child's life and program. How the parent enters into and functions within the circle of caregivers and educators is vital to the success of the child, as well as the program as a whole. The agency or program concerned must take this into account when devising its policies and in ensuring that its practices promote mutual understanding.

Communications from home to the agency, as well as from the program to home, form the core of this reciprocal relationship. This two-way exchange of information needs to include observations that the parent has made of the child at home. More than the exchange of information, there must be a sharing of values and personal goals. Miscommunication or lack of communication can be at the root of many disagreements that can disrupt the program and upset the families.

Daily, weekly, and, on a formal basis, monthly exchanges of observations and information are necessary. Some of these will be spoken exchanges, while other important data should be recorded in the child's portfolio. While gossip is counterproductive, some informal conversation and exchange of personal information can help the parent get a sense of the philosophy and practice of the educator. Likewise, the program for the child can benefit from the input of either or both parents.

Formal records can seem intimidating to parents, but the parents should be able, in an atmosphere of trust, to offer the agency staff a wealth of information about themselves, their child, their culture, and way of life. Some parents may be reluctant to complete long forms that ask intrusive questions; in this case, interviews can be less daunting. The information sought is intended to lead to a better and more appropriate program for each child. Personal and contextual information is particularly important for programs that offer care and education for children from diverse backgrounds. Getting to know the children's food preferences, sleep cycles, religious requirements, play patterns, and so on may seem odd at first, but these are all particular and individual to each child. Parents and educators need to talk, trust, and share with each other so that they form a true partnership; the child will subsequently feel comfortable in both the home and the program, which will, in turn, contribute to his holistic development.

Choice of Observation Method

There is a wide range of methods of recording information. As you read this book, you might want to try some new ways or practise some of those familiar to you. When choosing a method, ask yourself the following questions:

1. Are you playing a nonparticipatory role, or do you have responsibility for the children as you observe?
2. Do you have the language skills to enable you to write detailed narrative descriptions?
3. Why are you observing? What are you looking for?
4. Is your purpose in observing to increase your skill or to benefit the child directly?
5. Do you appreciate what the various methods of information collecting will tell you—and can you choose appropriately?
6. Have you developed strategies to summarize and make sense of the observational information collected?

   If in doubt about where to start, work through the methods presented in this book. They are offered in a sequence that is appropriate for observing students or for skill-developing educators. Since informal observation is what everyone has done without training, continue to do this. Your skill will improve as you record, and your casual observations will gradually take on greater meaning as you continue the process. Narrative recordings require little interpretive skill, and so may be the method of choice for the relatively unskilled. As you find new ways of charting behaviours, checking off behaviours on lists, and using styles that require inference in their recording, your understanding of child development will also expand. Your learning will accelerate if you study theories of child development at the same time as you improve your observations. Each will benefit the other.

   Child psychology can be established only through the method of external observation. (Montessori 1913)

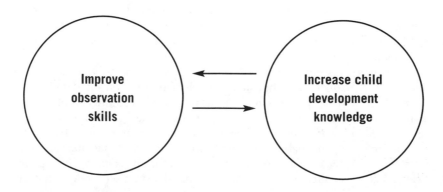

Observation as Part of a Formal Assessment Procedure

Early childhood specialists focus more on the process of the child's learning than on its products. Observation of the process can tell us much about the child that would not be revealed by viewing only such products as the child's artwork and writing. It is important, however, not to disregard the significance of such products. If you can gather information about the child from various sources, and in a variety of ways, you will be in a better position to make evaluations.

Formal **assessment** may require tests. (Chapter 11 deals with tests.) The best of these have an observation component. Children are in a better position to be evaluated fairly in a structured play situation, than in a testing situation. A restrictive "testing environment" can create stress. Children can demonstrate their skills more readily in a situation that resembles what they are used to. Members of an assessment team are wise to get their data through a variety of methods to ensure that they include naturalistic observations.

The **portfolio** technique combines the best of the evaluation styles. A portfolio can contain observations, charts, products of the child's efforts, test results, psychologists' reports, parental contributions, medical notes, and any other pertinent information. It forms a record that can be added to at any time. The portfolio forms long-term documentation of the child's education, health, and experience to which those involved with the child may refer. As the child grows, she may choose items for inclusion in her own portfolio to form a personal record of achievement. Looking back at the child's life experience can supply significant information about her patterns of behaviour.

TAKING A SPECIAL LOOK: Emerging skills

Whatever the developmental progress of a child, we need to support the skills that are emerging. Sometimes, when a child takes longer than average to acquire a new skill, the achievement seems even more amazing than it does for the child who had no particular challenge in that domain.

Observing the ongoing progression of skill development should lead us to respond. When we see new behaviours, we need to find ways of supporting them. We are not trying to get the child to develop faster—development is not a race! Rather, we are trying to ensure that we maximize the child's potential in a nurturing way.

Scientific Method

Science is a method of explaining the natural world. It assumes that anything that can be observed or measured is amenable to scientific investigation. (National Science Teachers Association 2003)

Science is also the orderly observation of events that cannot yet be manipulated, and, ultimately, the testing of many different such observations as the basis for theories to explain the events. (Humanist Association of Canada 2006)

Within most research institutions, it is an accepted idea that **scientific method** is used to both generate and solve problems. Observation is a key part of this process, which involves stating a hypothesis and then testing that idea. Notes are written throughout the process based on what the scientist sees happen. Logical thought processes help to draw inferences from the data. In the words of Rothchild (2007), "Observations are the meat and potatoes of science. We start a research project with observations made either in the field, the library, or the laboratory. How these observations are collected, classified, interpreted, and used as the basis of theorizing (from a hunch to a eureka) is, more or less, what science is about."

Ethics and human subjects

When we conduct research with human beings (and any meaningful observation and interpretation of behaviour is small-scale research), we must be mindful of **ethical** considerations. Clearly we cannot be intrusive or inappropriate, nor should we record observations without permission. Any time that we use our observation skills, we must remember that all persons are worthy of respect, most especially the children themselves.

We must work to a high standard of professionalism by

1. discerning our role as observer.
2. determining for whose benefit the observation is intended: research, the observer's skill, the child, the program, or the community; e.g., early development instrument.
3. seeking permission (see sample permission form on page 20).
4. being as objective as possible and avoiding bias.
5. selecting our subjects for observation and recording carefully.
6. recording significant observations.
7. using the appropriate recording method.
8. making only logical inferences from the observations.
9. responding appropriately to the observations and deductions.
10. disseminating the information we have produced.

(These issues are mentioned again in numerous places in the text.)

In research institutions the people who agree to be used in an experiment are called **human subjects**. Throughout the process, the subjects are observed and their behaviour, particularly their reactions to the test, is carefully documented. However, a review of any possible risks to the subjects in the experiment must be made with them, and their permission must be granted beforehand. Human research follows similar processes to those used in scientific research—scientific method—but researchers must conduct human research according to ethical processes for human subjects.

Informal observations carry a similar weight of ethical responsibility. Parents will be aware that their children will be observed in a childcare or school program; however, students and volunteers must seek parental permission, via the personnel responsible for their placement, before starting to record. Recordings of observations can be made in public schools, but it may be that permission must be sought from the principal and class teacher, as well as from individual parents. Taking photographs to support observations also requires permission; and with the fear of litigation, supervisors and principals may be cautious.

Observation at the core of the professional role with children

In the past, it may have been necessary to take steps to "prove" the need for observation as a central skill of educators and others working with children. Today that is not the case, and many important organizations offer occupational standards, job descriptions, program philosophy statements, policies, training standards, position statements, professional development guidelines, career laddering requirements, curriculum guides, and certification standards, each of which underscore the importance of observation for the purposes we mentioned earlier.

Here is a list of a few of the organizations in Canada, in the U.S., and internationally, that express support of observation at the centre of a professional role with children*:

- Canadian Child Care Federation—Occupational Standards
- Canadian Association for Young Children (CAYC)
- Child and Family Canada
- The Provincial/Territorial Associations supporting early childhood educators, e.g., Association for Early Childhood Educators Ontario, Early Childhood Educators of B.C., Manitoba Child Care Association, Early Childhood Educators of Quebec
- Canadian Teachers' Federation
- Resources for Infant Educators (RIE) (U.S.)
- Ontario Ministry of Training, Colleges and Universities Program Standards (and other provinces)
- Ontario Association for Childhood Education International (ACEI)
- National Association for the Education of Young Children (U.S.)
- Qualifications and Curriculum Authority (UK)
- YMCA
- Canadian Camping Association (CCA)
- Reggio Emilia (Italy)
- National Council for the Accreditation of Teacher Education (U.S.)
- Head Start (U.S. and Canada)
- High/Scope (international)
- The Search Institute (Developmental Assets)
- Association Montessori Internationale (AMI) (international)
- Association for Supervision and Curriculum Design (ASCD) (U.S.)
- Waldorf/Steiner Schools (international)
- Zero to Three (U.S.)
- Council for Early Childhood Professional Recognition/Child Development Associate (U.S.)

*These organizations have stated, in at least one official document, their position of the centrality of observation. We have included a sample from the sources mentioned above in the Instructor's Manual.

Observation and authentic assessment skill-building

We are each likely to develop observation skills at differing rates and in different patterns, but it is useful to monitor our progress and fill in the gaps of our growth. Below is a list that shows the skill sequence and progression of most professionals. A full version is available for dissemination from the Instructor's Manual.

PROFESSIONALISM

- Monitor your progress in observation and assessment skills.
- Seek permission to conduct observation(s)/develop portfolios.
- Enable parents to access your observations (this might be after showing them to your mentor or colleague).
- Follow professional protocols for confidentiality, handling, access, and storage of documentation.
- Seek support and feedback regularly; work as a team wherever possible.
- Be prepared to discuss the strengths and weaknesses of your recordings, summaries, and full analyses.

SKILLS

- Write reasonably objective accounts of one child's behaviour.
- Use basic narrative forms appropriately (focusing on one or more children).
- Review observational material (your own or written by others) to exclude bias.
- Use sampling methods appropriately.
- Define the behaviour category on which you are focusing.
- Select and use a prepared developmental checklist.
- Use the checklist to record observational information.
- Develop and use developmental checklists based on normative profiles.
- Select appropriate recording methods for various purposes.
- Record observations involving a group of children.
- Summarize observational data from each of the observation methods using a developmental framework.
- Make appropriate inferences based on your observations.
- Check your inference to see if each can be supported.
- Create a complex record-keeping system.
- Document accidents, potential child abuse, and serious occurrences according to appropriate protocols.*
- Demonstrate the ability to identify causes for concern.

*The needs of the children must always be met before the needs of the observer.

- Articulate why observation needs to be at the centre of child care practice (whatever the setting).

- Share observations with parents.

- Develop a strategy for having parents included in the data collection system.

- Use observational strategies to demonstrate how learning outcomes or program goals are being met.

- Institute a portfolio documentation system for each child.

- Advocate for observation, documentation, and portfolio assessment as a valid and reliable way of monitoring children's development (instead of using standardized tests).

- Dovetail institutional requirements for record-keeping with your own observational and assessment requirements.

- Review your observational data on a regular basis and work on your skill development.

- Ensure that all children are fairly represented in your documentation system.

- Display group documentation to assist children in reflecting on their learning and experience.

- Use computer software programs to record observational data.

- Write an IPP or IEP according to the child's needs.

- Keep observations, documentation, and portfolios up-to-date (all entries dated).

- Take steps to have the (older) children contribute to their own record-keeping.

- Gather contextual information on a frequent basis and use it to better understand the observations you have collected (family, community, and cultural information).

- Develop files containing pertinent health data and information related to the well-being of individual children (with updates when necessary).

- Schedule regular observation file reviews and developmental assessments.

- Avoid inappropriate discussion of children within the hearing of any child, colleague, or non-involved adult.

- Be prepared to hear and consider alternative explanations for children's behaviour.

- Review recent research, theory, and opinion related to children's development.

- Ensure that your use of normative assessments is fair and based on appropriate criteria from good sources.

- Select and use formal/standardized assessment tools when needed—especially with children who have special needs.

- Focus on making positive recordings—but do not avoid areas that need to be addressed.

- Label and explain a variety of "work" samples (children's artwork, creative activities, construction, etc.).

- Seek assistance
  - for the sake of the child and family to ensure the assessment process is fair and authentic.
  - for the sake of your own skill development.
- Link observations to
  - meeting the needs of individual children and those in groups.
  - program planning.
  - guiding children appropriately and according to their development.
  - extending spontaneous experiences.
  - directing the scaffolding of learning.
  - developing instructional strategies.

  - seeking extra resources.
  - seeking referrals (as appropriate to your level of responsibility).
- Think critically about your documentation and determine any gaps.
- Conduct regular program evaluation based on your observations, according to health and safety requirements.
- Conduct research using observation strategies within a project using action research and qualitative or quantitative methodologies.
- Design and implement a program evaluation using whatever criteria appear appropriate to access needed data.
- Develop a program plan as a result of a program evaluation process.

Summary

We all observe other people. Most of the time we do it informally. With practice, and with increasing knowledge about how children develop, we come to know what to look for in a child's behaviour, and we refine our observation skills. While it is necessary to know why we are looking intently at children—ultimately so we can support their development, protect them, or perform our role in their lives more effectively—we are constantly amazed at the individuality we see. Because children's behaviour is so complex, we find it challenging to understand just one child's actions, let alone those of a group of children. Our skill-building develops from looking at one child at a time to studying how children behave and interact within a group.

Systematic observation can be used as a type of "authentic assessment." In other words, we can appreciate the child's behaviour within a natural environment and without the stress that testing might produce. Adults play a variety of roles and assume different responsibilities in their work with young children. At times we can be most useful as nonparticipants who can stand back and notice more about the children's behaviour. At other times we are actively engaged with the children; we exercise most of our professional responsibilities when we operate this way. The parental role is paramount and any interaction with parents should demonstrate partnership with them.

Professionalism, which includes asking for permission to observe and record, is essential in any aspect of working with children. We must determine how we can be discreet and confidential in our conversations and in the record-keeping that is part of our job. We wish to be as objective as possible in our observing and recording, while leaving room for intuitive thinking about what we see.

Recording children's behaviour is part of the cycle of designing appropriate programs for them, both individually and in groups. For our programs to meet children's needs, we must use multiple observations as part of their authentic assessment. With good observational information, we can plan appropriate activities and experiences.

Key Terms

- accommodation
- assessment
- assimilation
- atypical
- authentic assessment
- behaviour
- bias
- confidentiality
- constructivist theory
- equilibration
- ethical
- exceptional children
- group level measure
- holistic
- human subjects
- nonparticipant observation
- normative profiles
- objectivity
- participant observation
- perception
- portfolio
- professionalism
- scaffold
- scientific method
- subjective

www.acei.org
The Association for Childhood Education International (ACEI), a national association whose philosophy is to promote and support the optimal education and development of children, from birth through early adolescence, in the global community.

www.cayc.ca
The Canadian Association for Young Children (CAYC), a national association focusing on the well-being of children, from birth through age nine.

www.cccf-fcsge.ca
The Canadian Child Care Federation (CCCF) aims to improve the quality of childcare services to Canadian families.

www.childcarecanada.org
The Childcare Resource and Research Unit focuses on early childhood care and education research and policy.

www.wikipedia.org
Wikipedia is the largest encyclopedia on the internet, but check for reliability. Look for sections on "scientific method," "observation" etc.

www.ascd.org
The Association for Supervision and Curriculum Development (ASCD) is an international association offering access to performance assessment resources.

www.newchildcare.co.uk
Although some of the terminology is different, this British site offers a good introduction to the key concepts of observation.

A group of children engaged in imaginative play.

2 Observing Development

Any activity can demonstrate a child's development in various domains. A careful observer of these children playing together could comment not only on their physical skills but also on their social, emotional, and communication skills.

With permission of the YMCA of Greater Toronto

And so we see that if we can develop a more delicate faculty of observation, we can really gain an insight into the true essence of existence.
Rudolf Steiner (1924)

All areas of a child's development can be assessed through play—physical, cognitive language, and social/emotional development.
Elementary Teachers' Federation of Ontario (2006)

...training teachers to observe children is perhaps best done in conjunction with a seminar or ongoing staff discussing, however informal, on child development. The two go hand in hand.
Sally Cartwright (2008)

The Development of Young Children

What we see when observing young children depends on what we know about how human beings grow and develop. The philosophy of observation and authentic assessment, and of this book, is based on the following principles.

Human beings, especially children,

- are unique and individual, and yet have characteristics that are common to all.

- need to form attachments and develop within a social network.

- tend to share patterns of maturational change.

- inherit many attributes and potentials, but their experiences of life influence how they develop.

- require early interactions and experiences that will decisively affect the structure of their brains and the type and extent of their adult capacities.

- are diverse in their appearance, patterns of development, beliefs, lifestyles, occupations, and needs.

- demonstrate individual temperamental styles that tend to remain fairly constant throughout life.

- develop within, shape, and are shaped by social contexts that are part of wider ecological systems.

- adapt to changing environments and circumstances, creating an individually constructed knowledge of the world.

- develop in patterns of continuous and discontinuous change, some elements of development increasing gradually and constantly and others changing in surges and plateaus.

- depend on having their basic physical and psychological needs met.

- are especially sensitive to particular kinds of stimuli at certain times in their development.
- undergo many changes during their lives, some observable and others internal.
- function in remarkably different ways and demonstrate a broad range of ways they can be creative, solve problems, and accommodate life experiences.
- are influenced by **social**, **biological**, and **psychological clocks**.
- demonstrate similar basic emotional expressions whatever their cultures or locations, whereas they learn social emotions within a context.
- continue to develop throughout their lifespans, each stage of which is equally significant.
- perceive the meaning of their lives and what is socially acceptable according to myriad different social, emotional, and spiritual factors.
- can be raised in environments that support and optimize development, but they cannot progress faster than their own timetables for development.
- may deviate from expected patterns of growth and development or have **special needs**, and may sometimes require special health, nurturance, or education interventions.
- are all worthy of respect.

DEFINITION: Child development

Child development is the dynamic process of change and progression that enables every individual to become increasingly independent, knowledgeable, skilled, and self-sufficient.

Underlying forces of development

Child development depends on maturational processes and environmental conditions that can optimize each individual's genetic potential. Theories of child development, such as those of lifespan development, consider human beings to be highly individual in appearance, style, and needs, while they share reasonably predictable patterns of adaptation and skills acquisition among most members of a population. Child-development models can help us understand the role we can play in observing young children and supporting their development.

The biological clock is determined by the individual's heredity. It shapes the person's pattern of **maturation**. The family and the wider community determine the social clock by their expectations. The complex inner self, beliefs, and motivations drive the psychological clock. As each clock "ticks," all three clocks interact with one other, influencing the development of the whole child.

At three years of age, Jerry, for example, is expected to be ready for nursery school (social clock). But he still wets himself because he does not yet have full bladder control (biological clock). Jerry wants to go to nursery school as the other children do, and he feels bad whenever they see him wet himself (psychological clock). Soon he will be able to control his bladder and will go to nursery school. His motivation will help his ability to read the signs of a full bladder.

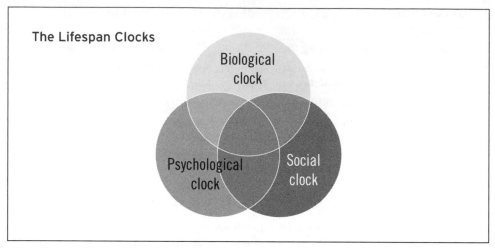

The Lifespan Clocks

Biological clock

Psychological clock

Social clock

The three "clocks" drive the process of development.

TAKING A SPECIAL LOOK: Developmental delay

For a variety of reasons, some children may have slower-than-typical development. The developmental delay may be general or specific in one or more domains. The caregiver or teacher may identify a cause for concern and approach the child's parents, or a parent may bring a concern to the caregiver's or teacher's attention. It then becomes the professional's responsibility, along with that of the parent, to observe the child closely, focusing on the particular area in question and the child's development in general.

Observing the Developmental Process

The developmental process is extremely complex, but our initial understanding depends on what we can see—surface behaviours. Using a developmental lens to watch children helps us to make sense of "what is going on" within the child and notice external features of development. Following this section are extensive lists to help guide your observations. Each focuses on one domain of development. Overlaps exist between domains, so do not be surprised when you see similar indicators in two or more domains.

When observing *physical* signs of development, you will notice that the indicators are easier to determine than in other developmental domains. Some domains require a greater degree of interpretation than others, such as with evidence of *moral* understanding or *cognitive* processes.

Supporting the lists of behaviours in each domain are research into maturational patterns, theories of development, and the reflection of various perspectives on development. Please remember that the lists

- are not progressive—they do not imply any sequence of development.
- offer indicators of typical development and, of themselves, cannot lead you to make any diagnosis. (Please see Chapter 10 to review developmental causes for concern.)
- are not complete, but they offer a wide range of behaviours that fall into each domain.

The lists are offered to help you

- learn about child development.
- connect what you observe with child development.
- lead you to categorize your observations into developmental domains.
- focus on a range of behaviours when you are observing an individual child.

This set of nine domains offers sufficient differentiation while at the same time avoiding the pitfall of creating too many domains:

1. physical development
2. sexual development
3. language and communication
4. social development
5. emotional development
6. temperament and personality development
7. moral development
8. cognitive development
9. spiritual development

Within each domain, we have further subdivided the observational **indicators** so that they are detailed but manageable for the observer. If you observe behaviours that are not included, and clearly belong to a certain category, add them to the inventory.

Physical development

Physical development has two basic aspects: the development of **gross motor skills**, which refer to the large muscles of the body; and the development of **fine motor skills**, which concern control of the small muscles. The **cephalo-caudal principle** explains that the typical sequence of bodily control starts with the head and proceeds downward from there. According to the **proximo-distal principle**, control usually begins at the centre of the body and proceeds to the extremities. **Sensory acuity** changes rapidly in the early months of the infant's life, with all five senses operating at an optimal level by the age of about two. Bodily proportions change throughout development, the head in infancy being larger in proportion to the rest of the body and the body gaining in proportional size through later stages.

Growth is an integral part of development and concerns increase in size. Even with good nutrition, a child may demonstrate an individual pattern of weight gain and height increase. The child's basic needs of food, shelter, clothing, and protection must be satisfied so that she develops physically in a healthy way. Children can fail to thrive if their physical needs are not met.

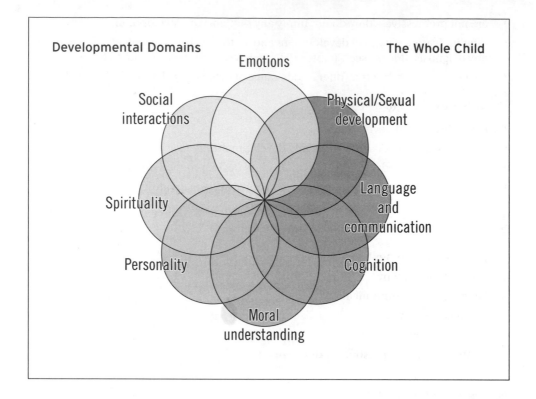

Developmental Domains   The Whole Child

Emotions

Social
interactions

Physical/Sexual
development

Spirituality

Language
and
communication

Personality

Cognition

Moral
understanding

Sequences of skill development are common to most children, but skills may be developed at differing rates. Physical development is the most easily observed group of developmental changes.

TAKING A SPECIAL LOOK: The use of norms

Looking at the typical behaviours of children at particular ages and stages gives us an idea of what is "average," but this **norm** does not imply that children "should" be at a certain level of achievement. The norm is just one way of viewing children's skill development, and it can give us an idea of how they are progressing. When we use the yardstick of the norm over a period of time, we can identify the children's rate of development in each domain. The fact that a child takes nine months to achieve skills that the average child accomplishes in about six months can tell us about the child's pattern of development.

If we can see that a child's skills are lagging behind those of other children his age, we may need to pay closer attention. Whatever the skills he demonstrates, we need to support that development, document further observations, and, if necessary, refer the child to a specialist.

What to Observe: Indicators of physical development

Appearance

- Skin tone, quality, and clarity; posture; facial expression; hair colour and texture; nail quality; eye brightness and clarity, pupil dilation; facial symmetry; ear positioning and cleanliness; sweat, personal odour
- Teeth: number, type, colour, and health
- Skin marks: freckles, spots, birth-marks; cuts, bruises; acne, milia; urticaria, heat rash, cradle cap, diaper rash, etc.
- Neck: angle and symmetry
- Abdomen: shape, protrusions, etc.
- Body symmetry
- Sexual characteristics
- Mouth and palate: shape, colour, and symmetry
- Fontanels (in children younger than two years)
- Leg positioning and straightness
- Foot position: inward-pointing, outward-pointing
- Physical disability

Bodily functions

- Body temperature
- Responses to foods: allergies, sensitivities, indigestion, colic, etc.
- Bowel movements: continence, colour, consistency, frequency, and amount
- Urination: continence, colour, frequency, and amount
- Bodily fluids: drooling, discharges, etc.
- Temperature regulation/sweating

Levels of consciousness

- Uptime, downtime, trance, and sleep
- Sleep: types, times, rhythms, and length

Fine motor skills

- Hand coordination
- Manipulative skills: holding, throwing, catching, squeezing, drawing, piano-playing, etc.
- Right- or left-handedness
- Drawing
- Writing
- Grasp (palmar/pinier)
- Cutting
- Colouring
- Threading beads
- Using two hands at once
- Releasing objects
- Building
- Opening
- Cleaning
- Manipulating

Gross motor skills

- Levels of activity and passivity
- Mobility
- Large-body skills: walking, running, jumping, kicking, etc.
- Endurance
- Use of outdoor apparatus
- Dance/response to music
- Stretching
- Balancing
- Rolling over
- Sitting up

- Crawling
- Walking
- Pedaling
- Climbing
- Rhythm

Measurements

- Appetite
- Weight
- Distribution of body fat
- Muscular tone and definition
- Alterations in body proportions
- Heart rate
- Respiration
- Right- or left-footedness
- Strength
- Fitness level
- Body proportion

Self-help skills

- Dressing, undressing, toileting, feeding

- Grooming
- Tying shoes/doing up buttons
- Body awareness
- Handwashing

Senses

- Use and acuity of senses: sight, hearing, touch, taste, smell, and multimodal sensory acuity
- Responsiveness to stimuli
- Sound production

Sport

- Interest in organized games
- Skill at particular sport (soccer, hockey, etc.)
- Effort at sport/activity/ball games

Other items

- repetitive behaviours: habits and patterns of physical behaviour
- Reflexive movements

Sexual development

Adults may have difficulty thinking of very young children as "sexual," because sexuality is associated with adult activity and reproduction. However, sexuality starts in infancy. In a baby, we see this in the attachments he makes with adults, the intimacy of close relationships, the sensuality of touch, multisensory experiences, and his physical discovery of his own body. Healthy child sexuality involves learning about bodies, their functions, and gender. Most importantly, **sexual development** involves nurturance and the meeting of a child's physical and psychological needs. It is necessary for children to learn by experience and example that sensations can be pleasurable and that sexual activity, at the right time and in the appropriate place, is enjoyable. Above all, the child needs to feel loved, to learn to build trusting relationships, to build positive attitudes, and to discover what behaviours are socially acceptable. Privacy, respect, and personal space are essential for healthy sexual development; children need to find out what behaviours they can demonstrate in front of others and what behaviours are private. Answering children's questions about sex must be appropriate to their individual development, as any learning experience about sexuality should be.

Observing the children's activity—such as the one pictured here—gives us some idea of their fine motor skill development, but it may also indicate their interests, personality, and social skills. Developing in one domain usually influences development in other domains.

With permission of the YMCA of Greater Toronto

The list below highlights elements of sexual development. Fortunately, most children demonstrate healthy development in all domains. If the observer has concerns about a child's health or behaviour that may indicate the possibility that the child has suffered abuse, the adult must report those concerns to a child-protection agency. We discuss this in Chapter 10, where we explore protocols and documentation associated with potential abuse and neglect.

What to Observe: Indicators of sexual development

Attachment

- Attachment behaviours
- Being soothed by touch/rhythmic movement
- Accepting adult touch
- Initiating attention
- Social referencing
- Establishing primary adult relationship
- Separation anxiety

- Responding to adult touch, hugs, cuddling, back rubbing
- Emotion expressed to or about parent
- Kissing (the way the child kisses parents, teacher, sibling, or child)

Being private

- Choosing to be alone during toileting/bathroom times
- Desire to be private

- Request for personal space for personal belongings

Asking questions

- Asking where babies come from
- Asking questions about bodies or sexuality
- Asking questions about adult bodies
- Asking questions about pregnant women
- Requesting information about gender and gender roles
- Responses to adult questions

Language

- Responding to adult cues
- Naming body parts
- Identifying body functions
- Expressing emotions
- Correct or incorrect statements about sexual intercourse
- Child's conversation about television, movie, video, or DVD sequences
- "Bathroom talk" ("poo-poohead")
- Telling or repeating smutty jokes
- Giggling or whispering ("Hazel loves Jason!")
- Communicating understanding of socially acceptable behaviour ("Only mommies and daddies do that")
- Using pet names for parts of the body
- Repeated mention of fairness
- Telling of "stories," real or imagined
- Use of sexual language
- Swearing or using sexual terms

Social behaviour

- Eye-gazing (gazing into space with or without focus, into another person's eyes, or at an object)
- Sharing/refusing to share
- Physical distance between child and adult or other child
- Need to see siblings
- Functioning within a group of peers
- Friendliness to strangers
- Eating patterns
- Adjustment to new situations

Sensory experience

- Responding positively to massage
- Sensory discovery
- Sensory repetition
- Exploring own genitals
- Touching (how, where, or the way the child touches others)

Curiosity

- Recognizing other children's body parts
- Sexual curiosity
- Masturbation
- Peering to see others' bodies
- Sexual discovery (access to books or other media)

Self identity

- Discovering parts of the body
- Recognizing own body parts
- Self-esteem
- Self-help skills
- Categorization of self ("I'm a boy")
- Pro-social or helping behaviours

Play

- Simulating "adult" sexual activity
- Doll play
- Adult role play
- Role reversal play
- Being "baby"
- Gender-related play
- Dressing up as member of the opposite sex
- Repetitive play
- Playing doctors and nurses to enable looking and touching
- Sex play (a version of imitating adults)

Other behaviours

- Fear of revealing body
- Drawings that have sexual content

- Assuming different postures for urination
- Removing clothes confidently
- Sudden phobias
- Showing embarrassment
- Unexpected displays of guilt, anger, shame, or sadness
- Exhibiting forceful behaviour to others/dolls
- Somatic symptoms ("I've got a headache")
- Response levels to stimuli
- Aimless behaviour or wandering
- Habitual behaviours (such as nail-biting)
- Relationship problem-solving
- Quality of sleep

Language and communication

Language development leads to two-way interpersonal communication. It includes not only hearing and the physical ability to produce sound, but the other sensory abilities. Language requires experimentation with sound, the repetition of human sounds, the attachment to adults, and various forms of reinforcement. There appear to be **sensitive periods** early in life for language development. It is thought that human beings are "pre-wired" to acquire language with certain conditions allowing it to flourish. The stages of first-language learning are clearly observable, but the underlying explanations of how language is acquired are more complex. Language learning is the precursor of literacy. Children exposed to more than one language may be at an intellectual advantage in later development.

What to Observe: Indicators of language and communication development

Early communication

- Crying: types and length
- Eye-gazing

- Eye contact
- Cooing
- Vowel-type sound production

- Says "mama" or "dada"
- Responding to "mother-ese" or "parent-ese"
- Talking about feelings
- Modulated babbling
- Attaching to adults
- Pointing
- Gesturing
- Protesting
- Drawing attention to self
- Experimenting with sounds
- Imitating sounds
- Rhythmic sound production
- Representing ideas

Two-way communication

- Negotiating
- Resolving conflicts
- Explaining ideas
- Looking toward a person for eye contact
- Listening to others
- Repeating consonants
- Taking turns
- Following instructions

Imitation

- Imitating sounds
- Repeating rhymes
- Imitating words
- Imitating phrases
- Imitating writing

Words and meaning

- Recognizing own name
- Understanding "no"
- Using 2-3 words
- Using ____ words

- Understanding sentences of _____ words
- Understanding "same" and "different"
- Defining object by its use
- Using language to think, plan, and imagine
- Using holophrases (single words that, when uttered, imply the meaning of whole sentences)
- Combining noun and verb; e.g., "Mommy go"
- Producing whole words
- Language with gesturing
- Uttering two-word phrases
- Using phrases of three or more words
- Creating stories
- Creating rhymes
- Storytelling
- Understanding instructions
- Expressing feelings
- Understanding the experiences and feelings of others
- Reporting and planning
- Lying and variations of telling the "truth"
- Comparing and interpreting
- Inferring
- Decoding
- Encoding
- Imagining
- Reasoning
- Predicting sequences
- Drawing conclusions
- Symbolizing (using symbols but not always ones that have meaning to others)

- Identifying body parts
- Understanding time concepts; e.g., "tomorrow"
- Creating words to suit own meaning
- Scribbling
- Using rhyming words

Play behaviour

- Game-playing
- Pretend-playing
- Role-playing
- Cooperating with other children
- Playing alongside others (parallel play)
- Communicating in associative play and activity
- Pretending

Writing

- Recognizing written letters
- Recognizing own name, in written form
- Writing own name
- Copying word shapes
- Early writing—scribbling/shapes
- Story- and letter-writing (simple or complex)
- Using phonetics
- Reversing letters
- Creating ways to spell
- Using conventional spelling
- Awareness of writing (lists, notes)
- Producing letter-like forms

Questioning

- Asking "How?"
- Asking "Why?"
- Asking "When?"
- Asking "Where?"
- Asking "What?"
- Asking for an explanation
- Making requests
- Asking questions
- Answering questions
- Clarifying mlsunderstandings
- Inquiring about people, places, objects, and ideas

Bilingual/multilingual language development

- Making pronunciation errors
- Mixing two languages
- Silent period
- Interacting with children of the "new" language
- Using whole phrases of "new" language
- Loss of first language
- Unusual grammar use

Relationship-building

- Social conversation
- Responding to social overtures
- Initiating social relationships
- Socially acceptable communication
- Listening to stories
- Singing

Grammar

- Over-generalizing
- Using rules of language
- Making grammatical errors

Young children can send out different **cues** or messages to us through their body language, gestures, and expressions. They have individual ways of communicating. Children who have some special needs may need to be supported with communication strategies and sometimes **assistive devices** so that they can be understood better. For example, a visually impaired infant may not maintain eye contact, smile, or imitate an adult in the same way that a sighted infant would. Caregivers will have to observe any visual responses she makes, and provide communications that she can perceive, perhaps through her other senses. If caregivers observe such a sensory deficit in a child, they should share their observations with the parents, who may have similar perceptions and seek further professional assessment. In this example, the child will probably need glasses.

This educator maximizes her social interactions with babies while she engages with them during sensory discovery.

With permission of the YMCA of Greater Toronto

Social interactions

Social development involves both the concept of self and the individual's relationships with others. Early **attachments** to primary caregivers are necessary for children to start building a sense of themselves. There may be particularly sensitive periods for the formation of these personal relationships, and long-term consequences if such relationships are not established. Children need other people so that they can learn what is socially acceptable. Much of this knowledge is gained through imitation. Social learning involves internalizing role models, so **social play** through pretend games is very important. **Social interactions** can be readily observed when children are at play, in domestic situations, or in their natural environment with other adults or children.

What to Observe: Indicators of social development

Self

- Cues for attention
- Egocentricity
- Stranger anxiety
- Separation of "self" from others
- Self-concept
- Personal achievement
- Identification of own needs
- Strategizing for meeting personal needs
- Categorical self
- Effort to win
- Believing independently

Relationships

- Eye-gazing
- Reciprocal communication
- Bonding to adult
- Relationships with primary caregivers
- Relationships with family members
- Multiple attachments
- Relationships with strangers
- Recognition of the existence of others
- Perspective-shifting
- Sharing skills
- Imitative learning
- Same-sex friendships
- Acceptance as member of a group
- Opposite-sex friendships
- Concern about group acceptance
- Showing security
- Making friends

Social responsibility

- Acknowledgement of similarities and differences
- Identification with group activities or beliefs
- Team activity and problem-solving
- Developing strategies for collective success
- Caring for others
- Unconditional love
- Empathizing
- Altruism
- Understanding fairness
- Understanding turn-taking
- Leading
- Protective towards others

Play behaviours

- Onlooker activity
- Solitary playing
- Parallel playing
- Genderless playing
- Playing associatively
- Pretend-playing
- Role-playing
- Cooperative playing

Emotional development

Emotional development involves the expression and control of feelings. All infants express basic **emotions** in similar ways. However, feelings become more complex as children understand more about themselves, others, and the world. A parent's relationship influences early emotions. Children experience typical stages of emotional conflict throughout childhood. At first, infants strive for a trusting relationship; then they focus on becoming independent and showing initiative, and struggle for a clear sense of self-worth. **Social emotions** express feelings shaped by social experiences. Emotions can be observed by interpreting behaviours, expressions, posture, and gestures; but inner conflicts and the subtleties of complex emotions may be harder to analyze.

What to Observe: Indicators of emotional development

Expressing feelings

- Facial expressions
- Eyes: openness, direction, pupil dilation, symmetry
- Showing basic emotions
- Eyebrows: shape and position
- Creases on forehead
- Mouth: open or closed, tilted
- Head tilt: direction and angle
- Nose: flared or relaxed
- Cheeks: puffy, pinches, etc.
- Skin: patchiness, colour, sweat, etc.
- Breathing: rate and depth
- Posture
- Change in emotional states
- Showing social emotions
- Expressions of love
- Use of comfort objects
- Fears
- Avoidance
- Recognizing own emotional needs
- Acknowledging the feelings of others
- Using words to express feelings
- Protesting when frustrated
- Showing signs of stress
- Imitating adult expressions
- Communicating desires and feelings

Relationships

- Empathic behaviour
- Attachments
- Separation behaviour
- Dependence/independence
- Perspective-changing
- Intentional communications
- Making friends
- Altruistic actions
- Sustaining friendships
- Cooperativeness

Play

- Regression and progression in play, language, or other developmental domain
- Pretend-playing
- Role-playing
- Fantasy-playing

Self-regulation

- Controlling impulses
- Self-regulatory behaviours
- Coping with crises
- Recovering from distress

Emotional intelligence

- Self-awareness
- Reading cues
- Resolving conflict

- Control of anger
- Labelling of emotions
- Congruence between stated feelings and behaviour
- Meeting own needs
- Responding to guidance strategies
- Using personal style to advantage

Other behaviours

- State of consciousness
- Constructive/destructive behaviour
- Withdrawal
- Emotive/non-emotive
- Patterns of sleep
- Eating patterns and appetite
- Speed of movement
- Gestures
- Response to stimuli
- Attention-seeking behaviour
- Egocentricity
- Building confidence
- Habitual behaviours
- Reactions to sensory experiences
- Creative activity or thought
- Responsiveness/unresponsiveness

Personality

Personality involves the individual's **temperament**, awareness of self, patterns of response, and ability to manage life's challenges. Temperamental styles tend to be observable soon after birth and are thought to remain fairly constant throughout life. However, life experiences can alter how people deal with their temperaments, and adults can influence how children see themselves and cope with events. Temperamental styles

What to Observe: Indicators of temperament and personality development

Self

- Self in relation to others
- Gender identity
- Self-respect
- Self-aware
- Categorical self
- Self-esteem
- Self-directed
- Body image
- Self-actualized

Temperament

- Activity level
- Rhythms and daily patterns
- Pace of activity
- Timing of responses
- Adaptability and openness to new experiences
- Extroversion or introversion
- Response to success or failure
- Response to being touched
- Level of sound production
- Agreeableness
- Consistency of reaction patterns
- General disposition (attitude)
- Intensity
- Response to new activity or person

- Typical mood
- Span of attention
- Persistence
- Adaptability

Personality

- Personal space (physical)
- Need to be with others or to be alone
- Pattern of self-control
- Pro-social or antisocial style
- Positive or negative perspective
- Leading or following others
- Sex-role performances
- Creativity
- Optimism or pessimism
- Confidence or diffidence
- Habits
- Honesty or dishonesty
- Seeking of emotional or practical support
- Conscientiousness
- Degree of autonomy/independence
- Distractibility
- Attention span
- Persistence
- Sleep and wakefulness
- Stability
- Sensitivity
- Personal preferences
- Organized/disorganized
- Content/frustrated
- Relaxed/stressed
- Calm/worrying
- Outgoing/shy
- Adventurous/timid
- Spontaneous/thoughtful

- Neuroticism
- Curiosity
- Impulsivity
- Eccentric/conformist
- Level of anxiety
- Independent/dependent
- Mood constancy/erratic
- Obsessive/laid-back

Responses

- Emotional stability or instability
- Intensity of reactions
- Responses to stressors
- Reality or fantasy
- Identification with adults
- Role-playing
- Style of responses to stimuli
- Mood quality and changes
- Responses to auditory stimuli
- Responses to visual stimuli
- Appropriateness of responses
- Altruism

Other behaviours

- Body type: ectomorph, endomorph, or mesomorph
- Narcissistic
- Compliance with social expectations
- Following rules
- Accepting consequences
- Inappropriate affect
- Egocentricity (beyond toddler)
- Fantasy/reality confusion
- Disorganized behaviour
- Self-defeating
- Passive-aggressive
- "Over-reacting"

have observable characteristics, whereas personality types can be difficult to label, because personal characteristics and patterns of behaviour need to be observed over a prolonged period. Chess and Thomas (1996) offer a useful model for identifying temperamental types for teachers and caregivers trying to respond to different temperamental styles (see page 175). A wide range of personality assessment processes are available, but there is merit in observing a child naturally rather than performing tests that disregard variables from situation to situation.

Moral understanding

Moral understanding involves the intellectual and social skills to understand the difference between right and wrong and be able to behave according to those principles. **Morality** develops from understanding social roles and responsibilities and may be shaped by religious beliefs and culturally determined roles. Because cognitive skills are required to be able to think from the perspective of others and to manipulate ideas about what is ethical or morally right, this developmental domain is difficult to observe. **Pro-social skills** are easier to observe, but the ability to behave appropriately or desirably does not necessarily indicate moral understanding. Stages of moral understanding can be observed through children's responses to moral dilemmas. The guidance children receive from adults and the role models they observe strongly influences moral development.

What to Observe: Indicators of moral development

Emotions

- Basic emotions: anger, contempt, disgust, distress, fear, rage, joy, sadness
- Emotional Intelligence (see emotional development)
- Response to praise

Challenging behaviours

- Aggressive behaviour
- Lying
- Cheating
- Behaving unsociably (the child might not yet be of a stage or disposition to absorb what is socially acceptable)
- Making incorrect assumptions
- Power playing

- Inflicting "punishments" on others
- Blaming others
- Entitlement
- Justification for wrong-doing
- Making excuses

Self-regulation

- Being honest
- Dealing with teasing
- Dealing with losing
- Saying "no"
- Dealing with mistakes
- Response to redirection
- Apologizing
- Regulation of bodily functions
- Deferring gratification
- Concept of self (see personality)

- Egocentricity
- Response to consequences
- Response to lack of consequences
- Impulse control
- Control over own emotions and behaviour
- Choosing to demonstrate "good" behaviour or "bad" behaviour
- Behaving according to social acceptability

Cognitive actions

- Perspective-taking (ability to understand the viewpoint of another individual—a cognitive function—as well as having a personal point of view)
- View of punishment
- Appreciating the concept of winning and losing
- Cause-and-effect understanding
- Understanding the role of authority
- Remembering parameters of behaviour
- Metacognitive processes concerning morality
- Linking events to causes
- Understanding "fairness"
- Identifying emotions and feelings
- Matching "punishments" and "crimes"
- Justifying behaviours and actions
- Internalizing religious beliefs
- Internalizing philosophical perspectives
- Making moral judgments on the basis of abstract ideas
- Stating personal beliefs

- Identifying "good" and "bad"
- Ethical challenges

Play behaviours

- Role-playing
- Superhero-playing
- Playing board games with rules
- Asking someone to play

Relationships

- Attachments
- Showing affection
- Competitiveness
- Bullying
- Dealing with bullying
- Seeking approval of others
- Response/imitation of role model
- Showing collective pride
- Taking on tasks for others
- Communication skills (see communication and language)
- Interpretation of social cues

Rules

- Listening
- Understanding specific rules
- Following rules
- Making up rules
- Making exceptions to rules
- Evidence of religious teaching
- Demonstrating manners (saying "thank you," "please," etc.)
- Accepting not being the centre of attention

Pro-social skills

- Taking turns
- Sharing
- Fantasy-playing

- Helping
- Collaborating
- Offering help
- Asking for a favour
- Initiating a charitable act
- Demonstrating respect for others
- Meeting the needs of an animal in their care
- Acceptance of others who have differing thoughts, ideas, and perceptions

Social emotions
- Pleasure-seeking or pain-seeking
- Pleasure-avoidance or pain-avoidance
- Social emotions: optimism, guilt, love, shame, envy, hurt, surprise, pride, jealousy, frustration, bitterness, horror, etc.
- Risk-taking
- Thrill-seeking

Cognition

Cognition involves the process of knowing, thinking, and understanding. Early learning is shaped by experimentation, play, imitation, stimulus-response, and reinforcement. Stages of cognitive development differ in their complexity, as well as in the amount of information that is learned. Infants' understanding is acquired through their sensory exploration of the world; it is highly egocentric. Later, thinking patterns change as children are able to deal with concrete ideas and some symbolism. Through intellectual stimulation and brain maturation, children gradually learn to deal with abstract ideas and multifaceted tasks. Information is processed according to these changing mental structures; the child creates an internal construction of the world. We can understand what children are thinking according to what they say, what they do, and the mistakes they make.

Recent advances in neuroscience are helping parents and professionals understand the importance of early experience and the dynamic capacities of the human brain. Cognitive development is an extremely difficult process to observe and to make appropriate inferences about. We can observe brain activity through various types of electronic scans and we can study it in the form of neurological activity, but this doesn't help us understand thinking in everyday situations. Theories of cognition can help us untangle the complexities of children's thought processes.

What to Observe: Indicators of cognitive development

Play
- Pretend-playing
- Role-playing
- Playing with ideas
- Playing games with rules
- Imaginative/pretend play
- Involvement in socio-dramatic play
- Involvement in "deep play" regarding fears and trauma

- Playing creatively
- Manipulating objects
- Playing with sand, water, malleable materials
- Using imagination in play
- Cooperating with others in play
- Playing with objects
- Imitative playing
- Playing using symbols

Math and science

- Classifying
- Sorting
- Matching
- Seriating
- Counting
- One-to-one correspondence
- Cardinality
- Sequencing
- Spatial relationships
- Patterning
- Discovering properties of materials
- Following sequences
- Estimating size, time, quantity, etc.
- Understanding time sequences
- Constructing
- Investigating a problem
- Designing objects
- Making models
- Carrying out plans
- Investigating nature
- Using research methods
- Identifying and solving problems
- Scientific discovery
- Categorizing
- Summarizing

- Stating or testing hypotheses
- Mathematical thinking: space, time, volume, weight, number, capacity, ratios
- Discovering

Thinking skills

- Constructing meaning
- Trial-and-error behaviour
- Use of symbolism
- Concrete thinking
- Identifying
- Organizing ideas
- Moral or ethical reasoning
- Moving from one idea to the next
- Decoding
- Encoding
- Using logic
- Predicting outcomes
- Convergent problem-solving
- Creative problem-solving
- Remembering people, objects, and places
- Considering others' viewpoints
- Goal-setting
- Producing ideas
- Using rational arguments
- Combining ideas
- Conserving ideas
- Decentring
- Imaging (creating a mental picture)
- Memorizing
- Comparing
- Contrasting
- Using intuition
- Using metacognitive strategies

- Developing strategies for problem-solving
- Recalling facts
- Learning by rote
- Creating rules
- Making free associations
- Attention span
- Curiosity
- Awareness of own thinking processes
- Brainstorming
- Refining solutions
- Identifying elements of "the mind"
- Deferring gratification
- Analyzing
- Assessing situations
- Synthesizing ideas
- Recognition of own learning style

Language and thought

- Emergence of language
- Use of language to express ideas
- Reponse to ideas
- Expressing a problem
- Reading and understanding
- Rhyming (to remember an idea)
- Using metalinguistic strategies
- Overextending rules
- Scribbling
- Attempting to spell
- Recording events
- Debating
- Paraphrasing
- Comprehending
- Making inferences
- Recording ideas

- Telling stories
- Making objective comments
- Making value judgments

Concept development

- Object and people permanence (the cognitive process by which a person can exercise complex recall and the ability to hold the idea of another person or an object in mind)
- Conserving ideas
- Concentrating or focusing on single ideas
- Identifying people, objects, and places
- Asking questions
- Discriminating
- Aesthetic understanding
- Concept of self and others
- Concepts: colour, floating and sinking, growth, change, money, shape, need and want, home, childcare or school, distance, measurement, time, routine, speed, weather, shopping, animals, plants, nature, towns, number, fairness, fractions, division, caring, belonging, more than/less than

Sensori-motor intelligence

- Reflexive behaviours
- Exploration
- Experimentation
- Sensory acuity
- Sensory discovery
- Attachment behaviours
- Responses to stimuli
- Imitation

continued

- Grasping and sucking
- Repetitive actions
- Coordinated sequences of action
- Discovery of new ways of achieving goal
- Symbolic functioning

Specific challenges
- Magical thinking
- Making errors

- Animism
- Loss of memory
- Errors in logic
- Conceptual errors
- Overgeneralizing
- Egocentrism
- Lack of conservation skills
- Attitude to learning

TAKING A SPECIAL LOOK: Patterns of development

Children gain developmental skills almost always in the same sequence, even though they may demonstrate them at varying rates. For a child with special needs whose development is somewhat uneven, you may observe that some of his domains of development are more advanced than the rest. Frequently, one aspect of development will affect another, so childcare professionals sometimes need to respond in different ways. For example, you may need to arouse the interest of a child who has a hearing deficit by providing visual rather than auditory stimulation. Watch closely to see the reactions to your stimuli and respond accordingly.

Spirituality

Spirituality is concerned with personal reflections, experiences that transcend the "here and now," a connection or relationship with a power or person outside the self, and an appreciation of the significance of people and things. Not all childcare professionals consider this developmental domain significant, and those who do may have difficulty defining it. For some, spirituality involves appreciating beauty, developing aesthetic values, and demonstrating care for the world and its people. For others, it is strongly associated with a religion or philosophy of belief about our creation, the nature of existence, and our role in the world. Spiritual development can involve an increased awareness, understanding, or practice in any of these areas.

Spiritual development is possibly the most challenging area of human development to observe. Philosophical thought obviously involves cognition, but there is more to spirituality than logic and mental gymnastics, and even that part of spiritual thought is not easily observed. Our observation of children's actions and words may only hint at a surface explanation for something that runs much deeper.

What to Observe: Indicators of spiritual development

Aesthetics

- Appreciation of beauty
- Appreciating art forms
- Recognition of aesthetics
- Interest in literature
- Engaging in movement and dance
- Poetry

Social responsibility

- Appreciating the efforts of others
- Pro-social behaviours (see previous categories)
- Trying to please
- Forgiving
- Striving for justice
- Advocating for peace
- Membership in a group
- Social advocacy
- Expressing ethical perspectives and behaving according to ethical principles
- Respecting people for their "good" qualities/role modelling

Emotion

- Expressing love
- Experiencing the intensity of emotions
- Accepting forgiveness
- Primary emotions (see previous categories)
- Social emotions (see previous categories)
- Becoming attached to an object
- Fearing consequences

- Overly strong sense of guilt
- Enjoying repetition
- Singing and chanting
- Feeling "at one" with the world/God/divine force
- Making attachments
- Expressing emotional experiences or ideas
- Being in a state of depression, sadness, bereavement, loss, etc.
- Feeling protected

Purpose

- Discussion of the meaning or purpose of life
- Searching for answers to the big questions of life (e.g., why are we here?)
- Enjoying myths and legends
- Analyzing why events happen
- Making meaning from traumatic events
- Finding meaning through experience
- Sensing purpose of life

Beliefs

- Philosophical thought
- Belief in the sanctity of human life
- Attributing "bad" things to the devil or Satan
- Acknowledging and respecting icons, symbols, altars, and other holy objects
- Belief in an afterlife

- Belief in the soul or other immortal element of human beings
- Belief in sacraments and other practical signs of spiritual occurrences
- Belief in being saved
- Belief in reincarnation
- Belief in God, the Divine, Krishna, the creator, mother Earth
- Belief in immortality
- Animism
- Belief in extraterrestrial forces
- Having pretend friendships
- Superstitious beliefs and practices
- Interpreting scriptures, holy books, and moral stories

Experience

- Levels of consciousness
- Meditation and prayer
- Listening to music
- Attunement to nature
- Wonder
- Joy
- Connection with predecessors
- Identification with culture or ethnicity
- Imagination
- Heightened sensory perception
- Experiencing success or failure
- Openness to subjective experience
- Experiencing collective guilt
- Seeing self as a small part of the world/universe
- Staring at a flower with wonder
- Connectedness with family, friends, etc.

- Romance
- The dream world
- Fun experiences
- Transcending the "here and now"
- Stillness
- Appreciating the "essence" of an experience
- Dreaming
- Giving thanks
- Celebrating
- Fasting
- Metaphysical thought
- Making a pilgrimage
- Knowledge of nirvana, heaven, hell, the underworld, etc.
- Worshipping
- Experience of death
- Mysticism
- Close personal relationships
- Knowledge or wisdom
- Healing
- Mindfulness
- Communication with the "creator"
- Atoning
- Acknowledging auras, karmas, atmospheres
- Communion/communing
- Love for people or for God
- Experiencing a "high" (non-drug-related)
- Visiting historic and holy places
- Living in the moment

Insight

- Insights regarding the future
- Premonitions

- Intuition
- Fantasy
- Magic and imagination
- Creative activity
- Listening to an inner voice
- Inspiration
- Interpreting dreams
- Sensing doom or fear of the future

Thinking

- Curiosity
- Symbolism
- Recognition of signs
- Imitating role models
- Internalizing values
- Magic thinking
- Anticipating events
- Discussing moral/ethical principles
- Being solitary
- Comparing and contrasting world religions
- Exploring social justice
- Punishment and retribution

- Identifying a moral in a story
- Interest in the supernatural or occult
- Identification of archetypes
- Determining personal values
- Understanding the relevance of morality tales
- Arguing from a specific religious or moral standpoint
- Perspective-taking
- Avoiding reality
- Attributing events to God
- Attributing unusual powers to objects of people

Ceremony

- Rituals
- Ceremonies/celebrations
- Rites of passage
- Birthday, anniversary celebrations
- Reciting mantras, creeds, scriptures
- Initiations

The interaction of domains of development

When we observe any child, we see a flow of behaviour that is not labelled as part of any one developmental domain. In fact, we should make sure that we do not think of any behaviour as solely representative of one domain; every behaviour involves interacting domains. Since no area of development should be considered without seeing how it might relate to the others, we need to observe carefully and consider the **whole child**. If, for example, we observe language skills, we must remember that they depend on social skill development, cognitive processes, emotional ties, and the physical skill of sound production. We need many observation and interactions before we can come close to understanding the whole child.

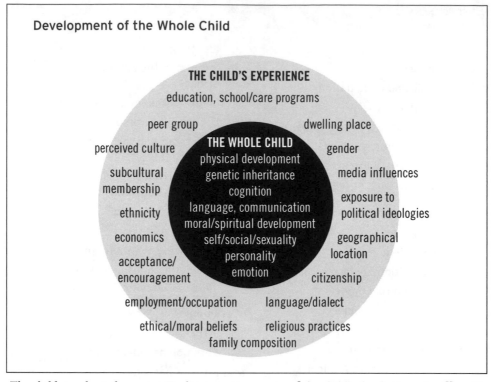

Development of the Whole Child

THE CHILD'S EXPERIENCE

education, school/care programs

peer group   dwelling place

perceived culture   **THE WHOLE CHILD**   gender

subcultural   physical development   media influences
membership   genetic inheritance
                    cognition   exposure to
ethnicity   language, communication   political ideologies
                    moral/spiritual development
economics   self/social/sexuality   geographical
                    personality   location
acceptance/   emotion
encouragement   citizenship

employment/occupation   language/dialect

ethical/moral beliefs   religious practices

family composition

The child stands at the centre. Each interacting aspect of the child's development is affected by all of the environmental factors that contribute to his experience of the world. You observe the behaviours that help you make inferences about the whole child's development.

Recording Your Observations of Children's Development

Your instructor will provide you with blank forms that will help you record developmental observations.

Start with a chart ready to input your observation. (Of course, you may not see what you are looking for if the child does not demonstrate it!)

Developmental domain	Category	Indicator	Observation/evidence of indicator

Example

Child's name	Jasmine
Age	8 months 2 weeks
Date	October 10, 2008
Observer's name	Rosie
Time	2.45–4.35 p.m.
Context	Child Care Centre, floor play
Domain(s) of Development	Physical

Developmental domain	Category	Indicator	Observation/evidence of indicator
physical development	gross-motor skills	sitting up	Jasmine sat propped by a cushion as she was handling some plastic bath toys. When the cushion moved because another child kicked it, Jasmine remained sitting without falling to her side. She remained still for several moments but when she heard the teacher she looked up and this caused her to twist around onto her tummy
physical development	fine motor skills	manipulating objects	Sitting surrounded by a semi-circular cushion, Jasmine reached forward and grasped a plastic train. She first held it to her mouth and then looked at it carefully bringing it up to her eyes. Passing the train from one hand to the other (L-R) repeatedly, she was distracted by another child's interest in "her" toy, and then held it close to her tummy with both hands.
physical development	senses	multi-modal sensory experience	Jasmine spent some time looking at other children as they were introduced to goop (cornstarch and water in shallow containers on the floor). She appeared hesitant as she waved her arm towards the goop. With apparent caution she stretched out her hand and banged it into the goop. It made a sound that seemed to startle her, but she persisted (did she understand cause and effect here?). Bringing her goop-covered hand toward her face, she spread goop under her nose and into her open mouth. She may have detected a smell (but does it have a smell?), and seemed to dislike the taste and the texture making an expression of distaste. She looked toward the teacher and made a repetitive "aah" sound indicating she wanted the goop experience to end.

An alternative approach is conducting an open-ended observation and then categorizing what you record using developmental domains.

Example

Child's name	Maya
Age	4 years 3 months
Date	October 12, 2007
Observer's name	Jon
Time	10–10.22 a.m.
Context	Home childcare playroom

Open-ended observation

Recording	Indicators of development (determine after you finish recording)
Maya is seated on the sofa next to Maria. They are undressing dolls. Maya pulls at the skirt of one of the Barbie dolls; "this is too hard" she says holding it up to the caregiver. "Have another go" suggests the Caregiver. When her next attempt fails to remove the skirt the caregiver suggests that Maya try to open the Velcro tabs on the skirt. Maya holds the top of the doll in one hand (L) and the skirt in the other (R) and pulled. The skirt comes off. "She's naked" Maya giggles, "I gotta find somut else" Maya says to Maria. "Give it to me" Maya shouts, but Maya appears persistent and continues with her efforts. Maya slides off the sofa onto the carpeted floor. Running toward the kitchen the caregiver warns her to "be careful". Maya looks in drawers, on the counter-top, and as she approaches the stove she sees a piece of aluminum foil. "Can I have it?" Maya asks. "Well,	gross motor skill—sitting fine-motor skill—manipulation language—declaration personality—persistence fine motor skill—manipulating materials cognitive skill—following instructions cognitive—concept of nakedness personality—humour language—makes request gross-motor skill—sliding to standing gross-motor skill—running cognitive—searching/keeping an objective in mind language—asking 3 word question

you can have a small piece of it" and she tears off a piece about 12cm square. Maya takes the foil and appears to explore its properties, crinkling it, smoothing it, tearing it, cutting it, and seeing how it bends. She tears the smooth part of the foil and bends it around the Barbie doll making a shiny skirt. "That's not straight," Maria offers, but Maya seems pleased with her efforts and holds the doll up for the caregiver's inspection. "I wanna do that" says Maria, and soon after Maya gives Maria a small piece of left over foil. "We could make other things with foil" suggests the caregiver, but Maya appears focused on her doll. "She's going clubbing" Maya says "and she look good . . . she dance" Maya giggles again.	cognition

Principles of Child Development

Understanding developmental theories

We should be aware of each of the developmental domains and also keep in mind some other important ideas that shape how we observe, what we see, and how we interpret that information. As we observe children, we come to realize that many of their surface behaviours indicate that much more is going on in their bodies and minds than we first supposed.

Behaviour as a key to development

The way to learn about young children is to be with them and to observe them. Observing a child's behaviours is the best way of appreciating the child's development and needs. Earlier in this chapter we explored the domains of child development and determined some of the things we might look for that fall within those domains. By watching the child in action in various situations, we can come to know and understand her better. All we see are surface behaviours; we cannot observe inner psychological and cognitive processes directly. However, we can draw inferences from the things the child does, what she says, and the mistakes she might make.

Behaviourists such as Watson and Pavlov focus on the demonstration of behaviours to help them understand their "subject"—the child. Their understandings can be useful to us, but appreciating some of the underlying motivations, thought processes, and feelings can help us understand the individual child more sensitively. Freud offers a **psychoanalytic** framework that provides further insights. Bandura, founder of the social learning approach, helps us understand the importance of imitation and role-modelling. Piaget, perhaps our most important developmental psychologist, supplies a complex model for grasping the dynamic processes that underpin the observable behaviours we can record. His word focuses on cognitive and moral behaviours as well as play. Vygotsky offers us a theory of development that focuses on the social aspects of development that he thought essential for language, thought and learning. More recently, Greenspan has delved into the child's emotional development and is a keen observer of children's behaviour that enables adults to enter into relationships with children and assist them to 'put right' any difficulties that have been experienced. Many other theorists also provide constructs that assist in our interpretation of the behaviours we see.

We need to ensure that we separate our observation of behaviour from our interpretations of it; the interpretations may be correct, but our own application of a particular theory to observed information may not lead to a complete, full, or correct analysis. It is better not to act too quickly. Learn to observe well before applying theories and creating inferences.

Ages and stages

Any casual observer will notice that children change as they grow. An adult is more than just a large baby; Infants become toddlers; in time they become preschoolers; and later they become school-age children. They increase in age, grow in height, gain weight, and develop in many ways as they acquire skills, construct knowledge, and acquire values and attitudes. These things happen simultaneously as all the domains of the child's development interact. The changes that we see follow a sequential pattern; in most cases, the child makes these gains progressively. Children do not always undergo these changes at the same **chronological age** (actual age), but the order of acquiring these skills remains much the same. We see that there are qualitatively different levels of development. For example, the toddler solves problems differently than an older child does. The periods of time that can be characterized in different steps we call stages. Ages and stages are not necessarily the same. Observing a child's behaviour indicates better her stage of development than does her age. Some stages refer to an approximate age range, such as "toddlerhood." Other stage labels refer to abstract ideas, such as "the sensori-motor stage." Significant stages of development, or the acquisition of particular skills, may be referred to as **milestones**.

Clarify your meaning when you use any stage description, because the meanings of such terms vary considerably. Variations come about because of culture, social expectations, research methods, legislation, and childcare and education program delivery.

Stage constructs

Model A: Broad stages commonly associated with childcare provision

infancy	birth to 12 months (or walking)
toddlerhood	12 months (or walking) to 30 months
preschooler	30 months to 5-6 years
school-age children	5-6 years to 11-12 years

Model B: Freudian stages/Psychoanalytical approach

oral stage	birth to 12 months
anal stage	12 to 36 months
phallic stage	3 years to 5 years
latency stage	5 years to puberty
genital stage	from puberty onwards

These are age approximations. Each stage involves complex interactions between the id, ego, and superego. These stages are for reference only; students should research Freudian ideas in order to gain an overview of his theory.

Model C: Erikson/Psychosocial approach

trust versus mistrust	birth to 12 months
autonomy versus shame	12 to 36 months
initiative versus guilt	3 to 5 years
industry versus inferiority	elementary years

These are age approximations. Each stage involves a profound inner conflict that has to be resolved. These stages are for reference only; students should research Erikson's ideas after they gain some understanding of the structure of his theory.

Model D: Piaget/Developmental psychology model

sensori-motor stage	birth to 2 years
pre-operational period	2 to 7 years
concrete operational period	7 to 11 years
formal operational period	11 years to adulthood

These are age approximations. Each stage involves development through qualitatively different ways of thinking and behaving. The stages are for reference only; students should research Piaget's theory in order to study its structure.

Model E: Allen and Marotz age/stage profiles

This is a model based on levels of maturation and developed from surveying large numbers of children. Gesell (1940) initiated this style of profile; Sheridan (1992) created a similar model using a different population of children. Other maturational profiles can be accessed for assessment purposes.

pre-natal	(first, second, and third trimester)
birth	
neonate	birth to 28 days
infant	1 to 4 months
	4 to 8 months
	8 to 12 months
toddler	12 to 24 months
	the 2-year-old
preschool child	the 3-year-old
	the 4-year-old
	the 5-year-old
school-age children	the 6-year-old
	the 7- and 8-year-old

Model F: Greenspan's milestones in emotional development

self-regulation and interest in the world	birth to 3 months
falling in love	2 to 7 months
developing intentional communications	3 to 10 months
the emergence of an organized sense of self	9 to 18 months
creating emotional ideas	18 to 36 months
emotional thinking	30 to 48 months

These are age approximations. Each stage involves significant emotional experiences and reactions. The stages are for reference only; students should research Greenspan's concept based on *First Feelings* (1985).

Key Issues in Early Development

Attachments   Bowlby (1965), Ainsworth (1972), and others have undertaken significant research on the necessity of early attachments. Caregivers should observe the processes of attachment and separation that children experience. Secure attachments are essential for healthy development in all domains. With infants, the attachment relationships with primary caregivers should be strong and well supported. With children of all ages, caregivers must observe how the children make transitions from one adult they know well to another adult, and they must find ways of supporting them through such separations. Strong emotional ties will lead to trusting relationships.

The child as the constructor of knowledge   Piaget's (1954) theory of developmental psychology offers a profound view of children's **construction of knowledge.** He observed and described play sequences that indicate that young children learn through direct experience. Their understanding must come from firsthand experiences; caregivers may orchestrate the events, but the children must play themselves. Piaget's theory reinforces the need to observe children's activities and to be present during those activities to ensure that the children can construct meaningful learning. Where necessary, caregivers have to intervene, reconstruct the physical environment, and then continue to observe.

The adult's role as facilitator of learning   Froebel (1974; orig.1826) describes the adult as a gardener in the child's garden. The garden metaphor is a useful concept in understanding child development. Teachers and caregivers must watch what is happening and supply the nurturance, tools, or practical help as required. They must be keen observers and learn when and how to assist the children's development.

The zone of proximal development and scaffolding   Vygotsky (1978) discusses a **zone of proximal development** that explains how children can be supported to acquire new learning. Through observation, caregivers identify what each child knows or can currently accomplish. The caregivers employ a variety of strategies to help the children perform at a new level of skill or acquire new knowledge. Bridging the gap between what each child can do with help, and then without assistance, allows caregivers to assist learning and allows the children to be successful. This principle underlines the need for careful observation and appropriate intervention in the children's activity.

Bruner (1966) developed a theory of **scaffolding** by studying how adults help children gain new language skills. He noticed that many mothers aided their children's language by extending the learning that the child had already gained. Mothers observed their infants closely and provided a "scaffold" for new language by using various support strategies. This model applies to many different situations in which caregivers observe children.

Neuroscience   Neuroscientific research currently under way is offering exciting insights into how the human brain works. This has major implications for parents and professionals involved with infants and young children. A number of reports, including *Rethinking the brain: New insights into early development* (Shore 1997), *The early years study: Reversing the real brain drain* (McCain & Mustard 1999), *Brain research and childhood education: Implications for educators* (Bergen & Coscia 2001), and *The early years study? Putting science into action* (McCain, Mustard, & Shanker 2007), have helped educators translate the highly technical and scientific data into material that is understandable and offers clear implications for practice. This is an area of research that is helping educators understand how children learn, when it is best to offer key experiences, and what is happening as children acquire new skills and knowledge.

Fortunately these reports have not significantly contradicted our previous understanding of development supplied by Piaget, Vygotsky, and other eminent figures. The reports are challenging to condense to essentials: educators need to reinforce their understandings of the immense capacities and the **neural plasticity** of the brain, and they also need to provide optimal learning environments to help maximize the brain's potential. However, **neuroscience** does not suggest that overly structured and targeted programs be developed for children; rather, science underscores the need to provide developmentally appropriate environments. We can observe children's responses to the experiences that we provide and mediate them according to the children's needs as they become apparent.

Play   Play is central to a child's development. Through **play**, there comes understanding about the world, relationships, and the self. Play behaviours offer observers insight into how the child perceives her world, her feelings, her social relationships, the physical and cognitive skills she has gained, and her interests and challenges. Play has many dimensions, and can be both mysterious and challenging to interpret. When we observe children playing we know that several aspects of their development are involved at any one time. Many of the great developmental theorists have studied the significance of play and they all agree that it is essential to learning and development. There are many theories of play, that is, explanations of why it occurs, its level of importance, its function, and its relationship to development. Play activity appears to spring spontaneously from the child, and this has been observed across all cultures. The well-respected expert on play and development, Fergus P. Hughes, claims that "play has been observed in virtually every human culture, past and present" (1999, p. 33). That said, it may take different forms that are culturally shaped. Our greatest difficulty is to know exactly what play is. There are many definitions of it, but Hughes offers us the useful idea that play has five essential characteristics: intrinsically motivated, freely chosen, pleasurable, nonliteral, and actively engaged in by the player (pp. 2–3). Doris Bergen has been an advocate for quality play throughout her working life. As one of a series of chapters on play (1998, p. 35) she explains how there has been increasing interest in studying play and this has been supported by better methods of studying it. Bergen suggests that "typical methods used for studying play include (a) naturalistic observation; (b) experimental manipulation and observation; and (c) self report/performance measures, such as interviews, questionnaires, and psychological or informational test" (p. 41). As this text offers skill development in most of those areas, we should feel comfortable being part of the process of studying play, as well as its link with development. One framework for studying play is to observe play activity and then refer to Parten's (1932) understanding of the stages of social play, to help you understand what you saw. These stages are: unoccupied (disengaged from play activity), onlooker (the outsider, or looking at the play of others for imitative purposes), solitary (playing alone in an egocentric manner), associative (playing alongside others but without understanding of the others' perspective), parallel (playing alongside another with similar intentions and actions), and cooperative (playing with shared intentions, role performances, social exchanges). These aspects of play tend to occur in that sequence, but children of all ages will engage in all these types of play. There are many more ways of considering play. A good place to start to understand these aspects is in Hughes's text *Children, Play and Development*, or *Play as a Medium for Learning and Development*, edited by Doris Bergen, although there are many other useful sources. The more you can understand about play the better able you will be to observe and record useful information.

Multiple aspects of intelligence   In recent years, interest had increased in Gardner's (1993) work on **multiple intelligences**. He hypothesizes that there are nine or more different forms of intelligence—spatial, logical/mathematical, linguistic, bodily/kinesthetic, musical, interpersonal, intrapersonal, naturalist, and existential. He suggests that, if we observe different children, we see that they think and operate differently. Teachers and caregivers should offer different learning experiences to accommodate all types of learning, without valuing any intellectual type over another. Each child will vary in both his approach to learning and the content of what he is to learn. The work of Goleman (1997; 2006) on **emotional** and **social intelligence** reinforces our need to observe and value ways to control, manage, motivate, and recognize emotions in others and to handle relationships. Both Gardner's and Goleman's theories clearly indicate that caregivers must observe and identify personal styles in order to meet the children's needs.

Sleep   Scientifically, sleep remains a great mystery. Some interesting studies have been conducted on the types and qualities of sleep, and the effects that they have on adults. Infant sleep studies have also enlightened us about the body's need for sleep and its regenerative powers. Studies have recently determined that many adults and children are getting inadequate, poor-quality, or too little sleep. Sleep hygiene may seem an old-fashioned concept, but it seems that negative sleep experiences are having a profound effect on children's learning and safety, and may negatively affect all-round development. The science of sleep can help our understanding of the processes of sleep, and watching children sleep may help us determine people's sleep patterns. At the same time, we must appreciate that adults need to provide an optimal environment for children that balances their stimulation and their relaxation, their social activity and their private space, and childcare professionals must ensure that children's differing needs for sleep, naps, downtime, and uptime be accommodated. Without adequate, good-quality sleep, children cannot benefit from the programs and experiences we offer.

Cultural diversity   Many of the children we care for and educate come from backgrounds very different from our own. This **cultural diversity** can be positive for us all. We benefit both from the breadth of experience of our community and from the multicultural climate that stops us from making assumptions about those who may seem to be unlike ourselves. When we observe the behaviour of people from different cultural groups, we must avoid employing **stereotypes** and generalizations from one family's behavioural patterns. Those behaviours may be particular to a family or even to an individual. Asking questions can supply us with really helpful information—a person will rarely reject a genuine inquiry—but approach the parent in an appropriate manner. Invite parents to participate in whatever way they can, and you will find you get to know each other better and provide a stronger bridge between the child's home and the childcare facility or school.

A pro-social ethos   Moral understanding depends on children's stages of maturation as well as their environments. Although parents are usually the strongest influence on their children's value systems, children also receive many strong messages from the media and from the other adults around them. Social learning theorists such as Bandura (1977) explain this process as imitation and deferred imitation, yet the way children construct their own set of values is more involved than mere imitation. A complex interplay between children and their environment enables them to search for meaning. Their cognitive level shapes how this happens; children can only internalize "right" and "wrong" according to their own personal realities.

Positive guidance strategies and strong role models can influence how children learn to behave; children acquire much of their moral and pro-social learning through conversation with adults. When we listen to what they tell us and respond thoughtfully, children know that we take their thinking seriously and care about them. In addition, we can observe their play behaviours and intervene to label a behaviour, clarify a moral issue, or nurse hurt feelings.

Ecological systems   Because human development occurs within a social system, caregivers must know about children's social networks and as much as possible about their

Children who come from other cultures can face social and linguistic challenges in North America. If such children also have special physical or developmental needs, caregivers and teachers must approach the assessment process with extra care. Methods of authentic assessment will allow a child to demonstrate his abilities and needs clearly. If at all possible, the child should be assessed in his native language to avoid misunderstandings and to ensure that a limited command of English is not interpreted as a limited ability to communicate or understand. Similarly, a person from, or at least familiar with, the family's culture should be present at meetings with the family, both to help the family understand the child's needs and to ensure that the family's beliefs and values are understood and respected by the caregivers and other professionals involved with the child.

broader ecological systems. Bronfenbrenner's (1979) **ecological systems model** of concentric circles explains how a child's development is influenced by a wide variety of social, political, economic, and religious aspects of the environment (see page 180). Caregivers should do their best to appreciate these interrelated factors that shape the development of the children they care for. Possible strategies include conducting sociological studies, observing local environments, keeping up to date with economic and employment issues, finding out about social challenges in the community, and establishing good communication with parent groups. Contextual questionnaires can supplement this data (see pages 266–68).

Early intervention   Until recently, it was thought inappropriate to interfere with a child's development in its very early stages. Any remediation or accommodation was thought unnecessary unless the child had a severe physical disability. The Greenspans' (1985) work, however, demonstrates great success in **early intervention** with infants and toddlers who are experiencing emotional and social challenges in their relationship-building. Recent studies show that "intensive, well-designed, timely intervention can improve the prospects—and the quality of life—of many children who are considered to be at risk. . . . In some cases, effective intervention efforts can even ameliorate conditions once thought to be virtually untreatable" (Shore 1997). Caregivers need to observe many aspects of early development, especially those involving how babies relate to adults. Early observation and identification of social difficulties may have lifelong effects.

Sensitive periods of development   The entire lifespan provides a time for a flow of change, and certain sensitive periods are particularly important for learning specific skills and acquiring cognitive processes. Observations of the imprinting behaviours of young birds led Lorenz (1937) to develop this theory, which can also be applied to other aspects of development. Language learning, in particular, is much easier for a young person acquiring a first or subsequent language. Bowlby (1965) believed that maternal bonding with a newborn needs to happen immediately after birth, or subsequent attachments will be spoiled.

Although some people debate whether a child will actually miss the stage or skill if he does not develop it during the sensitive period, it may not be possible for him to make up for some early deprivations. A neglected child who was not exposed to language or social learning may show severely reduced ability to gain a full language; in one such case, the child was able to say only a handful of words when she received concentrated teaching. Some mechanisms do exist to overcome certain short-term deprivations or limitations; in principle, however, some key experiences need to be provided at the right moments. We can observe the "prime times" (Shore 1997), critical periods, or whatever we may call the best time for particular experiences, when the child's response to an experience elicits a desired learning. Educators waste precious time when they try to "teach" a child something when the timing is not right for him.

Developmental diversity   As more children diagnosed with special needs are integrated into mainstream settings, we see a greater need to accommodate a wider range of development within any group of children. **Developmental diversity** can be positive for the individual and for society. At the same time, the integration presents a challenge in terms of curriculum and assessment. Observation skills need to be finely honed, and a wide range of assessment tools is necessary. Conducting some standardized assessments may be helpful, depending on the caregiver's role and responsibilities (see Chapter 11). It will always be necessary to read reports from educational psychologists and to be able to interpret the summary or results. Any **individual program plan (IPP)** that has been developed will have to be carried out. It is preferable that such a plan be a team activity; however, teachers can also find themselves carrying out the plans of psychologists or other interventionists, so they must be able to understand what is required and to observe and record the child's responses.

We have discussed ages and stages in this chapter. Now we revisit the age/stage approach, and consider the variety of individual developmental patterns. The age and stage profiles can be useful when we compare a child's demonstrated behaviour and chronological age with any of the stage charts—they give us an idea of where the child "is" in her development. The charts do not indicate what a child "should" be able to demonstrate; they illustrate what the "average child" can do at a given age. There is no such thing as the average child. It is appropriate to measure a child's performance in a constructive manner—but in terms of what competence she has, not what she cannot yet do! The concept of the norm is useful for parents and professionals as a benchmark and a reference point only; it is not acceptable to judge a child's development in such a way that the child "fails" in some manner.

The concept of "normal" is also open to misapplication. There are no "normal" children. The "norm" is an abstract measurement. Remember that many of the world's great thinkers have performed in ways considered well below accepted norms at some time in their lives. Focus on competence and the behavioural evidence of development, document this progress, and find ways of responding appropriately.

Health issues   In order to notice that a child is looking or behaving in ways that are different from usual, caregivers need to know about typical appearance and usual patterns of behaviour. Baseline observations are usually made on a daily basis. They can give us clear information about a child's state at the start of the day, which then acts as a useful reference point for later physical or behavioural changes. Pimento and Kernested (1996) suggest that caregivers take the time to observe and assess growth, personal hygiene, emotional health, developmental skills, and a range of physical and behavioural signs and symptoms.

Resilience and children's needs   Children do not always respond to the same situations in the same ways. Recent studies show that some children fare better in adverse situations than others. These children who do better despite difficult circumstances are considered **resilient**. Parents and professionals need to appreciate the factors that contribute to making children more resilient. We don't want children to experience difficult circumstances; but if challenges arise, we want them to cope well, adapt themselves to the situation, and go on to succeed in every aspect of their lives. Steinhauer (1996) considered the task of raising competent children a collective responsibility that benefits society, the child, and the family. The framework Steinhauer offers may seem like common sense, but it needs to be stated. Children have primary needs that include biological, physical, cognitive, and emotional/social elements. As he found in his work, and as is echoed in the work of many others, children often do not have these needs met and consequently fail to develop in ways that will enable them to become resilient.

When we think about basic needs, we might first think of the physical ones, such as air, food, protection, and so on. Recent studies have elaborated upon these items. Children's real needs appear to include enriched relationships and experiences as well. Brazelton and Greenspan (2000) have collaborated to produce a useful model. They identify significant needs of all children that are "irreducible"—an absolute minimum: the need for ongoing nurturing relationships, physical protection, safety, and regulation, and experiences tailored to individual differences; the need for developmentally appropriate experiences, limit setting, structure, and expectations; and the need for stable supportive communities and cultural continuity.

These **irreducible needs** seem much more than basic; if they are not met, society suffers along with the individual child and family. Brazelton and Greenspan urge that these needs be considered "the highest international priority, alongside human rights, as a 'right' for all. . . . [They] can serve as a framework (a report card) for nations and regions within nations and the international community as a whole to monitor current status and provide incentives for progress" (2000).

Developmental Assets   With the broad goal of increasing the resilience of all children, the Search Institute created several sets of **Developmental Assets**, each corresponding to children's different ages/stages. Each set includes a set of conditions in which children are enabled to develop in healthy ways. Many organizations and associations mandated to support children's needs, as well as childcare programs, schools, summer camps, and other settings, have adopted the 40 Developmental Assets as support to their program design and delivery. The Assets include family and community supports, so success depends on a collaborative venture. The Search Institute explains their strategy: "What's needed is an understanding of what actions and behaviors breed success, willingness and ideas to apply that knowledge, and most importantly, a desire to see young people grow up happy, healthy, and confident" (**www.search-institute.org**).

The Early Development Instrument (EDI)   Observing children so that accurate information informs policies and funding sources is a massive undertaking. It requires a well-designed methodology, good data collection, and competent analysis. One such group level measure is the Early Development Instrument. We mention it here not because you will soon be part of the observation process, but that you can appreciate the necessity for large-scale observations. The information required is similar to the observations you will be making, and focus on broad developmental data or a collection of observations leading to what is considered to be school readiness. Whether or not school readiness can actually be measured in another issue, and whether developmental information should be gathered for collective benefit rather than benefiting the individual is also open to discussion.

Linking Observation and Development

- The observer knows what to look for in each developmental domain.
- Recorded information is detailed and specific.
- Analysis of observation is more straightforward if data is already categorized.
- Data collection can meet the needs of educators to provide appropriate and individualized developmental programs.
- The approach is holistic.
- Observations are reviewed within the construct of developmental principles.
- Information is set into context.
- Observational information is recorded immediately.
- The observer learns more about development by observing.

Summary

As we learn more about children, we know more about what behaviours to look for, and how to interpret some of the behaviours we see displayed. All the time we are observing we need to hold in mind some basic philosophical beliefs about human beings. Our particular philosophical perspectives shape how we understand children. These beliefs indicate our own values and must be based on sound research, experience, and tested theories; they encapsulate how we think development occurs.

One way of understanding children is to think about their develement as it occurs in different domains. These include physical, sexual, language and communication, cognitive, emotional, spiritual, social, and personality domains. A childcare professional will learn to observe and identify behaviours in each of these domains. Even though we can identify behaviours that fall within these categories, many behaviours demonstrate an interaction among several different domains. The child is a whole person exhibiting integrated behaviour; her behaviour does not occur in separate, neatly labelled boxes. We can look for many behaviours, but children will often behave in unexpected ways; we need to be prepared to observe and record these too.

There are observable characteristics of development that can be readily seen by even a casual child-watcher. Studying children usually involves understanding the ages and stages of their development. Although there is a pattern of development common to all children, the rate of the progression of each child is highly individual.

Behaviourists tend to focus on demonstrated behaviour rather than motivators or other inner thoughts of the child. Social learning theorists suggest that imitative learning and the internalizing of role models explain some of a child's behaviours. Psychoanalytic thought leads people to consider the individual's deeper drives and motivations. Developmental psychologists also operate on this complex level of behaviour analysis. They appreciate the qualitatively different stages of thinking and behaving that emerge from a close scrutiny of actions. Surface behaviours tell us about acquired skills and indicate changes at a deeper level as well.

As science and research studies inform our work with children, we can create and revise our set of principles of development. We consider the child an active creator of her own knowledge and the adult plays a clear role in facilitating the child's learning. A prosocial ethos helps us to value and encourage moral understanding and appreciate it within a developmental construct. Children have a variety of ways of being smart, and children are stronger in some areas than others. We have to accommodate these multiple aspects of intelligence once we have observed them.

Neuroscience has updated our thinking about children and learning. Fortunately, it underscores much of what we already know about the importance of a child's early years to his later development. We appreciate the emotional needs of young children, particularly their need for attachment to certain adults. The cultural context of a child's upbringing and schooling influences his behaviour, attitudes, and thinking; these should be celebrated. The ecological system into which every child is born is unique. Educators must be mindful of that ecological system when trying to determine and meet the needs of children. There are some irreducible needs for all children, although the ways in which they are met may differ widely; these differences are both physical and psychological. When a child's needs are met she is likely to be more resilient when any challenges present themselves. Although there are some sensitive periods that are a prime time for a child to experience particular things, parents and educators can take comfort in the fact that there is also some flexibility in this development and in the child's brain plasticity. Early intervention programs can ameliorate the effects of previous damage. We can observe a wide range of development in any group of children, even children of similar ages. All children need to have experiences and programs designed for their particular capabilities.

In the past, researchers have theorized about child development on the basis of their observation of children. Additionally, applied neuroscience will offer insights into what is going on within a child. We aim to understand children from the inside and outside.

Key Terms

- assistive devices
- attachment
- behaviourists
- biological clock
- cephalo-caudal principle
- child development
- chronological age
- cognition
- construction of knowledge
- cue
- cultural diversity
- Developmental Assets
- developmental diversity
- early intervention
- ecological systems model
- emotion
- emotional intelligence

- fine motor skills
- gross motor skills
- indicators
- individual program plan (IPP)
- irreducible needs
- language
- maturation
- milestones
- morality
- multiple intelligences
- neural plasticity
- neuroscience
- norm
- personality
- play
- physical development
- pro-social skills

continued

- proximo-distal principle
- psychoanalytic (theory)
- psychological clock
- resilient
- scaffolding
- sensitive period
- sensory acuity
- sexual development
- social clock
- social emotions
- social intelligence
- social interaction
- social play
- special needs
- spirituality
- stereotype
- temperament
- whole child
- zone of proximal development

Weblinks

www.childstudy.net/cdw.html
Overview of the "Classic Theories of Child Development" of Freud, Mahler, and Erikson.

www.ecewebguide.com
This child development page offers pages about curriculum help, program management, anti-bias resources, and professionalism among others.

www.nncc.org
The National Network for Child Care (NNCC) site is categorized into age groups (infants to school-age), developmental domains, ages and stages series, brain development, observing, and assessing children, among others.

www.search-institute.org
The Search Institute offers several lists of Developmental Assets. They include asset lists for early and middle childhood.

www.earlylearning.ubc.ca
This site for HELP (Human Early Learning Partnership), an interdisciplinary research network, includes information about the EDI.

www.ncrel.org
Follow links to theories of Child Development & Learning, and other useful topics (North Central Regional Education Laboratory).

www.childdevelopmentinfo.com
Basic information on child development, including what to look for at each stage (Child Development Institute).

www.unicef.org
Child development from a human rights perspective. Indicates five key messages about child development and early learning.

3 Narratives

Recording anecdotal records can be useful when understanding a child's experience. Here a child appears to enjoy having her hand painted with Mehndi during the festival of Diwali.

Humans are believed to organize their experiences by narrative structure or the stories by which they explain and ascribe meanings to behavior.
Catheleen Jordan and Cynthia Franklin (2005)

Narrative [observations are] attempts to record as much as possible of what happens within the focus of the observation.
North Central Regional Educational Laboratory (2008)

Anecdotes of children must truly represent their behaviours, because the recorded observations will be a point of reference . . . for many educational decisions made by the team (of educators).
Sally Wylie, Humber College (1999)

In early childhood the most developmentally appropriate assessment approach is: observation and documentation of spontaneous play experiences
Thomas Armstrong, extrapolated from chart, "Summary of How Human Development Research Should Inform Educational Practice" (2006)

Narrative Observations

DEFINITION: Narrative observations

Narrative observations are written sequential accounts of what is perceived.

Describing behaviour

In most cases, recording a child's **behaviour** in a narrative description is a direct, non-interpretive method. The skilled observer can make an accurate record of the behaviour; for the less practised observer, the method can lend itself to making accidental **inferences** and **assumptions**. The greatest challenge of all narrative recording is to include sufficient detail to describe what happens and the way in which it happens, so that readers of the record can get an accurate impression. The goal is to record with as much detail as a video camera. (Using a video camera is covered in Chapter 7.) By looking for the minute details of behaviour, you as observer will see and hear details more closely than you would by recording the same behaviour on tape. The process of narrative recording makes you a better observer and furthers your own learning; it trains your eye.

Pestalozzi (1894) coined the term "Anshauug" to capture the "verbosity" of meaningless words and to help the adult appreciate direct observation of children. This term should be revived—or another like it—to assist teachers in writing what they see and only what they see!

Narratives can be helpful in observing and recording

- gross motor skills
- fine motor skills
- social interactions
- language
- play patterns
- interests
- the focus of attention

"But I can't write down everything," many students say—and they are correct! It is impossible to describe every muscle movement, blink of the eye, and breath of a child. Describe as much as you can of what is going on—you are exercising a degree of selection, whether it is inadvertent or owing to the limitations of language. But by recording, you learn to see more clearly.

Even when you intend to record all the nuances of the behaviour you are watching, in practical terms you must use whatever skill you have to write down as quickly as possible everything that seems significant. Your early observations will likely contain a lot of information relating to the child's **gross motor skills** and **language**. Later, you may add some detail about **fine motor skills**. As you practise, you will be able to add descriptions of posture and eye contact, and more details regarding the subtleties of communication. You will also develop your ability to "see" with new eyes.

Another observational concept useful to us is that of the teacher as **contemplative observer** (Brown 1998). The teacher contemplates—which provides a role model for the child—as she observes. This is not considered a subjective process; it is one that brings the observer closer to the child who is being observed. Coming from a Buddhist tradition, Brown suggests that teachers take time to eliminate the thought that constantly fills our minds. These thoughts "interrupt our direct experience. Observation is about untangling our experiences" (1998). To highlight this observational approach, Krishnamurti (1981) explains, "To understand a child we have to watch him at play, study him in his different moods; we cannot project upon him our own prejudices, hopes, and fears or mould him to fit the pattern of our desires." Although we may think of our observational role within the context of our homes, schools, or childcare centres, and all that those small communities demand of us, we might want to refresh our ideas about objectivity and decide on our own philosophical perspectives.

Finding the right words can be difficult when describing behaviour and expressing the quality of actions. A review of some of the components of narrative may help you:

1. **Adjectives:** These are the describing words, words used to qualify or define. Use them to describe how something is being done—for example, a "loud" noise made the "sleeping" infant start.

2. **Verbs:** These are the action words; they tell what is being done. These are the most important words in a narrative as they indicate the type of behaviour observed—she "skipped," he "ran," she "jumped," he "sorted" the counters.

3. **Adverbs:** These words describe the quality of an action or modify a verb—he rose "quietly" from the chair, not saying anything, straightening his knees "slowly," and twisting his ankles "sharply" as he passed the book to the teacher.

4. **Sequencing:** This can be a hurdle to those people who are not good at telling stories in the order in which they happen. Some cultural groups find this a particular challenge, as their language or tradition may emphasize different elements of a storyline. Writing down what happens, as it happens, can help with sequencing difficulties.

5. **Tense:** Purists would have us write what is happening in the present tense—"he squats down and picks up the book." Others are concerned that the tense be consistent— "he squatted down and picked up the book." Unless otherwise directed, use the tense that you find most comfortable.

6. **Observer bias:** The direct recording of behaviour in narrative styles allows less scope for **bias** than the interpretive methods, such as sampling. However, the observer risks seeing from a perspective that is slanted. Descriptive words may themselves seem biased—to describe a child as "smiling" may suggest happiness whereas the word "grin" may have broader connotations. The observer may feel subjectively about the observed child and consequently record as a fact something that might actually be a negative interpretation—for example, describing a child as whining might be a subjective observation. Selecting one anecdote rather than another may in itself express further bias—for example, the anecdote you select shows a preschooler being uncooperative when more often she is observed cooperating and sharing.

Biased data presented for analysis make for inadequate, invalid, subjective inference of little use. (See Chapter 1 for a more detailed explanation of observer bias.)

Types of narrative observations

Narrative observations can take the following forms:

A **running record** (see pages 81–87) is a written description of the child's behaviour. The observer should be physically separated from the child to be observed and without immediate responsibility for the child or for other children in the area; this is **nonparticipant observation**. The observer records exactly what the child says and does in sequence. The observer can attempt this method with little previous observation skill, but increased practice enables the observer to record more detail, to describe more accurately, to avoid assumptions, to be aware of personal biases, and also to make better use of the **data** that are collected.

An **anecdotal record** (see pages 87–92) requires that the observer, usually a practising teacher or a student teacher, write a brief account of a selected incident or behaviour soon after it occurs. These records are frequently used because they can be written up at the end of the working day and are an appropriate method of recording developmental stages. They require some expertise on the part of the recorder in choosing significant sequences of behaviour.

A **diary record** (see pages 93–95), or a day-by-day written account of the child's behaviour, which is dated and timed, may incorporate features of the running record or the anecdotal record as the observer thinks appropriate. This record can offer some of the **contextual information** that could help explain the behaviours observed. It may serve as a vehicle for an ongoing dialogue between caregiver and parents. Particularly useful for caregivers working with infants or children with **special needs**, this method enables rigorous record-keeping.

A **specimen record** (see pages 95–96) documents in precise detail the play or other behaviour of one child with such description and clarity that reading the account evokes a mental image of what the observer saw. This method may be carried out for a particular reason and may, therefore, be undertaken at a time designated in advance—say, to determine the child's attempts to communicate or to use a particular limb. Alternatively, the observation may have no specific focus but to offer an opportunity for thorough observation of the child in **spontaneous play** to investigate interests, choices, or **play patterns**. Most often, a psychologist or teacher not working directly with the child uses this intensive recording method.

A **running record (reading)** (see pages 97–101) focuses on observing a child's reading of text material. This book is careful to differentiate between a traditional running record, as described above, and a running record (reading), although there are educators who use the term "running record" to mean running record (reading). While the traditional running record tracks a child's observed behaviour in a narrative form, the running record (reading) is only linked to narratives in that it uses a narrative (story) as the required text for the child to read—and be assessed. The running record (reading) focuses on an individual child's developing reading skills. The child's reading of a narrative (story) is observed, and the educator documents coded responses to the child's efforts.

The concept of **personal narratives** covers a different type of narrative writing that includes self-observation, or what the teacher might think of as self-reflection. There are at least two kinds of personal narratives considered in this book.

The first is the teacher's own documentation of the experiences, programs, interactions with parents, involvement with children, teaching strategies, activities developed, and other elements of her own practice. Most importantly, this kind of documentation includes, as part of the writing, self-evaluations—reflections on what was successful or not, feelings about her responsibilities, and so forth. All of these contemplations contribute to serious teacher reflection, which is the essence of good practice. While the process of writing may start with anecdotal records, lists, and reminders, the narrative will be complete only when the teacher has examined his reality of experience.

Personal narratives frequently form part of a teacher's **professional portfolio**. This form of narrative allows the teacher to think critically, both objectively and subjectively, about his role and the experiences of those children and families for whom he is responsible. This is a **phenomenological** process—one that leads the teacher to construct a thorough, personal re-creation of his experience. Through writing the narrative, the teacher becomes more aware of his own needs and is able to focus clearly on how he sees the needs of the children in context; he can then plan for a continued relationship shaped by realizing his own philosophy of practice.

The second type of personal narrative is the one that is authored by a child. It shares some similarities with that of the teacher in that it encourages self-reflection and self-discovery, and it builds self-esteem that leads toward success. Clearly, very young children cannot write narratives. However, they can take steps toward personal narrative in oral (taped) recordings and they can also begin the narrative process through pictures. Teachers can assist children by writing the words each child speaks alongside his or her visual representations of the experiences. While early narratives seem to be little more than a few words and pictures, children who are encouraged to represent their world and their feelings about it are underscoring their own construction of their realities. Some personal narrative contributions can be included in the child's developmental portfolio along with teacher observations, samples of "work," and other evidence of development.

Personal narratives will not be discussed in further detail in this chapter as they fall outside a strict definition of observation methods.

Reasons for using narrative techniques

- to focus your attention on the details of a child's spontaneous activity
- to enter the observation session without preconceived ideas about what you will observe
- to get to know a child better
- to gather lots of information that can lead you to return and then target your attention on some area of interest
- to take time to step back from the program and observe in an open-ended way
- to help get into the child's experience (life-world—a phenomenological approach)
- to build your observation skills

Running Records

KEY FEATURES: Running record

- observation of one child
- open-ended
- written account recorded at time of observation
- detailed
- records most actions
- records all speech
- records whatever occurs
- naturalistic
- nonparticipatory
- as objective as possible

Writing descriptive sequences of children's activity is particularly useful for teachers or caregivers whose philosophy is **child-centred**. Open recordings enable observers to record whatever behaviours are demonstrated rather than look for specific categories of behaviour. Children's play is unstructured and directed by the children themselves. If we can observe children in action in their natural setting, we see the children being themselves.

Observing one child at a time can allow us to see more detail and make useful recordings. But the way the group interacts is also important, so you'll need to find ways of using a narrative form to capture this.

Observers face the challenge of recording whatever they happen to see, since the focus is not on specific behaviours. They must have good descriptive skills and the ability to record a number of behaviours in quick succession. A running record is the method students often choose when they start an observation course, because early attempts do not depend on a strong knowledge of child development.

When looking for a particular behaviour, you may well see it because you are expecting to. If you are looking for nothing in particular, you run the risk of not interpreting correctly what you do see—but you are more likely to be more objective.

Depending on when you undertake your running record, you are likely to see a variety of behaviours. As you write down what you see, do not include any inferences. Leave them for your **analysis**, where you will have to validate your comments. We discuss the reflective process, summarizing, and analysis of observations fully in Chapter 9.

In the effort to write what you see, you might find yourself writing "he played" or possibly "she went." Such phrases do not describe with sufficient accuracy what actually happened. Write down specifically how the child moves and what he does rather than using vague interpretive terms.

Running records are useful when planning parent interviews. Caregivers and parents work together better through sharing some substantial information. At this time, teachers may request the parents' informal observations and add them to the collection of information about a child.

Observation Sample 3.1

This sample running record offers an extremely objective and descriptive recording of the child's behaviour. A diagram aids the recording process. The student then summarizes the data and provides a self-evaluation.

All observations need to include sufficient background information, such as that given here on the first page, to make the recording meaningful. Permission to record must always be sought from the parents, as shown on page 2 of this assignment. Note that the permission form shows the child's real name, while the observation form uses a pseudonym to preserve confidentiality. How does this cover sheet support the observation assignment?

---

1 of 3

Observation Assignment

Front Page

Student name: ___Sue Fung___   Student number: ___000-888-000___

Section number: ___062___

Assignment method: ___Running Record___

Date due: ___February 12, 2009___   Date handed in: ___February 12, 2009___

Child's name (pseudonym): ___Patrick___

Child's age (years/months): ___2 years, 8 months___

Date of observation: ___February 2, 2009___   Time of observation: ___2:10-2:25 p.m.___

Setting: ___Daycare setting. Children are in free play time. There is a wide___
___choice of activities offered in the Toddler Room___

Parent's name: ___Mr. P. Yuen___   Phone # if released: ___N/A___

* *The observation recording is translated into English from the original made in Chinese.*

Each assignment has specific criteria. Please check with the assignment description and direction given in class.

Declaration by student

I have followed the assignment description and instructions given in class about confidentiality and privacy. I confirm that appropriate processes for making this observation have been undertaken and that permission has been gained from the parents. A copy of this observation will be given to the parents if they desire.

Sue Fung

_____
Signature of Student

Why is it necessary to use a form for permission? Wouldn't verbal permission be adequate?

Permission Form

Child Observations, Case Studies, and Portfolios

Student and Parent Agreement

Without written permission I will not observe and record information about your child. Please sign in the space provided if you agree that I may make observations and study your child. It would be helpful if you could initial each of the boxes if you are willing for me to undertake any or all of the techniques of information gathering.

I ___Sue Fung___ *(student name)* will not refer to the child in any written manner by his or her real name. Information recorded will be written objectively, treated professionally, and kept confidential.

___S. Fung___   ___Feb. 2, 2009___
(student's signature)   *(date)*

I ___Peter Yuen___
(parent's name)

agree to have ___Johnny Yuen___
        (child's name)

observed ☑   photographed ☒   audiotaped ☒   videotaped ☒

by ___Sue Fung___
(student's name above)

at ___University Settlement Recreation Centre-ESL family support division___
(agency/home)

for the purpose of study in child development at ___Cordial College___

(school/college) for a period of ___1 week___ *(weeks/months)* on the consideration that copies are made available to me, the parent, if I so request.

___Peter Yuen___   ___Feb. 2, 2009___
(parent's signature)   *(date)*

Is the level of detail recorded below sufficient? Is any content missing?

OBSERVATION RECORDING

Patrick is sitting with his legs beneath his buttocks; then he stretches both legs and sits on the floor. He holds a plastic strawberry in his left hand and a knife in his right hand, and he uses the knife to cut the strawberry in half. He grasps the two pieces of strawberry in his left hand and puts them on a plate. Then he puts the knife down on the floor; he picks up a cup with both hands, moves the cup toward himself and puts the straw, which sticks in the cup, in his mouth. It appears that he is sucking something from the cup.

He puts the cup down on his left side, and he bends his body forward and stretches his left hand to get a plastic tomato and holds it in his palm. He moves his upper body backward and turns it to his left side. He puts the tomato on the floor and uses his left thumb and forefinger to support the tomato. Then he holds the knife in his right hand and cuts the tomato. He releases one half of the plastic tomato from his left hand and uses his thumb and forefinger to get a plastic lemon. He puts it on the floor, supports it with two fingers and cuts it with the knife he is holding. He puts the knife down, grasps a half of plastic tomato and sticks it with the half of lemon. He holds the knife in his right hand and cuts the tomato-lemon, which is put on a plate and supported by his left thumb and forefinger.

He puts the knife down again, leans his upper body and stretches his left hand toward John, who is sitting opposite him. He frowns and grasps the plastic fruit that John is holding and pulls it toward himself. After getting the fruit from John, Patrick holds it in his left hand. He raises his left hand and uses it to hit John's head. After an instructor tells him not to hit others, he throws the fruit away.

He stands up, bends to the floor and picks up a cup using both hands. He straightens his body and walks to the instructor; he lifts the cup and has the straw touch her lips. The instructor asks him, "What's this?" He replies, "Orange juice, for you." After the instructor asks him to get an apple juice for her, he smiles and bounds to the place where all the plastic fruits and plates are located. He holds the cup in his left hand; he puts his right palm on top of the cover, seizes the edge by the forefinger, middle finger, ring finger, and baby finger of his right hand, and pulls the cover away. He moves the cup toward his nose; it seems like he is smelling something in the cup Then he uses his right hand to press the cover on top of the cup. He holds the cup with two hands, walks to the instructor and stretches both hands toward her, smiles, and says, "Apple juice." After the instructor has finished the juice, he throws the cup away, as he smiles and hums a tune.

He runs and then jumps into the play tent. He sits with his legs beneath his buttocks among balls and holds a ball in each hand. He raises both hands, looks up and says, "Cinderella" in a loud voice. He throws the balls away, leans his body forward and puts his hands on the floor. He stretches both legs; I think that he is trying to stand up. However, his right foot steps on a ball, and his body leans to the left. Then, he puts his hands on the floor again, stands up and jumps out of the tent.

He laughs and runs after John and says, "Goooo" in a high-pitched loud voice. He runs around the room, stops next to the slide and jumps up and down with both hands raised. At this moment, John is throwing balls from the tent. As the instructor asks John to stop throwing and pick up the balls, Patrick helps them to pick up the balls near him and throws them overhand into the tent. Then, he laughs and runs after John, follows John, creeps under the slide and lies with his chest down. He puts both elbows on the floor and both palms under his chin.

When snack is ready to be served, he creeps forward and puts both hands on the floor to help himself stand up. Then he runs to the right side of the room, grasps the back of a chair with two hands and walks with his body leaning backward. He puts the chair next to the table and sits down. He stretches his right hand and grasps a cup by using thumb, forefinger and middle finger. He pulls the cup toward himself; after the instructor asks him to wait for others, he pushes the cup forward next to the plates, moves his hands back and puts them on his thighs. While waiting for the instructor to allot the food, he puts his right hand on the edge of the table and says, "I want to eat." Then he pulls the plate toward himself with thumb and forefinger. He grasps a cookie by using his thumb, forefinger and middle finger and puts the cookie in his mouth. He holds his cup with his hands and moves it toward his lips.

Making regular **assessments** may mean employing the running record with other assessment or observational tools. These records may be presented at a case conference with the parents, at which a multidisciplinary or co-worker team may plan the required curriculum.

The running record is the method most frequently used for learning about children in every aspect of their development. Teachers, students, and parents gain; the process benefits everyone.

Good documentation requires a cover page for each observation. Review the example of a running record given in Observation Sample 3.1, which has a cover page, a permission form, and a short section of a longer recording.

TAKING A SPECIAL LOOK: Naturalistic observation of children with special needs

Narrative methods of observation and recording are sufficiently open-ended to make them suitable for children who have special needs. For example, Rianna—who was diagnosed with cystic fibrosis as a toddler and is now three years and five months old—has a fluctuating activity level. On some days, she is very mobile and plays alongside other children of her age; on other days, she is quiet, more reflective, and less active. Rianna's teacher is keen to record her development in each domain. A running record allows detailed recordings without any intrusion into Rianna's activity.

Using running records

Advantages

- This method can be used by untrained observers.
- Observation is less likely to be affected by bias when written at the time the behaviour occurs.
- A description of a child's behaviour can be used for a variety of purposes—developmental assessment, parent meetings, program planning, or learning about child development.
- Observational data can be used by other professionals for objective analysis.
- This method provides the opportunity to record all behaviour, including the unexpected.
- The record may indicate the need for further observation and/or assessment using other methods.

Disadvantages

- Successful recording requires fluent use of language.
- Observer bias may not be obvious where assumptions are made.
- The observer needs to be removed from responsibilities with the children.
- Writing the record can be a long and laborious task.
- Inferences may be difficult to draw from a bulk of data.
- Observation can be undertaken with only one child at a time.

There are various ways of recording running records. While the previous sample used a full narrative in paragraph form, others use a split-page format. This format enables the observer to log the time of events described. The left-hand "Observation" column is used for a detailed description of the behaviour as it occurs. The right-hand column allows for comments that clarify or explain what is happening. You might receive samples of the split-page format from your instructor.

Anecdotal Records

Although open to **subjectivity**, the anecdotal record is often used by psychologists, teachers, caregivers, parents, and students because of its focused efficiency.

The most basic forms are those that parents record in a **baby book** or log book of development. As the child gets older, caregivers and parents can use this method of formal record-keeping for meetings with parents or, most effectively, to maintain a log of developmental or behavioural changes. Students may learn from recording anecdotes while working with children or during opportunities to observe when they are not otherwise engaged with the children.

Jean Piaget recorded anecdotal observations of his own children in the 1920s. Later, his observations were more systematic and focused on asking children questions. His early observations enabled him to formulate his cognitive theory. Recording what seemed noteworthy enabled him to study the child's behaviour, by noticing the child's mistakes or misunderstandings.

The choice of event to record can challenge the untrained or inexperienced. Parents may be able to identify a significant behaviour worthy of recording because of the change it exhibits from previous behavioural patterns. The child may demonstrate a new strategy or an **emerging skill**. These would be opportune moments to record.

The anecdote dictates the degree of description required in its essential elements. You can test the appropriate level of detail by having other people read the anecdote, to see if they can appreciate its significance. There is no set length of narrative for an anecdotal record. Usually a paragraph or two is adequate, as the context and behaviour can be captured in that space. (See a sample anecdotal record on pages 90–92.)

Researchers and psychologists can keep anecdotal records and classify them according to behavioural types, social play categories, temperamental styles, cognitive activities, child's age, and so on. In this way, these records can be resourced or cross-referenced so that key elements can be drawn together as required.

Practising teachers may have a card index system, record information on tapes for each child, or keep a daily log book that parent and child can complete. Caregivers responsible for infants may find anecdotal records to be a particularly easy and effective way to pass information back and forth between home and agency.

Caregiving in a private home environment is particularly challenging because there is little time to write up observations. The anecdotal record enables the caregiver to make a few written notes while remaining a participant. Daily **baseline observations** can be recorded using the anecdotal method to provide a benchmark for later changes in a child's health or behaviour. Many childcare centres require that baseline observations be made at the start of each day as policy.

Time constraints make any written recording difficult for all those who work with young children. Toddlers' teachers may find the anecdotal record convenient and efficient. Fragmented bits and pieces of activity typical of the toddler can be written up as anecdotal records. If the caregiver is lucky, he can record these anecdotes at nap time.

Accidents, potential child abuse, or serious incidents may be written in anecdotal form. A court of law may require dated anecdotal records of a child's behavioural changes and health observations as evidence, considering those records important documentation.

TAKING A SPECIAL LOOK: Observing indicators of abuse or neglect

Observations may lead teachers and caregivers to think that a child has suffered some kind of abuse or neglect. It is not for them to investigate the situation; that is the task of the childcare protection agency, which must be notified if there is proof or evidence of abuse and also if there is reasonable cause for such concern.

Particularly useful observations in these cases include dated anecdotal records or diary accounts that detail the observation of physical marks, unusual or disturbing behaviours, anything significant that the child tells you, or artwork that the child has produced. Be very careful not to question the child, which can be counterproductive in the long term even though you might think that doing so could be therapeutic for her. Questioning can plant suggestions in the child's mind and could also undermine possible legal action. (See Chapter 10 for indicators of neglect and abuse.)

Using anecdotal records

Advantages

- A brief account of what happened is easy to record.
- Short anecdotes are efficient.

Lucas is counting the number of cups of water it takes to fill the cylinder. Later the educator will make an anecdotal record of this key experience, which highlights his mathematical understanding.

With permission of the YMCA of Greater Toronto

- The observer can record behaviour soon after it occurs.
- This is a useful means of recording behaviour for record-keeping and communicating with parents.
- Data can form a useful selection of significant behaviours.
- Almost everyone can use the anecdotal method.
- The observer can concentrate on more than one child.
- The observer can participate in the program at the same time.
- The record may form the basis of documentation for legal purposes.
- This method can be used as a learning tool for students.
- Anecdotal records containing baseline information can be made daily.

Disadvantages

- The observer needs to decide what behaviour is pertinent to record.
- Any time delay can increase observer bias.
- This method relies on the observer's memory.
- Selective recording can be biased.
- The record may offer insufficient contextual information.
- The observer must be skilled in recording most significant behaviours.
- The observer may find it irresistible to mix observed information with opinion.

The following pages provide a sample of a series of anecdotal records. As with running records, various formats can be used; select the one that works best for you and your responsibilities.

Observation Sample 3.2 uses a basic recording system, which can be used in a card index or in a log form for each child. An accident/serious occurrence form follows the sample.

Observation Sample 3.2

This student has used anecdotal records to record significant behaviours in different developmental domains. The summary comments make tentative inferences about the child's performance.

What do you think of the student's choice of events to record and how she has documented them?

Anecdotal Records

Observer's name: Sherry Lacroix

Child's name (pseudonym): Jenna

Age: 5 years, 4 months

Date: Monday, January 29, to Tuesday, February 20, 2009

Setting: Child Care Centre, Preschool room

      17 children and 2-3 adults

Purpose of observation: To observe the child in a natural setting to record behaviours unique to her. To select from the anecdotes the specific behaviours, and to use these for the purpose of contributing to the final analysis of her portfolio.

Date of observation: Monday, January 29, 2009

Time: 10:40 a.m.

Context: Preschool room during circle time with all the children.

Jenna is sitting down cross-legged in a circle with all of the other children; she is listening to the caregiver read them a story. After the story is finished, several of the children, including Jenna, put up their hands and offer questions and comments. Jenna puts up her hand; the caregiver asks Jenna what she would like to say. Jenna says, "I think Jeremy is having a very good day. I think he deserves a round of applause." The caregiver says that it is a good idea, and all the children clap their hands for Jeremy.

Summary: Jenna appears to be showing signs of some pro-social behaviour; she seems to be able to see things from another child's perspective and feel empathy for him. Jenna appears to have the ability to think about other people's feelings and show a sensitivity toward them. This can be seen in the above anecdote; Jenna seems to recognize the type of day a particular child is having and acknowledges it in her own way. Jenna appears to be becoming less egocentric; she now is able to put others in a primary role, showing increased pro-social behaviour.

Date of observation: Tuesday, January 30, 2009

Time: 11:15 a.m.

Context: The children are going to the gymnasium for gross motor activities.

The children walk to the gymnasium and sit down on the floor. Jenna puts up her hand; the caregiver acknowledges Jenna and asks her what she would like to say. Jenna asks, "Can we do exercises?" The caregiver says yes and asks her what kind of exercises they should do. Jenna pauses; she stands up with her legs straight and her feet slightly apart. Jenna bends at the waist and reaches her hands to touch her toes. The caregiver says,

"All right, let's touch our toes ten times." The children touch their toes. Jenna then says, "How about leg lifts?" Jenna lies down on the floor and demonstrates to the caregiver what she has said. The children follow Jenna and do five leg lifts.

Summary: Jenna appears to have improved her gross motor skills and coordination. She seems to be able to demonstrate specific exercises with relative ease and confidence. Jenna seems to use her cognitive abilities to think of different exercises, and to use her gross motor skills to carry them out in front of the class.

Date of observation: Tuesday, February 6, 2009

Time: 4:05 p.m.

Context: Preschool room at a table. Earlier in the day, Jenna and a caregiver had put together a puzzle; it was time for clean-up and the caregiver told Jenna they could do another puzzle later.

Jenna comes over to the caregiver she was playing with earlier in the day and asks, "Remember when you said we could finish the puzzle--well, could we finish it now?" The caregiver says yes. Jenna and the caregiver walk over to a table with two other children. Jenna picks out a Mickey Mouse puzzle containing 100 pieces. Jenna tries to fit several pieces together until she finds the one that will fit. The puzzle is completed and the caregiver asks, "How many pieces of the puzzle are we missing?" Jenna points to the empty spaces with her fingers; she replies, "One, two. Two pieces are missing." Jenna then says, "Let's keep this one together on the table. Let's do another one." Jenna stands up and walks over to the shelf and picks up another puzzle.

Summary: In the developmental area of social competence, Jenna appears to be able to interact positively with both adults and peers. She seems to be able to work cooperatively in a group all striving for one goal. Jenna appears to have a good sense of memory when she asks the caregiver about the puzzle they could not complete earlier in the day. Jenna seems to have an expanded concentration span to finish a large puzzle and wants to do another; she seems to be able to solve math questions the caregiver asks her. Jenna appears to have well-developed fine motor skills to fit together the small pieces in the puzzle. Jenna appears to enjoy cognitive games such as puzzles; this is seen when she remarks, "Let's do another one."

Date of observation: Tuesday, February 20, 2009

Time: 11:55 a.m.

Context: Just before lunch is about to begin, the caregiver asks the children to go to the washroom and wash their hands.

Jenna is sitting on the floor; she stands up and begins to walk to the door. Jenna stops and turns her head, looking behind her, then turns around and walks to a younger child who is standing still. She takes his hand and says, "Come on, Benjamin." Jenna takes Benjamin's left hand and walks with him out the door. The two children turn left and walk down the hallway and turn right into the bathroom. Jenna puts her hands under the fountain sink and washes her hands. She walks over to the paper-towel dispenser and pulls out one paper towel, dries her hands, and throws the paper towel into the garbage. Jenna turns around and walks toward the

Each anecdote is documented and summarized separately. What further considerations might follow this series of observations?

water fountain where Benjamin is standing. She bends down slightly, puts her arms around Benjamin s waist, and carries him over to the paper-towel dispenser. Benjamin grabs a paper towel; she puts him on the floor; he disposes of the paper towel. Jenna walks back to class beside Benjamin.

Summary: Jenna appears to have acquired many pro-social skills. She has developed a positive relationship with her peers; she shows sensitivity toward a younger, smaller child who has trouble reaching the paper-towel dispenser. She seems to be becoming less egocentric and has the ability to see things in a new perspective and help out when she can. Jenna appears to show her cognitive abilities when she responds to certain situations. She realizes the need for this child to get a paper towel; he cannot reach it, so she implements her own plan to fix the problem. Jenna shows her emotional development in a sensitivity toward others and in her general interaction with her peers; she seems to try to help others whenever the need arises.

Record of Accident/Serious Occurrence

Anecdotal Record						
Date	Time	Name of child	Incident	Teachers present	Action	Parent informed (sign)

This chart is useful when spread over the open pages of an accident book. Describe the incident as fully as possible—you might include a drawing.

Diary Records

Diaries may be the oldest of all narrative-recording methods. The diarist requires little technology or expertise and chooses to record what he considers significant. Diaries usually involve a series of anecdotal recordings; the degree of detail can vary. A diary may be an open communication or a private record of events.

The same diary technique can be used for keeping an up-to-date account of the development of an individual child or a group of children. The significant area of development is selected and written up on a frequent, usually daily, basis. The style is often anecdotal, but other forms of recording can be included. We can learn from the diary records of many figures in the history of education. Pestalozzi, Montessori, Steiner, Froebel, and Piaget, among others, offer us the legacy of their diary observations.

A parent may initiate a process of diary-keeping that produces a valuable document. Teachers and others may also want to keep an open diary as a dialogue between themselves and parents; the diary may encourage more parental involvement.

Developmental changes become evident when regularly documented, and patterns of behaviour are frequently revealed.

Using diary records

Advantages

- Observations are easy to record.
- This method leads to a daily record of behaviour.
- The diary becomes a valuable tool for communicating between parents and caregivers.
- The diary provides a valuable record or "keepsake" for parents and/or the childcare agency.
- This method may be used along with other methods of observation.
- The diary can be used as a learning tool for students as part of a child study.

- The record is useful in identifying behavioural changes and revealing patterns of behaviour.
- Observations may be written about one or more children at a time.
- Diaries can frequently help teachers review previous months' or years' programs and/or children's progress.

Disadvantages

- The choice of content might be subjective.
- The observer must be consistent in keeping the record daily.
- The need to interpret data is easily overlooked.
- Situations usually require further observation. A diary alone may provide insufficient information.
- Inferences may be drawn too easily.
- The selection of information may be influenced by observer bias.

Format for diary records

Daily log

Diary Record
Date: _____   Caregiver observation: _____   _____   Caregiver signature: _____   Parent signature/comment: _____
Date: _____   Caregiver observation: _____   _____   Caregiver signature: _____   Parent signature/comment: _____
Date: _____   Caregiver observation: _____   _____   Caregiver signature: _____   Parent signature/comment: _____

This system allows recording of a daily anecdote that is shared with the parent. You could include equal space for parent observations. Similarly, a parent can give the caregiver an update of what has occurred at home.

Infant observation log

Infant Observation Log

Child's name: _____   Date: _____

Age/D.O.B.: _____   Caregiver's name(s): _____

Feeding: _____

Diapering: _____

Sleeping: _____

Played with: _____

New interests/achievements: _____

Caregiver signature: _____

Read by parent (signature): _____

These sheets can be copied and left on a clipboard for each infant each day. After a week, the sheets can be kept in a binder, for each child, which the parent may want to keep. The "New interests/achievements" category can be completed as an anecdotal record.

Specimen Records

KEY FEATURES: Specimen record

- very detailed narrative that focuses on one child

- written account recorded at time of observation

- records *all* actions, including expressions, gestures, vocalizations, etc.

- may use codes for ease of recording

- requires skill and practice

- naturalistic or test situation

- the observer is nonparticipatory

The most detailed narrative recording, the specimen record, is described by Goodwin and Driscoll (1980) as "a comprehensive, descriptive, objective and permanent record of behaviour as it occurs." It is the most challenging of the narrative forms because of its comprehensive and open-ended nature.

An observer cannot undertake this type of recording while she has responsibilities for the child or other children. It requires skill on the part of the observer to record all the child's behaviours. All possible detail should be recorded, including all gross and fine motor movements, actions and reactions, details of posture, gesture, facial expression, and utterances, using the child's exact words.

Specimen records can use a variety of coding systems by which the observer captures details. Coding systems can be harder to read yet form a more detailed picture of the behaviour. They may be written by re-running a video-recorded sequence—particularly in a detailed movement study. Rarely if ever do practising teachers have the time or motivation to conduct this kind of observation. Sometimes, however, they will read specimen records prepared by psychologists; such records offer greater depth than normal classroom observation usually allows.

Using specimen records

Advantages

- The specimen record gives a rich, detailed narrative description of all behaviour.

- The data collected can be analyzed by one or more professionals.

- These records are useful for case conferences and may be used in research work.

- They are less likely to be affected by observer bias than other narratives.

- The record may focus on one category of behaviour or be entirely open-ended.

- This method provides an opportunity to observe unstructured play.

- The record may establish causes of behaviour.

- The observation may indicate development in one or more domains and show the necessity to employ other methods of observation.

- Specimen records may provide behavioural details that identify concerns not revealed through more superficial recordings.

Disadvantages

- The observer requires refined skills to record.

- The observer must be a nonparticipant in the children's program.

- This method depends heavily on the writing and language skills of the observer.

- The observer can observe only one child at a time.

- The observer record may incorporate complex coding in order to include sufficient detail.

- Professionals frequently keep specimen records without including full contextual information and may not represent the whole child fairly.

Reading Records or Running Records (Reading)

In some Canadian provinces and territories (and elsewhere) the process of recording and analyzing a child's progress in oral reading is called either a reading record or a running record (reading). This has caused some confusion because the term "running record" is a well-established method for recording observational information in a narrative form. Within the reading record—or running record (reading)—paradigm, the teacher uses a time-consuming process for documenting the child's progress in various aspects of reading.

Using running records (reading)

Advantages

- The process offers a means for teachers to document the progress of each individual child's reading skill development.
- This systematic approach to documentation can be used as comparative data.
- Running records (reading) are a tool to assist a teacher's provision of individualized teaching of reading.
- Children who need specialized reading support can be identified.
- The process avoids the use of standardized psychometric testing requiring additional professional support.
- The process is flexible: teachers can include aspects of reading that they consider significant or that are related to particular class projects and their curriculum.

Disadvantages

- The process is time-consuming.
- The recording may induce stressful reactions within both teachers and learners.
- The method lends itself to some degree of subjectivity.
- The teacher needs to have the rest of the class occupied while she focuses on one child at a time.
- Teaching/facilitating time is reduced if the focus is on assessment.

"Running Records [for reading skills] are assessment tools originally developed by Marie Clay, a developmental psychologist and world-wide authority on early reading" explains the Ontario Online Teaching Resource (2008). Some elementary teachers understand running records (reading) to be the essential technique for assessing the range of reading skills each child demonstrates. Commonly they seek evidence of proficiency in the child's reading out loud, in the stages before the child becomes a silent reader.

Before a reading assessment the child is told what will happen and if she will be asked questions after she reads. The teacher's role is to be neutral while sitting next to the student and observing her reading a set passage. Using a prepared worksheet, the teacher records how the child reads.

Typically, the recorder will document some or all of the listed elements of a child's reading skills (additional elements may be added):

- attention to the text
- expression
- confidence
- accurate reading of words
- incorrectly read words or miscues
- attempts at reading a word (decoding, using phonetics or alternative strategy)
- whole-word recognition
- self-corrections
- using clues from illustrations (if any)
- responding to context cues
- word insertions
- word omissions
- adult-offered words/teacher prompts
- requests for assistance
- starting over
- repetitions
- hesitations
- flow/fluency
- omitting a word, line, or sentence
- substitution/repeated substitution
- phrasing that reflects punctuation
- reversing word sequences
- altering correctly sounded words
- chunking words together (reading phrases)

Codes are frequently used to enable the teacher to record as much as possible. Checkmarks, first letters of the element sought, and letter or number identification of specific challenges may each allow educator to record interpreted information quickly and accurately. The ease of use of coding schemes comes with practice.

At the early reader level, questions about the passage that was read may also be included in a reading assessment. The meaning of words, retelling the story, identifying the main characters, repeating the sequence of events, the story's overall message, emotional responses to the story, relative enjoyment, familiarity with other stories, and aspects of comprehension are commonly evidenced through oral questioning.

The information gained from a running record (reading) helps the teacher to determine how successful she has been in teaching reading and how well the child is progressing. The teacher will also see if the text level is appropriate for the child at his stage of reading development. "Running Records [reading] can be used as a tool for diagnostic teaching that is responsive to those teachable moments when learners are ripe for specific instruction" (Shea 2000, p. 13).

At the beginning of the school year, the child's reading assessment is typically diagnostic—it tells the teacher what the child's prior knowledge and skills are in reading. As the year progresses, the child's reading skills are assessed in a formative way fairly regularly. As the school year ends, the child's reading assessment is summative—reading skills are reviewed over the year, as well as at this end-point.

The running record (reading) is one of a range of reading assessment tools. Teaching authorities that use the running record (reading) approach seem happy with its appropriateness, validity, and reliability, but others question the subjectivity and bias of the tool. However, there is little argument about the need for reading assessment tools, and teachers need ones that they can use with the whole class. It is possible that some think they cannot depend on standardized psychometric testing that requires additional professional support, time, and funding. Many educators are directed by the teaching authorities to produce reading assessments. Rather than feel that such directives are unimportant, teachers often feel passionately about the need to ensure that they undertake good reading assessments that guide their teaching and help them know who needs specialized reading support. From experience teachers know the difficulties when children's reading is delayed. "Identifying children at risk of reading problems in the early primary grades is critical because more than 75% of students who are not identified until grade three never catch up with their peers," says Natalie Rathvon (2004, p. 23).

There are several different approaches to offering reading support to children who are in need of it. All the adults in the child's life need to take part in supporting the child's reading skills. Parents, early childhood educators offering before- and after-school programs, resource teachers, camp counsellors, and others must become aware of the need for very early reading support. **Pre-reading skills** can be gained through play, domestic life, and particular games and puzzles; these skills form the foundations of later reading success whatever the age of the learner.

Using running records (pre-reading)

Those children not yet reading might be assessed for their pre-reading skills. Although these might be harder to identify and record than specific reading skills, they are essential for the later development of reading skills. Rather than being taught pre-reading skills, children gain these skills through general experience. "Programs that teach children to identify letters might make a child seem ready to read but reading readiness is so much more," suggests Susan Carney (2007). The Surrey Public Library in BC summarizes these six areas of pre-reading: motivation, vocabulary, the knowledge of things, print awareness, phonological awareness, and narrative skills. Early in childhood, children can acquire many skills and strategies that might not appear to be associated with literacy, but do actually help them to read. The following specifics are some of the behaviours that the observer might seek when recording information about a preschooler, kindergartener, or any pre-reader. A running record (pre-reading) may use a coding system similar to that of a running record (reading) system as mentioned above.

When handling a book, the child might offer evidence of

- enthusiasm for looking at books.
- attention to the book.
- holding the book the "correct" way.
- sound articulation.
- talking to him- or herself about a book (after looking at it or being read its story).
- turning pages.
- associating words with print symbols.
- preferences for board books, picture books, or "story" books.
- pointing at pictures.
- pointing to and labelling objects in an illustration.
- care and protection of books.
- identification of letters.
- whole-word recognition.
- recognition of phrases.
- sounds related to letters of the alphabet.
- left-to-right sequencing.
- seeking adult assistance with the book.
- using the illustrations or story to create pretend play sequences.
- oral vocabulary.

In domestic or play situations, the child may develop pre-reading skills through

- enjoying story-time.
- recognizing symbols and signs.
- sharing books.
- doing puzzles.
- solving problems.
- looking at family photographs and being told about them.
- labelling pictures.
- creating art.

- talking in many contexts.
- following instructions.
- associating books with comfort (being read to/sharing/cuddling).
- linking spoken words with text.
- pretend reading.
- "reading" to others (imitating the adult).
- asking questions about the book.
- pretending to be the teacher.
- responding to adult questions.
- responding to the questions of other children.
- learning nursery rhymes.
- imitating adults reading to themselves.
- noticing aspects of the text environment.
- forming letters.
- sorting items.
- playing with patterns.
- sequencing/ordering.
- decoding.
- routines.

Recording Narrative Observations

Steps to take to record, summarize, and analyze a narrative observation

1. Decide on your reason for using the narrative method.
2. Choose one of the narrative styles that fits your purpose.
3. Check that you have parental permission.
4. Prepare a method chart to meet your needs.
5. Write the observation as it happens, or as you select behaviours to record after they occur, in a rich, descriptive narrative.
6. Write up your "neat version" of the observation as soon as possible, making only additions that you are certain help your description without changing the content. (Translate into English, if necessary.)
7. Review your data, sort it, and summarize the information according to developmental domains. (List, without explaining, behaviours you have observed in each domain.)
8. Consider your reason for making the record(s), and explain the observed behaviours with reference to valid norms and theoretical models.

9. Make inferences about the behaviours following the process of analysis outlined in Chapter 9.

10. Develop an action plan or learning prescription based on your findings.

Ways to make narrative recording easier

- **If your handwriting is a problem:** Try using a tape recorder. Speak your observation into it, using rich, descriptive language. Write up the observation as soon as possible, before you forget any of the details.

- **If English is your second language:** Try writing your observation in your first language, using the method as described. You may have to translate your work if it is for an assignment or for record-keeping. Be aware of how translation can affect objectivity.

   Or tape-record your observation in your first language to capture the detail and then translate as you put it down on paper.

- **If you cannot write fast enough:** Try using a map to indicate the child's movements to accompany your observations.

   Or videotape the observation and take your time in writing your version on paper, using the pause and replay buttons frequently until you have the descriptive narrative written down.

   Or observe the child with another observer recording simultaneously. Afterward, sit down together and discuss your perceptions. If possible, write a narrative together.

   Or use a form of shorthand. If you do not know standard abbreviations, study or invent your own. Try using "R." instead of "Richard," "chdn." instead of "children," and so on.

- **If your language lacks sufficient descriptive powers:** Write your observation in point form and add the adjectives, adverbs, or whatever is missing soon afterward with the help of a teacher or colleague who observed at the same time or from whom you can get language support.

   Or prepare lists of adjectives, adverbs, and even verbs, and use appropriate terms to write up your observation.

- Work with another adult and share your observational data, but avoid accepting another person's biases.

- While practice may not make your observation skills perfect, it helps!

   Each of the above strategies can help students or teachers who have particular difficulties in writing. Always acknowledge the skill-building ideas you employ in your actual observation, as they may affect the accuracy of your recording.

TAKING A SPECIAL LOOK: Terminology for exceptionality and differences

Positive language can help shape our attitudes toward children with special needs. A child is a person first and foremost; her individual identity should come before any descriptive term denoting ability or any professionally diagnosed condition. It is more sensitive and appropriate to speak of "a child who is partially sighted" than to say "a blind child." Observe children and describe their behaviours from a positive perspective. Avoid subjective descriptors that are disrespectful.

Inappropriate language can be demeaning, teasing, impersonal, or judgmental; it often ignores the child's potential and focuses on disability rather than ability. Appropriate language considers the child first and then describes her condition, family, ability, or behaviour as objectively as possible.

The language we use sends a message about our beliefs and attitudes.

More positive and appropriate	Negative and inappropriate
Dana has epilepsy.	an epileptic
Percy has hearing aids.	the deaf kid
Bert's social skills are sometimes inappropriate.	a "behaviour" child; a misfit
Kinga needs special help with...	a slow learner
Dora has learned to tie her shoelaces.	educable retarded; trainable
Rivka has a developmental delay.	a below-average child
Cory (child's name alone)	spotty Scotty (or other rhymes)
Ho is new to the country.	a "chink" (or other demeaning references to country of origin)
Sharina's skin is a rich brown colour.	ethnic children
a child who has exceptionalities	a special-ed kid
a child who has a disability	a handicapped child
a child who has a disorder/delay	an abnormal child
developmentally delayed	a "retard"/"retarded"
a child who is unwell	a sick kid
cultural diversity	multiculturalism
different	damaged, imperfect, or abnormal
Shania has attachment difficulties.	She's clingy.
Richard has Down syndrome.	He's got mongolism.
Cathy mimics adult behaviour.	Cathy is cute/sexy.
developmental diversity	normal and subnormal
focus on ability	focus on inabilities
focus on person	focus on disorders

living with HIV/AIDS	dying of AIDS
inclusion	exclusion
building on competence	identifying failures
celebrating successes	pinpointing "incorrect" behaviour
authentic assessment	dependence on standardized tests
assessment based on multiple observations	assessment based on one observation

Narrative recording can be used to record situations such as this intimate sequence where an adult and two children share a moment with a book.

With permission of the YMCA of Greater Toronto

Summary

There are a number of different methods of documenting observations in written form. Each of these narratives—running records, anecdotal records, diary accounts, specimen records, and running records (reading), as well as personal narratives—has its strengths and weaknesses. Deciding which method to use depends on the observer's reason for recording.

Teachers and others who want a detailed account of behaviour prefer the running record, yet accept that they cannot record every tiny nuance of the behaviour they observe. Typically, teachers aim to write running records that incorporate as much detail as possible.

The final observational recording method outlined in this chapter is that of the running record (reading), a process for recording a child's reading skills that can be adapted to document a child's pre-reading skills. This method should not be confused with the regular narrative style called the running record. It can be included as a narrative only because it uses text material as the basis for assessment, and elementary teachers sometimes call it a running record.

Whichever narrative method we select for documentation, we must use appropriate positive descriptive language that avoids judgments, assumptions, and inappropriate labelling. Our use of language needs to be careful and professional because it alerts others to our beliefs, values, and perspectives.

Anecdotal records are useful for those professionals and parents who want to record what they think important after it has occurred. The long stream of behaviour and the interactions between children typical of the level of activity within classrooms, childcare centres, homes, and play spaces make it difficult for adults to collect as much information as they might like. The anecdotal record is quick, focused, and efficient.

The specimen record is the most detailed type of written record. Although it is potentially revealing, its detail makes it cumbersome and time-consuming, and typically the data need to be coded.

The final observational recording method outlined in this chapter is the running record (reading), a process for recording a child's reading skills. This method can be adapted to document a child's pre-reading skills. Running records (reading) should not be confused with the regular narrative style called the running record. A running record (reading) can be considered a narrative only because it uses text material as the basis for assessment, and also because it is sometimes called a running record by elementary teachers.

The diary recording offers the observer the regular opportunity to document a series of observations. Over time these records may become more revealing than at first obvious. Clearly the diary allows greater flexibility in the selection of observational information, and this is also its challenge—the diary-recording process is open to unfocused recollections, biases, assumptions, and unsupported inferences. However, neither the professional who wants to view what is happening nor the parent who wants to document the daily progress of his child should discount its usefulness.

Personal narratives can take two different forms: one for the teacher and one for the child. The teacher's personal narrative is a full document containing observations and reflections that merge fact and opinion. This might form part of a teacher's professional portfolio as well as provide information about the effectiveness of her role and responsibilities. Through visual representations, oral recordings, and adults' assistance, children can become more reflective about their learning in a way that can lead to success in making their own records. Neither of the personal narrative forms constitutes typical observational methods.

The writer's biases can compromise each of the narrative styles. (The observer's bias is particularly evident in anecdotal records, in the observer's choice of a particular sequence to document, and in the difficulty in separating observational information from opinion.) Also, whichever narrative method we select for documentation, we must use appropriate positive descriptive language that avoids judgments, assumptions, and inappropriate labelling. Our use of language needs to be careful and professional because it alerts others to our beliefs, values, and perspectives.

Key Terms

- analysis
- anecdotal record
- assessment
- assumption
- baby book
- baseline observations
- behaviour
- bias
- child-centred
- contemplative observer
- contextual information
- data
- diary record
- emerging skill
- fine motor skills
- gross motor skills
- inference
- language
- narrative observation
- nonparticipant observation
- personal narrative
- phenomenology
- play patterns
- pre-reading skills
- professional portfolio
- running record
- running record (reading)
- special needs
- specimen record
- spontaneous play
- subjectivity

Weblinks

http://betterkidcare.psu.edu/AngelUnits/OneHour/obToolkit/obToolkitLessonA.html
An overview of narrative methods of observing and recording with video examples, which Penn State University calls a Toolkit.

http://learningdisabilities.about.com/od/glossar1/p/observations.htm
Explains the use of narratives and other observations as part of assessments of children who have special needs.

www.phenomenologyonline.com/
Gives examples of phenomenology, especially good for phenomenological studies on children.

www.uft.org/chapter/teacher/special/anecdotal_recor/
The United Federation of Teachers (US) offers a tutorial on anecdotal records, their use, and the necessity for teamwork.

www.iss.k12.nc.us/writing/personal.htm
The basics of writing a personal narrative, with skill-building assistance.

www2.scholastic.com/browse/article.jsp?id=4148
The professional portfolio and how it allows the creator to demonstrate what they know and can do.

www.readinga-z.com/guided/runrecord.html
Offers a way of using a running record (reading) to assess a child's reading progress.

4 Samplings

Children in a Kindergarten/ Reception class have their sewing displayed so they can see it and share it with their parents. If these pieces are demonstrations of their best work then they might be used as work samples.

With thanks to Wanstead Church School

Event samples are observations focused on particular events that build up a pattern of a child's behaviour over a period of days or weeks.
Childcare UK (2008)

Time sampling can be more objective than narrative records. It is less time consuming, and it offers a way to observe and record two or more children simultaneously.
North Central Regional Educational Laboratory (2006)

A Functional Assessment assumes that the behaviour in question serves a purpose of "function" for the child. Simply put, it "functions" to get the child something she or he wants . . .
Lynda Orr and Geraldine Cavallaro, Child and Family Canada (2000)

It [work sampling] enhances student motivation by emphasizing what children can do instead of what they cannot do, and by involving students in the process of assessment.
Rebus Inc. web site (2005)

Focus Questions

1. For what reasons might you select a particular sampling technique?

2. If you could identify a trigger or cause of a behaviour, what use could you make of the information?

3. When you reveal a pattern in a child's behaviour, what might it tell you?

Learning Outcomes

By reading this chapter and applying the ideas to practice, learners will

• select and use sampling techniques to identify patterns of behaviour.

• use recorded sampling data to analyze behavioural patterns.

Sampling Observations

DEFINITION: Sampling observations

Sampling observations are those in which (a) examples of behaviour are recorded as they occur, (b) behaviours are recorded as they are demonstrated at previously decided intervals, or (c) "work" samples are gathered.

Sampling behaviours or events is an indirect or interpretive style of observing children. Practising teachers may choose to record them frequently because of their very specific nature and their speed in producing results. Recording information while involved in activity with the children can be challenging; you can do some samplings without disengaging yourself from the children for any significant length of time. Gathering examples (or samples) of the products of a child's work can provide insight into that child's interests and thought processes.

Reasons for using one of the sampling methods

• to determine patterns of behaviour

• to seek specific information about the duration, severity, and causality of behaviour

• to determine how many times a behaviour occurs, and in what context

• to look at the possible triggers of a behaviour

• to develop strategies to support positive behaviour

• to use as a tool for evaluating challenging behaviours

Samplings can be helpful in observing and documenting

- patterns of behaviour

- what triggers or causes a behaviour

- examples of the products of a child's activity

Samplings may assist in

- avoiding negative behaviour sequences

- behaviour reshaping

- evaluating both the process and the products of behaviour

Some educators fail to see the benefits of samplings, because they consider them only useful in special education settings. Reluctance to use what might have once been considered a technique associated with behaviourism might also prevent teachers from recognizing their potential effectiveness. Samplings can be used within a variety of child-centred and responsive early childhood philosophies. Their most significant benefit is that they can focus on positive behaviours and highlight a child's emerging competence.

Event Sampling

Event sampling is a method of observation that records occurrences of behaviours called **events** or target behaviours, which are examples of a previously selected category of behaviour. Event sampling most frequently focuses on one child at a time, but it may be constructed to record behaviours of a number of children simultaneously. Varying formats mean that the following aspects of the behaviour can be highlighted:

- frequency: how often the behaviour occurs
- duration: how long the behaviour continues
- causality: what conditions brought about the behaviour
- severity: the degree to which the behaviour can be considered serious or a cause for concern
- triggers: what situation or conditions set off the behaviour

Event sampling is frequently used to analyze behaviours that present a challenge, but it can be used for other observational purposes as well.

ABC format

The ABC format is possibly the most useful of the event sampling methods:

A: the **antecedent event**—the "happening" just before the behaviour example cited

B: the **behaviour**—the example of the category of behaviour you are looking for

C: the **consequent event**—the effect, consequence, or event that occurs after the example given

KEY FEATURES: Event sampling

- focuses on behaviour of one child

- defines the behaviour to be sampled

- records occurrences on a chart

- aims to establish behavioural causes and patterns

- naturalistic

- participatory or nonparticipatory

- interpretive method of recording

Event samplings can indicate clearly the causes of the behaviours recorded. With the ABC format, the trigger or cause of the behaviour may become apparent through application of the ABC format. By viewing the antecedent, we can see whether there is an identifiable pattern in which responses are elicited by particular stimuli. The child may initiate the stimulus–response pattern; but the teacher's behaviour, a routine occurrence, or an environmental factor could also produce the pattern. This method enables the observer to see possible effects as well as causes of the behaviour. See examples of event samplings using the ABC format in Observation Samples 4.1 and 4.2.

Behaviour categories

Sampling techniques involve categorizing sets of behaviours. Choosing, and then defining, the behaviour category can be troublesome. Behaviour is a continuous flow of activity, and it is hard to segment; so observers must be clear about what they seek to watch and to record. Categories can be broad or specific according to needs, as long as they are precise. To clarify your thinking, ask yourself, "What range of behaviours am I expecting to see?" The commonality of the set of behaviours should become apparent.

An **operational definition** of the behaviour to be observed is essential for the success of the observational recordings; without it, the observation will be built on quicksand. More than a list of behaviours that fall within a broad category, the definition must offer a clear explanation of the behaviour to be recorded.

Remember that it can be useful to use event samplings with both positive and negative behaviours. Here we look at an operational definition of an obviously negative behaviour.

For example, if you expect to see examples of hitting, biting, and shouting, you will see that the common denominator of these qualities is anger or aggression. Consider the following definitions of "anger" and "aggression":

Anger: a behaviour in which the individual demonstrates rage and passionate resentment

Aggression: a behaviour in which the individual demonstrates acts of violence or anger in words

It is useful to create your own definition of aggression. Your definition could be more open-ended and, therefore, likely to cover other examples of behaviours you might see.

You might identify narrower categories if you are looking for a very specific behaviour. In that case, you might choose a precise category. If you are seeking examples of altruism or empathy, you will not choose a category such as social behaviours.

Another more positive behaviour category that might be observed:

Pro-social: This is a behaviour in which the individual demonstrates his understanding of another individual's feelings. Examples of this behaviour include helping others, showing altruism, sharing, indicating concern for another person, and contributing to a group effort.

Defining the behaviour you want to observe both limits the parameters of the observation and supports its objectivity. You may discover that the examples of behaviour that fall into a category may be more than you anticipated—and the operational definition would allow for that.

A special targeted way of looking for the reasons for, or purpose of, a behaviour is called **functional assessment**. This precise event sampling leads to the development of an intervention to help change the child's behaviour that is the focus of the observation. You aim to establish priorities of the troublesome behaviours so that you target the most challenging ones first. Teachers and psychologists work together with parents, team members, and, if possible, the child herself, to identify the frequency, intensity, and context of the behaviour.

The most successful sequence for preparing to make an event sampling (using any recording format) is to

- determine your reason for recording the sample (e.g., to pay greater attention to a child's cognition).
- select the type of behaviour that might be useful to record (e.g., identification of mathematical understanding).
- refine your behaviour category (e.g., mathematical thinking).

- define the behaviour operationally (e.g., this is a behaviour in which the child indicates understanding of numeracy, sorting, sequencing, seriating, weight, balance, spatial concepts, and time).
- predetermine the kind of examples you are seeking (e.g., examples include, but are not limited to, symbolic representation, labelling textures and colours, discovering, counting, one-to-one correspondence, adding, placing objects in a sequence according to specific criteria, sorting items according to one or more criteria, using measurement tools, estimating results, representing mathematical ideas, determining distances, using spatial ideas in creative or other media, using weights and a balance, or comparing and contrasting numbers).
- prepare the event sampling chart as per your needs.
- date, time, and describe examples of the behaviours as the child exhibits them.
- summarize the data you collect.
- determine how successful you were in highlighting the behaviour, as per your original purpose/reason for the recording.
- analyze the examples separately and in their entirety.
- write a report that highlights your key findings.

Seemingly happy as he eats his lunch, Damien, who has Down syndrome, suddenly burst into tears a moment after the photograph was taken. An event sampling of these occurrences revealed a significant behaviour pattern.

With thanks to Centennial College Child Development Centre

The ABC format enables the observer to record the behaviour under examination as it occurs, giving information about what was observed immediately before the sample behaviour and what happened afterward. By detailing the surrounding events the observer gains clues to the possible causes or triggers for the behaviour, gains a **tally** of occurrences, and can produce a detailed set of information that may be helpful in understanding the behaviour of the child.

Using event sampling

Advantages

- This method of recording is quick and efficient.
- The targeted behaviour can be charted in convenient units.
- Information can be recorded more quickly than with narrative observations.
- Sampling may be blended with other methods—with a detailed narrative account, rating scale, and so on.
- This method may reveal behavioural patterns, frequency of behaviour, and cause and effect of behaviour and event.
- It is possible to observe and record more than one child at a time.
- The results are easily converted into appropriate program planning and/or behaviour modification strategies.
- An observation can be recorded at the time or soon after its occurrence.
- Teachers interacting with children can record as they interact within the program.
- Sampling may offer information about the duration of particular behaviour.
- Sampling may indicate the severity of the recorded behaviour.
- Consulted professionals can select some basic formats and, with only a little instruction, parents and caregivers can carry out those formats.

Disadvantages

- Sampling lacks the detail of narrative recordings.
- A high degree of selectivity and inference is required in categorizing observed behaviour.
- Sampling breaks up the natural continuity of behaviour into separate units.
- This method may encourage judgmental inferences.
- Sampling relies on the repetition of behaviour—not useful for infrequently observed behaviours.
- Any time lag in recording data might lead to inaccurate documentation.
- Sampling relies on the skill of the observer to choose an appropriate methodology, define the category of the behaviour, and evaluate the child's behavioural patterns.

TAKING A SPECIAL LOOK: Behavioural challenges

Sometimes a behaviour makes us wonder what is making the child act this way. We can be so frustrated that we believe the behaviour is happening more often than it actually is. Consider this situation an excellent opportunity to conduct an event sampling. This will enable us to examine the possible cause or triggers of the behaviour, try to determine how significant the behaviour is, and see how frequently it really is happening.

For example, Karl, aged five years and seven months, has been diagnosed as visually impaired, so various strategies have been employed to help him become independent. Recently, Karl seemed to withdraw from the other boys with whom he usually played. Sitting alone, he would rock himself back and forth, bang his head repeatedly, and sometimes rub his eyes and shake his hands in front of them. After carrying out an event sampling over several days, documenting each occurrence of these solitary and self-destructive behaviours, the teacher could see a pattern and a possible cause: the behaviours denoted a decrease in Karl's visual acuity. Karl could not sustain the relationship he had previously had with the other boys because he could not see well enough. The teacher's observation led to his referral to an ophthalmologist. With a much stronger prescription for his glasses, Karl regained some of his sociability and entered into activities with the other children.

In Observation Samples 4.1 and 4.2, you can see two event sampling observations that use the ABC format. Because of space restrictions, we have not included the front page and permission forms for the second event sampling, but these should always be included in real situations.

Observation Sample 4.1

This observational recording is a clear example of an ABC event sampling. The operational definition is clear, and the examples of behaviour are specific. The analysis explains the behaviours in paragraph form. Note how the observer has outlined the assignment on the first page and included a signed permission form from the parents. The child's identity is kept confidential through the use of a pseudonym in the observation.

Is there any other information that might support the observation that follows?

Observation Assignment

Front Page

Student name: *Donna Francisco*   Student number: *000-111-000*

Section number: *061*

Assignment method: *Event Sampling (ABC format)*

Date due: *October 24, 2007*   Date handed in: *October 24, 2007*

Child's name (pseudonym): *Margaret*

Child's age (years/months): *1 year, 11-1/2 months*

Date of observation: *Oct. 8 and Oct. 15*   Time of observation: *Throughout one day*

Setting: *Toddler room at childcare centre and main entrance hallway at the centre*

Parent's name: *Wayne and Jane White*   Phone # if released: *(203) 987-6543*

Each assignment has specific criteria. Please check with the assignment description and direction given in class.

Declaration by student

I have followed the assignment description and instructions given in class about confidentiality and privacy. I confirm that appropriate processes for making this observation have been undertaken and that permission has been gained from the parents. A copy of this observation will be given to the parents if they desire.

Donna Francisco
_____
Signature of Student

If the permission form is stored with the observation, how might confidentiality be compromised?

Permission Form

Child Observations, Case Studies, and Portfolios

Student and Parent Agreement

Without written permission I will not observe and record information about your child. Please sign in the space provided if you agree that I may make observations and study your child. It would be helpful if you could initial each of the boxes if you are willing for me to undertake any or all of the techniques of information-gathering.

I _____Donna Francisco_____ *(student name)* will not refer to the child in any written manner by his or her real name. Information recorded will be written objectively, treated professionally, and kept confidential.

_____Donna Francisco_____   _____Oct. 1/07_____
(student's signature)   *(date)*

I _____Wayne White_____
  (parent's name)

agree to have _____Jennifer White_____
              (child's name)

observed ☑   photographed ☑   audiotaped ☑   videotaped ☑

by _____Donna Francisco_____
   (student's name above)

at _____Grenadier Child-Care Centre_____
   (agency/home)

for the purpose of study in child development at _____Northern College_____

(school/college) for a period of _____2 weeks_____ *(weeks/months)* on the consideration that copies are made available to me, the parent, if I so request.

_____Wayne White_____   _____October 1/07_____
(parent's signature)   *(date)*

Read the recording of the observation. Does the analysis reflect the pattern of autonomy that the student is seeking?

Event Sampling

Child's name: ___Margaret___   Observer: ___Donna Francisco___

Age/D.O.B.: _1 yr, 11-1/2 mos/Oct.30/05_ Date(s): ___October 8 and 15, 2007___

Behaviour: _Autonomy_

Operational definition: _This is a behaviour in which the child displays initiative_
to perform tasks independently to help herself achieve something specific.

Examples of behaviour: _Self-help skills: for example, independent toileting or_
identifying her need to have her diaper changed/sit on toilet; feeding
self; washing/drying own hands without help; dressing self

Reason for observation: _To see if Margaret is succeeding in her attempts at_
autonomous behaviour(s).

Time	Antecedent event	Behaviour	Consequent event
(October 8)			
9:45 a.m.	Sitting on floor playing with "linking stars."	Turned to caregiver and said, "I need help with this one."	Caregiver showed Margaret how to attach the star and handed it back to her, and she tried to put the pieces together.
2:45 p.m.	Margaret sitting on floor pulling on her sock.	Said to caregiver, "I am fixing my sock."	Caregiver said, "You did it all by yourself, Margaret!"
3:45 p.m.	During gross motor activity in hall, Margaret went to her cubby and took out her hat.	Margaret pulled her hat onto her head.	Looked at caregiver and said, "Look, I put on my hat!"
3:50 p.m.	Children had just re-entered toddler room to find a place at the tables to sit for snack.	Margaret, sitting at her place at the table, said to caregiver, "I want juice please; I want milk please."	Caregiver poured a cup of milk for Margaret and put it in front of her. She picked it up with both hands and drank.
(October 15)			
11:10 a.m.	Margaret, while seated at the table at lunchtime, was sorting through the plastic bibs.	Margaret chose a green bib.	Margaret said, "I want this one," while she was trying to put it on for herself.

Time	Antecedent event	Behaviour	Consequent event
11:20 a.m.	Margaret's lunch was placed in front of her.	Margaret picked up her spoon, scooped up some pasta, and put it in her mouth.	Margaret successfully placed food in her mouth and ate it.
2:30 p.m.	Margaret had just awakened from her afternoon nap.	She walked to the caregiver standing at the door and said, "Change my diaper?"	Caregiver said, "Yes, Margaret, let's change your diaper."
2:40 p.m.	Margaret returned to the toddler room after having her diaper changed.	She walked to her cot and picked up her shoes.	Margaret sat on the floor and tried to put her shoes on, saying, "Put shoes on."
3:35 p.m.	Caregiver had just placed coats on the floor in preparation for going outside.	Margaret went to where her coat had been placed and picked it up.	She tried to put her coat on, putting her right arm into the sleeve of the coat. She looked at caregiver and said, "I need help."

Observation Analysis

This is the age of the drive for autonomy. Children at this age are often heard to say, "Me do it myself!" They are striving for independence, while still needing lots of support from caregivers and parents. They make many attempts throughout the day to do things for themselves, and it is important that caregivers recognize their attempts in a positive and supportive way. According to Erikson, this is the stage of a child's social/emotional development where the struggle for autonomy versus shame and doubt takes place (Barrett, 1995, p. 264). To avoid power struggles with toddlers, which may impede their ability to achieve autonomy, caregivers need to offer children "yes" choices instead of those requiring "yes or no" answers. Leading them to the choices one wants them to make in a positive manner (e.g, "I bet you can put the blocks away all by yourself!") is much more effective than making direct demands. When children feel that they have made decisions to perform specific tasks on their own, it contributes to their ability to think for themselves.

Throughout the observation period, Margaret displays many attempts to make decisions and do things for herself. The observation was limited to observing "self-help" skills and there were many to see. Each of the behaviours recorded shows that Margaret consistently tries to perform tasks for herself and that she is aware of the order and routine in her day. For example, she tries to put on her socks, her coat, and her shoes at different times in the day. Once she completes the toileting routine after nap, Margaret knows that it is time to put on her shoes, and she looks for them as soon as she re-enters the room. While she still requires the assistance of an adult in her dressing routine, she knows what to do and consistently practises the skills she needs to do these things for herself (October 8, 2:45; 3:45; October 15, 2:40; 3:35).

The caregivers in the room recognize the importance of facilitating and supporting the children's self-help skills. For example, coats are placed separately on the floor of the toddler room when it is time to go outside. This gives the children the opportunity to find their own coats and attempt to put them on. Words of encouragement are also given consistently throughout the day, as when Margaret is successful at pulling her own sock back up her foot when it is falling off (October 8, 2:45). In each behaviour recorded, Margaret's attempts at independence are recognized and positively reinforced. As she makes her attempts to help herself, she often seeks the attention of a caregiver. Caregiver responses support her attempts, and she knows that her requests for support/help will receive a positive response resulting in the help she needs. For example, she asks for help with her coat; she receives milk at snack time as she requests; her need for a diaper change is acknowledged verbally and accommodated immediately; and her success with the sock is verbally acknowledged. At the same time, care-givers do not interfere with Margaret's attempts to help herself until she asks for the help. Margaret is consistent in her requests for help and asks immediately when she requires adult assistance (October 15, 2:30; 3:35).

Margaret's attempts at self-help skills are developmentally appropriate for her age (almost 2 years old): "Self-help skills improve during this time period (18 months to 2 years). As far as dressing is concerned, toddlers can do a few things for themselves, but for the most part, they require the assistance of an adult" (Barrett, 1995, p. 213). Finally, "Erikson believed that if toddlers are allowed to learn to do things for themselves, such as walking or dressing and feeding themselves, they gain a feeling of autonomy. If they are not allowed to do so, feelings of shame and self-doubt will haunt their sense of themselves, and they will have trouble with the next phase of development" (Barrett, 1995, p. 204). Margaret's positive approach to helping herself and her comfort level at asking an adult for help are indicators that she is achieving success in her drive for autonomy, paving the way for the next stage of development, "initiative versus guilt," which she is moving into on the eve of her second birthday.

References Cited

Barrett, K.C., et al. (1995). Child development. Westerville, OH: Glencoe.

Biracree, T., & Biracree, N. (1989). The parents' book of facts: Child development from birth to age five. New York: Facts on File.

Martin, Sue. (2007). Take a look: Observation and portfolio assessment in early childhood. Don Mills, ON: Addison-Wesley.

Woolfson, R.C. (1995). A to Z of child development: From birth to age five. Toronto: Stoddart.

Additional methods charts for event sampling

Frequency count

Event Sampling

Child's name: _____   Observer: _____

Age/D.O.B.: _____   Date(s): _____

Behaviour: _____

Operational definition: _____

_____

Examples of behaviour: _____

_____

Reason for observation: _____

_____

Time	Tally count	Total

Here the observer records the occurrences of the selected behaviour as they happen. A practising teacher can employ this method efficiently, without a break from her responsibilities with the children. No detail about the behaviours can be recorded.

Duration chart

Event Sampling

Child's name: _____   Observer: _____

Age/D.O.B.: _____   Date(s): _____

Behaviour: _____

Operational definition: _____

_____

Examples of behaviour: _____

_____

Reason for observation: _____

_____

Day/date	Time (from—to)	Total in minutes

This chart gives the observer a sense of the duration of the selected behaviour, although no other explanation of the occurrences of behaviour can be offered. The observer might find it advantageous to calculate average duration as well as to analyze the pattern of behaviour examples.

Group samples

```
                          Event Sampling

Names: _____    Ages/D.O.B.: _____
       _____                 _____
       _____                 _____
       _____                 _____
       _____                 _____
       _____                 _____

Observer: _____    Date: _____

Context: _____

Behaviour: _____

Operational definition: _____
          _____

Examples of behaviour: _____
          _____

Reason for observation: _____
          _____
```

Time	Antecedent	Behaviour	Consequence

Recording information about more than one child at a time has its practical limitations. Here the observer can record a set of examples of a preselected category of behaviour. It is wise to limit the breadth of categories used in this method or the set may provide too many examples. In other variations, the observer can simply document the frequency of the behaviour, record the behaviour's duration, or, if the observer is not directly involved with the child, apply the full ABC format.

Severity recording

Event Sampling

Child's name: _____ Observer: _____

Age/D.O.B.: _____ Date(s): _____

Behaviour: _____

Operational definition: _____

Examples of behaviour: _____

Reason for observation: _____

Inference Coding Rating Scale

1	3	5	7	9
Mild		Moderate		Severe

Date	Time	Behaviour	Rating	Comments

This chart uses a combination of an event sampling technique and a rating scale. Charting the severity of behaviour can reveal more information than some other sampling methods, because the observer is required to evaluate the behaviour's severity as he records it.

Complex behaviour sampling

Event Sampling

Child's name: _____ Observer: _____

Age/D.O.B.: _____ Date(s): _____

Behaviour: _____

Operational definition: _____

Examples of behaviour: _____

Reason for observation: _____

Inference Coding Rating Scale

1	3	5	7	9
Mild		Moderate		Severe

Date	Antecedent event	Behaviour example	Consequent event	Duration	Severity	Comments

This chart can be too demanding for the caregiver of a medium or large group of children. Parents, student observers, and psychologists whose focus is on only one child at a time find this an appropriate method of recording detailed information. It is particularly useful for challenging behaviours for which guidance strategies need to be developed as part of **behaviour modification**, *cognitive therapy, or another management or therapy technique. Your instructor will be able to provide you with blank forms for samplings.*

Time Sampling

Time sampling, sometimes called interval sampling, is a method of observing and recording selected behaviours during previously set periods. These observations can be used for recording information about one or more children simultaneously. Time samplings are usually structured to record behaviours at regular intervals though they may also be undertaken at randomly chosen times. See sample time samplings, recorded in two different ways, in Observation Samples 4.3 and 4.4.

KEY FEATURES: Time sampling

- focuses on behaviour of one child
- records behaviour at preset time intervals
- records behaviours on a chart
- aims to identify behavioural patterns
- naturalistic
- participatory or nonparticipatory
- interpretive method of recording

Time intervals for samplings

Time sampling observations need to be set up even more rigorously than event samples do, because the interval at which the behaviours are to be sampled must be structured in such a way that they produce the information required. A sampling made over several days at 15-minute intervals may give information about an infant's pattern of sleep and wakefulness, but it may not give such useful insights into a 7-year-old's levels of concentration. Those experienced in doing time sampling suggest that, as a rule of thumb, the younger the child, the more frequently she will select shorter time intervals. This tendency, however, is not a hard-and-fast rule; circumstances may suggest other timings.

Using time sampling

Advantages

- This method provides frequency data about behaviours.
- Information can be recorded quickly.
- Time sampling is more likely to allow for a representative sample of behaviour appropriate for students and researchers to use.
- Results tend to be more reliable over time.
- Time sampling provides an overview of a wide range of behaviours.

Disadvantages

- Time sampling does not provide qualitative information.
- The recordings may be misinterpreted because of the lack of contextual information.
- Behaviour observed infrequently may not be recorded effectively.
- Sampling relies on the skill of the observer to structure observations appropriately to elicit the most important information.

    We include a sample of time sampling for you to review. Samplings offer some very specific information.

Observation Sample 4.2

The following time sampling offers greater detail than a snapshot sampling because it is supported with contextual information and relevant comments. The comments include some inferences, but they address things pertinent to the stated focus of the observation. In what ways is this time sampling successful in addressing the reason it was undertaken? Are there any parts of the time sampling that might have been recorded more effectively?

Time Sampling Observation
Five Arches Child Care Centre

Child's name:	Jordan
Age:	3 years 8 months
Context:	Preschool Room. Most of the morning period is scheduled for free choices in play. 16 children, ratio preschoolers: 1 ECE, + 1 part-time unqualified assistant
Observer:	Carrie (Lead Early Childhood Educator)
Date/s:	September 8, 2007
Sampling intervals:	5 minutes
Sampling length:	3 hours (36 samples)

Reason for observation/previous observation: Jordan has recently had a new brother join his family. Although he seems to enjoy his brother, Max, and tells everyone about him, his behaviour appears to be more erratic than usual. Jordan also appears to be having challenges with some social skills that previously were of little difficulty. He does seem to pay less attention to activities, and the other ECE and assistant teachers say that he tends to flit from one play situation to another.

Why a Time Sampling might help: A Time sampling may help me to take a snapshot of Jordan's social skills and, at the same time, provide us with a pattern of his play activity.

Specific focus: 1. Social skill performance
2. play activity/focus

Time	Behaviour observed	Comments and explanations
8:50 a.m.	J easily leaves his Mom without apparent distress and goes to the side window where he can see her walking away, pushing Max in a stroller	Typically J leaves his Mom without a stressful parting, but his usual pattern is to go join the group of boys (this group has more boys than girls). ?jealous of new baby
8:55	stands by window staring; his face seems expressionless	Most days J enters into play quickly and enjoys taking on an empowered superhero or likes to play "Daddy" in domestic play. ? underlying resentfulness of Max spending time with Mommy— not J
9:00	looks toward what is happening and he seems to observes others as they play in the indoor sand tray	more usually J enters the play rather than watches it, but the sand tray hasn't been offered for a time because there is sand outside in warmer weather. ? J might feel that his family, and therefore his security, is in jeopardy
9:05	tries to take a plastic funnel from another boy	the other child's response was to let J have it – but J soon set it down J may sometimes feel conflict but he usually shows greater self-regulation
9:10	stands back from sand tray with solemn expression looking at the group of preschoolers as they chatter about what they are doing	perhaps J doesn't want to play or he is overwhelmed by the noise, talk, and action going on around the sand
9:15	wandering around room	appears to move aimlessly but he may be acting as more of an observer than a participant in play or the choice of activities offered
9:20	staring at two girls trying on hats and looking at the mirror (which causes them to giggle) but J's face seems expressionless	it is possible that J doesn't feel like having fun and so cannot relate to the giggling girls
9:25	responds to ECE's request for all the children to sit on the rug. Sits down alongside others without much enthusiasm	there does not seem to be any difficulty in J following instructions although he appears to lack his usual enthusiasm for many aspects of the program
9:30	sits without engagement as ECE tells the story of the Three Bears using hand puppets	this behaviour is unusual. At story time J is more likely to be interrupting, moving to the front, getting excited about the story or waiting in anticipation of what is to happen in the story especially if it's a story well-known to him like this one.
9:35	older girl screams as J pulls her hair	Most of the children remain seated on the mat. The girl in front of him is a little taller and J may not have been able to see the ECE very well. The ECE does not seem to see what occurred. The girl whose hair was pulled screams until she gets attention from an assistant who is setting out a new activity immediately behind the group (the ECE story teller

		remains unfazed and continues with the story). J looks toward the assistant and the girl with her – with what seems to be contempt – as the adult sits the girl by her side and rubs her back.
9:40	Another boy pushes J	J had just shuffled forward on his bottom appearing to get a better view – the push J received may have been accidental
9:45	crying. Tears roll down his face but he does not seek support	the ECEs make eye contact with one another as a response to J's tears. After a few moments an ECE approaches J and asks him what is wrong. J says nothing is wrong.
9:50	at the window J looks out and appears mournful	this dismays the ECE (and myself although I do not know him well)
9:55	does not go to snack table when the teacher invites children to help themselves	Snack is set out so that children can help themselves when they want something to eat or drink
10:00	sits by the side of an ECE at a craft table without participating in the printing that the teacher demonstrates	J usually gets very messy as he enjoys the activities that are provided; J may get some pleasure in watching. It feels as though he is somehow punishing himself, but that cannot be true
10:05	accepts a hug offered him by ECE	sensing the tension experienced by J, the ECE tries to offer him some support and empathy – but it is short lived
10:10	Remains seated by ECE	it is as though being in close proximity to the ECE that J is comforted
10:15	carries and then pushes a child-sized chair to the window. As he does this he holds a wooden train under his right arm	this is the same window – his expression doesn't seem to show any affect
10:20	brings a number of toys from the shelves and piles them by the window	gaining some command over toys might give J some feeling of control over what is happening to him
10:25	tells others that it is his window "mine winnow" he says repeatedly and puts his arm up so as to prevent others from coming near	J claims the space around the window as being his – and, interestingly, most of the other children respect his need to be alone in his small domain
10:30	Remains alone at the window with the increasingly large pile of toys	J stands guard as though he has enabled himself to be in charge of the window area
10:35	claims the toys are all his "mine", "mine" he exclaims repeatedly as any child approaches	the children stay away from J seeming to understand his demand to claim the toys as his own, and the window his space
10:40	from the dress-up area a girl comes up to J and offers him a pretend "cup of tea"	he took the 'tea' and pretended to drink it

10:45	"my mommy 'as offee" he says into the air around him	the girl walks away quite quickly chatting to others
10:50	staring out the window but J stops for a pretend drink	he appears to 'forget' his sadness for a minute while in symbolic play
10:55	a little excited when he sees a Mom walk past	This is not his Mom and his face fades to neutral
11:00	sitting in the chair J rocks back and forth	the ECE may not be aware that J is self-soothing
11:05	roaming around the room	J appears to lack motivation
11:10	follows ECE as she washes her hands, he is asked if his hands need washing and he shakes his head	Possibly J seeks emotional support from being in close proximity to an ECE
11:15	Observes several boys as they attempt to build a 'castle' out of wooden blocks and several large cardboard boxes	the block area is where J usually spends long periods of play time
11:20	hears request from a child to pass him a block but seems to ignore what he is asked	J is acting differently, but that doesn't mean that he would typically comply with requests
11:25	invited by a boy to play in the 'castle' - but J is unresponsive	this is something he might easily have done in the past
11:30	sits on floor near the castle as ECE sings a 'tidy up' song	J seems to know the routine and what is expected, but he probably wasn't feeling like helping
11:35	sits at lunch table next to ECE who is serving mashed potato with chicken	J accepts his portion and puts the plate in front of himself ? he may be unsettled because there are new plastic plates that have partitions
11:40	plays with food but eats very little. ECE encourages J to eat and comments on how well the other three children are eating. She says "you must be hungry" to the group	Not having an appetite is not usually J's approach !
11:45	sitting at the empty lunch table looking around room	? seems sad and a bit cut-off from adults and children
11:50	puts his head on his arms folded on the table	? is he tuning-out what he doesn't want to be involved with

Analysis

Special focus #1 Clearly J's social skills are challenged- most probably by the birth of his new brother- but there could be another issue we are not yet aware of.

#2 J's engagement in his usual play activities has been reduced, he is acting as more of an observer than a full participant

Developmental information: Although there is some evidence of regression in social skills associated with J's lack of involvement in play, this is most probably a transient issue.

The observer role is appropriate at this stage of development, and we know that J has previously been involved in more complex social play including associative and parallel play. We know that J is capable of richer play sequences, but his emotional issue is preventing this richer depth of play. The lack of play could become a serious issue, but the ECE team is confident that as he adjusts to his new role of big brother, he will catch up and regain the play behaviours associated with his stage of development. It is good that J accepts some comfort from others, and that he has not completely shut down. Although he wants and needs his Mom he is learning that his desires are not always the first to be addressed; this is a difficult life-lesson. J does need clear behavioural parameters but not to make a great fuss about his apparently short-term change of behaviour.

Identified patterns: #1 J has a mild regression of everyday social skills (that is expected to correct itself)

#2 I saw him in a repeated 'observer role' in play rather than a full participant (when more comfortable J's role will revert to previous levels- or advance to more cooperative play)

#3 J has a significant pattern of introversion (seemingly temporary style change)

#4 J shows some unhappiness - although he did show some negative responses to his situation he is able to express his feelings

#5 J has the trust relationship necessary for a secure attachment to Mom/Dad and further (multiple) attachments to others (ECEs etc) but has repetitious negative reactions to the existence of Max because, perhaps, his place in the family is threatened

#6 J may be in a 'rebellious child mode' unconsciously

#7 J moves from one activity to another fairly quickly until he finds something that meets his surface emotional needs

Observation shared with parents: Yes

Parental comment: "Thank you for doing the observation- what you have seen fits with what J is like at home. We feel bad that J seems unhappy but your assurances that J will soon go back to his earlier level is helpful. We do worry that J's issue with the baby will increase until he does Max some harm."

Mom

Agreed action/response: Explain and apply behavioural parameters, offer warmth and comfort when needed, keep J in the preschool program so that he has the opportunity to get back into deeper play when he is ready, send consistent messages between parents and professionals, provide a 'helping' role for J with Max, give J something that he can hold and smell that he can remember Mom, put up family pictures, offer doll play with appropriate props, tell stories about brothers and families, support regressive behaviours without approving of them (so J doesn't think regression 'works' for him), avoid enabling J to get his needs and wants met through less mature behaviour, and carefully monitor J's progression or regression in social and other situations at home and in the preschool program.

Additional method chart for time sampling

Group interval recording

Time Sampling		
Names: _____ Ages/D.O.B.: _____		
_____ _____		
Observer: _____ Date: _____		
Context: _____		
Behaviour category: _____		
Reason for observation: _____		
#	Child	Behaviours (Time/units/intervals)	Comment (Total)
1.			

A group of children can be observed in this time sampling. The detail of activity that can be recorded is quite limited.

How to Use Event or Time Sampling
Deciding what sampling methodology to use

1. Become aware of the various techniques; know their advantages and disadvantages, and what information they can give you.
2. Assess your need for a sampling: What do you need it for? These are some of the most obvious uses:
   - to help you learn about sequences of development
   - to support understanding of an individual child's behaviour
   - to look at the behaviours a group of children demonstrate
   - for formal record-keeping
   - to support communications with parents, colleagues, and other professionals
   - to help evaluate the program offered to an individual or group
   - to provide information for behaviour modification plans or for learning prescriptions
3. Choose the method of preference, use it, and evaluate its usefulness for the required purpose.
4. Practise using sampling techniques and build skills in the component parts of objectivity, clarity, and accuracy of recording, checking with others on their perceptions of the validity of your work.

Event sampling versus time sampling

Event sampling	Time sampling
• can be used to study any event or behaviour	• can record any demonstrated behaviours
• is less likely to give information about frequency of behaviour over longer periods of time	
• is more likely to give qualitative information	• may make it easier to quantify behaviour
• may indicate causes of behaviour	
• may indicate effect of child's action	
• is often used by practitioners	• is often used by researchers
• includes every natural occurrence of target behaviour	
• may offer information about duration of behaviour	• may offer behavioural pattern
• may indicate severity of behaviour	
• can be user-friendly and easily carried out by parents and paraprofessionals	• may require professional background in child development to structure behaviour-coding systems

How to record a time or event sample observation

1. Decide on your reason for sampling behaviour.
2. Select the behaviour category or time frequency that applies.
3. Prepare a method chart to meet specific requirements.
4. Write your operational definition of the behaviour category, if necessary.
5. Record as soon as possible the precise details of the examples of behaviour observed.
6. When sufficient examples are recorded for your purpose, take time to analyze your findings.
7. Write your objective **inferences** as clear statements—but support your statements.
8. Use the inference statements to devise a plan or learning prescription.

The analysis: Interpreting data collected from process samplings

Remember that your inferences rely heavily on the **objectivity** of your recording. Before you start to analyze the data, evaluate its **validity** and **reliability**. Review the effectiveness of the sampling before you proceed to analyze the content. Some samplings require you to select specific behaviours. Your decision to observe a particular behaviour may prove ineffective because you didn't see the behaviour you expected. The operational definition of the behaviour category can also cause difficulty—perhaps you could have selected a suitable category without defining it clearly to cover the samples you include.

Patterns of behaviour, such as this one when a baby imitates her caregiver, can be recorded easily using a sampling method.

With permission of the YMCA of Greater Toronto

Focus the **analysis** on some of these issues:

1. determining the **frequency** of the events
2. considering what prompted the events (which may be different from the actual cause)
3. finding a **cause** for the behaviour
4. measuring the **duration** of the events
5. examining the developmental significance of the events
6. evaluating the necessity of responding to the events
7. identifying the pattern of behaviours and/or events
8. determining further observation and assessment needs

Using inferences drawn from the analysis

Other than for purposes of dry record-keeping, there is little point in recording copious numbers of observations without putting them to some use. There are many reasons to record samplings, and often more than one reason for each observation.

Having checked the inferences for their detail and general objectivity, you will be ready to make use of your analysis.

You can use the inferences in a similar way to those produced by other methods of observation (see Chapter 9, pages 310–24). Samplings are frequently used as forerunners to devising a learning prescription or an individualized program plan for children.

- Melinda's family came on "meet the teacher" night. Melinda showed her parents around the room and introduced them to the teacher. Both her parents and the teacher thought that Melinda had behaved very well and praised her beautiful manners.

- Ellie was just past her second birthday, and her parents were concerned that she had not yet said a "real" word but tended to repeat the same string of sounds. Her caregiver saw Ellie point at the shelf above her crib and say "bo-bo" repeatedly. "That's your bunny rabbit, bunny rabbit," the caregiver said. Ellie later said "bun-bun," and the caregiver said, "Yes, your bunny rabbit," and gave it to her.

- Craig, at 6 months, liked to hold his own bottle. But he didn't like to hand back the bottle when it was empty. His mother played a game with Craig in which they passed items back and forth. The next time his bottle was empty, he handed it to his mother.

These examples suggest that behaviours can be reinforced through positive feedback or some kind of reward. More structured behaviour modification also employs **reinforcement**. Be aware that this method is not used everywhere, because of concerns about manipulating behaviour. The following example illustrates how sampling can be used in a classroom where behaviour modification is practised.

Gareth, aged 7, has been diagnosed with a social adaptation difficulty, based on detailed narrative observations, a psychological test, and meetings with his parents and teacher. Recently, he has faced some new challenges in sharing art materials. He snatched items from other children, and the class disintegrated into a fight. He also took home a pair of scissors, which he used to cut up an album of family photographs. When Gareth met with the psychologist, his parents, and his teacher, they decided that he would be "rewarded" for behaving appropriately and "corrected" for behaving inappropriately. Gareth agreed that he wanted to "behave himself." In the following days, he demonstrated positive behaviour, such as helping hand out the snack, waiting in line for the washroom, and helping a younger child find his lost coat. Each time the teacher observed such behaviour, she recorded it on a sampling chart and allowed Gareth to have "privileges," such as staying outside for longer than the rest of the class or being first to select afternoon activities. For each negative behaviour, Gareth was asked to do a clean-up job, made to sit away from the other children, or denied his choice of book at circle time. Gareth understood this plan, which seemed to reinforce some of his better behaviours; his behaviour overall was being modified to what was considered socially acceptable.

Work sampling

A **work sample** is the product of the child's activity. Although the term "work" might make us think of formal classroom activities, the term also applies to items a child might produce during times of creativity and play. Typically these "work samples" might include

- paintings
- early writing and letter formations
- card-sewing or fabric-sewing
- project work
- group-made creative materials
- pictorial representations (early math)
- story-writing
- tape recordings of early reading or music-making

- drawings and diagrams
- pattern-making
- weaving
- collages
- models
- masks
- mathematical work, scale drawings, etc.
- photographs of large-sized constructions

Parents, teachers, other professionals, or students who are studying the development of one or more skills may wish to collect work samples. They may do so rather than compiling a complete portfolio (see Chapter 8 on portfolios) or to enrich a rounded portfolio. In collecting most effectively, consider

1. what the child produces on a regular basis.
2. the child's "best" work (using her own opinion of her efforts).
3. items that illustrate **progression** or **regression** in skill development.

The **products** of a child's play activity may not give us an accurate picture of that child's process of discovery and learning in creating them. Adults can focus too much on the product because they need to identify art that is **representational** or that corresponds to their idea of what is beautiful or worthwhile. Too much emphasis on the products of a child's activity may lead children to think that what they produce is more important than the thinking they put into their activity. Educators prefer to honour both the child's work and its products.

The Work Sampling System is a trademarked performance-assessment system that is "used in preschool through fifth grade. Its purpose is to document and assess children's skills, knowledge, behavior, and accomplishments across a wide variety of curriculum areas on multiple occasions in order to enhance teaching and learning" (Meisels et al. 1997). Teachers who wish to adopt a systematic approach to work sampling and reporting may find that this system meets their needs for observing, documenting, and assessing learning. Those wanting a more open-ended work-sampling approach might establish their own systems to fit their own philosophies and the outcomes expected of their programs.

When used successfully, work samples can offer

- a glimpse (for adults) into the thinking of the child as he created the work.
- a time when the child and the adult discuss the child's work and how it was created.
- concrete examples of the child's progression and skill development over time.
- a collection of materials to share with parents and families that helps re-create a learning experience.
- the feeling for the child that her work is valued.
- additional insights into the developmental portfolio process.

Functional Assessments

Functional Assessments may be shaped on either of two different paradigms, but each seeks to observe particular aspects of a child's behaviour.

1. *Functional Assessment aimed at observing and recording the individual's ability to function and perform self-help and self-care skills, and manage to perform the necessary tasks of domestic living*

   "An assessment of function [or functional assessment] involves a practical investigation into an individual's ability to perform activities of daily living—tasks that are usual for them," explains Aruna L. Mitra, who is an occupational therapist with experience working with children and adults who have a variety of disabilities. In these observations and recordings, samplings are often used, but a variety of observations help the assessment to be more thorough. The summary and analysis of the recorded data help to determine the supports that are necessary for more effective functioning.

   One of the standardized functional assessment processes is the Child and Adolescent Functional Assessment Scale (CAFAS) that is currently used in many U.S. states and in Ontario, where it is funded by the Ministry of Child and Youth Services, giving it some credibility. Currently it is being piloted in BC. Connexus, a community-based training and professional development agency focused on Family and Children's Services in that province, suggests that the "program is useful for case planning and program evaluation. CAFAS is a reliable assessment tool suitable for child care workers, social work professionals, intake workers, psychologists, and mental health professionals, etc." Dr. Kay Hodges, a clinical psychologist, developed the CAFAS to assess the degree of functional impairment in both children and adolescents with emotional, behavioural, or substance-abuse problems.

2. *Functional Assessment aimed at observing and recording the child's behaviours that appear to be challenging to others or dysfunctional for themselves, and to determine their purpose and try to change behavioural patterns*

   Functional Assessments may include a number of different observation tools, but use of the ABC Event Sampling format is most common. Why do we need an assessment of function? "The goal of functional assessment is not to simply 'punish' misbehavior, but to alter the environment to promote children's appropriate behavior and to teach them more adaptive and acceptable ways to get what they want," says John W. Maag (2008) (**www.scwablearning.org**), who is the author of several books on the education and parenting of children who have emotional and behavioural disorders. The idea behind functional assessment is that all behaviour is deliberate and is done to obtain a desired outcome. Children do not always realize that their behaviour has an implicit goal; often the behaviour is part of an unconsciously driven pattern. The educator and parent assist the child to learn appropriate ways to get what he wants. Maag outlines the goal of functional assessment as rearranging the events that occur before a child misbehaves (the antecedent), changing the consequences that the behaviour generates in order for the behaviour to be more likely appropriate, and teaching the child a replacement behaviour that accomplishes the same purpose as the original dysfunctional behaviour had.

   Learning Together Every Step of the Way and the City of Toronto's Early Childhood Services team have produced a practical guide to ABC Functional Assessment that includes concrete examples of the documentation necessary, similar to the ABC

Event Sampling method. That said, they are clear that "Understanding and changing behaviour is never simple. However, describing the behaviour that concerns you, and gathering good information that occurs and under what conditions, is the first step to your success" *Learning Together* (undated online resource).

Summary

There are three main types of sampling. The first focuses on recording an event and the time in which it occurs (event sampling), the second looks at what behaviour is happening at designated times (time sampling), and the third considers the products of a child's activity (work sampling). Each sample offers a glimpse of a child's behaviour—concentrating on the frequency, duration, and severity of a particular behaviour, or on what behaviour is occurring at predetermined times, or on seeking what the child has produced in order to supply us with insight into the child's skills and general behaviour.

Samplings of each kind can give us a hint of the interests, significance, and development of the child being observed. The decisions that need to be made about how to sample behaviour are challenging, but the results can offer insights into the possible cause of the behaviour, the recurrence of the behaviour, and, most importantly, possible means of managing the behaviour. The samplings can help a child to understand better his own behaviour and so acquire skills of self-regulation. Most educators can discern patterns of behaviour from the samplings that lead them to make appropriate decisions about interventions, guidance, and curriculum.

Event samplings make it possible to discern patterns of behaviour and identify behaviour triggers and causes. This means of recording depends on the observer's identifying and developing an operational definition of the behaviour under examination. Time samplings often highlight a suspected pattern of development that needs careful guidance. Both of these techniques are the traditional sampling methods used by a variety of behavioural specialists, educators, and psychologists.

Work sampling is a method of gathering samples of a child's "work." The term "Work Sampling" is the registered name of a system for collecting children's work as part of a portfolio. However, sampling children's products is a widely used technique in the portfolio-documentation process, and it includes a variety of observation and documentation approaches to each assessment.

Functional assessments either focus on observing and recording an individual's ability to function in a particular way, or look at the purpose (or function) of a child's challenging behaviour in order to alter it.

Key Terms

- analysis
- antecedent event
- behaviour
- behaviour modification
- cause
- consequent event
- duration
- event
- event sampling
- frequency

Continued

- functional assessment
- inference
- objectivity
- operational definition
- product
- progression
- regression
- reinforcement
- reliability
- representational
- sampling
- tally
- time sampling
- validity
- work sample

Weblinks

www.newchildcare.co.uk/Event.html
The site offers a brief introduction to event sampling and other observation methods.

www.stats.gla.ac.uk/steps/glossary/sampling.html
Here you can find many advanced sampling techniques defined and described.

www.ericdigests.org/1996-1/early.htm
This well-recognized site offers an explanation of work sampling and discusses the work sampling system.

www.schoolsuccess.net/Products/highscope.cfm
There is the possibility here of touring the work sampling system, as well as reading outlines of other sampling approaches to assessment.

http://cecp.air.org/fba/
Here we have an outline of functional assessment use within a US agency called Centre for Effective Collaboration and Practice.

www.child-dev.com/drupal/node/88
Dr. Cynthia Jackson offers a practical guide to behavioural change by using observational methods such as time and event sampling, along with other strategies.

www.ericdigests.org
Search for "work sampling" for an overview of S. J. Meisels's system.

www.scwablearning.org
Search for "functional assessment" for an article by Dr. J. W. Maag focused on changing inappropriate behaviours.

5 Checklists

When school-age children select their own activities their interest is deeper and their involvement is often much longer. On a developmental checklist an observer can see if the children are demonstrating fine motor skills.

With permission of the YMCA of Greater Toronto

The observation Checklist is most appropriately used in situations where teachers wish to record information on explicit student behaviours, abilities, processes, attitudes, and performances.
Children First: A Curriculum Guide for Kindergarten Saskatchewan Education (2004)

The observation checklist is a strategy to monitor specific skills, behaviours, or dispositions of individual students or all the students in the class.
Kay Burke (2004)

Caution is advised in the administration and interpretation of assessment measures with young children. Norm-referenced tools compare a child's abilities to other children's abilities. Norms used, however, in standardized tests can be based on the development and experiences of a group of children that are generally not representative of current diversity within our early childhood settings.
Rachel Langford for the *Checklist for Quality Inclusive Education* (1997)

Checklists make it easier to collect and organize information.
BC Ministry of Education (web site 2005)

Focus Questions

1. How could you record behaviours quickly when you are looking to see whether a child exhibits a particular skill?

2. If you listed some behaviours, how could you determine whether they were in an appropriate developmental order?

3. If you had to observe and record using a ready-made checklist concentrating on gross motor and fine motor skills, how would you know whether the checklist was any good?

Learning Outcomes

By reading this chapter and applying the ideas to practice, learners will

- develop appropriate checklist criteria and formats.
- use prepared checklists as tools to identify the developmental characteristics of young children.

Types of Checklists

DEFINITION: Checklists

Checklists record the presence or absence of particular predetermined behaviours demonstrating skills, attributes, competencies, traits, reactions, achievements, or stages of development.

The observer may use a checklist she has prepared for a certain purpose, a prepared checklist by a well-known authority, or a checklist written by a group of users who have a common reason for observing.

In this interpretive style of observing, the observer records a demonstrated **behaviour** by checking off the item on the checklist. This may be done at the time the behaviour was demonstrated or a short time afterward.

CHILD DEVELOPMENT FOCUS

Checklists may help the observation and recording of

- physical skills (gross and fine motor)
- self-help and social skills
- emotions and temperamental style
- cognitive skills
- language and communication

A knowledge of the **patterns of development** is essential for observers using checklists. These recordings can be only as useful as the items in them are sound; reference to recognized authorities on child development will support the writing of the checklist criteria. The items in the checklist must be **developmentally appropriate** and designed to supply the information the observer seeks.

The "homemade" checklist

The "homemade" checklist is a useful tool for teachers or students to record developmental information about one or more children quickly and efficiently. Observers may want information about the children's skills in particular areas such as **language**, **fine motor skills**, **gross motor skills**, or shape recognition. A list of such skills, developmentally appropriate and complete, will give the observer some insights into a child's **skill acquisition**. These results may be used as part of a program-planning change if teachers think that new activities or experiences might enable the child to gain the skill.

Parents might want to keep a record of the sequence in which, or dates by which, their children achieve particular **milestones**. In this case, a checklist can be prepared to indicate key achievements; these can then be checked off when they occur, and they should also be dated.

KEY FEATURES: Homemade checklist

- designed to record developmental information about an individual child

- lists expected behaviours

- used to check off observed behaviours

- interpretive method of recording behaviours

- naturalistic or "set up"

- participatory or nonparticipatory

Developmental Checklist

Child's name: _____   Observer: _____

Age/D.O.B.: _____   Date: _____

Context: _____

Source of checklist: _____

Age/stage designation: _____

Age/level	Behaviour	Date	Evidence

Prepare the checklist before you need to record the evidence. You might want to use a developmental profile to select items. Make sure you state the source of the checklist items.

The prepared checklist

Many well-designed checklists are available for use with young children. For ready-made observational tools, the same criteria apply for appropriate categories. If the items are not developmentally appropriate or do not fit the job you need done, then they will not produce useful information.

Teachers, psychologists, caregivers, students, or parents may wish to carry out checklist observations for different reasons, but they might find part of a prepared checklist sufficient for their purposes; they do not have to use the whole schedule.

Besides a specifically prepared checklist, you can look for checklist criteria in a variety of resources, including the Internet. You can also use developmental profiles or schedules for this purpose.

Reasons for using a checklist
- to gather large amounts of observational information efficiently
- to help focus the observer's attention of specific areas of development
- to target the presence or absence of particular behaviours or skills

KEY FEATURES: Prepared checklist

- uses a standardized list of behaviours to record information about an individual child
- behaviours listed have been checked for their validity and reliability
- interpretive method of recording behaviours

Features of a Checklist

A checklist can give you worthwhile information if the items it indicates are appropriate to the child. To work out the usefulness of a checklist, you will need to assess its appropriateness, **validity**, and **reliability**.

Theoretical perspective

All checklists have an underlying perspective, set of values, or beliefs. Even a simple list of behaviours indicates that the teacher considers those behaviours important. The way items are selected, the sequence in which they are written, and the way they are observed and documented are all shaped by the adult's beliefs, even if those beliefs are not articulated. If an authority of some kind developed the checklist, that list will also reflect a perspective on what is important and will reflect beliefs about the way children develop. Because all checklists are **theory-bound**, those we use or develop must reflect our beliefs about children and their development.

Teacher Observation Form and Checklist for Identifying Children
Who May Require Additional Services

Child's name: _____   Recording teacher's name: _____

Birth date:_____   Date: _____

LANGUAGE	Yes	No	Sometimes
Does the child			
1. use two- and three-word phrases to ask for what he or she wants?	☐	☐	☐
2. use complete sentences to tell you what happened?	☐	☐	☐
3. when asked to describe something, use at least two or more sentences to talk about it?	☐	☐	☐
4. ask questions?	☐	☐	☐
5. seem to have difficulty following directions?	☐	☐	☐
6. respond to questions with appropriate answers?	☐	☐	☐
7. seem to talk too softly or too loudly?	☐	☐	☐
8. Are you able to understand the child?	☐	☐	☐

PREACADEMICS	Yes	No	Sometimes
Does the child			
9. seem to take at least twice as long as the other children to learn preacademic concepts?	☐	☐	☐
10. seem to take the time needed by other children to learn preacademic concepts?	☐	☐	☐
11. have difficulty attending to group activities for more than five minutes at a time?	☐	☐	☐
12. appear extremely shy in group activities (for instance, not volunteering answers or answering questions when asked, even though you think the child knows the answers)?	☐	☐	☐

MOTOR	Yes	No	Sometimes
Does the child			
13. continually switch a crayon back and forth from one hand to the other when colouring?	☐	☐	☐
14. appear clumsy or shaky when using one or both hands?	☐	☐	☐
15. when colouring with a crayon, appear to tense the hand not being used (for instance, clench it into a fist)?	☐	☐	☐
16. when walking or running, appear to move one side of the body differently from the other side? For instance, does the child seem to have better control of the leg and arm on one side than on the other?	☐	☐	☐
17. lean or tilt to one side when walking or running?	☐	☐	☐
18. seem to fear or not be able to use stairs, climbing equipment, or tricycles?	☐	☐	☐
19. stumble often or appear awkward when moving about?	☐	☐	☐
20. appear capable of dressing self except for tying shoes?	☐	☐	☐

SOCIAL	Yes	No	Sometimes
Does the child			
21. engage in more than two disruptive behaviours a day (tantrums, fighting, screaming, etc.)?	☐	☐	☐
22. appear withdrawn from the outside world (fiddling with pieces of string, staring into space, rocking)?	☐	☐	☐
23. play alone and seldom talk to the other children?	☐	☐	☐
24. spend most of the time trying to get attention from adults?	☐	☐	☐
25. have toileting problems (wet or soiled) once a week or more often?	☐	☐	☐

VISUAL OR HEARING

Does the child

	Yes	No	Sometimes
26. appear to have eye movements that are jerky or uncoordinated?	☐	☐	☐
27. seem to have difficulty seeing objects? For instance, does the child			
• tilt head to look at things?	☐	☐	☐
• hold objects close to eyes?	☐	☐	☐
• squint?	☐	☐	☐
• show sensitivity to bright lights?	☐	☐	☐
• have uncontrolled eye rolling?	☐	☐	☐
• complain that eyes hurt?	☐	☐	☐
28. appear awkward in tasks requiring eye–hand coordination such as pegs, puzzles, colouring, etc.?	☐	☐	☐
29. seem to have difficulty hearing? For instance, does the child			
• consistently favour one ear by turning the same side of the head in the direction of the sound?	☐	☐	☐
• ignore, confuse, or not follow directions?	☐	☐	☐
• pull on ears or rub ears frequently, or complain of earaches?	☐	☐	☐
• complain of head noises or dizziness?	☐	☐	☐
• have a very high, very low, or monotonous tone of voice?	☐	☐	☐

GENERAL HEALTH

Does the child

	Yes	No	Sometimes
30. seem to have an excessive number of colds?	☐	☐	☐
31. have frequent absences because of illness?	☐	☐	☐
32. have eyes that water?	☐	☐	☐
33. have frequent discharge from			
• eyes?	☐	☐	☐
• ears?	☐	☐	☐
• nose?	☐	☐	☐
34. have sores on body or head?	☐	☐	☐
35. have periods of unusual movements (such as eye blinking) or "blank spells" that seem to appear and disappear without relationship to the social situation?	☐	☐	☐
36. have hives or rashes?	☐	☐	☐
wheeze?	☐	☐	☐
37. have a persistent cough?	☐	☐	☐
38. seem to be excessively thirsty?	☐	☐	☐
seem to be ravenously hungry?	☐	☐	☐
39. Have you noticed any of the following conditions:			
• constant fatigue?	☐	☐	☐
• irritability?	☐	☐	☐
• restlessness?	☐	☐	☐
• tenseness?	☐	☐	☐
• feverish cheeks or forehead?	☐	☐	☐
40. Is the child overweight?	☐	☐	☐
41. Is the child physically or mentally lethargic?	☐	☐	☐
42. Has the child lost noticeable weight without being on a diet?	☐	☐	☐

Source: K.E. Allen, C. Paasche, and A. Cornell, *Exceptional Children: Inclusion in Early Childhood Education*, 2nd ed. © (1998). Reprinted with permission of Nelson Thomson Learning: A division of Thomson Learning. Fax 800-730-2215.

Developmental sequences

Most checklists used by educators have lists of behaviours that form the criteria for what they want to look for when they observe. The checklist should indicate

- the domain of development to which it applies.
- the age/stage of development for which it is intended.

The behaviours listed must be in a developmental sequence that is consistent with current knowledge about the step-by-step progress made by most children—what is considered the **norm**. There should also be scope for recording behaviours that fall outside this typical sequence. This detailed developmental sequence allows the observer to record specific behaviours that might otherwise be lost. The success of this method of recording depends entirely on the adequacy of the developmental criteria and should not be considered an open-ended observation.

Ideally the checklist should offer space to record "evidence" of what was actually observed that makes the recorder think that the child demonstrated the behaviour. This evidence elaborates on the "present" or "absent" checks.

The child skills checklist in Observation Sample 5.1 below uses prepared checklist items and offers the opportunity to document evidence in several developmental areas.

Appropriateness

To judge the suitability of a prepared checklist, determine

1. that the checklist covers the areas of behaviour you wish to record.
2. that the items cover a suitable developmental span of behaviours in the selected domain.
3. that a sufficient blend of behaviours will be recorded to show a pattern, rather than simply whether a behaviour is absent or present.
4. that the checklist will fit your purpose—in the form of reports, record-keeping, program planning, identifying a concern, and so on.

Validity

Checklist items must measure effectively the behaviours that they intend to assess. First, look at a checklist's broad categories and consider how they will provide information in those areas. There should be a sufficient number of subcategories, graduated in their level of difficulty. Without these, the criteria will likely not measure what you desire. (See also Chapters 4, 6, 11, and 12 regarding the notion of validity.)

Reliability

Prepared checklists will usually have been tested for reliability, but do not assume this. While standardized measures may be useful in many situations, their reliability may be affected by a built-in **bias** not easily detected. Most significant, but least easily detected, is a cultural bias that can lead an observer to believe that a child is either more advanced or less skilled than he actually is. Even supposedly "standardized" measures may not have eliminated these biases. For example, if you were to assess self-help skills as part of competence, you could find that some children lack experience dressing themselves because this is not considered a desirable early skill in their cultures of origin. Similarly, when a child's first language is not English, it is unfair to evaluate her communication skills in English. She may be far more competent in her own language; consequently, her cognitive skills may also be more advanced than your observations might suggest.

To be reliable, a checklist should evaluate a child's behaviour in a way that does not fluctuate from one observation situation to the next. Look for some short-term consistency among outcomes of the checklist recordings. Observers recording information about a child should produce consistent results.

Review the child skills checklist for preschoolers in Observation Sample 5.1. To what extent is this observation appropriate, valid, and reliable? Might there be biases in the checklist itself and/or the evidence documented? How effective is the checklist's key?

Checkmarks

We use **checkmarks** to record whether we have seen a behaviour. A simple ✓ is not really enough, because it does not offer any detail. In addition to writing some "evidence" you might develop a code to assist your documentation. Educators find the following marks useful, and you can develop your own as well. Remember to date everything!

Skill demonstrated	SD
Not yet demonstrated	ND
No opportunity to observe	NP
Attempts unsuccessfully	AU
Can perform with support	CS
Emerging skill	EM
Seen by third party	3D

Observation Sample 5.1

The recorder has selected a checklist appropriate for the developmental level of the child. The prepared checklist allows room for supporting evidence when items are observed. This sample shows excerpts from the complete checklist.

How might parents and professionals work together to complete a "Child Skills Checklist" for a preschooler?

Child Skills Checklist for Preschoolers

Child's name: Jimmy   Observer: Cody

Age: 5 years, 9 months   Dates: 25 and 30 June and 2 July 2007

Setting: Laboratory School

Key: A–agree   D–disagree   N–not observed

* Observation of daycare teachers   ** Observation of mother

Item	Evidence	Date
1. Self-identity		
A Separates from parents without difficulty	Mother tells him goodbye; he says bye and continues to play*	30 June
A Does not cling to classroom staff excessively	Plays at the assigned areas on his own	30 June
A Makes eye contact with adults	Looks teacher in the eye as she explains how to stop the tricycle	30 June
A Makes activity choices without teacher's help	Hollers out, "I want to paint!" after the teacher explains their options for play	25 June
D Seeks other children to play with	Will seek out an activity, not a playmate	25 & 30 June
N Plays roles confidently in dramatic play		
A Stands up for own rights	Teachers say he often expresses anger if he does not get his way*	30 June
A Displays enthusiasm about doing things for self	Holds up his artwork to show another student	30 June
2. Emotional development		
A Allows self to be comforted during stressful time	During play, when Jimmy is running around wildly not listening to the teachers, he allows an instructor to pull him onto her lap; he remains there until he is more settled	25 June
A Eats, sleeps, toilets without fuss away from home	Uses the bathroom and eats lunch at the daycare centre with no fuss	25 June
N Handles sudden changes/startling situations with control		
D Can express anger in words rather than actions	Jimmy has hit teachers and peers when he is angry or is not getting his way*	30 June
D Allows aggressive behaviour to be redirected	Teachers say it is difficult to redirect his anger and aggressive behaviour when he is upset*	30 June

Item	Evidence	Date
A Does not withdraw from others excessively	Eager to do activities even when they involve the entire group	25 June
A Shows interest/attention in classroom activities	Asks teacher to read a story again that involves imitation	25 June
A Smiles, seems happy much of the time	Often smiles while playing	30 June

3. Social play

Item	Evidence	Date
A Plays by self with or without objects	Plays with a paper airplane while other children are around or alone	2 July
A Plays by self in pretend-type activities	Pretends his tricycle is an automobile	30 June
N Plays parallel to others with or without objects		
A Plays parallel to others in pretend-type activities	Pretends his tricycle is an automobile; other children are present	30 June
A Plays parallel to others constructing or creating something	Colouring and cutting out a picture at a table with other children	30 June
A Plays with a group with or without objects	Pretends to dig in sand with a shovel during a circle reading activity	25 June
N Plays with a group constructing or creating something		

...

7. Cognitive development: classification and seriation

Item	Evidence	Date
A Recognizes basic geometric shapes	Can identify triangles, squares, and circles**	30 June
A Recognizes colours	Can identify the main colours	2 July
A Recognizes differences in size	Will tell his mother he wants a big cup not a small cup**	30 June
N Recognizes differences in musical tones		
D Reproduces musical tones with voice	Will sing a song but does not noticeably change his tone**	30 June
N Sorts objects by appearance		
N Arranges events in sequences from first to last		
N Arranges objects in series according to rule		

8. Cognitive development: number, time, space, memory

Item	Evidence	Date
A Counts by rote to ten	Counts by rote up to one hundred**	30 June
A Counts objects to ten	Can count at least up to ten with a one-to-one ratio**	30 June
A Knows the daily schedule in sequence	Has to make his bed and brush his teeth after breakfast so that he can play before he goes to school**	30 June
N Can build a block enclosure	Child has never tried to build one; he builds bridges and airplanes with Lego**	30 June

Item	Evidence	Date
A Knows what happened yesterday	Can recount events of days that have passed**	30 June
A Can locate an object behind or beside something	Finds the Slinky that is behind a bigger toy	25 June
A Recalls words to song, chant	Can repeat/sing popular country songs that he hears frequently**	30 June
A Can recollect and act on directions of singing game	Participates in a group activity that involves singing and acting out parts of the song	25 June

9. Spoken language

Item	Evidence	Date
A Speaks confidently in classroom	When the teacher asks the group a question about a story she is reading, he answers the question with, "It's a wave."	25 June
A Speaks clearly enough for adults to understand	Same as above	25 June
A Speaks in expanded sentences	Tells his mother, "I have an airplane. Ben made it for me."	2 July
A Takes part in conversations with other children	Talks to a child sitting next to him while he is colouring a picture	30 June
A Asks questions with proper word order	Asks the teacher, "Can we go in this room to play now?"	2 July
N Makes "no" responses with proper word order		
A Uses past tense verbs correctly	Tells the teacher, "I used my feet to stop the bike."	30 June
N Plays with rhyming words		

10. Written language

Item	Evidence	Date
N Pretends to write by scribbling horizontally		
N Includes features of real letters in scribbling		
A Identifies his own name	Can point to things that have his name and recognize his name written**	30 June
N Identifies classroom labels		
A Knows some of the alphabet letters	Knows the entire alphabet and can recognize most of the letters**	30 June
A Prints real letters	Can print his first name**	30 June
A Prints letters of name	Can print his first name**	30 June
A Prints name correctly in linear manner	Can print his first name**	30 June

Item	Evidence	Date
12. Imagination		
<u>N</u> Pretends by replaying familiar routines		
<u>N</u> Needs particular props to do pretend play		
<u>N</u> Assigns roles or takes assigned roles		
<u>N</u> May switch roles without warning		
<u>D</u> Uses language for creating and sustaining a plot	Mother says she's never heard him make up stories about an event**	30 June
<u>N</u> Uses exciting, danger-packed themes		
<u>A</u> Takes on characteristics and actions related to a role	Makes sounds like a car while riding a tricycle	30 June
<u>D</u> Uses elaborate and creative themes, ideas, and details	Mother says she's never heard him make up stories about an event**	30 June

Source: Janice Beaty, *Observing Development of the Young Child,* 4th ed. © 1994. Adapted by permission of Prentice-Hall, Inc., Upper Saddle River, NJ.

Checklist Observations

Recording observations

Observers need to interpret the checklist criteria and match the observed behaviour to each of the items. Observers mark the presence or absence of the behaviour; behaviours may be coded as noted above. This recording may be done all at one time, or over a period of a few days, if a wide variety of behaviours is sought.

Checklists may also form part of a complex developmental assessment. We then focus on basic developmental checklists useful for educators and parents. See Observation Samples 5.1 and 5.3 for sample checklist observations.

Items are usually checked off as a result of the child's spontaneous activity. Occasionally, the child will not demonstrate some desired behaviours, so the observer may set up a situation in which the behaviour may occur or organize a more formal "testing" situation to elicit the desired response. In any situation, the observer should record the contextual information that might have had an impact on the behaviour.

Checklists are frequently used to evaluate information gathered from informal observations, and they may be compiled from a narrative recording or from other documentation as well. The direct method is more likely to generate accurate results.

How to record a checklist observation

1. Decide on the purpose for using the checklist method and review its underlying theory.
2. Choose a prepared checklist or devise a list of behaviours that fits your purpose.
3. Assess the checklist for its developmental appropriateness, validity, and reliability.
4. Prepare the checklist and place it where you can record the behaviours as they occur or soon afterward.
5. Check off the items you see demonstrated and use codes where appropriate.
6. Date all entries.
7. Make a note of any areas about which you are uncertain because of difficulty in interpreting the criteria or because the behaviour is just emerging.
8. If more than 80 percent of the items are checked, you may find that the child's behaviour has developed beyond the scope of your checklist. If so, use a more advanced checklist.
9. When behaviours are not demonstrated, set up experiences so that you will see them. Document the results.
10. Make appropriate, validated **inferences**, remembering that the absence of a behaviour does not necessarily indicate that the child is incapable of performing the behaviour.

Using checklists

Advantages

- Recording is quick and efficient.
- This method can be used in a variety of settings.
- All details need not be recorded.
- A clear picture of the presence or absence of behaviour is given.
- The observer can choose the criteria to observe.

- The observer can record observations while responsible for the care of the children under observation.

- The observer can choose to record information about more than one child at a time.

- Coverage of a range of developmental aspects may offer an overview of the whole child.

- The information produced can be used for program planning.

- Prepared checklists that are valid and reliable may be available.

- This method can identify concerns when an individual is not performing in keeping with the norm.

Disadvantages

- Recording is so simple that errors are not easily seen. The detail and context of the observed behaviour are lost.

- Recording may require a degree of inference or interpretation.

- Criteria can easily be inappropriate, invalid, or unreliable.

- Criteria may reflect a theoretical perspective other than the one that the observer holds.

- Interpretation typically focuses on what the child cannot do rather than on the skills she has mastered.

- The checklist requires evaluation and preparation beforehand.

- A checklist tends to represent a selection of isolated fragments of behaviour.

- Information about a child's skill development does not necessarily translate into appropriate goal-setting or -planning.

- Checklist criteria may be difficult to validate for developmental appropriateness.

- This method typically relies on norm referencing, which some educators consider a dubious tool.

- Recorded behaviours may require a qualitative description in addition to a statement of presence or absence.

- The absence of a behaviour does not necessarily indicate an inability to perform the behaviour.

- Recording might be affected by emotional conditions or illness that might not be evident.

- Teachers and parents tend to "remember" behaviours and record them as present from previous occasions; these may be expectations rather than objectively recorded examples.

Group checklists

The efficiency of checklists is increased when the observer uses a recording format that documents several children's behaviours at once. The teachers of a joint preschool/kindergarten program developed a homemade **group checklist** to provide them with an overview of the children's gross motor skills. Observation Sample 5.2 shows how a teacher recorded a large amount of information relatively quickly. The observer's skill must be good to ensure accuracy and the reduction of bias. This kind of format lends itself to effective program planning because the range of children's skills is the starting point for how the program can build on each child's emerging competence.

Observation Sample 5.2

The educator has created a group checklist as a way of overviewing her group's gross motor skills. As well as noting the presence or absence of skills, she has made a few explanatory notes. This recording system allows the teacher to pull together information associated with the program being offered, and see how well the children are doing in relation to the curriculum delivered. What other uses might there be for this style of recording?

Group Checklist
Date(s): October–November 2005   **Age Range:** *Preschoolers/Kindergartners*
Observers: Leah (Teacher), Soheila (Teacher), Steve (ECE), Mary-Lou (Resource Teacher)
Focus of Observation: *Gross Motor Skills*
Criteria: Skills identified in curriculum for joint preschool/kindergarten program   Y = Yes;   N = No

Children's Names	Walks	Runs	Skips (alternating feet)	Kicks large ball	Jumps on the spot	Hops on one foot	Balances on one foot	Walks on straight line	Climbs ladders/trees	Climbs stairs (alternating feet)	Walks backwards	Walks a balance beam
1. Aariz	Y	Y	not yet	Y	not yet	not yet	Y	Y	Y	Y	seems confused	a few steps
2. Wyatt	Y	Y	not yet	Y sometimes	not yet	not yet	Y	fairly well	attempts	not yet	not yet	not yet
3. Parveen	Y	Y	not yet	not yet	not yet	not yet	Y	needs practice	seems fearful	not yet	Y	not yet
4. Daniel	Y	Y	not yet	Y	Y	Y	Y	Y	stays at the top	Y	Y	Y with little fear
5. Dawind	Y	Y	not yet	Y	Y	not yet	not yet	nearly!	2 steps	one at a time	not yet	doesn't want to try
6. Elena	Y goes with mom on hikes	Y	not yet	Y	Y	not yet	Y	Y	Y	likes to go backwards	Y	Y
7. Timmy	Y	Y	not yet	Y	Y	Y	Y	Y	Y	Y runs upstairs	Y	not yet
8. Haifa	Y	Y	not yet	Y	not yet	not yet	not yet	fairly good	Y	Y	Y	Y
9. Esther	Y	Y	Y	not yet	not yet	tries hard	not yet	makes effort	Y	Y	Y	Y
10. Toby	Y	Y	not yet	Y	not yet	not yet	not yet	didn't try	didn't try	Y	Y	not yet
11. Jo	Y	Y	not yet	Y	Y	Y	Y	Y enthusiastic	Y	Y	Y	Y
12. Brady	Y difficult because of spina bifida		encourages others!	encourages others!	encourages others!	encourages others!	encourages others!	encourages others!	holds clothes while others try	N	N	N
13. Cory	Y	Y	not yet	not yet	not yet	not yet	not yet	attempts	Y	Y	Y	not yet
14. Caitlin	Y	Y	Y	Y	Y	not yet	Y	Y	Y	Y	Y	Y

Observation Sample 5.2 (continued)

Children's Names	Rides a trundle toy	Rides tricycle	Dribbles large ball	Lifts large items (strength)	Team game skills	Spontaneous physical activity (interests)	Swims	Floats	Doggy paddle	Jumps in water	Challenges self
1. Aariz	Y	Y	Y	Y	Y	enjoys outdoor play with climber	not yet	not yet	not yet	–	
2. Wyatt	Y	but trundles	not yet	Y tries hard	not yet	prefers indoor play	may fear water	–	–	–	imitates others
3. Parveen	Y	trundles only	Y	Y helps to prepare for circle	not yet	needs adult encouragement	no opportunity	–	–	–	often diffident
4. Daniel	Y	Y	Y	Y	N	responds to ideas and then plays independently	Y	Y	Y	Y	initiates physical challenges
5. Dawind	Y	Y	not yet	reluctant	Y but slow to join in	active near teacher	not yet	–	–	–	gradually more confident
6. Elena	Y	Y	Y	pushes, pulls, and picks up!	Y tries	bold risk-taker outdoors	Y	Y	Y	Y	wants to race others
7. Timmy	Y	Y a few metres	not yet	Y	Y	imitates older boys	not yet	not yet	Y	not yet	not very self-directed
8. Haifa	Y	can go fast	not yet	Y	Y	greater risk-taking recently	–	–	–	Y	more confident
9. Esther	Y	recent skill	not yet	only watches	not yet	demands adult "watches" her	Y	–	no	–	wants audience and direction
10. Toby	Y	says "that's for girls"	Y	– he's a "bodybuilder"	Y	constantly moving; needs challenges	not yet	plays in water	–	–	risk-taker
11. Jo	Y	Y but finds it hard to take turns	Y very agile	Y helps adults move furniture	Y	prefers action with girls	Y	not yet	Y	not yet	imitates
12. Brady	N	N	N	N	N	N	has found role as cheerleader	wants to try	N	N	positive attitude
13. Cory	Y	Y confident on trike	Y	not yet	not yet	wants adult alongside	no opportunity	no opportunity	–	–	follower
14. Caitlin	Y	Y shows others how to cycle	Y	Y	Y	confident	Y	not yet	Y	Y	risk-taker and encourages others

The analysis: Interpreting the data collected from checklists

Inferences should not be drawn from the information unless the checklist has been assessed for its suitability and the recording has been made with **objectivity**. A typical **analysis** might cover the following areas:

1. Draw deductions from the pattern of skills present on or absent from the checklist. Highlight the strengths demonstrated.

2. Make inferences about the child's skill level using comparisons with expected performance. This **norm-referenced assessment** needs to make clear supporting statements that are thoroughly validated.

3. Depending on the reason for making the observation, evaluate the effectiveness of the checklist and examine its outcome.

   a. Focus mainly on what the child can do.

   b. Look at any supposed "lack" of skill development. Ask yourself whether the child has not acquired the skill or the skill was perhaps present but not demonstrated.

   c. Verify the checklist with information from others.

   d. Consider the child's behaviour within his cultural experience and expectations.

   e. Follow up with a variety of other observation methods and attempt to match the outcomes.

   f. Develop an **individual program plan (IPP)** that devises activities and experiences to enhance the child's skills.

   g. Ask the parents, school, or another interested party to offer insights or other informal observations to help explain the behavioural pattern recorded.

   h. If the child demonstrates all the criteria, little information about the stage of development can be elicited. Use another checklist more developmentally appropriate for that child.

   The checklist sample that follows as Observation Sample 5.3 uses a norm-referenced list of criteria. The novel feature in this observation is that the recorder has been able to document the child's language in the Chinese language and script. Evaluate the effectiveness and potential for bias in this example.

Observation Sample 5.3

This school-age child has been observed using a checklist developed from a normative profile. The recording contains quotations in the child's (and recorder's) first language. The observer found a way of addressing language differences in her recording.

How might you complete a developmental checklist if you do not share a common language with the child?

DEVELOPMENTAL CHECKLIST

Observer: Ki Wan A Yau

Child's name: Mei Lin
Age/D.O.B.: 8 years, 8 months (July 10, 1999)

Date of observation: March 2-16, 2008
Time of observation: throughout day
Setting: March 2-16 at her home and her aunt's home; March 4, 9:25-11:30 a.m. in her classroom and gym

Source of checklist items: Allen, K.E., & Marotz, L.R. (1994). *Developmental profile and growth pattern* (Appendix 2). In *Developmental profiles: Pre-birth through eight* (2nd ed., p. 171). Albany, NY: Delmar.

Designated age/stage of checklist items: 8 and 9 years

Key: ✓   Observed

✓$_2$ Observed by caregiver or parent

N   No opportunity to observe

✗   Behaviour not yet demonstrated

Behaviours	Key	Date	Evidence
1. a. Have energy to play	✓	March 4	She showed she had energy to play in gym. She climbed a rope, walked across a balance beam, jumped up and bent her knees on a boxhorse, turned somersaults.
b. Continuing growth	✓	March 2	Now, her height is 130.5 cm. Since last June, her height has increased 3.5 cm.
c. Few illnesses	✓	March 6	Last winter, she only had one cold.
2. Use pencil in a deliberate and controlled manner	✓	March 4	She can hold a pencil and marker using a tripod grasp. I saw this when she was drawing pictures in her journal.

Behaviours	Key	Date	Evidence
3. Express relatively complex thoughts in a clear and logical fashion	✓	March 2	She used macaroni to make a bracelet and talked at the same time. Quote: Chinese language: 她對媽說：「我用這條繩去度手腕的長度。」(她再度橡根，然後將通心粉串上)又說：「陣間我會油上顏色。」媽說：「你串好，十分難上色。」她說：「我要知道用幾多，然後拿出來再上色。」 Translation: She said to her mom, "I use this string to measure the length around my hand." After she had done, she cut a rubber band and threaded macaroni one by one. She said, "I will paint them later on." Mom said, "If you thread them all, you will find it difficult to paint afterward." She said, "I want to know how many I will use, then I will let them out and paint them."
4. Carry out multiple (4-5) step instructions	✓	March 13	Quote: Chinese language: 媽對她說：「Tracy，去廚櫃拿一個碗和碟，放在枱上。然後去雪櫃，取兩隻蛋，兩塊HAM。打蛋於碗內，至起泡，用剪刀把HAM剪絲。做完後，話我知，我會教妳炎蛋。」 Translation: Mom said, "Mei Lin, get one bowl and one small plate from the cupboard and put them on the table. Then, get two eggs and two pieces of ham from the refrigerator. Break the eggs into the bowl and stir them with a fork until bubbles appear. Cut the ham into stick-size pieces on the plate with scissors. After you finish, tell me. I will teach you how to cook it."
5. Become less easily frustrated with own performance	✗	March 5	She was frustrated with her own performance when she did paper folding to make a turtle because she didn't remember exactly the steps.
6. Interact and play cooperatively with other children	✓	March 14	She talked to her cousins when they played games together. They played Monopoly cooperatively. She waited for her turn patiently.

Checklists **155**

Behaviours	Key	Date	Evidence
7. Use eating utensils with ease	✓	March 4	She can use her right hand to grasp chopsticks and left hand to grasp a bowl at the same time to eat food. She uses her right hand to grasp a knife and left hand to grasp a fork at the same time to cut food.
8. a. Have a good appetite	X	March 5-16	She could eat half a bowl of rice, lots of vegetables and meats.
b. Show interest in trying new foods		March 15	Mom mixed salad and tuna fish. She did not want to eat it.
9. Know how to tell time	✓	March 4	Quote: Chinese language: 在校裏, 我同她:「recess 幾時完?」她說.存束十. Translation: I asked her when she finished recess in her school. She said "10 to 11."
10. Have control of bowel and bladder functions	✓	March 2-16	She has control of bowel and bladder functions. I saw this when she went to the washroom regularly and independently without any problem.
11. Participate in some group activities a. Sports	✓	March 4	In gym, she participated in the group routines.
b. Plays	✓₂	March 4	Every Monday, she joins the folk-dance club after school.
c. Games	✓	March 16	She played games with her cousins.
12. Demonstrate beginning skills in a. Reading	✓	March 6	She read a book to her baby sister. Sometimes she reads books borrowed from the school library.
b. Writing	✓	March 12	I saw this when she wrote letters to her classmates using handwriting.
c. Math	N		
13. a. Want to go to school	X		
b. Seem disappointed if must miss a day	X		

Summary

Checklists may be either developed by an educator or borrowed from a prepared standardized measure. A checklist is only as useful as its appropriateness for the age/stage of the child, its focus on the appropriate domain of development, its reliability in measuring what it intends to measure, and its effectiveness in improving the child's development. Essentially the checklist records the presence or absence of the skills, attributes, or other characteristics of development.

In practice, checklists usually offer more useful information if they are accompanied by clear evidence, or note exactly what it was that made the observer check off or mark the item. Although completing this kind of checklist can take longer, such detail improves the checklist, makes it easier to share with others, and leads to strong curriculum decisions.

Prepared checklists can offer educators and parents a valid and reliable measure, while "homemade" checklists can be tailored to the particular needs of the educator and children. All checklists require that their criteria be interpreted and those items related to the actual behaviours observed. These requirements can be harder to meet than is apparent at first. An experienced observer makes these necessary interpretations better. Practising the use of narrative recordings helps you complete checklists as well, because the latter hones your skills of recording without interpretation.

Checklists are created according to a theory about how children develop; not all will be appropriate or reflect your philosophy as educator. When selecting and using a checklist, take care to ensure it actually measures what you consider important. As with other observational recordings, collect data using a variety of different methods and at different times. Use the checklist to prompt action in terms of general curriculum design along with individual program planning.

These children are enjoying experimenting with dough and comparing it to flour without water—this provides evidence of their parallel play. Open-ended activities like this one allow the teacher to document each of the children's skills on a prepared checklist.

With permission of the YMCA of Greater Toronto

Key Terms

- analysis
- behaviour
- bias
- checklist
- checkmarks
- developmentally appropriate
- fine motor skills
- gross motor skills
- group checklist
- individual program plan (IPP)
- inference
- language
- milestones
- norm
- norm-referenced assessment
- objectivity
- pattern of development
- reliability
- skill acquisition
- theory-bound
- validity

Weblinks

www.circleofinclusion.org/english/guidelines/modulefour/social/g.html
This useful site has a number of observation strategies, including checklists, and is designed to document developmental information about children who have special needs.

http://parentcenter.babycenter.com/behavior-observation-checklist-kindergarten-to-first-grade
This checklist could be useful, but notice how it is framed in a negative way. It intends to identify children who might have ADHD; be really cautious about using it. Also, can you find ways of checking its validity and reliability?

http://www.sasked.gov.sk.ca/docs/kindergarten/kindstu.html
This is a reputable site that reinforces the necessity for observing and recording information about children. It includes an example of a checklist. It's designed for kindergarten children, but do you think it is also usable with preschool children in childcare who are of kindergarten age?

www.sasked.go.ca/docs/ela/assessment/assessment01.html
Saskatchewan Education offers many different checklists designed to monitor elementary children's developing skills. Some are applicable to younger children, especially those in preschool or kindergarten.

www.language-express.ca
Language Express Pre-school Speech and Language is involved in early identification, direct assessment, treatment, and support in transitioning to

school, and other speech-language services. The site offers a checklist for parents and caregivers to help in early identification.

http://scholar.google.ca
This is an excellent starting point for researching academic articles of many kinds. Try entering "Cautions in Using the Child Behavior Checklist" and you will reach an article by Perrin and others outlining a critique of a checklist.

www.investinkids.ca
Information on early development with seven profiles from birth to age 5.

www.zerotothree.org
Follow Professional and Parent for information about development up to 36 months. Profiles useful for developing checklists. Focus on childcare providers, pediatricians, and parents.

www.search-institute.org
Identifies 40 developmental assets for several age/stage groups; could be formatted as checklists.

www.dcmsonline.org/jax-medicine/2000journals/march2000/EIPchecklist.htm
American Medical Association developmental checklists (birth to 36 months) designed for early intervention.

www.sasked.gov.sk.ca/docs/kindergarten/kindshar.html
Techniques for sharing evaluation information with parents and family members.

www.bmcc.org/Headstart/As_I_Am/appendix.htm
"Observing Skills for Living" checklist.

6 Charts, Scales, and Pictorial Representations

Understanding a child's family and social context can help an observer interpret the child's behaviour. Family trees and other social maps can be used to chart the child's relationships.

Bar graphs are one of the many techniques used to present data in a visual form so that the reader may readily recognize patterns or trends.
Statistics Canada (2005)

Observational data can be more meaningful if it is represented visually.
Child Studies student (2008)

Educators, like many other people, tend to appreciate information presented in visual formats. It is much easier to follow a mapping of children's movements using a diagram or a graphic representation of observational data than it is to read very long narratives or detailed checklists.
Dr. Pat Corson (2005)

Focus Questions

1. How might you devise a quick and efficient method of recording information about a child's daily routine?

2. How might a map of a room, outdoor play space, or other children's area be used to benefit the program or an Individual child?

3. After interpreting data from observations of a whole class, the teacher wants to present the findings in a graphic manner. In what ways could this be done?

Learning Outcomes

By reading this chapter and applying the ideas to practice, learners will

- identify a variety of techniques to record observational data.
- recognize a range of graphic data displays.

Features of Charts, Scales, and Pictorial Representations

DEFINITION: Chart

A **chart** is a visual representation of information (observational or other) on a prepared form for recording basic information.

DEFINITION: Scale

A **scale** is a form of measuring information that uses lists of behaviours (or other items) and rates them according to predetermined values, or visually represents information based on rated behaviours.

DEFINITION: Pictorial representation

A **pictorial representation** is any form of recording or interpretation that uses a visual way of demonstrating data.

Charts, scales, and pictorial representations are all interpretive methods of recording observational data. These methods depend heavily on the recorder's **objectivity**; there are few ways of validating the accuracy of the recording. These forms of recording can enable teachers to collect information that might be impossible to record using more time-consuming methods. Alternatively they may be used to present observational information after it has been analyzed, or as part of the analytical process itself. (See page 178–87 onward for these uses.)

Some charts and many pictorial representations and scales are completed soon after the activity is over. Their easy use enables teachers to record some of the essence of what was observed without having to write down all the details. This recording requires professional skill in deciding what is relevant to record and what is not. Almost any untrained person could complete a rating scale or chart; some of the information might be useful and accurate, but it might not all be reliable. While the outcome may look fine, the chart may lack the objectivity of a professional's work. These observations alone should not be used to determine a child's program plan. They can be used in addition to other observation methods, as they may help in providing a fuller picture.

CHILD DEVELOPMENT FOCUS

Visual representation may assist in determining

- social relationships
- typical patterns of behaviour
- contextual influences on development
- mobility/movement
- personal preferences/personality types
- cognitive skills

Useful recording methods

Charts, scales, and pictorial representations are methods for recording observational data, or ways in which observational information is presented after analysis. They are all visual representations of information. The following are the most useful categories for the observer:

Observation charts (pages 163–71): These are prepared blank forms with labelled and sectioned categories used for charting behaviours, relationship dyads (connections/interactions between two individuals), routine events, and other significant information as it is observed.

Observation scales (pages 172–78): Commonly called **rating scales**, these are lists of behaviours or traits prepared in advance for scoring at the time of or after observation. These can be open to subjective recording. They may include forced choices, semantic differentials, **numerical scales**, or **graphic scales**.

Social maps (pages 178–87): Pictorial presentations of the composition of the child's family, history, social relationships, or life experiences are all helpful to the observer. These may include sociograms, ecomaps, genograms, family trees, and flow diagrams or pictorial profiles. Information is gathered from the child, family members, or those in other social relationships and is presented as a chart or diagram.

Mappings (pages 187–91): Trackings or mappings are records of a child's movement or activity within a specified room, zone, or space. By recording the path of movement on a prepared map of that space, the teacher documents evidence of the child's mobility, interests, and attention span. Mappings may also support a teacher's evaluation of the use of space.

Interpretive graphic representations (pages 191–200): In analyzing observational recordings, observers might wish to explain their findings visually. Graphs, block charts, and pie charts are simple methods designed to make evaluative comparisons.

KEY FEATURES: Charts, scales, and pictorial representations

- easily understood depictions of information
- visual representations of observational data
- interpretive methods of recording information
- may focus on one or more children
- usually naturalistic
- mostly nonparticipatory

Observation Charts

Many teachers choose to record behaviour on observation charts, because the method is quick and efficient, and they can do so while they continue to participate in the children's program. Routines and sequences of a child's day may be recorded to help indicate the child's personal rhythms and adaptation to a changing environment, and to assist a caregiver in responding to the child's needs.

Using a prepared form or chart, the caregiver can check off when particular events have occurred, such as sleep, rest, feeding, periods of activity, diaper-changing, or bowel or bladder evacuation. The pattern of feeding, wakefulness, sleep, and toileting can give clues about the child's health and well-being. Observers often use these charts for infants, but do not underestimate their use with toddlers and older children. Identification of behavioural patterns can help the caregiver appreciate the child's needs in a **holistic** sense. A sample infant chart can be found in Observation Sample 6.1.

The effectiveness of charting observations relies on the philosophy on which the chart is based, the appropriateness of the chart in covering a range of predictable categories, the accuracy of the recording as the observer interprets what she sees, and the consistency of interpretation among the adults using the chart.

An obvious limitation of charts lies in their simplicity, as they offer little opportunity to explain behaviour. It is tempting to make efficient use of a chart and to avoid analyzing the resulting patterns and identifying any need for intervention. As records, charts should be used, not just stored. While we must observe indicators regarding individual needs, health, well-being, and disease in order to respond to a child's needs, we must also consider this information within its family and social context, as well as understand its impact on the interrelated aspects of the child's growth and development.

Participation charts can give teachers a good indication of the interests, motivation, and focus of individual children or groups. While they frequently quantify involvements, they offer little opportunity to describe the quality of activity. Some charts allow for recording the number of children involved in a specified activity; others count activity in designated time slots or enable the teacher to determine who has participated. Charts may be designed to increase the children's own responsibility by having the children themselves check off what they have achieved.

Charts may be designed to increase parent–teacher communication or facilitate exchange of information between caregivers. Separate charts for each child may be useful for focusing on an individual, and group charts can help with program planning. In the latter case, exercise caution in making assumptions about the "average" or the "majority's" responses, and in planning a curriculum on that basis. "Averages" may in fact apply to nobody; the groups of children may have levels of competence and participation above or below that average, and your programming may not suit any of them. Similarly, focusing on the "majority" may leave out children who have other needs.

Caregivers, social workers, or teachers may make observations related to the children's health and symptoms; the information may then be offered to health professionals. A non–health professional can chart symptoms only if trained in what to look for. Children with a variety of special medical conditions—such as asthma, anemia, or cystic fibrosis—may be in mainstream settings and need close observation and appropriate intervention when they exhibit particular symptoms. Many of these children may have mild conditions, others much more severe; in all cases, parents and caregivers should share observational information, and a connection with the health professionals should be maintained.

The Information Chart for Infants of Observation Sample 6.1 offers an overview of each day's key events, but cannot provide much detail.

TAKING A SPECIAL LOOK: Health observations

Baseline observations should be made every day. These informal observations act as a foundation for measuring a child's change of behaviour or appearance later in the day and are particularly useful for children with special conditions that need to be monitored. These observations can be recorded as anecdotal records or on prepared charts, but they are sometimes undocumented observations.

Observation Sample 6.1

This information chart provides daily information for parents and caregivers. A comparison of these charts as the weeks pass will provide more information about the infant's development.

Are there any other categories that you might include on this one-page chart?

Information Chart for Infants

Child's name: _Adrienne_

Age: _9 months_

Date: _January 18, 2008_

Observer: _Scott_

Parents: _Lynn and Malcolm_

Other caregivers and students: _Michelle P., Jennifer, Carolie, Darlene, Michelle C._

Who brought the child to the centre? _Malcolm_

Time: _8:10 a.m._

Liquid intake	a.m.	Formula: 8:30 – 4 oz; 9:15 – 2 oz; 11:15 – 1/4 cup
	p.m.	Formula: 1:00 – 6 oz; 4:35 – 4.5 oz. Water: 4:15
Solid intake	a.m.	8:30 – Cheerios; 11:15 – macaroni and cheese, breadstick, 2 oz. peas, 1/4 banana
	p.m.	2:50 – 4 oz. peaches mixed with 1 tbsp. of cereal
Sleep	a.m.	9:30–10:25
	p.m.	1:32–2:36
Health indicators	a.m.	Diaper rash, runny nose
	p.m.	Diaper rash, runny nose
Urination/diaper change	a.m.	10:30 wet; 11:55 wet
	p.m.	1:00 wet; 2:38 wet; 4:10 wet
Bowel movements/diaper change	a.m.	None
	p.m.	None
Behaviour notes	a.m.	Very happy (11:15 lunch – all smiles)
	p.m.	Happy *on walk Adrienne became slightly upset – carried rest of the way
Play activities	a.m.	Gross motor room, different types of boxes, floor toys – crawling
	p.m.	Jello cube play on the floor
Climate/environment	a.m.	20°C room
	p.m.	7°C walk, partly cloudy, mild; 20°C room

* NOTE: Only three infants in today.

Who picked up the child? _Malcolm_   Time: _5:45 p.m._

Using observation charts

Advantages

- Can be used for either one child or a group.
- Charts may enable observers to record behaviours quickly and efficiently.
- Behaviour may be recorded during or after observation.
- Charts may include routine information as well as behaviours—for example, feeding, diapering.
- The format is user-friendly.
- Observations are usually easy to interpret.
- Charts may identify behavioural patterns.
- The format is useful for information exchange between caregivers and parents.
- Charts frequently offer health as well as developmental areas for observation.

Disadvantages

- This method requires a prepared chart that includes all predictable categories.
- Charts often require inferences to be drawn at the time of recording.
- The format may encourage observers to concentrate on domestic routines rather than responses and learning.
- This method may be used for efficiency rather than depth.
- Charts tend to offer only superficial information, limited to expected observation categories.
- The format may encourage simplification of developmental issues.
- Charts should not be relied on as the sole source of observational information.

Types of observation charts

The following pages show several types of charts that can document general behaviour, social relationships, and health. The Information Chart for Infants of Observation Sample 6.1 can be used to record a week's worth of data by adding a column for each day. Using such a chart the caregiver keeps an ongoing record of observations. The format allows for a change of caregiver while sustaining the information flow. The notes, however brief, can form the basis of a log, which can show developmental changes over weeks. The chart may also aid the caregiver's memory, prompting oral anecdotal accounts to support the information. This kind of record offers essential information to parents.

Daily Program Implementation Chart

Children's names: _____   Age/D.O.B.: _____

_____   _____

Date: _____

Observer(s): _____

Activity area	Materials	Objectives	Observation
Creative			
Language			
Sensory			

This chart underlines the notion of a dynamic, ongoing process of observation and activity planning. The activity area will always show a response to the previous day's observations; the following day, these observations would be used to determine the new plan.

Activity Response Chart

Observer(s): _____   Date.: _____

Zone, activity, or room area	Children's names				
	1 _____	2 _____	3 _____	4 _____	5 _____

The activity response chart shares some features with **event sampling** but uses only a **tally** or checkmark to identify each child's involvement in an activity. As an alternative, have a separate chart for each activity or learning centre and check off the name as a child participates.

Activity/Routine Chart for Infants

Name: _____

Age/D.O.B.: _____

Date: _____

Context: _____

Observer: _____

Time	Activity/routine	Imposed (I)/Choice (C)	Feeding	Personal care	Rest/sleep	Outdoor activity	Play	Other
6:00 a.m.								
6:30 a.m.								
7:00 a.m.								
7:30 a.m.								
8:00 a.m.								
8:30 a.m.								
9:00 a.m.								
9:30 a.m.								
10:00 a.m.								
10:30 a.m.								
11:00 a.m.								
11:30 a.m.								
12:00 p.m.								
12:30 p.m.								
1:00 p.m.								
1:30 p.m.								
2:00 p.m.								

The pattern or rhythm of a child's day needs to be considered with reference to the context and any imposed routine. Infant schedules may be structured or responsive; if flexible, the pattern will reveal the child's natural rhythm and may help indicate the child's personal style. This chart includes a column to indicate whether an activity is adult directed or chosen by the child. This chart is a form of **time sampling** *(see Chapter 4).*

Immunization Record

Immunization type	Date	Reaction	Given by

Parents may keep an immunization-record card for their own benefit, to be aware of their children's immunization needs. A medical practitioner may sign the record. Agencies may wish to see this record with verification of the information.

Patterns of Relationships Within a Group

Date(s)/times: _____

Context: _____

_____

Observer(s): _____

Children's names: Ages/D.O.B.:

A:_____ _____

B:_____ _____

C:_____ _____

D:_____ _____

E:_____ _____

F:_____ _____

G:_____ _____

Child	A	B	C	D	E	F	G	H	I	J
A	■									
B		■								
C			■							
D				■						
E					■					
F						■				
G							■			

To complete this chart, observe the children in various activities in which they are free to choose their companions. Record interactions between children with a tally mark in the appropriate box. When two children interact for longer than five minutes, put a different mark. Patterns of interactions will enable you to identify children who are isolated from the rest and those who have made social relationships. This chart could also focus on initiating and responding to invitations to play. For example, if C initiates play with F, record "CF," but if F invites C to play, record "FC." You can classify positive, negative, or neutral interactions (with a colour-coded tally) to add a further dimension. This practice requires further interpretation, which has to be recorded during the process.

Components of Participation Chart

Children's names: _____ Ages/D.O.B.:_____

_____ _____

Observer: _____

Activity: _____

Names	Physically involved	Follows instructions	Attempts to solve problems	Cooperates in action/ verbally	Creative/ constructive	Keeps on task

This chart can be used to record participatory information about an activity for a group of children. Do not assume that each component of participation is, of itself, always positive. Appropriate and valid participation may include solitary activity, experimentation, and even destruction! Chart results can be useful if analyzed without judgments or assumptions.

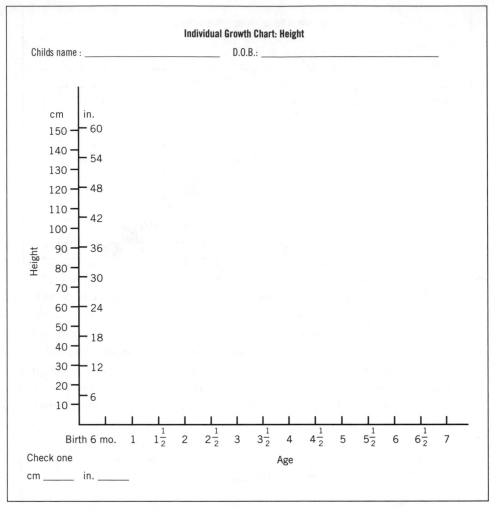

Individual Growth Chart: Height

Childs name : _____   D.O.B.: _____

Height

cm	in.
150	60
140	54
130	
120	48
110	42
100	
90	36
80	30
70	
60	24
50	18
40	
30	12
20	6
10	

Birth 6 mo. 1 $1\frac{1}{2}$ 2 $2\frac{1}{2}$ 3 $3\frac{1}{2}$ 4 $4\frac{1}{2}$ 5 $5\frac{1}{2}$ 6 $6\frac{1}{2}$ 7

Check one

Age

cm _____   in. _____

A child's height can be plotted on this chart. A pattern of growth is a useful consideration when evaluating aspects of gross motor-skill development.

A similar chart can be used for weight. Plotting a child's weight gain can help parents and professionals determine the child's overall pattern of change. Comparisons with norms can be helpful if those using the information understand the range of what constitutes an average; undue emphasis should not be placed on slight variations from a norm.

TAKING A SPECIAL LOOK: Children born prematurely or at low birth weight

Many babies, with expert pediatric assistance, survive premature birth, and some of them are extremely small. Other babies have low birth weights for other reasons. More than their size presents a challenge; many of these babies also have a range of medical and developmental difficulties. You will need to consider birth size and developmental history when you are interpreting your observations of infants, toddlers, and also older children. For example, some children may be developing at an appropriate rate, but their actual skill performance might match that of the norm for a younger child.

Symptom Chart for Chronic or Special Medical Conditions

Child's name: _____ Age/D.O.B.: _____

Observer(s): _____

Diagnosed condition: _____

Date(s) from: _____ to: _____

Reporting line: _____

Date	Behaviour symptom	Number of times observed	Severity	Comment

The parent, caregiver, or teacher may need to record observations of a child's specific behaviours or symptoms as they occur. If a child with a special medical condition is integrated into a childcare setting, the caregivers need to be taught to identify the behaviours that are important to record for that child, and they should ensure that such information is reported appropriately.

Observation Scales

You can rate observed information according to the degree to which a quality, trait, skill, or competence is demonstrated in various ways. The simplest rating scale may use a checklist-style inventory of items (see Chapter 5) accompanied by a scale that elaborates a yes/no response. The scale may contain opposites on a **continuum**, numerical ratings, choices of levels of behaviour, or pictorial or graphic representations. More complex rating scales may have established criteria for grading a performance or demonstration of skill. Each type of scale is scored at, or soon after, the time of observation. Some require evidence to help validate the scoring.

All rating scales require the observer to make **inferences** at the time of recording. The complex inferences required in identifying a child's behaviour, labelling it, and evaluating the quality of the child's performance require considerable skill. The components of the inventory itself, coupled with the form of evaluation that goes with it, may not be sufficiently valid. It can be difficult to assess the **validity** and **reliability** of a rating scale; too often, a scale is chosen because of its apparent ease of use rather than its technical merit or appropriateness. A scale can be only as good as the philosophy, theory, and research on which it is based. Allocating a grading or scale to a checklist may alter its intrinsic reliability if it was not designed to be used that way. Also be aware that evaluating skills based on a pre-set scale presumes that the performance will fall within the bounds of that grading system. The scale shown as Observation Sample 6.2 is accompanied by a discussion of Tasha's personality.

Using observation scales

Advantages

- Scales can be used to record information about a wide range of behaviours and styles.
- Recording is efficient.
- Little training is required to implement the use scales at a basic level.
- This method can be used to measure behaviours not easily measured in other ways.
- Scales may be used to record information at the time of observation or shortly after and they allow for the observer's continued participation in the program.
- Scales may offer a large amount of information about children quickly.

Disadvantages

- The validity of items may be questionable.
- The format offers little contextual information.
- For effective choice and use, thorough training is necessary to evaluate behaviour.
- The rater needs to make qualitative judgments of behaviour.
- The position of items on the inventory may affect scoring.
- Inferences must be made rapidly and without full validation.
- A scale may be inconsistent in its wording or lead to assumptions about so-called **positive** and **negative behaviours**.

(continued on page 175)

Observation Sample 6.2

This semantic differential scale is used to record observations on a child's personality. The attached personality profile comments on the validity and reliability of the rating scale and elaborates on the results.

The observer used the following attributes as a guide to considering Tasha's personality. Can you see any concerns related to these items on the semantic differential scale?

Personality Attributes Rating Scale

Child's name: _Tasha_   Observer: _Salma_

D.O.B.: _5-5-99_   Age: _7 years, 8 months_

Circle the number that describes the degree of the attribute:

Attribute	3	2	1	0	1	2	3	Attribute
Outgoing	3	(2)	1	0	1	2	3	Reserved
Sensitive	3	(2)	1	0	1	2	3	Insensitive
Confident	3	(2)	1	0	1	2	3	Lacking confidence
Aggressive	3	2	(1)	0	1	2	3	Passive
Dominant	(3)	2	1	0	1	2	3	Submissive
Flexible	3	(2)	1	0	1	2	3	Inflexible
Patient	3	2	1	(0)	1	2	3	Impatient
Responsible	3	2	(1)	0	1	2	3	Irresponsible
Dependent	3	2	1	0	(1)	2	3	Independent
Imaginative	(3)	2	1	0	1	2	3	Unimaginative
Relaxed	3	(2)	1	0	1	2	3	Tense
Responsive	3	(2)	1	0	1	2	3	Unresponsive
Introverted	3	2	1	0	1	(2)	3	Extroverted
Generous	3	(2)	1	0	1	2	3	Mean
Trusting	3	(2)	1	0	1	2	3	Suspicious
Controlled	3	2	(1)	0	1	2	3	Uncontrolled
Serious	3	2	1	(0)	1	2	3	Easygoing
Courageous	3	2	(1)	0	1	2	3	Timid
Intelligent	(3)	2	1	0	1	2	3	Less intelligent
Emotionally stable	(3)	2	1	0	1	2	3	Emotionally unstable

Signature _Salma Ahmad_   Relationship _Student teacher_

Tasha's Personality

Validity of the rating scale: There are more "positive" attributes on one side of the scale than the other. This makes me think that my responses may have been skewed a little. Also, a few of the items are presented as opposites when they are not, according to my own definitions. I am not entirely confident that the scale can measure what it is meant to measure.

Reliability of the rating scale: I think that there needs to be a way of indicating what exposure to the child is necessary before undertaking the rating. I might have been influenced by the fact that I have known Tasha for only a short time. If her mother or teachers scored Tasha's personality with this scale, they might come up with different responses.

Strengths of the rating scale: The rating scale prompts me to evaluate some elements of personality that I might not have considered otherwise. I see it as a kind of checklist with a way of stating to what degree the attribute "fits." This kind of rating scale is very quick to do and could be replicated by other adults to determine common perceptions.

Weaknesses of the rating scale: There may be some bias in my scoring because the items are not effectively random. Also, my results cannot be validated on their own. My current positive outlook on life may bias me to see Tasha more positively than I would at another time. A few items are not typical of most personality inventories; for example, intelligence seems inappropriate as a dimension of personality.

My profile of Tasha's personality: Personality is a matter of relatively enduring behavioural characteristics. These are difficult for me to determine in Tasha because I have not observed her with her family or anywhere outside her class. I have seen patterns of behaviour that have repeated themselves. Some are sufficiently predictable that I have to alter my teaching strategies so that she cannot always be the leader of an activity! I think that Tasha tends to be warm and receptive to new ideas, but this wasn't scored on the rating scale. Her warmth may be seen as pro-social behaviour that is developmentally significant, as well as part of her personal style. Focusing on what the scale did indicate, I see Tasha to be very imaginative in her artwork and sociodramatic play. She frequently has ideas for new dramas that she initiates and draws her peers into. She is willing to cooperate with others, but she is persistent in wanting the play to go her way. Tasha leaps into new situations without being daunted and appears confident in approaching unfamiliar people. Her trusting nature could be potentially worrisome, so she needs close supervision. Curriculum challenges may allow Tasha to use some of her dispositions in new areas. I am hopeful that she will soon expand her artwork into storytelling because the necessary pre-reading skills are emerging. We are using a lot of stories in the classroom; she responds and acts out some of them in her play.

- Scoring may not be consistent over time.
- Scoring may depend on the observer's interpretation of an item.
- Evaluation should not stand alone as the sole information-gathering technique.
- Observer **bias** can take a variety of forms.
- Observer bias is not easily detected.
- There may be a tendency to rate well-known, liked, or attractive children higher (and some children lower for the opposite reasons).
- There may be a tendency to overcompensate for known and recognized biases.
- There may be a tendency to avoid extreme scores.
- Results can be affected by the order of inventory items.

Types of observation scales

1. **Forced-choice scales:** Observers choose between predetermined ranges of behaviour to identify levels of functioning. The observer is forced to select a choice that is given.

   ### Example

   handwriting (Circle the category most applicable.)

messy, illegible most of the time	some letters readable but untidy most of the time	some words readable but quite untidy most of the time	words legible, varying tidiness most of the time	phrases legible, tidy most of the time	clear, legible sentences most of the time

2. **Semantic differential scales:** With a semantic differential scale, the observer chooses between two terms that mean opposite traits, or at one of 3, 5, 7, or 9 points between them. Typically seven categories are used between the extremes. The categories may be numbered or may appear on an open continuum. See Observation Sample 6.2 for a sample semantic differential scale.

   ### Example

   a. cooperative ☐☐☐☐☐☐ uncooperative

   b. sociable ☐☐☐☐☐☐ unsociable

   c. honest ☐☐☐☐☐☐ dishonest

   d. skilled ☐☐☐☐☐☐ unskilled

   e. extrovert ☐☐☐☐☐☐ introvert

3. **Numerical scales:** The inventory items may be rated according to a number system. Each item is graded in relation to a predetermined set of criteria. Assigning a number to a skill can indicate the level at which it is performed. Pre-assigning the grading can help ensure objectivity in the structure of the scale, although it does not ensure objectivity in the grading.

Example A

How well does the child dress herself/himself? (Choose one of the categories.)

1. Competent in all respects, including doing up buttons, laces, zippers.

2. Puts on clothes, tries to close fasteners, but lacks sufficient skill to complete task.

3. Attempts to put on clothes, cannot do fasteners, and needs help.

4. Does not attempt dressing.

Example B

Preschool physical skills. (Circle the number as appropriate.)

1 = poor skill				5 = highly defined skill
runs	1	2	3	4	5
skips	1	2	3	4	5
hops	1	2	3	4	5
climbs stairs	1	2	3	4	5

Example C

Communicates wishes and needs verbally.

1. Makes self understood with phrases and gestures.

2. Clear articulation in full sentences.

3. Attempts to make self understood with some success.

4. Attempts infrequently to make self understood.

5. Does not attempt to communicate wishes and needs.

Circle one: 1   2   3   4   5

4. **Graphic scales:** These points on a line indicate the degree to which the item is applicable. This evaluation form is frequently depicted as a scale between "always" and "never." Descriptions may also be used for clearer evaluation.

Example A

Speech fluent and grammatically correct.

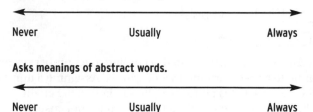

Never   Usually   Always

Asks meanings of abstract words.

Never   Usually   Always

Example B

Response to new activities:

$\longleftarrow\joinrel\relbar\joinrel\longrightarrow$

positive, inquiring,	erratic, inconsistent,	negative, uninterested,
and exploratory	varying attention,	does not respond to
approach, long	relatively easily	stimulation
attention span	distracted	

5. **Likert scale:** Evaluating a statement in terms of your agreement or disagreement of that statement is often achieved using simple phrases; this is called a Likert scale. A Likert scale is the total score of the responses of each Likert item. Interviews and questionnaires might use a Likert scale to find out individual preferences, beliefs, and perspectives.

Example

I feel good about my progress in writing.

1. strongly agree

2. disagree

3. neither agree nor disagree

4. agree

5. strongly agree

6. **Guttman scale:** A Guttman scale requires Yes or No responses to a series of related and sequential statements/questions. Use of the Guttman scale is usually limited to structured interviews and questionnaires. It is designed to see what responses an individual has to a number of situations, policies, or ideas as measured by a cumulative scale.

Example

1. Children should be smacked if they are naughty.

2. Children should be reprimanded if they are naughty.

3. Children should be guided to another activity if they are naughty.

4. Children should be allowed to play to stop them from being naughty.

5. Children should be allowed to do what they want because no child behaviour is naughty.

Children respond to the same situations in different ways. The style of response particular to an individual depends on his **temperament**. Although you may see fairly typical patterns of responses from a child, sometimes you will be surprised when he acts "out of character." Observing what is typical and also what is unusual for a particular child helps you determine his environmental influences and how he is coping.

Chess and Thomas (1996) review nine categories of temperament and three temperament "constellations." These categories can be scored on a rating scale—mild, medium, high—to develop an individual child's profile. The child is rated on activity level, rhythmicity (regularity), approach or withdrawal, adaptability, threshold of responsiveness, intensity of reaction, quality of mood, distractibility, and attention span and persistence.

Social Maps

The complexities of children's social contexts can make professionals very wary of delving into their backgrounds. Recognize that conclusions drawn quickly can lead to very inappropriate judgments and assumptions. Nothing can replace the sensitive observations and recordings of an observer who has taken the time to delve into the home life and social background of a child to understand who she is and appreciate the range of factors that affect her growth and development. Social maps can offer a backdrop against which you can increase your understanding of what you observe directly.

The child's social context can be represented in various ways. These maps are not intended to replace more detailed study; they may help support an in-depth study. Diagrams can show key life experiences, family trees, social relationships, or factors affecting the child's world, providing a structure to help make sense of the whole. In themselves, they offer little detail of the child's life.

Family trees

Sentimental interest often motivates a person to research a **family tree**. Such research, however, may also produce some understanding of a child's genetic inheritance, life patterns, and history, which in turn can help medical professionals, social workers, caregivers, teachers, and the child himself. A family tree provides historical background information gained through interviews, diaries, and archives. Name searches can be part of the research; surnames can help in tracking family members, though they should not be relied on in determining a person's complete ancestry. Names are passed down through generations differently, according to cultural and other norms, so check on such information at the start of your research.

Families have become increasingly mobile since the last century. Immigration frequently complicates research. Information recorded in passenger-ship lists and diaries can assist in tracing ancestors. Adoption, multiple partners and offspring, name changes, wars, changes of location, inadequate local record-keeping, translations, fires

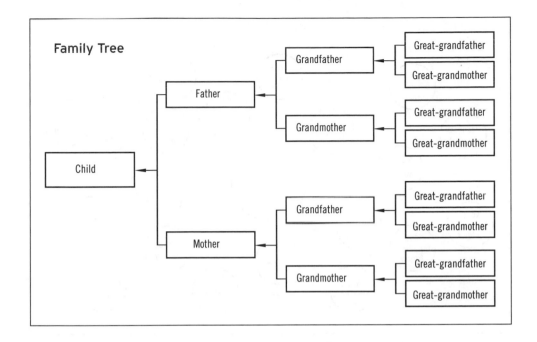

Family Tree

and other natural disasters, and individuals trying to cover up their ancestry are some of the common challenges we face in formulating a family tree. A typical tree may look like the above diagram—a family tree does not have to resemble a real tree!

Ecomaps

An **ecomap** is a diagram showing a child's social world in the form of a diagram. It includes the significant people, activities, and organizations in the child's world, and the relationships between the child and each of the elements of her environment. For social workers, an ecomap can facilitate an understanding of how the child functions within her environment and how her family's demands and resources compare. Teachers, caregivers, and parents may find the exploration of the child's ecosystem enlightening through understanding how the immediate social setting (the family) and the more remote social settings (childcare, school, media, clubs, and so on) help shape the child's development. The Observation Sample 6.3 is an example of an ecomap.

Urie Bronfenbrenner's **bioecological systems model** of human development (1979) helps us recognize and see as important each system operating within a child's environment. Each of these systems, or domains, is represented by one of several concentric circles. The model allows professionals to construct an individualized representation of the child's world—from which they can study the interplay between a child and each of his interacting environments. Bronfenbrenner's work helped shape the Head Start programs for children; his appreciation of the impact of positive and negative environments on young children's development inspired others to explore his systems theory and use it in various applications.

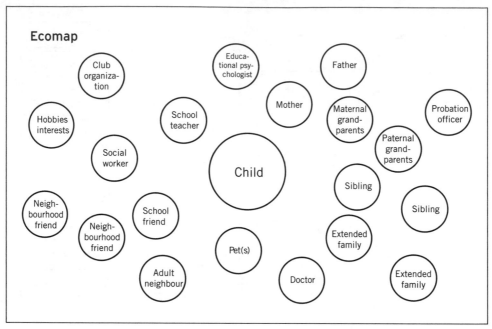

Ecomap

Club organization

Educational psychologist

Father

Mother

Maternal grandparents

Probation officer

Hobbies interests

School teacher

Social worker

Child

Paternal grandparents

Sibling

Sibling

Neighbourhood friend

School friend

Neighbourhood friend

Extended family

Pet(s)

Adult neighbour

Doctor

Extended family

Source: Department of Health, Great Britain (HMSO). *Protecting Children: A Guide for Social Workers Undertaking Comprehensive Assessment* (p. 85).

Ecomaps enable educators, social workers, early interventionists, and others—often working in a team—to conduct **family assessments** by "gathering specific, valuable information related to the current state of a family or individual being assessed" (**www.ohiocla.com** accessed July 2008). The aim is to determine, and then present, information about the strength, quality, and impact of the key connections in the individual's life. An ecomap can be part of a family assessment process, and it's a visual one that is not dependent on narrative description. Risk assessment is sometimes a part of family assessment; the process likely depends on a wide variety of sources of data and visual representations such as a flow diagram, ecomap, family tree, and a genogram. Although professionally facilitated, the family assessment—including risk assessment—embraces family members as part of the assessment team. A new resource is available to assist with ecomapping: "Using Ecomapping to Understand Family Strengths and Resources" (2008). The authors clarify the purpose of ecomaps: "In short, practitioners use ecomaps as a mechanism to establish rapport with families" (p. 18).

Ecomaps were originally created in 1978 by Dr. Ann Hartman, who wanted better ways of representing relationships in her practice as a social worker. She applied the idea of mapping to social relationships and devised a way of ensuring that the visual representation of social connections added value to narrative descriptions. Hartman understood that what went on in relationships were transactions, and was driven to want to display these visually so that adults and children could better understand the relationships that were significant to them. **Transactional analysis** (TA) (Berne 1961) had previously been developed as a way of understanding social exchanges. Three main ego states—that of parent, adult, and child—were theorized to be the psychological make-up of each individual in a transaction. In TA "the unit of social intercourse is called a transaction" (Berne 1964, p. 29).The purpose of TA, according to current perspectives (Newell & Jeffrey, 2002), is to look at a subject's communication, behavioural patterns, and personality, with a view to bringing about change that benefits the individual's functioning. TA has its own visual representations, the most basic image being like an outline of a snowman: three stacked circles, each of which depicts one of the three ego states. Relationships are shown as occurring between two "snowmen" side by side. Arrows from one to the other indicate "transactions." Applications of TA can be found in several fields, including education, social work, psychology, and psychiatry.

Domains (social systems) to be included on ecomap

a. family relationships
b. non-family relationships
c. neighbours/those in close proximity
d. social groups
e. community services
f. education/care

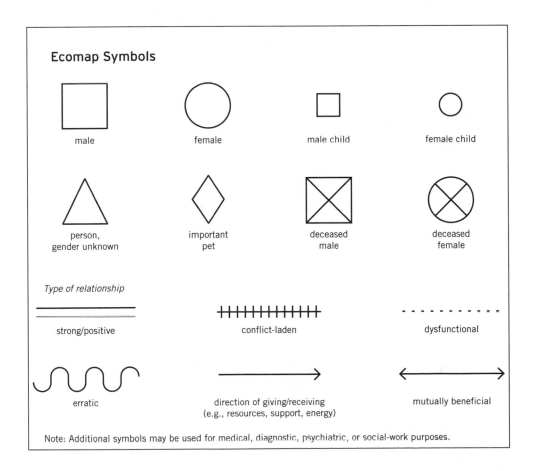

Observation Sample 6.3

This sample ecomap represents the people and organizations that make up a child's world. The annotations provide further information to help the observer understand the child's relationships and their influence on his development.

What information should the observer have recorded that would have produced this ecomap?

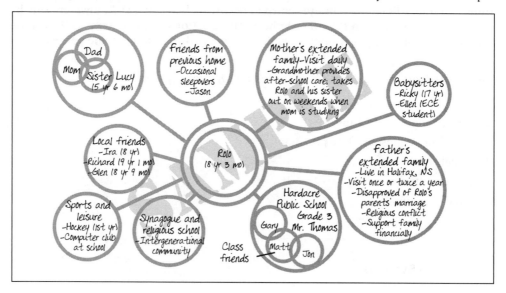

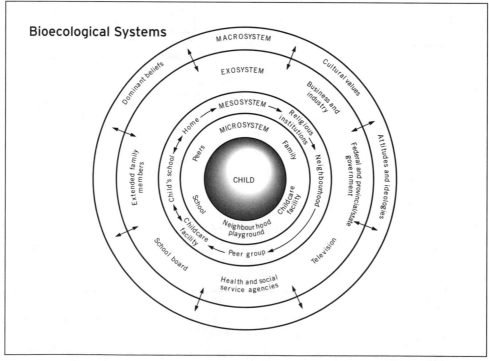

Source: Based on Urie Bronfenbrenner, *The Ecology of Human Development: Experiments by Nature and Design* (Cambridge, MA; Harvard University Press, 1979).

Genograms

According to McGoldrick and Gerson (1985), "a **genogram** is a format for drawing a family tree that records information about family members and their relationships over at least three generations." It is created through interviews, discussion, and research with the child's family members. Family structure and composition may be shown in a variety of forms, there being no "standard" format. A genogram may include critical family events, dates of birth, marriages, adoptions, custody arrangements, partnerships, separations, divorces, and deaths, and details of places of residence, occupations, and other significant information. It provides a clear view of complex family scenarios, patterns, and lifestyles. It is not intended to detail day-to-day interactions or to be a snapshot of how the family functions. Social workers often find the genogram a valuable tool.

The process of collecting the data from family members may be as important as the final product. Adults in the child's life may find the genogram enlightening themselves,

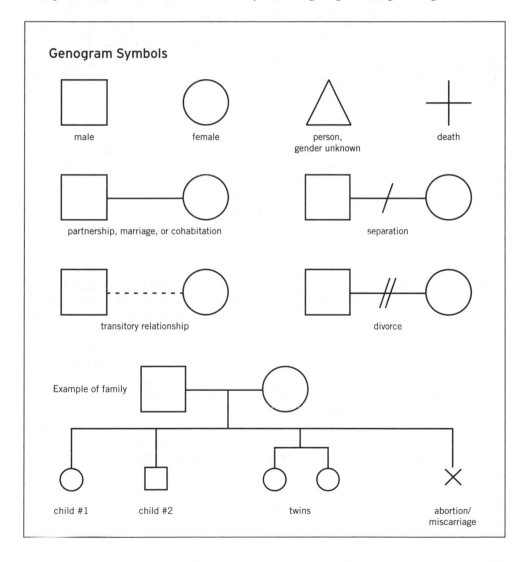

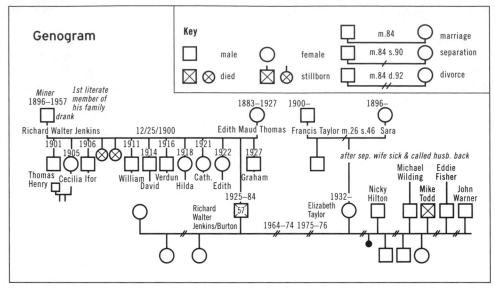

Source: From Monica McGoldrick and Randy Gerson, *Genograms in Family Assessment*. © 1985 by Monica McGoldrick and Randy Gerson. Used by permission of W.W. Norton & Company, Inc.

as it provides them with an overview of the connections between the family members and can identify possible stressors. In preparing the genogram, sensitivity to the privacy and range of styles and practices of families is essential. Both the researcher and family members must agree on the symbols to represent birth order, individuals, relationships, and living arrangements before starting to represent their data.

Sociograms

Sociometry is a research technique used for identifying children's acceptance by their peers and exploring their social status. A **sociogram** visually represents the child's perceptions of acceptance within his own group. The most important source of information for a sociogram is the child's behaviour in relation to other children. Observing children in many social situations over an extended time period is essential. A child in an organized setting may be asked to name the child who is his "best friend" or "person he does not especially like" or "like best" or "admire most." Alternatively the child may be asked who she wants to sit with or who she wants to play with. Results depend on the phrasing of the question and may be influenced by what the child thinks the adult wishes to hear. Information gathered from group members is pieced together and presented in a diagram. Popular children and those who are solitary or isolated may be identified more quickly; some unexpected connections may come to light at the same time, leading the teacher to observe interactions more closely. Over a period of time, the sociogram may change quite radically. You may choose to use a sociogram at designated times during the year to assess the dynamics of your group. The children must be old enough to understand the questions posed, be able to give clear answers, and be mature enough to have formed social relationships within the group. The interactions or "friendships" of younger

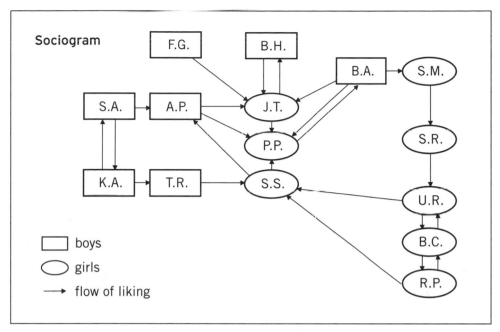

Sociogram

boys
girls
→ flow of liking

Information collected from a class of 8-year-olds (seven boys, eight girls). The children were asked, "Who are your two best friends?" The sociogram may indicate whether some of the children are isolated.

children tend to be transitory, because the children are not yet able to communicate, appreciate the perspectives of others, or form social attachments with their peers. For these children, a sociogram would reveal little.

Sociometric processes were first developed in the early 1930s (Moreno 1934 & 1960) in an attempt to understand not only what interactions are made, but the reason for them. In addition to a sociogram, a matrix can be created to represent complex group interactions; this is called a **sociomatrix**. "Measurement of relatedness can be useful not only in the assessment of behavior within groups, but also for interventions to bring about positive change and for determining the extent of change" (Hoffman 2002).

Life-experience flow charts

A person's significant life experiences can be reduced to a list of dates that offer a structure for understanding chronology, while providing no contextual information to explain why the events occurred. A **life-experience flow chart** explores the context, identifies key experiences, and labels and shows a sequence of events. The flow chart can reveal structure and patterns in a child's life. Teachers and caregivers can use such charts to help them appreciate the child's cultural identity, traumas, life stages, and happy experiences. As a result, they may become more sensitive to the child's needs and understand the child's own perception of reality.

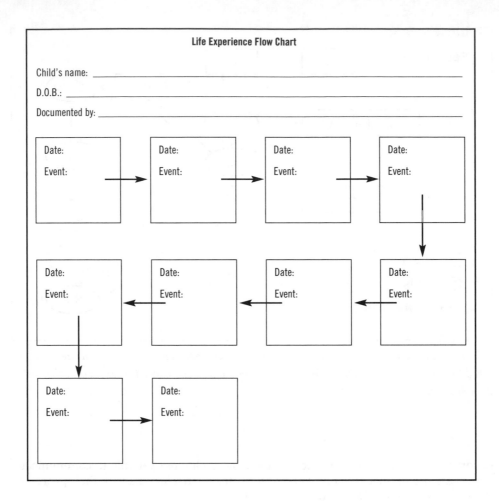

Life Experience Flow Chart

Child's name: _____

D.O.B.: _____

Documented by: _____

| Date:
Event: | → | Date:
Event: | → | Date:
Event: | → | Date:
Event: |

| Date:
Event: | ← | Date:
Event: | ← | Date:
Event: | ← | Date:
Event: |

| Date:
Event: | → | Date:
Event: |

Using social maps

Advantages

- Social maps are relatively easy to create.
- Social maps give a visual overview of the child's situation/context/environment.
- Families are usually helpful in supporting access to information.
- Social maps may appear clear and concise.
- The information is easily accessible.
- Individual and group contexts can be examined in this way.
- The child may be involved.
- The process of drawing up maps may have a therapeutic purpose.

Disadvantages

- Social maps depend heavily on professional sensitivity.
- The format can be overly simple and insufficiently supported by contextual information.
- Social maps rely on the accuracy of the information collected.
- Objectivity of recording is required.
- Inferences may be difficult to draw.
- Training may be needed to analyze family patterns.
- Inaccurate assumptions may be made by unqualified people.
- If support is not available, the child may be unnecessarily vulnerable.

Mappings

Sensitivity to the planning, set-up, and use of the children's environment leads educators and caregivers to evaluate what they provide (see Chapter 12). Part of a qualitative assessment of the use of space will be to create a mapping of the room or outdoor space in order to see how well it meets the needs of the children. The evaluation may consider the effectiveness of the learning environment, the aesthetics of the space for children and adults, the contrasts of activities in different areas, the degree to which the space allows for appropriate mobility and safety, the space's flexibility of use, and the construction of the environment on the basis of agreed philosophy of care and education.

Trackings can follow the movement of groups of children to see how they interact, move, and use the different parts of their environment. By tracking individual children, you may notice what interests them, their mobility, their concentration span, and their range of movements between activities. You can evaluate caregivers' roles within the room or play space by tracking their movements within the available space as well.

A simple line on a map can follow the movement of a child. Arrows can show the direction in which she was moving. You can represent movement back and forth in the same place with arrows in both directions showing the number of times the child travelled through that space. A circle containing the number of minutes or seconds can show how long a child stayed at a particular activity. More than one child can be tracked on the same map if the observer has sufficient skill and uses a different-coloured line for each child.

A narrative description of the details of a tracking can explain the diagram recorded. This dual technique means the observer can elaborate on the "tracks" so that she can make a more qualitative evaluation later. The sample tracking given in Observation Sample 6.4 includes a narrative account.

Observation Sample 6.4

This mapping tracks a child's movements in order to assess his participation in a program. The accompanying narrative provides details that will help the observer draw inferences from the mapping.

Although this mapping provides useful information, it may not offer a complete answer to the observer's reason for observing Peter. What should the observer do next?

Tracking in School-Age Program   1 of 2

Child's name: ___Peter D._____   Observer: _____Rena_____

Age/D.O.B: ____7 years, 2 months_____

Context: ___Peter has recently come, with his sister Kate (6 years), to an after-school program in a housing complex. Both started the program less than three weeks ago. Mom and Dad have recently separated and there is now nobody at home until approximately 6:00 p.m., when Mom returns from work.___

Reason for observations: ___We tracked Peter's movement to help us determine the level of his interaction in the program. There were concerns about Peter remaining in an onlooker role while other children were playing.___

Narrative account of tracking

Peter came out of the room just after 4:00 p.m., a few minutes after arriving from school. Standing at the door, he looked around outside at the children. Walking to the storage room, he said "Hi!" to his sister, who was talking to some girls. After a moment, Peter came out of the storage room carrying a ball, bouncing the ball as he walked. Peter looked up to see where everyone was and dropped the ball. Standing momentarily, he watched a girl playing catch by herself against the wall. When she finished, only a moment later, Peter took over her position and bounced his ball against the wall. A boy called to him from a swing. He went over to the swing and had a conversation about school until the other swing became available. Snack arrived a few moments later, so Peter left the swing in response to the caregiver's request. Walking slowly to the picnic table, he sat down, but was sent in to wash his hands. Following instructions, Peter came back after a few moments, ate a snack that was offered to him, but declined the drink. Walking around the backs of three seated children, he went to sit under a tree for some minutes as he watched the others staying at the picnic table. Another boy came up to him. They talked and walked together to the baseball diamond.

Peter's movements are tracked on the attached map.

Tracking Peter in the Outdoor Space of the School-Age Childcare Program

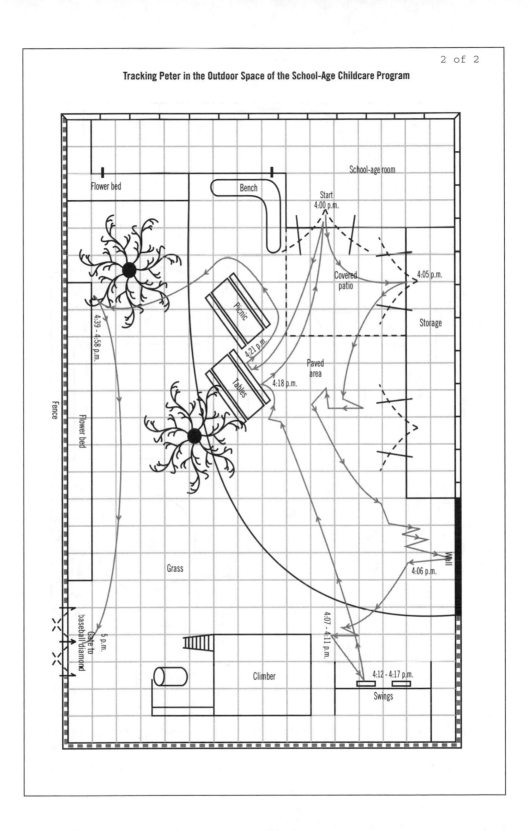

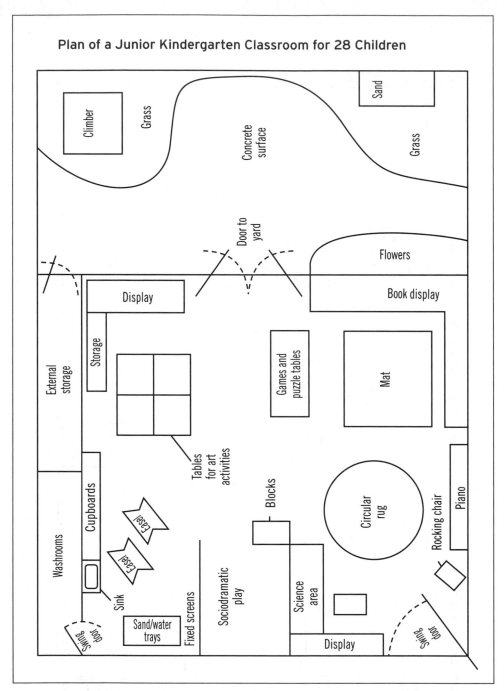

Plan of a Junior Kindergarten Classroom for 28 Children

This mapping could be used by a teacher to evaluate the use of space—for example, to consider whether all curriculum areas have been included or whether activities are allotted appropriate space. The plan could also be copied and used to track the movements of individual children.

Using mappings

Advantages

- Mappings are easy and efficient to record.
- The tracking can focus on an individual child or the actions of a group.
- Mappings may be used to analyze traffic, use of space, or safety considerations.
- Analysis can help to identify
  - mobility
  - attention span
  - interests/motivation
  - child–child interactions
  - child–adult interactions
  - participation in specific areas of the program
- Maps can be layered to show change, compare activity levels, or identify traffic problems.

Disadvantages

- The space or room must be mapped beforehand.
- It is difficult to record the action of more than one child at a time.
- Qualitative evaluation is difficult without an accompanying narrative.
- Reasons for behaviour may not be revealed.
- Inferences must be drawn on little data.
- Participants in a program may find it difficult to make an accurate tracking.

Mapping templates

A mapping can show both the physical layout and the use for which each area is intended. Such blank maps can be used for observation or environmental evaluation. See Observation Sample 6.4 for a sample observational tracking of a child's movements.

Interpretive Graphic Representations

Rather than recording direct observational material, interpretive graphic representations aim to demonstrate numerical results, percentages, comparisons, variables, proportions, or other quantifiable outcomes from observation or evaluation. Pictorial representations are used to understand and analyze the content of assessment **data** (information). While there is a danger that observers could oversimplify such information without appreciating its context, the representations are intended to support the conceptualizing of large amounts of information.

Graphic representations are mathematical and statistical ways of presenting data clearly and objectively. Often easier to understand than to create, they may require some practice before they can be relied on for accuracy.

A wide variety of techniques might be used. Charted tally marks can form simple graphic representations. Block graphs, **bar charts**, flow diagrams, **pie charts**, chains-of-events charts, **xy scatter graphs**, line charts, area charts, organizational maps, triangular charts, 3-D plots, **Venn diagrams**, cycle organizers, spider maps, fishbone-mapping graphs, picture diagrams, genetic maps, percentile charts, and picture symbols can all be used to present data. A sample graphic representation is given in Observation Sample 6.5. (For a more detailed explanation of these representations, refer to Tufte [2001].)

Observation Sample 6.5

This bar-line graph does not identify particular children or order the results. Such a graphic representation allows observers to make comparisons and consider trends without commenting on specific children.

Why might the observer have recorded these data? How do these data relate to the standardized norms for this age/range?

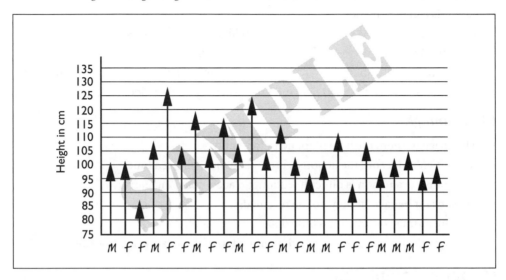

Using graphic representations

Advantages

- Graphic representations can display simple, easy-to-understand information.
- Certain formats may offer trends and comparisons.
- Mathematical data analysis may be more objective than anecdotal reports.
- Information from various sources can be pulled together.
- Large amounts of data can be represented meaningfully.

Disadvantages

- Graphic representations rely on valid and reliable data collection.
- Users may need to understand statistics in order to interpret the information.
- Results are quantitative rather than qualitative.
- Graphic representations may encourage comparisons with other children rather than an analysis of changes in the child's own performance.
- Results can be used for unwise program planning or other inappropriate purposes.

- Comparisons may foster unnecessary parental anxiety.
- Trends may be analyzed without contextual information.
- Research psychologists may be able to use graphs more readily than practitioners.

Conducting research into child behaviour

Beyond carrying out their primary role, educators conduct research into the finer nuances of children's behaviour so that they can respond to the children more fully, understand the ways they learn, and consequently furnish them with improved learning experiences. Such research may be either **quantitative** (considering behaviour in terms of counting repetitions of actions or the number of children behaving a particular way) or **qualitative** (looking at the subtleties of individual children's behaviour in particular circumstances).

Both approaches to this research rely on accurate, skillful observation and information-recording. Without either of these elements, the researcher cannot analyze the data and draw useful conclusions from them. The research analysis may be presented in the form of a graphic representation, particularly in quantitative research. The numerous types of graphic representation include those listed above, many of which are self-explanatory.

To pursue qualitative inquiry, refer to Creswell (1998) or Ely et al. (1991) as starting points for effective research. Other inquiry methods that are more quantitative in style are described in Best and Kahn (1989).

Action research, a favoured **research method**, is a branch of qualitative research that teachers frequently carry out while attending to the children more directly. The teacher observes, records, and analyzes the program, curriculum, environment, interactions, or the children themselves. The information generated can assist the teacher's planning and lead to program improvements. It can also have larger implications when those data are shared with other teachers. To some extent all teachers are conducting action research as they carry out their roles and responsibilities. However, some present their data collection and findings more formally.

As discussed previously regarding basic observations of children, all research into human behaviour must be conducted ethically, confidentially, and with informed consent. Gain permissions for any research beyond the day-to-day notes teachers record in their roles as employees. Make the research data available to the participants—in this case, their parents. Educators should ensure that they do not use information gained while performing their roles as teachers in the interests of other research without obtaining the necessary permissions and using pseudonyms for the children being observed.

Types of graphic representations

The following examples show several of the most common types of graphic representations and suggest the types of data for which such graphs can be useful.

Bar chart or histogram

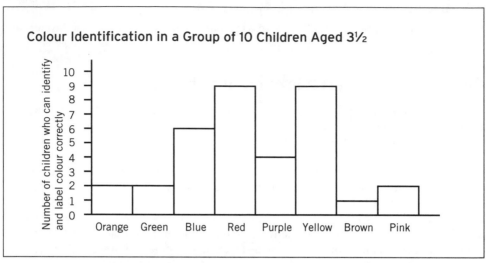

Colour Identification in a Group of 10 Children Aged 3½

*Information charted is not designed to show which child knows which colours; the intention is to determine the number of children who can identify each colour. The bar chart or **histogram** can be used to present a variety of data.*

Pie chart

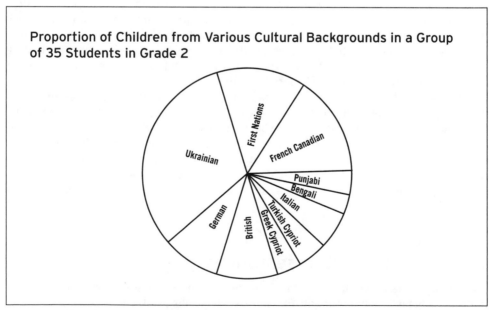

Proportion of Children from Various Cultural Backgrounds in a Group of 35 Students in Grade 2

This particular chart indicates heritage rather than origin or place of birth. A pie chart may need a key to explain the items. The "whole" must be identified; otherwise the proportions of the whole are meaningless. Percentages can be written into the pie for extra clarity.

Pareto chart

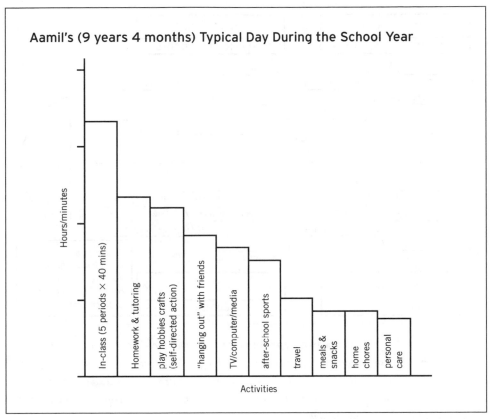

Aamil's (9 years 4 months) Typical Day During the School Year

Hours/minutes

In-class (5 periods × 40 mins)

Homework & tutoring

play hobbies crafts (self-directed action)

"hanging out" with friends

TV/computer/media

after-school sports

travel

meals & snacks

home chores

personal care

Activities

The **Pareto chart** is a form of bar chart but it displays its blocks/bars in descending order. This example represents the waking hours of a child. Aamil completed a log book to track his activities, a video camera tracked him while at home, he completed a questionnaire, and a researcher conducted several lengthy observations.

Ishikawa or Fishbone Representation

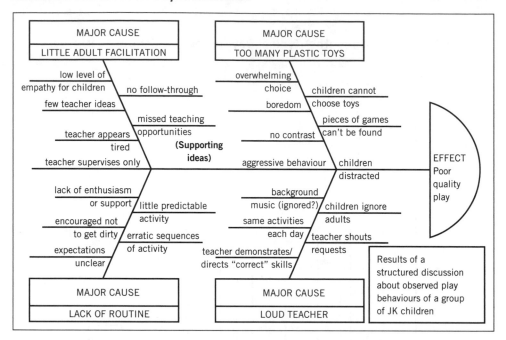

MAJOR CAUSE	MAJOR CAUSE
LITTLE ADULT FACILITATION	TOO MANY PLASTIC TOYS

low level of empathy for children

no follow-through

few teacher ideas

overwhelming choice

children cannot choose toys

boredom

missed teaching opportunities

pieces of games can't be found

teacher appears tired

no contrast

(Supporting ideas)

teacher supervises only

aggressive behaviour

children distracted

EFFECT Poor quality play

lack of enthusiasm or support

little predictable activity

background music (ignored?)

children ignore adults

encouraged not to get dirty

same activities each day

teacher shouts requests

expectations unclear

erratic sequences of activity

teacher demonstrates/ directs "correct" skills

MAJOR CAUSE	MAJOR CAUSE
LACK OF ROUTINE	LOUD TEACHER

Results of a structured discussion about observed play behaviours of a group of JK children

This is an example of the **Ishikawa representation**, *sometimes known as a fishbone. The diagram helps users to establish a possible "cause" and "effect" relationship. Initially designed as a quality management tool, it might also be applied to childcare and education contexts— especially in overcoming challenges to designing and implementing high-quality environments (see also Chapter 12 on Environments.)*

Sarina's life timeline indicating key events

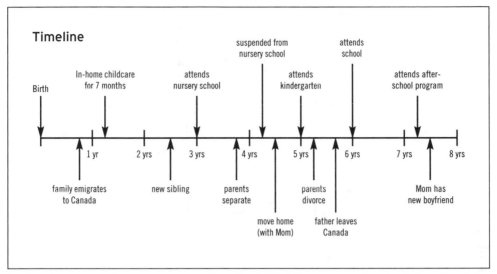

Rather than using only a narrative to explain the child's life experience, this visual **timeline** helps educators and others to understand Sarina's life and use it as a skeleton to fill out the details of her experience. The data were collected from parent questionnaries and personal interviews.

Observation sample

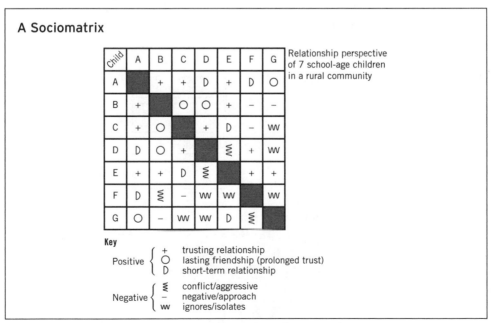

This **sociomatrix** displays the complex relationships of a group of school-age children. Because each axis contains the same 7 children, we can see for each of the children how they perceive their relationships with the others. The data were collected from observations and questionnaires.

Heirarchy diagram

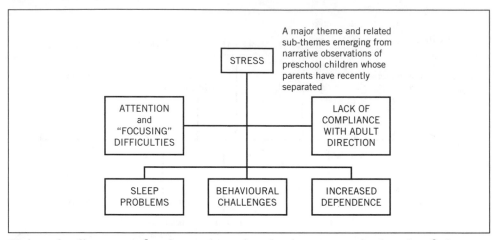

Heirarchy diagrams *often depict relationships, but here a researcher has identified a theme and two layers of sub-themes. The raw data included parent interviews, the children's developmental portfolios, and lengthy observations of preschool children in spontaneous and adult-directed contexts.*

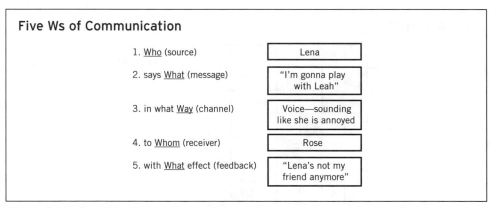

*Although the **five Ws of communication** seem very simple, a series of similar communication analysts' statements can help an observer determine dominance, articulation, methods of conveying ideas, projections of emotion, the difference between "sent" and "delivered" messages, and many aspects of relationships. Draw data from narrative or recorded observations.*

Concept map

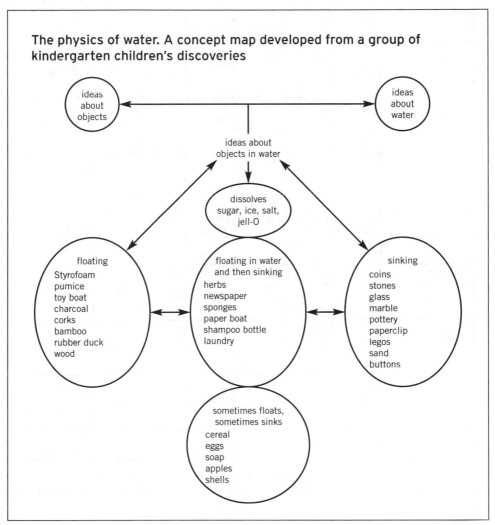

The physics of water. A concept map developed from a group of kindergarten children's discoveries

ideas about objects ← → ideas about water

ideas about objects in water

dissolves
sugar, ice, salt, jell-O

floating
Styrofoam
pumice
toy boat
charcoal
corks
bamboo
rubber duck
wood

floating in water and then sinking
herbs
newspaper
sponges
paper boat
shampoo bottle
laundry

sinking
coins
stones
glass
marble
pottery
paperclip
legos
sand
buttons

sometimes floats, sometimes sinks
cereal
eggs
soap
apples
shells

*A **concept map** has few rules. In this example, created for the children themselves, as well as for program documentation, is depicted a group's conceptual understanding.*

Issue	Monday	Tuesday	Wednesday	Thursday	Friday	Total	Note
frustration: sharing difficulty	卌 卌 卌 ||	卌 卌 卌	卌 卌 |||	卌 卌 ||||	卌 卌 卌 卌	79	developmental challenge— toddler need support
frustration: not having desired object	卌 卌 卌 卌	卌 卌 ||||	卌 卌 卌	卌 卌 ||	卌 卌 卌 卌 |||	84	? insufficient #^{s} of toys
frustration: not having desired person	卌 卌 ||||	卌 |||	卌 ||	卌		卌 |||	43	attachment/ separation anxiety
frustration: not getting 'own way'	卌 卌 ||	卌 ||||	卌 ||	卌 ||||	卌 卌	47	typical challenge of stage
frustration: cannot communicate effectively	卌 卌 卌		卌 卌 卌	卌 卌 |||	卌 卌 卌	卌 卌 卌 ||	81	reduction in challenge as language develops
frustration: having to wait	卌 卌 卌		卌 卌 |||	卌		卌 ||	卌 卌 卌 |||	70	? egocentricity
frustration: other	卌 卌 ||	卌 卌	卌 |||	卌 ||	卌 |||	45	individual frustrations: personality related?
TOTAL	107	84	74	75	109		peaks, on Mon–Friday

*A **Check Sheet** can assist an observer to demonstrate patterns of behaviour within groups, as well as individually.*

Summary

Charts, scales, and pictorial representations each have a visual component and need to be interpreted. They also serve a variety of different purposes, including the display of observational data or representation of an analysis of that data. At the day-to-day level, educators may gather information about the children with whom they work using easy-to-manage graphic forms. They may also be conducting action research with those (and possibly other) children. This might be a more comprehensive data-gathering process and would require that the person collecting the data understand complex research methodologies. Whatever the observer's intentions, each of these forms incorporates some kind of observation strategy.

Prepared charts can help with recording observational information efficiently. These are often used for focused observations of individuals and children. Rating scales are the most frequently used type of scale. The observer can record information from observations as he conducts them, without influencing what is happening with the children. Scales indicate the degree of a specified characteristic in a child; several useful forms employ numerical or semantic differentials. Graphic scales visually represent the degree to which an attribute is present.

Social maps can reveal relationship patterns among groups of children or within families. Through family trees the educator, parent, or older child can show the family relationships over generations. Ecomaps consider the particular social networks within which the child lives; these networks include the individualized microsystem, mesosystem, exosystem, and macrosystem of a particular child. Genograms provide complex generational maps of the structure, composition, and relationships of a family. The use of Likert or Guttman scales can also be helpful when rating attitudes or preferences and styles. Sociograms are visual representations of a child's perception of himself within a social group. Life-experience flow charts document the significant life experiences of a child. Mappings are particularly useful for teachers who want to examine the use of the space available to them for their classes; through these they can track the movement of individuals or of groups of children.

When a large amount of information needs to be recorded, a prepared chart or scale can be used. At the water trough, each child plays differently, revealing some aspects of his her personality. Later, the educator can use a semantic differential temperament scale to record her observations.

With permission of the YMCA of Greater Toronto

Interpretive graphic representations can take numerous forms, many of which are borrowed from mathematics. These include bar charts, diagrams, 3-D plots, spider maps, Venn diagrams, area charts, and visual organizers. Those conducting research may represent their data, ideas, analysis, and theories using a variety of interpretive measures. Acquiring the skill of using computer software to manage observational data can be helpful for educators, as well as researchers. Clearly, using a keyboard to document narratives and other observations is essential. However, more complex software is available that helps with the management of large amounts of data. Some programs can assist with identifying themes in qualitative research and then presenting them in charts and tables; other software programs help with representing data visually in a variety of formats. Read the representations carefully and appreciate precisely what they indicate within the context of particular research.

Key Terms

- action research
- bar chart
- baseline observations
- bias
- bioecological systems model
- chart
- check sheet
- concept map
- continuum
- data
- ecomap
- event sampling
- family assessment
- family tree
- five Ws of communication
- forced-choice scale
- genogram
- graphic scale
- Guttman scale
- heirarchy diagram
- histogram
- holistic
- inference
- interpretive graphic representation

- Ishikawa representation
- Likert scale
- life-experience flow chart
- mapping
- negative behaviour
- numerical scale
- objectivity
- observation chart
- observation scale
- Pareto chart
- pictorial representation
- pie chart
- positive behaviour
- qualitative
- quantitative
- rating scale
- reliability
- research method
- scale
- semantic differential scale
- social map
- sociogram
- sociomatrix
- sociometry

Continued

- tally
- temperament
- timeline
- time sampling
- tracking

- transactional analysis
- validity
- Venn diagram
- xy scatter graph

Weblinks

www.genopro.com
A site that offers information and free trial of genograms/family trees.

www.archives.ca/02/0201_e.html
ArchiviaNet is the National Archives of Canada's online research and consultation tool.

www.deakin.edu.au/~agoodman/sci101/index.php
Presentation of data and other major forms of non-quantitative charts in the form of graphs. Click on "Graphical data presentation."

www.statisticscanada.com
Search for "pie charts" and other types of visual representations.

www.graphcharts.com
Resources to assist with creating pie charts, line graphs, and bar charts.

www.familytreesearcher.com
A starting point, with links, to developing family trees.

www.smartdraw.com/specials/genogram.htm
Download ecomap and genogram software.

www.graphic.org/goindex.html
Descriptions, examples and uses for a number of graphic tools.

www.eduplace.com/graphicorganizer/
Houghton Mifflin Harcourt Education Place offers examples of a wide variety of ways to present data.

7 Media Techniques

A video recorder can be unobtrusive and can help students in learning to observe. Here, an in-class observation opportunity is recorded so that replay can assist in making accurate inferences.

Researchers have tools, child researchers need new observation tools.
Jean-Baptiste Labrune (2006)

Getting down to a child's level will not only make them feel more comfortable with you but eye-to-eye contact is also extremely engaging in a photo. The expressions you capture from the child's perspective will look much more natural than if you're hovering over them.
Staticphotography.com (2008)

We now recognize how computers can be used to manage very large collections of data and assist in the understanding and construction of meaningful information and interpretation.
P. Theroux, teacher in Alberta (2008)

In the past, portfolios were collections of work stored in binders, file folders, or boxes. Today, computers are used as an effective tool for developing and storing portfolios given their ability to store and process large quantities of content, and because they can effectively support and guide the portfolio process. These computer-based portfolios are called digital or electronic portfolios (e-portfolios).
Anne Wade, Philip C. Abram, and Jennifer Sclater (2005)

Features of Media Techniques

DEFINITION: Media technique

A **media technique** is any method of recording, storing, or analyzing observational data that is achieved by mechanical, electronic, or technical means.

An ever-widening range of methods of observing and **recording** information is becoming accessible to those working with young children. If used properly, these techniques offer the chance to gather information more quickly and effectively. They require the same degree of sensitive perception as traditional methods, because the choice of whom to observe and what to record remains the observer's. An observer requires varying amounts of skill to use the different media techniques. For example, the automatic functions of many analog cameras, digital cameras, or video cameras may mean you need little training before you start to employ them; practice is the most effective way of improving the quality of your productions.

Media techniques can provide a quicker, more efficient, more accurate, more detailed, and possibly longer-lasting and more meaningful record of the child, and one that can be more readily replayed. Not all the technologies available offer these benefits, however, so do not assume that technically assisted observations are, of themselves, preferable to narratives or samplings. Consider them a useful addition to our range of information-gathering tools.

It is tempting to let a videotaped observation "speak for itself." Even if the observation is self-explanatory when recorded, it becomes increasingly meaningless if not labelled, dated, explained, summarized, and analyzed as any other significant data would be. We can choose the most effective methods of media techniques of observing and recording by acknowledging their limitations.

One of the newer uses of technology is for electronic portfolios. These are discussed in Chapter 8 as one type of portfolio documentation. They have many advantages over traditional documentation, but they demand technical skill, as well as appropriate systems.

CHILD DEVELOPMENT FOCUS

Media techniques may assist with observing and recording

- complex social interactions

- long sequences of conversation

- detail of posture, expression, and gestures

- physical skill acquisition

- language acquisition

- cognitive abilities

KEY FEATURES: Media techniques

- use various technologies to assist recording

- provide efficient ways of documenting behaviours

- may provide comprehensive information

- are usually naturalistic

- are participatory or nonparticipatory

- may assist the organization and analysis of observations

Media tools: Recording and communicating using current technologies

Gaining skill in using a variety of media tools may help improve observation accuracy and detail. Following is an overview of many available technologies; test them to see their usefulness for your purposes.

The following chart will help you to select media that meets your observation and recording needs. A few examples offer data management functions in addition to recording.

A guide to current media types, features, potential uses, and the challenges they present.

Type and example	Features	Potential uses	Challenges
audio-recording	• Uses magnetic tape to record sound • Tapes are reusable	• Recording communication skills, language, social interactions, music, and sound productions • Children can use audio recordings to assist in language development while the educator observes	• May pick up background noise • Conversations may be difficult to track if children move around • Permission to use/store audio recordings
VHS video camera, videotape, recorder, and player	• Camcorder takes moving images • Analog system • Cassettes may be used in camera VHS • Tapes reusable	• Quicker than hand-written observations • Captures a lot of detail (not filtered by the eye of the observer as are traditional direct methods) • Recording behaviour related to all developmental domains: physical, social, emotional, cognitive, such as looking at social play, relationship dyads, group interactions, discovery learning, the creative process, and observing "challenging behaviours" as they arise	• Tapes becoming less available • VHS recorders and players being phased out • Permission needs to be sought to record/use material—and, maybe, with more than one child • Open-ended nature of recording means that key aspects of activity may be missed • Recordings capture "everything" but do not always focus on the particular child or specific activity you need to observe

(*continued*)

Type and example	Features	Potential uses	Challenges
VHS video camera, videotape, recorder, and player (continued)		• Children are often interested in viewing themselves; this can reveal aspects of their self-concept • Because recording is inexpensive and easily accessed, the camera can become a regular part of the program rather than an unusual addition	
camera + processed film	• Film allows for black-and-white or colour images • Automatic and manual functions • Some claim greater flexibility for "art" photographers	• Capturing images of children in activity, portraits, individual, and group pictures • Identifying children • Program documentation • Supplement to portfolios • Photos can support a narrative or other observation	• Greater use of digital media is reducing use of traditional cameras • Pictures often require greater expertise for a good result • Time needed to process film • Images may fade over time • Having adequate film and batteries available • Cost of film • Permission to take and use particular pictures

Type and example	Features	Potential uses	Challenges
digital camera photography	• Mostly small cameras with complex features but easy-to-use functions • Very portable • Easy to take & share pictures via email • Immediate pictures can be seen through LCD display • Camera can be ready to point and shoot at any time • Compact cameras have increasingly wide range of zoom, flash-range, image stabilizers, apertures, speeds, storage, face recognition, # of megapixels, exposure options, automatic focus • Memory card can be reused multiple times • Images can be loaded directly to computer • Allows editing, cropping, etc. • Jpeg compressed files allow user to transfer many images and for them to retain their quality	• Same as above + • Greater range of pictures, photographs in lower light, so allows better indoor pictures—such as children playing indoors in the winter • Faster speeds allow action pictures—such as children playing sports • Responsive to different conditions • Because images can be deleted immediately and more taken, the chance of getting useful pictures is increased	• Familiarity with the camera's functions • Sorting/deleting/labelling the vast quantity of images created • Having adequate memory and batteries • New cameras available; choice is difficult • Permission to use digital photographs in e-portfolios and other educational purposes a greater challenge because of the quantity of material and because images may contain several children • Aligning the camera with the computer and its software is essential if you need to store or move images to places other than the memory card • Memory cards must be cleared for new images (so images must be stored or lost)

(*continued*)

Type and example	Features	Potential uses	Challenges
digital camera photography (continued)	• A camera for documenting aspects of children's activities may have a memory of around 1 gigabyte, not be too small, appear robust–and even be waterproof!		
digital video recording/camcorders (including HD video, MiniDV, disk-based, models with hard drive, camcorders with flash memory)	• As above with digital moving images • Memory card can be reused • Mpeg compressed files allow video segments to be transferred keeping their initial quality • More lightweight and portable than earlier models • Camera features have improved since early models were developed • Sony dominates the market • Check to see if it has quick review, backlight, auto focus, low-light compensation, infrared sensitivity,	• Great scope for capturing long sequences of play and other activity • Has most of the same uses VHS videotape has • Greater versatility in recording moving images in challenging contexts • Can capture large quantity of material that can be edited • Children can use the cameras themselves and document their own learning • Sequences of recordings can be used as part of formal assessments	• Permission for recording/labelling/use/storage • Having the video camera ready at the right time • Taking time to edit material

Type and example	Features	Potential uses	Challenges
digital video recording/ camcorders (continued)	digital still capacity, title generator, time and date stamp, time code, programmed recording (self-timer), and remote control		
closed-circuit television (CCTV)	• Video recording— often on a re-recordable loop • Can be made accessible via intranet or Internet to security-protected individuals who need passwords to look in on their children during their day at camp, childcare, etc.	• Parents can view children whenever they are under professional care. • Can replay tapes to review any element of the program. • Often this technology is used for security • Nannies may be unwittingly monitored	• Video sequence is not contextualized or explained • Vast permission/access issues • Can seem to some as a form of spying on others
sound systems & video systems	• Evenly distributed microphones (and/or video cameras) set up in childcare or other space • Recording and playback facility available • Large-screen for presentation/ student teachers • One-way-mirrored booth may assist non-participatory observation	• Capture the voices, sound productions, intonations, communication skills, acquisition of parts of language, & emotional expressions • Good to share with parents • Replay for analyzing individual progress or aspects of group functioning	• Confusing collection of sounds/ images, too much visual/auditory data to process • Interactions, although very important, may be difficult to report in an individual narrative, sampling, or other observation methodology • Permissions must be sought,

(continued)

Type and example	Features	Potential uses	Challenges
sound systems & video systems (continued)		• Student educators can learn • May be part of a learner-support strategy so that students can learn about children's development, curriculum, guidance, or other aspect of the children's program (often called a lab-school) • May offer large-screen playback for demonstration and critique of teacher strategies • Can be used for recording children's plays and concerts • Children can see themselves and critique their performances	but this may be easier within the confines of a childcare agency or other institution
Telephone (land line) & voice mail	• Land-based analog telephone communication and in-built voice messaging system • A cordless phone is not a cell phone; it receives messages from a nearby telephone	• Communications with parents, conversations about the child/program, & leaving messages for those who are "out"	• Check on privacy issues–leaving a voice mail message may be inappropriate • Need to be sure that the parent is free to talk when you call

Type and example	Features	Potential uses	Challenges
cell/mobile phones & text messaging	• Digital wireless telephone service (sometimes called a mobile) that depends on connection to a local transmitter • Each area (or cell) is equipped with a low-powered radio transmitter and receiver that connect signals among cell-phone users • As a "smart phone" it can connect with the Internet • Written messages (texts) that may include codes and short-forms for speed • Text messages are independent of the internet and therefore cost less	• Quick way of connecting with parents and others, can seek assistance in haste • Text messages inexpensive way of sending short pieces of information • Messages can be sent without dependence on the Internet	• Ensure privacy issues are addressed • Cell phones cannot receive messages if they are out of range of a transmitter
spy cameras	• Analog or digital cameras (including audio facility) set up in hidden places • May be linked to time switches	• Recording the actions of a caregiver or other person left alone with a child, student, or client • May provide evidence of an adult's performance—or a child's behaviour	• May be both inappropriate and illegal (see notes on CCTV)

(continued)

Type and example	Features	Potential uses	Challenges
Computers: Personal computers (PCs) IBM & Macs Laptop computers Word processing	• A computer is built around a microprocessor for use by an individual or group of people (perhaps using passwords) in an office, childcare centre, school, or home • A PC has separate monitor, keyboard, mouse, and processor (and also a hard drive) • The hard drive contains the computer's memory capacity • System software enables the computer to perform actions (such as operating functions, debugging, & file management tools) • Applications software enables programs to operate (such as word processing, games, graphics, spreadsheets) • Businesses, (including childcare centres, schools, early interventionists, and other human-service fields) use PCs for word	• Limit access to confidential files; ensure passwords are allocated • Write up (type) narrative observations (word processing) • Date and then file observations and other materials (see below) • Create a file for each child/family • Keep records of parent meetings, written communications, and any advice or direction that was offered • Ensure you record narratives, rating scales, samplings, infant charts, video segments, scanned documents and artwork, photos, parent-written observations, individual Program Plans (IPP) & Individual Education Plans (IEP), emergency & authorized information, enrollment tracking & scheduling, child-health	• Make a list of your childcare responsibilities and functions to help you decide what computer capacity and software programs are needed • Make a choice between IBM and Apple systems (search details to make a full comparison) • Compare prices • RAM or memory capacity needs to be discussed prior to purchase (do not underestimate your needs, although extra capacity can be added) • Ensure that the system software that is needed is loaded at the time of purchase • Review different specially designed childcare software and research the capacities with reference to your program needs • Request a demonstration and be aware of ongoing technical support costs

Type and example	Features	Potential uses	Challenges
Computers (continued)	processing, accounting, desktop publishing, running spreadsheets, and database management • Home use is typically for games, photo records, written correspondence, filing, financial record-keeping, Internet searching, & e-mail • A laptop computer (or notebook) is a small battery or AC-powered personal computer that is easily transported and used in a wide variety of places. It has a screen and keyboard and may have the same memory and functions and use the same software applications as a large PC. A laptop is portable and no more than 10 cm or 3 inches thick. Laptops can have Internet and e-mail like a PC	histories, immunization tracking, waiting lists, developmental screenings and their results, formal assessments, whole portfolios, daily reminders to families, attendance tracking, notices, budgets, evaluations of educators, employee records, staff scheduling, menus, parent evaluations, financial matters (including subsidies, purchase orders, and invoices), program logs, letters & e-mails • Use large memory to keep documents over time	• Look for user-friendliness, if it's Canadian, how well it supports observation and portfolio processes, its flexibility and efficiency, how easily technical support can be accessed, if it can be used on multiple sites, its levels of security, compatibility with existing programs, program breadth, how well it can be customized to your needs, training requirements, if it will generate the reports you need, the graphics and visual presentations of data, if and how well the program can be linked and can monitor the use of the computer by children • Before buying any software, read the box/data sheets and check out the system requirements

(continued)

Type and example	Features	Potential uses	Challenges
Computers (continued)	• Apple Macintosh offers both PCs and their own laptops • Linked computers allow networks to be established		• Application software packages should be purchased as needed (remember: they have licence restrictions) • Additional hardware such as webcams or speakers add to the cost, but the prices are lower than they were a few years ago • Staff training may be needed • Access, privacy, passwords, and ethical issues must be addressed before educators can use the system
computers, Internet, & URLs	• Viewable pages that are shared from a computer	• Educators can research, communicate, and even advertise their programs • Resources that assist with observation and portfolio development become accessible • Millions of sites created by individuals and organizations are viewable from all over the world	• Creators are solely responsible for content, and sites are generally never censored. Thus sites may be appropriate or may be incorrect, inappropriate, or obscene • All material on the Internet can be viewed by anyone with no restrictions and, as such, placing information on

Type and example	Features	Potential uses	Challenges
computers, Internet & URLs (continued)		• Can facilitate sharing of Information to a larger audience	a site may create privacy issues
computers & webcams	• Small, inexpensive digital video camera. Many computers are now provided with one.	• Enables continuous digital video to be shared with one or multiple viewers over the Internet, or recorded onto the owner's computer	• Video is often very low quality and may not be of great use • Privacy issues if the video is left on and those being viewed are not aware. • As with all digital media, software, and storage devices, it allows easy sharing of information, but it's much harder to control distribution as anyone with brief access can copy it
computer PowerPoint	• Software that enables a slideshow-like presentation to be created	• Provides templates for users to create presentations in a slideshow-like format that may be readily shared with others or viewed on a large projected screen • Can integrate written ideas/ observations, digital photographs, even video or Internet links	• Requires comfort with working on a computer and familiarity with the software • If appropriate permissions are not set within the software, can easily facilitate plagiarism as another viewer could extract the information • As with all digital media, software,

(*continued*)

Type and example	Features	Potential uses	Challenges

computer
  PowerPoint
  (continued)
			and storage devices, it allows easy sharing of information, but it's much harder to control distribution, as anyone with brief access can copy it

computer scanner	• Digital photocopier-like device attached to a computer	• Allows digital images of documents or photographs to be created • Allows archiving and sharing of these digital images	• Requires familiarity with use to optimize the image created • As with all digital media, software, and storage devices, it allows easy sharing of information, but it's much harder to control distribution, as anyone with brief access can copy it
computer Photoshop	• Software that permits editing of digital images	• Allows editing, labelling, and dating digital images in a variety of ways–many suitable for portfolios	• Quite expensive and complex to use. There may be cheaper/simpler alternatives • Allows users to edit images to an extent that they may not accurately represent what actually occurred
intranet	• Computer network within a building or institution	• Allows sharing of ideas, e-mail, digital documents	• Only works within that institution or building and not outside unless connected to the

Type and example	Features	Potential uses	Challenges
intranet (continued)		• Seeking group support for analyzing observations	Internet (see "Computers Internet") • As with all digital media, software, and storage devices, it allows easy sharing of information, but It's much harder to control distri-bution, as anyone with brief access can copy it.
computer printers	• Devices attached to a computer that allow paper copies of digital files to be gener-ated	• Available in vari-ous types, the most common being laser and ink jet	• Vary greatly in quality and expense. Expensive printers/supplies needed to gener-ate good-quality printed photographs
CDs, DVDs, Blu-ray	• Disk-shaped digital storage media	• May come prere-corded with soft-ware or information or come blank to create stable, long-term, sharable storage for digital files, images, or documents. • Generally inex-pensive and so good to create multiple copies of material for storage or sharing	• Vary in cost and quality and may degrade over time despite manufac-turer's claims. Best to research to find best prod-uct for your uses. • As with all digital media, software, and storage devices, it allows easy sharing of information, but it's much harder to control distri-bution, as anyone with brief access can copy it.

(*continued*)

Type and example	Features	Potential uses	Challenges
memory cards, Memory Stick, CompactFlash, SD/MMC, xD	• Also known as flash cards: small electronic devices that can be inserted into digital cameras for the storage of photographs	• Equivalent to reusable film. Very stable, resilient form of storage and reusable 1000's of times • Available in different capacities and several different types for differing cameras	• Although dropping in price, quite expensive and, as such, better for temporary storage • Different cameras may require different types of cards, so not always sharable, although some computers may now have multiple card readers. • As with all digital media, software, and storage devices, it allows easy sharing of information, but it's much harder to control distribution, as anyone with brief access can copy it.
Bluetooth	• Type of local computer network	• Short-distance local/personal, wireless form of computer networking that allows connection of small devices to each other, including cellphones, headsets, printers, etc.	• Subject to wireless interference and may have security concerns if devices left in a state that others may connect to

Type and example	Features	Potential uses	Challenges
jpeg & mpeg	• Digital File formats	• Common formats for digital photographs and video respectively	• As with all digital media, software, and storage devices, it allows easy sharing of information, but it's much harder to control distribution, as anyone with brief access can copy it.
USB drive (thumb drive, flash drive)	• Small thumb-size (or smaller) device for digital storage	• Getting much cheaper and available in varying capacities • Near universal compatibility make them a way to carry large digital files between computers.	• Older computers may need software installed to use them, thus making them less convenient • As with all digital media, software, and storage devices, it allows easy sharing of information, but it's much harder to control distribution, as anyone with brief access can copy it.
Internet search engines (e.g., Google, Ask Jeeves)	• Access to the Internet	• Essentially massive Internet catalogues that allow search terms to be entered and web sites containing those terms retrieved	• Ability to find web sites depends on entering appropriate search terms

Using media techniques

Advantages

- These methods offer detailed information not possible with traditional methods of recording.
- The observations recorded may show more **objectivity** than those requiring the observer's description.
- A large quantity of information can be recorded quickly.
- The recordings can be analyzed by many professionals individually and collectively after the event.
- The observations can supplement and validate other traditionally recorded observations.
- Information that replays a "real" situation can be shared with parents.
- Data can be stored efficiently.
- Some programs can sort, store, and even analyze observations.

Disadvantages

- The costs can be high.
- The availability can be limited.
- Training is required.
- These methods can encourage quantity recording at the expense of well-analyzed quality recording.
- Knowledge of the recording may influence the children and alter their behaviour.
- **Confidentiality** issues are challenging to resolve.
- Storage and retrieval systems need to be established.
- Issues such as **professional responsibility**, ethics, and privacy may arise.

Ethical issues

In the past it was much clearer who was responsible for what. Confidentiality was clear-cut; particular information was to be recorded and shared between parents and professionals only. Now personal information in the form of photographs, digital portfolios, scanned images, video-recordings, and other stored data has exploded in volume. Questions remain as to why and when this information should be made available, and to whom. Some of the technologies permit limiting access electronically, but this is not entirely reliable.

Members of the observation and assessment teams observing young children may also be more numerous than before. With parent helpers, assistants, technical resource people, and paraprofessionals, as well as the teaching team and consultants, the sheer volume of people accessing personalized data, as they are being collected, is potentially large.

Consequently, gaining permissions to collect or use those data, and ensuring their confidentiality, is not easy. Some parents might reasonably withhold their permission to feature their own children in a group video sequence because they do not want others to know about their behaviour. These people may feel the whole world is watching their children and their teachers! These concerns are not reason enough to avoid using technologies altogether to assist in record-keeping and the closer observation of children. All those involved with children must work together to develop policies to ensure confidentiality within certain parameters. Neither the educators nor the parents should feel that they are constantly being scrutinized in every aspect of their lives.

One use of video cameras causes particular problems: the hidden camera. Some education institutions use them for safety purposes or for a random documentation of activities. Although this may have become accepted practice, it does raise the invasion-of-privacy issue. Intrusively observing and recording personal information about parents, children, or educators is not acceptable. There is a fine line between educators observing children at a distance without their knowledge and intruding in the private lives of people. As technologies develop, we can expect more **ethical issues** to arise. We will have to address these with proactive policy-making born of a common understanding of what is in the best interests of the children.

If parents feel the need to monitor their in-home caregivers or educators minute to minute, the two parties would appear to distrust one another. Video-recording the caregiver to ensure that a child is properly cared for is ineffective; parents will know there has been a problem only after some event. Sensational video footage has been shown on television of caregivers abusing the children in their care, and this has caused some alarm among those employing nannies. It is not recommended that parents record their in-home care providers. Instead, before hiring, parents should interview prospective caregivers, observe them in action, request and check references, and suggest a probationary period with the parents and the caregiver working together. Once a sense of trust has been established, parents can feel more comfortable about offering a contract. By that point both parties will have clear expectations. If you feel that you must video-record the caregiver and your child, explain this at the outset of offering the employment, and do it to capture some of the moments of your child's development you would otherwise miss or lose. Ideally, ask the caregiver to use the technology to make records to share with you later.

As an educator, you may encounter concerns arising from bad experiences related to recordings that make some parents particularly reticent to share information, have photographs taken, or use recording devices that collect material about their children. If your explanations of your purpose in making the recordings cannot satisfy a parent's concerns, then you must limit such documentation to the minimum necessary. As a parent you will need to build trust and confidence in the educators before you can feel comfortable sharing some information. Explain this to the teachers who are requesting your permission.

Another serious issue concerns access by other parties, governments, employers, and other powerful agencies to information about individual children and their families. While relatively unlikely, some people will particularly resist sharing personal data that might fall into "Big Brother's" hands. This fear should not be discounted, even if you consider the likelihood far-fetched. Again, limit the exchange of information and reduce documentation to only what is strictly necessary. As an educator, you may find this frustrating because you think that having more information about a child will help both you and the parents appreciate who she is and what she needs. While the authentic-assessment approach honours family information as integral to understanding the behaviour that the educator observes, parents may have valid reasons to shy away from what they believe would put them in a vulnerable position. Current technologies exacerbate the problem, as they can store so much more information than was possible earlier, and unauthorized and unwanted people could gain access to it.

Going "green"

Two conflicting forces are producing a particular challenge for us in this century. The first force is the fact of our developing new media at an astonishing rate and at the same time making obsolete many objects that previously had a much longer lifespan. The second force is our ecological responsibility and effort to lessen our carbon footprint. If we are to take the best of the technological advancements, we must find ways of reducing waste, such as reusing what we have, replacing items only when necessary, re-purposing items that can be adapted, and recycling when possible. How we get rid of technological waste has to be addressed. There are projects that attempt to address this issue, but the responsibilities of some of the big manufacturing companies are not being recognized as they should.

Photography
Uses for recording information

You will need to consider your intentions and the possibilities associated with the use of photographs. You can likely use photography in one or more of the following ways to help you perform your responsibilities or support your learning about children:

- as part of a **life book** to support a child's appreciation of his own "story"
- as evidence of a child's growth and changes in physical appearance
- to record significant life experiences and rites of passage
- to support traditionally recorded observations
- as part of a child's developmental **portfolio**
- to document stages in the process of an activity or project
- to record episodes of a child's activities
- to keep information about the products of a child's activity
- for file identification
- as a safety measure to ensure security
- to aid a child's memory of situations

General principles

Some basic guidelines might be helpful if you choose to use photography to support your child observations.

1. Choose a camera that fits your level of competence and your purpose.
2. Keep the camera ready to use, battery charged, stored safely, and close to where it will be needed.
3. Practice taking pictures.
4. Get the children used to your taking photographs.
5. Be aware of your reasons for taking a photograph.

6. Design and use a consistent format for labelling and storing the photographs.
7. Ensure that every photograph is treated as a confidential document.

The basics of photography

Taking photos for use in childcare and education does not substantially differ from taking family photos. Just as you and your family will regard your photos as records of significant events or stages in your life together, so will childcare professionals taking photos of your children use those photos professionally. In making any kind of photographic record, you aim to capture what you consider pertinent in a way that is accurate and easily understandable. Some people have a natural flair for photography, while for others even the "point and shoot" camera presents challenges!

Here are some suggestions for increasing your skill and artistry with this tool.

Choice of traditional SLR, or analog, camera Many good pictures have been "lost" because of the time it took to set up a complex camera's speed, angle, and focus. Gifted and skilled photographers will get some marvellous results investing in expensive paraphernalia and lots of time, but most adults working with children want to capture a moment spontaneously. They may prefer a camera that is relatively small in size, has automatic functions and a built-in flash, and is loaded with a film intended to work both indoors and out.

With an automatic pocket camera, you can often take a perfectly adequate photograph that you might have missed with a camera with various attachments. A camera that meets the following specifications is ideal and can be used by any member of the work team:

- small, pocket-size with firmly attached cord for wearing around neck or tying to something
- automatic loading and automatic wind
- automatic shutter/exposure and automatic flash
- clear indicator for number on roll of film
- battery-tester buzzer
- clear and accurate indicator of image through lens
- relatively inexpensive

The importance of lighting Adjust your technique to the lighting available. Ensure that there is sufficient light for your proposed shot and supplement it with the flash if necessary. Avoid taking photographs while looking toward the sun. The sun should be behind you, preferably not casting long, sharp shadows. The degree of light can be deceptive: light in snow and evening sun are particularly difficult to evaluate without a light meter. Indoor lighting can seem stronger than it actually is and can also make your photograph turn out in strange, unpredictable colours. You may not know this until you have your pictures processed (developed).

Instant cameras Instant cameras are frequently called Land cameras—after Edwin Land, who invented them—or Polaroid cameras—after the company that developed, manufactured, and marketed them.

Photographing the structures made by children is useful for later discussion with the children. Photos can also be useful addition to written observations and portfolios.

With permission of the YMCA of Greater Toronto

Instant photographs have some obvious advantages. They enable you to

- tell immediately if you have taken an appropriate photograph without waiting for processing.
- avoid waiting for film processing and sending, delivering, or collecting film.
- date and label the photograph immediately and more accurately, and rapidly share information with the subject of the picture, parents, and other professionals.

Photographic processing If you have a darkroom and the appropriate equipment, you might want to develop and print your own film. More likely, you will use a commercial processing service.

The cost of service varies considerably, often according to the time you choose to wait for the processing: the faster the service, the higher the charge. Although photography experts may argue about the types of process and their results, your choice may be more a matter of personal preference than objective choice. You will also have to decide on the size of photograph, the finish, and the number of copies. It is a good idea to log the details of your photographs as you take them, because of the time lag between taking in the film and turning it into photographs.

Digital cameras **Digital cameras** store images on a memory card rather than on film. No processing is required, as the images can be downloaded and viewed (as well as stored) on a computer. They can also be e-mailed as "jpg" files and burned onto CDs and DVDs. If you need conventional prints, you can make them from the stored file, either at a photo processing lab or at home or in the office, using an appropriate printer and photo-quality paper. Many digital cameras have video and audio capabilities.

Taking photographs for observational purposes

When to take a picture (being natural) Your purpose is likely to "capture a moment" of a child in action, to record interests, skills, relationships, learning, reactions, or to take a picture for some other educational consideration. Be patient; try not to attract the child's attention or disturb his activity in any way. The child's play and learning experience are always more important than the actual photograph. You cannot record the essence of the action by trying to direct what the children are doing for the sake of the camera. If you start to interfere, you become intrusive and work against the professed philosophy of early childhood education.

To achieve **naturalness**, to record a child's interactions within a natural setting, there is a longer list of what *not* to do than what *to* do. It may be helpful for the children to access "play" cameras or even to try their own photography. Their familiarity with the technology may help them accept your use of the camera around them more easily.

Capturing natural expressions Getting down to the child's level is very important in understanding what the child is doing. The child's eye level is exactly where you need to be; that angle allows you the most open view of the child's expression and allows you direct eye contact, which can help personalize the moment, if that is what you wish. Less appealing is an angle that looks down at the child and distorts the action rather than showing it as the child sees it. You may have to lie on the floor, squat, kneel, sit on a child's chair, or adopt some other uncomfortable position.

When children try to pose, they tend to overact. If you take several pictures within a short period of time, you are more likely to get a useful shot. At moments of discovery and engrossment, the children are less likely to be influenced by your presence, and the result should be more successful.

Recording child development To record a child's development, take regular and deliberate, rather than occasional or random, photographs. You might like to record a chart of your photographs so that you can see developmental progression. What you want to do is take photographs of the child when she is involved in activities.

Using photographs to supplement other observational recordings can be helpful because they can give a more real sense of "who" the child is when you review the data.

Photographs for record-keeping You may wish to establish a photographic record system that uses a predetermined labelling system. Include the child's name and age, the date of the photograph, the names of other children/adults in the photograph, and the situation depicted. For observational purposes, you might have the photograph mounted on an accompanying form with additional information on the **context** of the photo. Try to avoid writing directly on the back of a printed photo, as the photo suffers from being handled and the writing may rub off or show through on the front. You could apply self-adhesive labels to the photos if you wish to cut down the bulk of paperwork, but even a preprinted label will not save the picture's being lost in a file folder with other information. If you have available shelf space, you could keep the photographs in albums, one for each child, with labels below each picture. You can also keep the photos filed in special boxes designed for file index cards and present them as wonderful gifts to the children's parents when their children leave the agency.

Although archived images take much less space when they are on a CD or DVD, when digital images are plentiful, tough decisions need to be made about what to store. Before starting to load pictures onto a computer it is best to decide the reasons for keeping the images.

A sample photographic observation with contextual information is shown in Observation Sample 7.1. Often photos are more useful from an educational perspective if they capture spontaneous activity. Here, the process of taking the picture involved social interaction. Software that allows educators to create individualized files that include digital images is available.

Observation Sample 7.1

This photographic record could be put in a photo album or in the child's portfolio. The comments provide a context to explain the significance of the picture.

In what ways might you use photographs to document the behaviour of children in a preschool program?

Name: <u>Ashley (second from right)</u>   Age: <u>5 years, 7 months</u>

Date: <u>May 27, 2008</u>

Others represented: <u>(from left) Kayleigh, Elizabeth, Lashonda</u>

Situation: <u>On the bus on the way to an outing at the Museum of Science</u>

Comments: Ashley tends to be a loner. Her home life is unsettled (her parents were recently divorced and her grandmother, whom she is very close to, is quite ill), and this seems to have contributed to her reluctance to form close relationships with the other children. Elizabeth, who lives next door to Ashley, sometimes invites Ashley to be part of her group. Perhaps because she was excited about the trip, Ashley let herself be drawn into the fun with the other girls on the bus, as seen in this photo. Observation of Ashley's interests may help her teachers find other activities to draw her into social interactions with other children.

Observer: _____ Josh _____

Video-Recording
Uses for digital or analog video

There are a number of purposes for recording the child's activities or environment:

- to replay particular scenes when time allows in-depth observation
- to share information about the child's development with parents
- to create a long-term record of a child's progress
- to assist in observing groups of children so that attention can concentrate on each child's involvement and interactions
- for research
- to record important happenings or rites of passage in the child's life so that the child himself can review significant parts of his own life
- to support observations recorded in more traditional ways
- to re-create the child's activities and interactions to support a multidisciplinary evaluation
- to assist in evaluating the child's **environment**

As Meghan plays with blocks, an educator (reflected in mirror upper left corner) takes photographs of the children.

With permission of the YMCA of Greater Toronto

General principles

You can gain skill in video-recording quite quickly once you get started.

1. Survey the market of available recording equipment, identify the features you need, and consider your finances.
2. Familiarize yourself with your recording device and its functions.
3. Allow plenty of time for practice.
4. Build your vocabulary to include video terminology.
5. Desensitize the children who will be your subjects before making recordings you intend to keep. You might have the children actively participate in video-making.
6. Determine your purpose for recording.
7. Avoid **subjective** shooting that centres on what is "cute" or on children acting up for the camera.
8. Investigate possibilities for editing your video-recordings.
9. Design and use a format for labelling and storing the camera's memory.
10. Ensure that every recording is confidential.

The basics of video-recording

Some beginner's tips to get you started:

- Read and use the owner's manual so that you can appreciate the camera's features.
- Try using a tripod to hold the camera or brace yourself against a firm object to avoid a bouncing effect.
- Use an autofocus or practise focusing manually. Be aware that the camera will focus on the nearest object when set on autofocus.
- Practise using the zoom to accustom yourself to the feeling that you are lurching back and forth, but do not overuse this feature.
- Compose your video-recording so that the context, or background, is clear before you go into a close-up.
- Set or move the camera at different angles in relation to the subject to create more interesting images.
- Record movement that cannot be captured by a still camera.
- Hold static shots, particularly at the beginning and end of a sequence.
- When panning across an area (left to right or right to left), move smoothly to direct the viewer's attention, and limit the angle of movement to 90 degrees.
- Follow the children's action at their level for a more insightful view of their world.
- The pause button enables you to exercise a form of in-process editing. Practise using it.
- Try to capture meaningful sequences of activity.

Videotapes Blank tapes are not all the same. They vary in length, cost, quality, and type.

Video-making skills To learn how to make video-recordings, you may want to read how-to manuals, but your starting point will probably be trial and error. Awareness of the most common mistakes will not necessarily help you avoid them, because you need to see how they come about before you can rectify them. Familiarize yourself with the functions of the recording device on a tryout basis. Short of dropping the device or applying physical force to it, you are unlikely to do it any harm.

In *Learn to Make Videos in a Weekend* (1993), Roland Lewis suggests that the 14 basic skills of video can be learned in two days. He describes the sequence of holding and moving the camera through lighting and composition to editing and adding titles and soundtracks. Another good reference is John Hedgecoe's *Complete Guide to Video: The Ultimate Manual of Video Techniques and Equipment* (1992), which is written for the newcomer and provides helpful detail.

Additional video-recording features

- **Age subtitles:** It is possible to program some cameras to memorize an individual's birth date so that her actual age can appear on the video.
- **Date/time:** Cameras may record the date and time of the recording on the screen.
- **Title superimposer:** A memory function in the camera can record a title or picture over a scene.
- **Self-timer:** A timer allows the camera operator to "get into the action" for participant observation.
- **Insert edit:** New recordings can be made over the old with a sophisticated, dedicated insert-edit facility that you can pre-set to the point at which you want to add the new material.
- **Macro close-up/zoom:** Cameras allow varying degrees of close-ups. On some, this function can be controlled automatically.
- **External mike socket:** This feature can help pick up sound when the fixed microphone is too far away to pick up language.
- **Audio dub:** The recorded sound can be replaced with a narrative or voiceover on some models.
- **Auto exposure:** The iris diaphragm automatically adjusts the size of the aperture to suit the available lighting.

Making video-recordings for observational purposes

When to make a video-recording As you develop your skill, you will start to see opportunities for recording the activities of the children in your care. You may find the flow of their action makes it difficult to decide when and what to record; the amount of time you have may well dictate your choice. It can be a challenge to maintain your supervisory role, participate in the activity, and also record what is happening. You can solve this problem if you have systems of shared care, time designated for recording, or a small, undemanding group of children. Somehow educators who are committed to video-recording usually manage to do it!

You may want to record some of the more domestic and routine elements of the children's day. In only a short time, these routines evolve as the children develop, and mere memories of them can be lost. Recording typical behaviours may be as rewarding as seeking new advances in development. The dated record will help you see developmental changes over a period of time. Capturing children's **spontaneous play** can be the most revealing and meaningful subject of video-recording. You can shoot what happens without any fuss by having the camera available in the children's play area. Indoors and out, you can record a variety of play sequences and social interactions.

Video-recordings may centre on the activity of one child. You will seldom record that child in isolation; she will usually be involved with others. If you make a recording, you must decide how to pick out the individual child's behaviour from the general flow. Knowing how to edit forms the foundation of effective individual record-keeping.

What video-recordings can highlight Here are some suggestions for the types of observations you could record on videotape:

- any of the features of audio-recordings (see page 236)
- play patterns
- body language/eye contact
- program effectiveness
- use of space
- group interactions and behaviour
- gross motor skills
- manipulative skills
- children's responses to activities
- discovery and curiosity
- experimentation with objects and materials

- mood changes
- independence skills or autonomy
- process of play and learning
- products of activity
- creative activity and artwork in progress
- social groupings
- styles and preferences
- separation or other anxieties
- any other aspect of development that can be revealed by other observation methods

TAKING A SPECIAL LOOK: Observing and recording sign language

American Sign Language (ASL) is the form of **sign language** used most commonly by people who are considered deaf (this does not always mean people who are completely nonhearing). Observing and recording the communication of children who use sign language is even more challenging than observing children who use spoken language!

To record sign language and other gestures, video-record the child and transcribe the recording. You can also write a full narrative description that includes all the child's gestures, as well as any facial expressions and changes in posture; you will likely have to devise a coding mechanism in order to capture all the detail. Or you can record the use of sign language with a commentary that includes the meaning of the signing, rather than in a narrative that describes the signing in full.

Videotapes for record-keeping Video-recordings of any kind can form a history of children's development, activities, or festivals. If you've used videotapes, you can store the tapes, labelled and filed vertically in chronological order.

An educator's videotapes that record the activity of groups of children may require editing, but they can be very useful for program planning for the group. These tapes can be stored simply and accessed by staff when necessary. They may also provide very good teaching material for student educators and caregivers.

Most important is record-keeping of such tapes for the individual child. Keep these recordings with, or alongside, an observation file or portfolio, and consider them an integral part of your observation and assessment system. To make these individual tapes, you must have an effective editing facility.

Confidentiality and professionalism must apply to the use of videotaped or -recorded observations. You may need to use a permission form that addresses video-recordings specifically.

Labelling and dating are often difficult with videotapes because they offer little space for detail. A reference card showing the same counter numbering as the tape itself could accompany the video in its sleeve or box.

Because technologies change rapidly, you may want to consider how one recording format can interface with another so that data is not inaccessible.

Digital video Editing digital video is much easier, because it can be transfered to a computer directly, edited online, then returned to its original format. Computerizing records allows you to organize the material into files and to send short clips, perhaps to parents.

Use of webcam This delightful newer technology allows parents to see and monitor their child at any time of the day. Basically it's a video camera that allows images to be viewed live on the Internet. The use of webcams has become widespread, and offers parents reassurance that all is well with their child. From their perspective, this adds accountability to the program for their child. From the educators' perspective, it ensures that practice is always optimal. Similar recordings can be made for staff viewing, which enables educators to review and improve their work.

Video Recording Log

Name:		Group:	
Date	Counter #	Context	Comment

Audio-Recording

Uses for recording information

You may have any of the following purposes in making audio-recordings:

- to support any traditionally recorded observation
- to record the educator's **narrative observation** of a child's behaviour
- to record a child's or children's verbal communications
- to facilitate close analysis of a language sample
- to record a child's or children's explorations and production of sound and music
- to keep records of a child's language, music, or reading skill development
- to communicate with parents in sharing direct recordings or anecdotal observations
- as part of a child's developmental portfolio
- for the student teacher to learn about the language, music, humour, and thinking skills of children

General principles

The following steps will help you get started with audio-recording:

1. Consider your needs and purchase an audio-recording device that is resilient and portable.
2. Set up the device in a convenient place and use its portable feature to go where the children are when necessary.
3. Give yourself lots of time to practise recording.
4. Familiarize the children with recording and playback.
5. Organize time for replay and analysis.
6. Determine your purpose in recording.
7. Consider the possibilities of editing your recordings using specialized equipment.
8. Accept failures.
9. Design and use a format for labelling and storing the audio-recordings.
10. Ensure that every audiotape is considered a confidential document.

The basics of audio-recording

Some beginner's tips:

- An extended microphone with a jack will pick up distant sounds more clearly.
- Use the pause button for in-process editing.
- Set up your recordings in an area that minimizes sounds of background activity.

- Use a Dolby noise-reduction system if one is built into the recorder for better, clearer replay.
- Keep recorders in a dry place, in moderate temperatures, and away from magnetic fields.

Choice of audio-recording device You may be familiar with a range of these, from the old reel-to-reel, cartridge, and cassette systems to the new digital audio recorders, many of them small and hand-held with built-in microphones. Others have jacks for distant mics.

Laboratory schools and agencies with built-in sound systems that allow students and teachers to "listen in" will be at an advantage. Not all of these systems are built for recording, so you might want to check into this. A good sound system has microphones a little above the children's heads, fairly evenly spread across areas where the children are active. Observers listen from a distance, usually from a one-way mirrored observation booth with speakers or headphones. Observers can select the microphone they wish to use and pick up the sounds they want. If your school or agency has an additional recording facility as well, you can store a lot of useful information this way.

You can use dangling microphones if you are doing straightforward recording. One mike might give you a "flat" sound recording, while two or more give a stereophonic quality and can record a group of children more effectively. A mike propped up on a table usually picks up too much white noise. When the children move around, you might try the reporter's technique of following them with a hand-held microphone.

Making audio-recordings for observational purposes

When to make an audio-recording You will need to decide what to record according to your purpose. The children may become so familiar with the audio recorder that it does not bother them. You can desensitize them to the equipment by allowing them to record and replay by themselves, or by sharing your recordings with younger children. The replay may elicit squeals of delight from the preschoolers, but younger children may be confused when you replay their language.

You might like to make an audio-recording at many times during a child's day. Try not to miss the normal, average, and domestic aspects as well as the more structured peak-programming times. Be prepared to record spontaneously, and also acknowledge that you will have to be patient. Here are some suggestions on what to record:

- circle times
- greetings, separations, and reunions
- group singing
- experimentation with sounds and instruments
- book corner—conversation, reading, storytelling
- spontaneous play activities
- crib sounds
- interactions with adults
- sociodramatic play
- imitative play
- transitions
- bathroom routines
- individual singing or reciting rhymes
- music activities
- hearing children read

- bilingual children's conversation
- toddlers' emerging language
- problem-solving activities
- outdoor play
- outings, picnics

- at home with parents/siblings/friends
- formal assessments
- examples of school-agers' jokes
- portfolio-assessment meetings

What audio-recordings can highlight While this list is not comprehensive or ordered, it offers some ideas of what you might look for in analyzing your recordings:

- pronunciation
- reading strategies
- MLUs (mean length of utterances)
- pitch discrimination
- experimentation with oral sound production
- rhythm of speech/length of phrase
- accent/cultural patterns
- phraseology/speech patterns
- use of parts of speech/grammatical errors
- communication difficulties
- egocentric speech/egocentricity
- expression of ideas
- overextensions
- misunderstandings
- social relationships
- humour and incongruities
- moral views and attitudes

- social role play
- developmental level of thinking skills
- demonstration of feelings
- solitary activity/isolation/talking to self
- memory
- sequencing of stories or events
- imagination
- use of rhyme
- musicality
- concentration length
- interests
- play level
- fantasy or realism
- logic
- friendships and peer interactions
- imitation or repetition
- conversation with adults
- sibling interactions

Audio-recordings for record-keeping Like any other observational material, audio-recordings must remain confidential. You may wish to have individual and group recordings. Remember that individual children's records are more effective in helping you determine developmental levels and programs in response to children's various needs and skills. Where you have the recordings of a group, you will find it almost impossible to edit them to make individual files. Instead, you can write a narrative account from the recording. Although it may be difficult to get complex language down on paper, you can replay the recording many times, and capture all the detail your written account needs.

Audiotape Recording Log

Child's name: _____ D.O.B.: _____

Date	Counter #	Sequence	Narrative documents Yes No	Comment

Computers and Recording and Storing Data

Uses of computers for recording and storing data

Computers can be used to retain data from observations, in various readable and presentable formats. Any of the available word-processing programs allows for easy input and storage, so you can retrieve and display the records quickly or print them in a wide range of styles. They also facilitate the addition of new data as part of an integral record (always a problem with handwritten notes), as well as the insertion of changes. One concern here is that it may not be obvious that these additions and insertions were made to the original recording later. Work around this drawback by using "read-only" protection and passwords to control access.

Files can be sorted alphabetically and/or by date. Mail management programs such as Microsoft Outlook allow you to send documents electronically between locations.

Memory A personal computer or laptop will have a large hard-drive memory capacity. The memory increases with each new model, with today's models storing many times more than those made only a few years ago. Computer memory capacity—RAM, or random access memory—is measured in megabytes or gigabytes, although there are other aspects of memory. Rarely is a computer's memory full.

Text and other data can be stored using a number of different memory devices in addition to the hard drive. A CD is a compact disk that can have large amounts of visual, text, or other data burned onto it. Most computers can perform the steps necessary to both record and read a CD. A CD-ROM is a read-only disk. They are commonly used to play music, but their use can go far beyond that, and for our purposes assist with the management of large amounts of observational material. A newer technology, the DVD (digital versatile, or video, disk) has a much greater storage facility. There are various forms of DVDs, some of which have been abandoned in favour of others using different "platforms," but they all have the capacity to store complex high-resolution audio-visual information.

Small and therefore portable memory devices allow data to be easily accessible. The memory key, memory stick, or flash drive is a tiny hard drive that can be plugged into a computer's USB port (a universal serial bus). This is the entry point for peripheral devices such as memory sticks or linkages to cameras.

A digital camera, either video or still, will have one of a number of different **memory cards**. There is a variety of types of memory devices. A memory card (sometimes called a flash memory card or a storage card) is a small storage medium used to store data such as text, pictures, audio, and video for use on small, portable, or remote computing devices. Most of the current products use flash memory, although other technologies are being developed. There are a number of memory cards on the market, including the SD card (secure digital card), the CF card (CompactFlash card), the SmartMedia card, the Memory Stick, and the MultiMediaCard (MMC). These cards are of varying sizes, and each is available in a range of storage capacities that typically relates to the price. The CompactFlash card is about the size of a matchbook, while the MultiMediaCard and Secure Digital card are each about the size of a postage stamp. Simple hookups between a recording device and a computer allow for data to be managed, sorted, and stored. The capacity of a memory device is measured in **megabytes**, or MB (one million bytes).

Data is stable on these memory cards, is not threatened by a loss of power source, and does not need to be periodically refreshed. They have no moving parts and, therefore, are unlikely to suffer mechanical difficulties. Newer cards are smaller, require less power, have higher storage capacity, and are portable among a greater number of devices. Because of these features, memory cards are influencing the production of an increasing number of small, lightweight, and low-power devices.

Memory cards offer a number of advantages over the hard disk drive: they're much smaller and lighter, extremely portable, completely silent, allow more immediate access, and are less prone to mechanical damage. In comparison, however, the hard disk still offers a compelling advantage: currently, a memory card (for example, CompactFlash) with a 192 MB capacity typically costs more than a hard drive with a capacity of 40 GB.

(This information about memory cards was supplemented by information from **SearchStorage.com**, a web source for Information Technology professionals.)

Organization and management Gathering large amounts of observation and other data is highly commendable, but knowing what to do with it and making sense of the information is even more important.

A computer's hard drive allows filing systems to be established that can assist in sorting the information. However, it is likely that individual files need to be kept about each child, and these may be saved to a CD when the data has been sorted. Sorting involves separating out information about each child, and within the files that are then created, summarizing each child's observation according to developmental or other domains. The next step is to analyze this data. We discuss this in Chapter 9, where we review the whole analytical process. The computer can be a tool to manage the data, but only a few software programs can help with the analytical process.

Managing files demands discipline in creating folders, keeping to a folder system, accessing and updating existing files rather than creating new ones, and ensuring that the team is familiar with the system and records who makes which entry. Other data can be even more complex and use more file space than expected. Video sequences are particularly demanding of space.

Software programs Most computers come pre-loaded with word-processing programs (Microsoft Word and Corel WordPerfect are the most common) and spreadsheet software (Microsoft Excel). Other widely used programs include Microsoft Access (for databases), Microsoft PowerPoint (for presentations), and Microsoft Outlook (for e-mail management). Educators and parents can use these to document their observations and their most necessary information in the form of more traditional methodologies, such as narratives, samplings, and checklists. Even complex portfolios can be managed using these tools.

Some purpose-designed software programs also meet the needs of observers and researchers. For example, the Creative Curriculum has a new integrated assessment system based on their developmental continuum, which has a software-reporting tool, CC-PORT. Another software package available through a Weblink, **earlylearner.net**, makes it possible to document portfolios, and recommend activities and support resources. This is available to schools and childcare centres; another version is available for parents.

The COR (child observation record) assessment tool, which focuses on a child's current competency in a range of developmental areas, was created by High/Scope and offers a software program that enables anecdotal records and other observations to be recorded and managed prior to assessment. As with other software a licence to use the product is necessary.

Other software systems claim application to early childhood observation recording management, including Galileo, which is a "complete electronic **assessment** and **curriculum** system with online and offline capabilities that links planning, individualization, outcome documentation, and program enhancement for preschool educators and other stakeholders" (Galileo web site **www.ati-online.com**/). Some assessment software offers a means of scoring cumbersome assessment material in an efficient manner. The Battelle Development Inventory (BDI-2) is such a tool (Newborg 2004). Another commonly used assessment tool that includes software that makes the recording, management, and scoring an easier process is the Brigance Comprehensive Inventory of Basic Skills (CIBS— Revised) for pre-kindergarten to grade nine.

When selecting a program that must meet the needs of your early childhood program, consider

1. upfront and ongoing costs.

2. licences and restrictions.

3. how well the software integrates into your philosophy of observation and assessment.

4. whether or not the software is sensitive, unbiased, and individualized, and uses naturalistic observational information.

5. what results or outcomes you need.

6. how access and confidentiality can be assured.

7. how much time is saved or wasted.

8. what the program can do that your previous system(s) failed to do, if anything.

9. how the program could lead to improved child environments and better curriculum design.

10. how adaptable the program might be to future practical or technological change.

Research An interesting project using multiple cameras to gather observational information about children's behaviour was conducted by several Japanese researchers (M. Hirano, K. Shintani, H. Nakao, S. Ohta, S. Kaneda, and H. Haga 2007). The child observation support system (COSS-MC) was used to observe children in nurseries and kindergarten programs. Observing the environment from multiple directions and then recording motion pictures simultaneously, teachers could then select appropriate sections and build one streaming video for each child. This would appear to get around the issue of confidentiality. The multiple input from several peripheral devices was managed using a software package developed by the research team. If this application were made available, it might have broad use in childcare and school settings.

Labrune (2005) sought a method of recording observations using multiple sources and multiple senses. His work posed the question of how we can document the process of a child's creativity. Although seemingly outlandish, his ideas called for full child direction and participation, and Labrune envisaged several types of mechanisms that would allow for such an idea. These ideas are in the early stages, but today's observers may be able to create new means for capturing ideas, processes, and thoughts, as well as the more clearly visible and audible parts of children's activity.

Another program, ecore (classroom observation software) developed by John Tenny, tracks a teacher's response to misbehaviour. **Research** into the effectiveness of new software still needs to be done; it looks promising but has not been tested. Whether the expense of the software is justified is another matter—costs are usually cited on a per-child basis.

For research, some people have found software programs that do more than store information. Some programs can actually manage data, sort it, and produce printouts that can add meaning to data collection. NUD*IST—yes, that's its name!—is one of these programs. However, it requires complex coding of qualitative data and tedious inputting. You may find the results useful for some projects once you collect enough material to warrant investing in the program.

Scanners Scanners let you save documents and images on the computer's hard drive as facsimiles of the originals. This is extremely useful as a means of retaining a child's file copies of letters, forms, work samples, and photos.

Sharing Information with Parents Using Technology

The guidelines for communication remain the same with whatever **media** you're using for transmission of data. Keep the following points in mind:

- Use the technology to gather more data, manage it more effectively, and analyze it more thoroughly—rather than as a fancy way of showing off your program!
- Frame all communications positively and focus on a child's progress.
- Avoid communicating anything through technology that you wouldn't say to a parent's face.
- Ask parents what they want to discuss or see.
- Remember that communication is a two-way process; you need to receive as well as send information.
- Make face-to-face communications a priority; technology should not take you away from personal interactions.
- Ensure privacy and limit access to any personal information.
- Make sure that you have permission to collect and store all information.
- Consider ethical considerations seriously.
- Personalize the information you transmit rather than sending cold data.
- Provide opportunity for parents' feedback and family discussion.
- Ensure that you include all team members in the communication circle.
- Communicate regularly during, rather than at the end of, a major project.
- Avoid comparing any child with another or commenting on the other children.
- Explain the purpose of your observations, record-keeping, and assessments.
- Present the information and your perspective professionally.
- Document the parents' responses.
- Develop your ongoing plan with the parents.

Summary

Every year, new technologies and modifications of existing ones appear and become more accessible to the mass market. We can be dazzled by them and want to use them in our programs for children as novelties. For observation and recording purposes they may offer us significant advancements beyond traditional paper-and-pencil methods. Yet we need to use them carefully and spend money on them wisely, so that the medium does not take over the children's activity and our time as educators. Children must remain our focus!

All the media techniques available obscure the "real time" activity of the children who exist in the here and now. At the same time, traditional approaches using narrative, sampling, or other documentation cannot match the amount and quality of recording of children's activity possible through these newer technologies. We need to learn about what and how to record, and to acquire some understanding of the potential of each technology. Try to learn these skills outside your actual observation time as educator rather than devote precious program time to it.

Recordings made by any media are just that—recordings. They are not really observations and they are not interpretations of a child's activity. We must not expect the technology to "speak for itself"; educators must narrate what they record, find ways of categorizing the data, and develop ways to analyze what they have collected. The tools merely allow us to gather more information about children. We don't learn more if we don't do something with the information!

Simple audio-recordings can offer educators unparalleled detail of conversation compared to other methods. They also allow us to replay the material and make sense of what we hear. Even though the video sequences of activity offer such a quantity of data that they may leave us no further ahead in our interpretation than when we were observing those same sequences in real time, they can allow us to focus on one type of behaviour or on one child at a time, by replaying a scene over and over again. We can gain insights this way that would otherwise be lost because we cannot process all that information as it actually happens.

Computers enable parents and professionals to record information quickly, easily, and accessibly. They can also allow parents and other team members access to that information through the same technology. Through video facilities linked to the computer we can gain a limited-access view of the children while the parent is at work or at home and the child is in childcare or in school. This suggests a new type of parent involvement.

Digital portfolio systems are now being developed that move our authentic assessment process into new territory. We still have to consider whether we are using technology to fulfill our needs, or using it simply because it is there. We have yet to determine how much it enhances our observation, documentation, assessment, and curriculum design.

The new media present us with new ethical, professional, and privacy issues, in the form of new twists on concerns about confidentiality, questions regarding access to data, and the question of who takes responsibility for the storage and later dissemination or destruction of the records. Whether "outside" professionals such as consultants should have access to recordings has not been established; the boundaries need to be drawn. When personal information is recorded, risks always arise regarding its inappropriate use. What should the ethical criteria be?

This chapter has discussed the types and potential uses of various technologies. It is hoped that readers will want to practise using them and develop their own recording methods with or for children in their care. Financial considerations may limit their incorporation into all programs; some schools and childcare programs have found ways of overcoming this through budgeting for specific funds, applying for grants, or using their own hardware. We are in the earliest stages of using these technologies to record children's behaviour. Many educators use cameras for portraiture only rather than activity. We have yet to develop ways of making technologies fit our purpose, or to actually design or alter existing technologies to meet our needs as observers. Finding effective means of recording, of sifting through large quantities of material, and of analyzing the data so produced is an ongoing challenge.

Key Terms

- assessment
- confidentiality
- context
- curriculum
- digital camera
- environment
- ethical issues
- life book
- media
- megabytes
- media technique
- memory cards
- narrative observation
- naturalness
- objectivity
- portfolio
- professional responsibility
- recording (technological)
- research
- sign language
- spontaneous play
- subjective

Weblinks

www.privacylawyer.ca/
Fraser's overview of federal, provincial, and territorial legislation on privacy.

http://electronicportfolios.com
Information on constructing and developing electronic portfolios.

www.geocities.com/Athens/Olympus/7123/camera.html
Tips for using digital cameras in the classroom.

www.hp.ca/portal/hho/dpc/learn/learn.php
A manufacturer's guide to learning how to use digital technology.

www.lexar.com/dp
Help with digital photography.

www.tru.ca/faculty/wlroberts/
Free access to a software program that collects data (naturalistic observations) and analyzes children's interactions.

www.howstuffworks.com
Explanations of how various media devices are used, along with their functions.

8 Portfolios

Portfolios document a child's development for the benefit of both educators and the family. Here a parent and an educator discuss what they have learned from the child's portfolio.

With permission of the YMCA of Greater Toronto

Documenting children's work is a widely accepted aspect of professional teaching. Individual and group portfolios allow teachers to maintain a record of children's development across disciplines and support discussions of their progress in parent–teacher conferences. In early childhood programs, where developmentally appropriate practice is a priority, documentation can play a major role.
Sara Wilford (2005)

Similar to the portfolio approach, [in Reggio Emilia] documentation of children's work in progress is viewed as an important tool in the learning process for children, teachers and parents.
Eric Ching (2003)

Although each child's portfolio is different they should all provide evidence of the child's progress. The portfolio is therefore the assessment procedure . . . It is the portfolio that provides an overall picture of the child.
Sophie Ioannou-Georgiou & Pavlos Pavlou (2003)

Focus Questions

1. How could you gather information about a child in a way that offers thorough, objective recording but does not rely on standardized tests?

2. How could you ensure that your records about a child's development are as thorough and complete as possible?

3. When would a child be able to contribute to record-keeping about his or her own experiences and learning?

Learning Outcomes

By reading this chapter and applying the ideas to practice, learners will

- understand the philosophy of authentic assessment.
- collect contextual data along with observations and samples to create a developmental portfolio.
- select materials suitable for reflection and analysis as part of an assessment cycle.
- explore documentation systems that display the processes and products of children's experiences and learning.
- advocate for portfolio documentation as part of authentic assessment.

Features of Portfolios

DEFINITION: Portfolio

A **portfolio** is a record-keeping device in which observations, health and social information, test results, work samples, and other significant information about an individual child are stored. The system enables educators to keep records over a period of time, add items as necessary, evaluate the child's performance, evolve plans to meet the child's needs, and review progress. A portfolio offers a **holistic**, or all-round, picture of a child and, therefore, the best data for assessment.

While the child study is undertaken primarily to support a student's learning, the portfolio is done to help a practising teacher find out more about the child, for the child's benefit. In spite of this difference, they have many features in common.

Performance assessment, authentic assessment, and portfolios

Performance assessment is a simple and straightforward practice, with a philosophy behind it that needs to be understood. Performance assessment depends on the child's demonstrating or performing something that shows her understanding of it. It is a way to "show what you know" through demonstration. This way the educator can appreciate the knowledge, skills, and dispositions (attitudes) that the child has gained. Rather than being tested on that knowledge in a more formal way, the child shows her ability as she goes about her day playing and learning. The teacher's task is to document these performances in a way that is meaningful. This may involve observing and recording, videotaping, or keeping product samples.

Performance assessment is a form of **authentic assessment**. The assessment is authentic (or genuine) because it occurs naturally and without stress. An educator applies authentic assessment appropriately when the child's learning experience is also authentic, when the child is self-directed and the process of her learning is considered more important than its products or test results. When developmentally appropriate practice lies at the core of curriculum design, then developmentally appropriate assessment must be aligned with it.

Authentic assessment can take many different forms depending on what the educator thinks is genuine. It is in the interest of the children, families, and the educators to agree on the child's learning experiences and the way those will be assessed. If the educators and parents are comfortable with a philosophy and practice that is developmentally and culturally appropriate to that child, they will want to keep within that philosophy to measure how well the children are performing.

Some educators use the term "performance assessment"; teachers of older children probably use it more often. They may work with the children to develop ways to show what they know. However, the broader term *authentic assessment* is used within childcare and early-years education. It includes all the informal data-collection methods discussed in this book, especially portfolio assessment.

Using portfolios as an assessment approach offers an even broader view of the child and her abilities because it looks beyond separate observations and bits and pieces of information. Portfolios offer a holistic understanding of the child's development within the context of "who she is." The portfolio itself becomes an assessment after the data have been gathered. The adults, and the children themselves—if they are mature enough—reflect on the materials and analyze the learning behind them. This should lead to education and developmental decision-making that benefits the children.

Why some educators are moving to strengthen authentic assessment

Testing versus authentic assessment

There is a movement in education that values **standardized tests** and considers them preferable to portfolio assessment, or to authentic assessment generally. Proponents believe standardized tests offer comparisons at a program level and even support healthy competition between children. These supporters think that standardized measures will increase performance levels, improve accountability, and offer a fair way of measuring performance.

This is not true. As Sacks states in *Standardized Minds* (2000), "Evidence strongly suggests that standardized testing flies in the face of recent advances in our understanding of how people learn to think and reason. Repeatedly, in the research conducted over the past few years, especially in the grade school arena (K–12), one finds evidence that traditional tests reinforce passive rote learning of facts and formulas, quite contrary to the critical thinking skills many educators now believe schools should be encouraging." Although Sacks confines his remarks to the school system, there is no reason to think that the narrow approach of standardized testing is any less abhorrent for younger children!

Later in his book Sacks recommends an approach to assessment that counters the problems entrenched in standardized measurement: authentic assessment. Many educators and researchers support authentic ways of assessing learning. Among them is Gardner, who offers insights into the multiple ways of being smart—the Multiple Intelligences theory. Katz and Chard have researched Italy's **Reggio Emilia**'s documentation process, which is a living monument to authentic learning and documentation.

Global perspective

It is well known that education in Finland is of a high calibre. Finland is one of several countries that lead in exemplary practice in both childcare and education. Pedagogy there binds together learning and assessment, both of which are integral to successful authentic assessment practice. Finland's approach incorporates assessment in a way that complements the authentic learning that occurs in the classroom. Many countries—especially Finland—demonstrate and profess a confidence in authentic assessment that is solid and that emphasizes a new look at the ecological context of development and overall learning.

Around the world authentic assessment is often seen as a reaction to the biases and difficulties embedded in more "traditional" approaches, or what we think of as formal assessment. However, authentic assessment existed long before the testing movement or examination boards. Skills or knowledge acquired in school or everyday life were "tested" when the learner had to demonstrate her new competence—this was in fact authentic assessment! An apprentice carpenter demonstrates his success by his cabinet-making, house-building, or creation of sample objects that highlight his skills. Traditionally, a child's reading ability was monitored by a demonstration—reading a story. More complex learning might require more detailed observations, demonstrations, and perhaps conversation with the learner about any underlying concepts or theories. Mathematical problems, scientific experiments, or even philosophical ideas were assessed using methods that fitted the kind of learning. These might include examining the products of the learner's work, listening to debates between learners, evaluating learners' pieces of writing, reviewing presentations or demonstrations, and observing the candidates in action. Educators used, authentically, whatever method allowed their learners to show what they knew or demonstrate the skills they had acquired.

Swedish early childhood provision before school-age (birth to age six/seven) is not compulsory although it is encouraged. In childcare programs the educators are free to use whatever assessment process they think appropriate. Their philosophy and pedagogy leads most to use observations, and many collect information for portfolio assessment. The government offices of Sweden, called the Regeringskansliet, are responsible for the development and administration of national assessment protocols in the early school years. Typically these are criterion-referenced (measuring performance against a specified yardstick), but data collection includes a broader view than relying on testing alone.

In the states and territories of Australia there is no formal assessment prior to school, but practice varies from place to place; there is widespread use of portfolio assessment, including observational studies. Tasmania has a system of pre-compulsory education and assessment—the Kindergarten Development Check. How data is collected for this varies, but its approach is largely authentic.

Although Hungary's education system has changed with the turn away from communism observable in the past decade, its education system has developed in a structured way. Prior to starting school, children may attend preschool programs, and the five/six-year-olds must gain a kindergarten certificate before starting school. Although this sounds rigorous, the actual assessment is based on authentic assessment principles, and teachers are required to record many observations and other data.

In Britain there has been pressure from educators whose approach is child-centred to use paper-based or online portfolio assessment as a supplement to standardized tests. Even in a school climate of imposed standards (National Curriculum 1992) and testing, many educators have held to the notion of authentic assessment and have used portfolios to round out their documentation. At the centre of the testing versus authentic assessment debate, there is, in the UK, as elsewhere, a conflict between **formative** (monitoring the process of learning) and **summative** (measuring the end-products of learning) assessment. While there is a place for both, formative assessments help us understand the pattern, style, and richness of each child's development in every domain, and summative assessments let us know the child's competence in specific learning areas. These summative assessments are often used as a check that the educator has been teaching the specified content, rather than as a means to understand individual children or develop curriculum that is culturally and developmentally appropriate. England's standardized curriculum has as many flaws as have the mandated curricula of other jurisdictions, but there has been a commitment to create digitized portfolios, as well as use standardized tests. Although Margrave (2008) claims that "international evidence confirms the prominence of the testing culture in England's Primary Schools," the Qualifications and Curriculum authority is studying "e assessments"(electronic assessments) across the curriculum.

Scotland's curriculum (separate from that of England and Wales), "The Curriculum for Excellence" (2004), was shaped by teachers and mandated by the Scottish HMI—Her Majesty's Inspectorate. It outlines specified outcomes for preschool children through to 16+ years. Their system is interesting in that it crosses the typical boundaries between childcare and education seamlessly. This approach appears more adaptable to diverse teaching approaches, including the teacher's discretion about some elements of assessing learning and the development of individual portfolios. The Scottish approach can be characterized as "assessment as part of teaching."

In the United States, approaches to authentic assessment vary from state to state and even within each state. The so-called reform movement and believers in "back to basics" hold that standardized testing improves standards and accountability; their stronghold is sizeable and supported by the No Child Left Behind Act of 2001 (NCLB). However, there are regions where authentic-assessment practices are strong. It seems ironic that the back-to-basics followers have moved further away from the authentic assessment that occurred before educators meddled in it with pseudo-scientific testing methods.

Canadian approaches to authentic assessment vary just as much as they do in the United States and other jurisdictions, being strongest in childcare and early education. Some boards of education in Canadian provinces and territories have adopted forms of

outcomes-based learning (OBL) along with performance assessments. Other forms of authentic assessment can be found through the education system, practices differing even within the same school. Only where there is institutional support can authentic-assessment approaches be really successful.

A full chapter on measuring outcomes can be found in the Instructor's Manual. Readers are guided to collect observational data associated with predetermined learning outcomes.

In addition to discussing the use of authentic assessment and portfolio use according to country, we can look at the philosophies of Montessori, Reggio Emilia, and Waldorf (Steiner), which emanate from Italy (Montessori and Reggio Emilia) and Germany (Waldorf). Although there are dissimilarities between these philosophical approaches to education, each has an interesting and similar sympathetic approach to assessing children's development, and all three document children's experience, achievement, and critical elements of their development. Pope Edwards has researched these three philosophies in practice, and says that

> In all three approaches, children are assessed by means other than traditional tests and grades. Instead, parents receive extensive descriptive information about their children's daily life and progress and share in culminating productions or performances. Portfolios or other products of children's individual and group work may be displayed and sent home at key intervals and transitions. (Spring 2002)

There are other well-recognized philosophical approaches to education and assessment that typically use a form of portfolio assessment. (It should be remembered that practice is not necessarily in a pure form following exactly the same procedures). Friedrich Froebel offered a philosophy that valued the process of unfolding development, and typically Froebel programs and schools use portfolio documentation for program planning as well as individual assessments.

Although Froebel, Waldorf, Emilia, and Montessori have used various types of authentic assessments, including performance-based assessment and portfolio documentation, most of the education based on their respective philosophies takes place in independent childcare centres and schools, rather than mainstream public schools. The late Susan Isaacs, John Dewey, Jean Piaget, A.S. Neil, and others shared some views on children's development and its assessment; they also helped shape the educators of today and their approaches to assessing learning. Today's thinkers, such as Howard Gardner, Steven Pinker, and Lillian Katz, are also making some inroads with both the public and independent systems, and have helped shape ideas about the brain, experience, and how learning occurs, as well as the assessment of learning and children's development based on real-life performances that are observed and understood.

It is frustrating for many educators to find that their own political systems—which claim to be intent on improving their education systems—remain intent on using overly structured teaching approaches and unsatisfactory, limited, and restrictive assessment practices. These rely more on the testing of narrow realms of learning, rather than attempt to capture the child's real experience, understand the child's ever-changing development, and come close to who the child is and what he might need.

Steps toward improving assessment

Over the past two decades or so research has bolstered the argument for the use of authentic assessment, particularly the use of portfolio documentation. For those of us who consider authentic assessment an essential element of practice, as is developmentally and culturally appropriate practice, this news is good. We have a better appreciation of the need to align curriculum and assessment and have them complement each other.

Following are a few reasons opposing educators give for authentic assessment being inappropriate:

- It's too time-consuming.
- I don't understand it.
- What I've been doing has been working OK.
- It's too soft, fluffy, and imprecise.
- It fails to offer grades and numerical scores.
- I need to put children in groups according to ability.
- Parents expect graded reports.
- I don't have the discretion to assess the way I want to do it.

When you have read this chapter, come back to discuss these reasons and see what you agree with and what responses you might make to educators who give these reasons.

What is needed before the use of portfolio assessment is commonplace:

1. Lessons must be learned from best practices in authentic assessment.
2. Further research needs to be undertaken to determine the future potential of authentic assessment.
3. Educators need to appreciate that authentic assessment must be aligned with authentic learning (and vice versa).
4. Demonstration sites practising authentic assessment and portfolio documentation need to be used as learning places for teachers, parents, politicians, and community members.
5. Governments must be persuaded (using good evidence) that "back to basics" (and along with it, the dependence on only standardized scores) is a negative reversion to practice prior to our current understanding of children's development and learning.
6. Childcare centres and schools must demonstrate the advantages of authentic assessment to all their stakeholders (parents, educators, community members).
7. Authentic assessment, including records of achievement throughout the education system, needs to show how it benefits children, families, educators, and even future employers.
8. There needs to be improved understanding about how children develop and learn—and consequently how they should be assessed
9. There needs to be a shift away from a dependence on standardized testing.
10. The trust in educators, that they know best about this area, needs improvement.

Before implementing a portfolio assessment system or any other authentic assessment approach, it is worthwhile to discuss the issue fully and appreciate the help you will need, the hurdles you must overcome, and more importantly, the benefits you can expect.

The most obvious form of portfolio is one created mostly in a paper-based way. As you will read in this chapter, that is the most common at present. While there are many reasons to go this way, be aware that there are ways of avoiding gathering endless piles of material that need to be sorted, stored, and accessed. Technology now allows for the traditional paper-based portfolio to be digitized. Also there is software available that enables the user to gather specific items. As you review such programs, ensure that they meet your philosophical perspective; they may appeal to you merely because of their glossy appearance and speed of documentation rather than for more genuine reasons.

Barrett shifted the authentic-assessment process into a new technology-assisted generation. Companies even market trademarked portfolio systems—such as Focused Portfolios and the Work Sampling System—developed for those teachers who want a ready-to-use process for documentation. So that authentic approaches to learning and assessment are easily recognizable, names like "The Mindful School," "Total Talent Portfolios," "School-wide Enrichment Model," and "Essential Schools" are coined, denoting the kind of authenticity each represents. Each of these names is intended to conjure a vision of authenticity and exemplary practice. In another irony, the systems that these companies recommend may lead educators to impose structures that actually disallow the flexible authenticity that was their selling point! Many software programs are available—we do not want to influence your purchases by emphasizing brand names.

Educators who start to develop, or continue developing, authentic assessments tend to demonstrate the following characteristics. They

- are motivated.
- can articulate their beliefs about authentic learning clearly.
- are independent.
- are practitioners who reflect on their role as educators.
- work cooperatively with parents and team members.
- find time for what they think is important.
- develop their own systems for managing data.
- value critical thinking.
- exhibit role-model dispositions they want the children to demonstrate.
- facilitate the environment without dominating it.
- share power effectively.
- advocate authentic assessment.

Educators who use authentic assessment methods do so because they

- dislike standardized tests and consider their use unfair.
- regard authentic assessment as part of authentic learning.
- may have had negative personal-assessment experiences themselves.
- understand how children learn.
- focus on children's success—perhaps by being less competitive.
- recognize the damage done by labelling a child.
- contextualize learning.

- consider formative assessment usually more important than summative assessment.
- want to gather information from multiple sources.
- consider individual programming important.

- consider conceptual, broad real-world learning central to their philosophy (rather than narrow memory-based skills).
- wish to align curriculum and assessment.

We can appreciate that a move to portfolio assessment, or any other kind of authentic assessment, is challenging. The shift means change at the philosophical level as authentic assessment is an integral part of authentic learning.

We know that changing surface practices are unlikely to work effectively. On one level, having a mosaic of educational practices within one institution may sound desirable, as such an array might reflect the separate beliefs of each educator. However, only a cohesive approach, along with a shared philosophy of learning and assessment, can produce a community of successful learners within any place of learning, be it a school or a childcare environment. An authentic approach is vital.

The portfolio philosophy

KEY FEATURES: Portfolio

- is part of authentic assessment
- contains a variety of observations, samples, and contextual information
- documents development over a period of time
- considers development an individual and holistic process
- analyzes and assesses development sympathetically within the individual's context
- is mostly naturalistic

A portfolio is much more than a collection of information. It is an attitude and a process. While it is relatively easy to describe the potential contents of a portfolio, it is more challenging to generate enthusiasm for the concept of portfolio evaluation and record-keeping and to get each member of the team to participate in the process of data collection.

Several principles underlie the portfolio philosophy:

- The process of a child's experience is important and individual to that child.
- The most effective way to record information about a child's experience is to observe the child in a natural setting—that is, at home, in a childcare centre, or at school.
- Information about a child is most usefully supplied by parents, teachers, caregivers, and others who play a role in the child's life.

- Portfolios provide the opportunity to record data about a child's experiences and evidence of the products of his work.
- Portfolios enable the parents, teachers, and caregivers in a child's life to be involved with both the formative assessment and the summative assessment of his performance, skills, and competence, based on a valid collection of data.
- Portfolios encourage teamwork and cooperation among all those concerned in the care and growth of the child, in support of meeting his needs over the years.
- Portfolios offer the possibility of recording family health and contextual information, which puts the behavioural data into a framework.
- Portfolios encourage the child's involvement in the record-keeping process and selection of items for inclusion, a sense of responsibility and ownership for his behaviour, and a sense of control in determining the education experience in the long term.
- Portfolios are flexible in meeting the requirements of those adults caring for the child as they can contain various types of information.
- Portfolios may include input from additional professionals, as desirable; psychologists, social workers, and others may add to the portfolio to expand the information base and frequently they can validate the findings of the primary caregivers and parents.
- Portfolios encourage professional **accountability** by providing documentary evidence of evaluation processes and program planning.

With practice, teachers and caregivers will see the value of the portfolio process. Those who say they observe all the time but do not record their observations will recognize that portfolios can help them do their jobs more effectively with the investment of only a little time and effort.

Furnished with information from a variety of sources, the teacher may be better equipped to understand children's needs and to see how their families and contexts should determine how those needs are met. Agencies that subscribe to the portfolio philosophy usually find that the practice supports close work with parents and a cooperative style of teaching. At a time when parents, boards of education, and other administrative bodies are demanding greater professional accountability, the portfolio provides good documentation of evaluation, planning, and practice.

Contents of a portfolio

CHILD DEVELOPMENT FOCUS

Portfolios may assist in observing, recording, and analyzing

- holistic development
- the process and products of development
- a child's culture and context in which she is developing
- a child's development in relation to the norm or goal achievement

Teachers and caregivers vary in their philosophies regarding record-keeping. The portfolio approach is flexible enough that all practitioners can adapt it to their needs.

The following list suggests the items a portfolio might contain. Those employing the system will want to choose those elements that suit them, their skills, the agency or school, and the child.

- health records (parent questionnaire, information from a physician)
- notes forwarded from previous care-giving agencies
- psychologists' reports
- social workers' notes
- photographs of special moments in the child's life
- photographs of things the child has made
- special items the child has selected
- artwork samples
- samples of the child's writing
- the child's own records-of-achievement journal
- a learning log of the child's lifetime experiences
- questionnaire responses
- **anecdotal records** (see Chapter 3)
- **running records** or **specimen records** (see Chapter 3)

- **event samplings** and **time samplings** (see Chapter 4)
- **developmental checklists** (see Chapter 5)
- contextual information (parent questionnaire, objective notes, **genogram**, **ecomap**, **life-experience flow chart**, etc.) (see Chapter 6)
- infant **charts** (see Chapter 6)
- **rating scales** (see Chapter 6)
- photographs of the child (passive or in action) (see Chapter 7)
- audiotapes of the child's language, reading, or music (see Chapter 7)
- videotapes of the child's activities (see Chapter 7)
- assessment results from standardized tests (see Chapter 11)
- summary of skills (see Chapter 9)
- **analysis** (see Chapter 9)

Using child studies to learn about development

A child study contains in-depth information and an analysis of one child's life and behaviour. Students frequently conduct child studies to understand more about child development. This can be a good way to get to know and understand an individual child. The study may include any of the contents of a developmental portfolio, with emphasis on an analysis of the child's development at one particular point. The study is usually more for the benefit of the student than that of the child; by carrying it out, the student develops skills in gathering data, selecting pertinent material, and analyzing all the information within a developmental framework.

Advantages

- A child study provides the opportunity to study one child in depth.
- The study reveals each aspect of the child's development in relation to that of the other children.
- Contextual information helps the observer make inferences that are more valid.

- The observer appreciates the changing process of development by gathering information over a period of time.
- A variety of observations and accumulated information can produce a more accurate picture of the child.
- The detail of analysis can surpass the detail produced by any other evaluation method.
- As a strong learning experience, a child study supports the student later in carrying out portfolio assessments in practice.

Disadvantages

- A focus on one child cannot be the basis for generalizations about all children.
- The observer's close connection with the child may mean that the inferences that the observer draws are more subjective.
- The process is time-consuming and cumbersome.
- The study may not lead to any direct benefit for the child studied.
- All children in the group cannot be studied in the same depth.
- The student may make inappropriate inferences that are not challenged.
- The observer may not evaluate the large volume of material in sufficient detail to offer adequate feedback.

Using portfolios for ongoing evaluation and record-keeping

Advantages

- A portfolio provides for a comprehensive record-keeping process.
- A portfolio allows a variety of observations and information to be kept together.
- Professionals and parents can see the records and make additions.
- The record can be used at any time.
- Information is stored over a long period and can be passed on from one agency or school to the next.
- The process includes deliberate parental involvement.
- A portfolio provides for the most rigorous, thorough, and developmentally appropriate assessment because its contents are so diverse.
- Informal and formal records may be kept alongside each other, which helps identify program intentions.
- A portfolio provides for ongoing assessment. It allows for more immediate responses than some other assessment procedures.
- The system can be adapted to whatever the child's needs and abilities.
- Both the process and the product of the child's experience can be recorded.
- The child values the portfolio-assessment process, as it validates the importance of his activity.
- Keeping portfolios accommodates a wide variety of teaching and caregiving philosophies.

Disadvantages

- A portfolio requires effort to be kept up-to-date and this is time-consuming.
- A portfolio can become more of a sentimental memory box than a valid assessment tool.
- A substantial amount of file space is required.
- The focus may be deflected from the process of the child's learning to overzealous record-keeping.
- Information may be stored without having been evaluated regularly.
- The criteria for inclusion of items in the record may not be clear.
- Teachers need training in what to look for when choosing samples.
- Meetings may be required for teamwork planning.

Types of Portfolios

Baby book

Perhaps the most commonly used portfolio is the **baby book** that parents keep. Parents can use ready-made albums or create their own to record the significant happenings in their children's lives and to map out developmental **milestones**. Some parents may wish to maintain the book until the children reach school age, or even until the children leave home. These records might contain some of the following:

- a list of homes/accommodation where the child has lived
- a family tree
- copies of newspaper headlines on the day of his or her birth
- a lock of hair
- hand- and footprints
- lists of favourite foods, toys, etc.
- feeding and sleeping records
- caregiver information
- developmental milestones
- photographs
- religious information
- lists of gifts
- name information, record of naming ceremonies
- "firsts": words, events at daycare or school, party, steps, etc.
- artwork
- anecdotes, funny things the child said or did
- health and immunization records (dates of infectious diseases)

Some items might be included for sentimental reasons, to give the parents a concrete reminder of the child's early years. The book could also serve as a way of storing health or developmental information that may be required later.

Life book

A **life book** can be started at any stage of a child's life. It attempts to capture the individual nature of the child's own story. Initiated by a parent, guardian, social worker, adoption and fostering worker, or other childcare employee, the book can be passed on, with the child, from one person to another involved in the child's care. The child can benefit directly from such documentation. Changes, both happy and sad, should be included so that the child can reflect on her own experiences and story. Agencies may use this kind of portfolio to support mental health, particularly when the child is undergoing transitions in parenting, home, or caregiving, or other potentially traumatic changes.

A life book may contain some of the following:

- photographs of the parents/guardian
- a family tree
- pictures of significant people
- personal narratives
- pictures of significant places/homes
- small sentimental objects
- lists of favourites: foods, games, objects
- birthday greetings
- mementoes from outings and other special occasions
- developmental charts
- health information, immunization schedules
- letters from friends and family members
- tape recordings of people, music, etc.
- religious affiliation records, initiations
- club membership cards, friendship souvenirs
- artwork

Learning log

While a **learning log** is not in itself a full portfolio, it can form part of a solid record documenting a child's learning. The log, written by a teacher or, later, by the child, tracks the child's activity and thinking. There are two parts to this kind of log. One records the program plan, curriculum activity, or experience, and the other records how the child responded to the experience—that is, what he or she "learned." The log system requires a teacher to be diligent in record-keeping. It can provide a detailed analysis of what the child is learning. For the child who has a diagnosed **special need**, this type of record-keeping can supply data to be interpreted as part of the planning process. For teachers with large numbers of children in their care, or for whom curriculum planning is more spontaneous, this method might not be as useful as others.

Older children capable of documenting their own experiences may keep logs, under their teachers' direction, in which they record their responses to classroom or other activities. Either the teacher or the child can maintain a more informal type of log, a **record of achievement**, an anecdotal record of skill development and achievements. The record of achievement allows for reflection and critical thinking, as well as actual achievements.

Learning Log		
Date	Curriculum experience	Response

Child study

The student's assignment may require certain components or focus on particular aspects of development. Through the child study, the student appreciates the complexity of the child's context and development. As discussed earlier, the child study gives the observer the chance to study a child for the benefit of the observer's own learning rather than for the child's benefit. The student focuses on one child as objectively as possible, and to achieve a more personal view of that child's experience and development. Critics of the child-study approach say that it tends to be subjective and produces information that cannot be considered statistically significant. While this criticism may be valid to a degree, child studies can also offer educators important insights into the individuality of the developmental process.

Curriculum-based portfolio

Teachers can base their records on the formative evaluation of the children in particular curriculum areas. Formatted to record information about the curriculum experiences offered and the group and individual responses to the experiences, the curriculum portfolio documents the process of curriculum development, an evaluation of its effectiveness, and data on which to base further planning.

A teacher who is responsible for one or more particular aspects of the curriculum usually develops curriculum-based portfolios. Various choices present themselves:

- What is the purpose of the portfolio and how should it be constructed?
- Should the portfolio document the process or the products of learning?
- Is it best to follow the progress of individual children or the learning of the whole group?
- How might the portfolio develop over time?
- Who is going to collect, select, and reflect on the contents?

Curriculum-Based Class Portfolio			
Date	Curriculum area/activity	Group response (anecdotal record)	Individual outcomes

- What is a useful assessment cycle and an appropriate time frame for collecting and analyzing the contents?
- To what extent will the children be involved with the portfolio processes of collection and reflection?

Educators who use curriculum portfolios do so to improve their delivery of the curriculum. They might focus on a content area, such as math, science, or language arts, or on a more general notion of documenting whatever learning the children demonstrate. These portfolios often become part of a teacher's own **professional portfolio**, showing clearly what he or she does best.

Professional portfolios

Society increasingly demands that educators be accountable in all aspects of their roles. At the same time teachers want to monitor their own professional and personal development, evaluate their performance, and determine future directions for themselves. The professional portfolio provides teachers with an open-ended tool to

- document the learning of the children for whom they are responsible.
- include observations and samples of the children's work while linking the curriculum and program goals.
- record pertinent information associated with their own teaching and learning experiences.
- store memorabilia associated with teaching, such as thank-you cards, letters of appreciation from parents, and other items such as photographs and newsletters that represent their time with a group of children.
- keep letters of reference, certificates, grade reports, and professional-development attendance sheets.
- write a personal-philosophy statement.

- evaluate the delivery of the program.
- comment on each artifact included in the portfolio.
- demonstrate the achievement of a professional standard, licensing standard, program outcomes, and other professional benchmarks.

The process of portfolio development is often considered an enlightening professional development activity. Through the refinement of collecting the materials, careful performance evaluation, and forward planning, the teacher becomes a more **reflective practitioner**. This person plans carefully, reflects regularly, is sensitive to feedback, adapts to people and circumstances as they change, and furthers his or her professional career at the same time.

Learning-assessment portfolio/record of achievement

Either a teacher or a child, as he matures and moves into adolescence, can keep an individual learning-assessment portfolio to detail the child's own learning. This kind of portfolio documents general experiences, as well as more formal learning situations. Experience is described in terms of the **competencies** the child has achieved as a result of that experience. These **learning outcomes** are then analyzed to establish what the experience has enabled the child to do.

Teachers and learners at all stages of their education find the learning-assessment portfolio a useful device. The process of recording and examining experiences forces the individual to really learn and to evaluate that learning.

An early childhood educator may wish to log a child's experiences day by day and evaluate the effectiveness of the program by determining and recording her newly acquired competence. This requires practice in recording behaviourial information, but once having mastered it the educator ensures that the portfolio tracks the child's learning.

With help, older children can log their own experiences and what they have learned from them. Identifying what has been learned helps the child consolidate what he has learned.

More mature children may want to explore their experiences to express their learning outcomes in terms of acquired competencies. Learning to evaluate their own experiences and determine their skills will equip them eventually to gain credit and access to college and university programs, and may prove useful one day in job evaluations too. This idea is gaining more and more acceptance in education. To start this process in early childhood settings will help the child who is growing up in the currently changing education and work environments.

Program-documentation portfolios

The idea behind program documentation is to record the evolution of learning of a group of children. This is a key part of the project approach that centres on project-based learning (see Chard 1999).

A **project** is defined as "an in-depth investigation of a real world topic worthy of children's attention and effort" (Chard 2005). This approach to learning, experiential and action-based, focuses on children's own inquiry. Every project has several phases, but typically a project ends in "communicating, sharing and presenting their work . . . by personalizing new knowledge." A project has both a process and products. Typically, the process is documented using a variety of observations, project mapping, photographs, and other materials that are produced. The end products may also include the items used throughout the process, but mainly they offer various forms of explanation of what has been learned by the participants, such as plays, demonstrations, models, and performances. These, when recorded, form a portfolio.

The Reggio Emilia philosophy, also a complex form of documentation, values the work of the group of children as well as the activity of each individual child. The documentation supports "learning made visible," a term describing the photographic records, narrative descriptions, children's artwork, and individual and group depictions of learning. The documentation also allows families to become more involved with their children's education, supplies educators with a tool for reflection, and at the same time encourages children to think critically about what they have been doing. This reflective process is known as **metacognition** (thinking about thinking) and it is crucial to complex project development.

The Reggio Emilia approach has taken project-learning and documentation to new levels of success—ones that many educators are trying to replicate in their North American classrooms and childcare centres. The interest in Reggio Emilia may reflect the need for educators and children to be motivated and engaged in learning and assessment in ways that the current systems of direct instruction and standardized tests do not make possible. Howard Gardner and others from the Harvard Graduate School of Education have undertaken Project Zero, a research project that explores how people learn and work together in groups by observing the work in Reggio Emilia, Italy. The findings of their study are presented in the book *Making Learning Visible*, which examines how to keep records in the context of individual and group learning.

Another form of assessment based on documentation has been developed that seamlessly blends together curriculum and assessment. Well-prepared early childhood educators employ the *YMCA Playing to Learn* curriculum with young children in appropriately designed environments. The philosophy behind it is somewhat eclectic, being informed by Froebel in the 1890s, Vygotsky from the 1960s, Yardley and Erikson in the 1970s, and Suzuki, Gardner, Katz, and several other 1980s and 1990s educators. More current, up-to-date neuroscientific findings are also reflected in this curriculum approach. It emphasizes play as the means of learning, incorporating curriculum and assessment into the program simultaneously by means of thorough documentation. As with the Reggio Emilia approach, *YMCA Playing to Learn* promotes displaying, as well as documenting, children's work—their play—so that play is honoured, shared, and reflected on. The documentation process contains the following elements:

- anecdotes based on day-to-day observations (see Observation Sample 8.2)
- ongoing developmental review
- representative samples of children's work
- photographic and audio-records of the processes and products of children's learning
- notes from colleagues who also teach the child
- notes from conversations with parents and, on occasion, other professionals

Observation Sample 8.1

This is an example of a project built from the children's interests. It might be included in a program-documentation portfolio. Although it seems complex, it was carried out by a group of four- and five-year-olds. How the project was documented is explained; both the teacher and children contributed to recording the information. How does this project differ from a teacher-directed theme, and how does the documentation contribute to the children's learning?

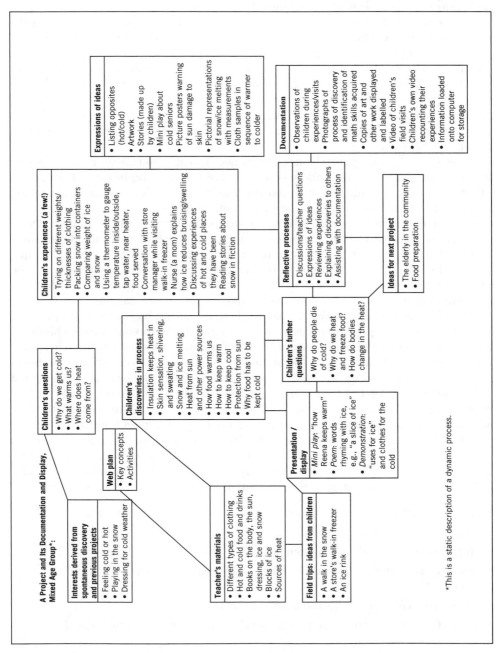

A Project and Its Documentation and Display, Mixed Age Group*:

Interests derived from spontaneous discovery and previous projects
- Feeling cold or hot
- Playing in the snow
- Dressing for cold weather

Children's questions
- Why do we get cold?
- What warms us?
- Where does heat come from?

Web plan
- Key concepts
- Activities

Teacher's materials
- Different types of clothing
- Hot and cold food and drinks
- Books on the body, the sun, dressing, ice and snow
- Blocks of ice
- Sources of heat

Field trips: ideas from children
- A walk in the snow
- A store's walk-in freezer
- An ice rink

Children's experiences (a few)
- Trying on different weights/thicknesses of clothing
- Packing snow into containers
- Comparing weight of ice and snow
- Using a thermometer to gauge temperature inside/outside, tap water, near heater, food served
- Conversation with store manager while visiting walk-in freezer
- Nurse (a mom) explains how ice reduces bruising/swelling of hot and cold places they have been
- Discussing experiences
- Reading stories about snow in fiction

Children's discoveries: in process
- Insulation keeps heat in
- Skin sensation, shivering, and sweating
- Snow and ice melting
- Heat from sun and other power sources
- How food warms us
- How to keep warm
- How to keep cool
- Protection from sun
- Why food has to be kept cold

Children's further questions
- Why do people die of cold?
- Why do we heat and freeze food?
- How do bodies change in the heat?

Presentation / display
- *Mini play:* "how Reena keeps warm"
- *Poem:* words rhyming with ice, e.g. "a slice of ice"
- *Demonstration:* "uses for ice" and clothes for the cold

Expressions of ideas
- Listing opposites (hot/cold)
- Artwork
- Stories (made up by children)
- Mini play about cold seniors
- Picture posters warning of sun damage to skin
- Pictorial representations of snow/ice melting with measurements
- Cloth samples in sequence of warmer to colder

Reflective processes
- Discussions/teacher questions
- Expressions of ideas
- Reviewing experiences
- Explaining discoveries to others
- Assisting with documentation

Ideas for next project
- The elderly in the community
- Food preparation

Documentation
- Observations of children during experiences/visits
- Photographs of process of discovery and identification of math skills acquired
- Copies of art and other work displayed and labelled
- Video of children's field visits
- Children's own video recounting their experiences
- Information loaded onto computer for storage

*This is a static description of a dynamic process.

The *Playing to Learn* curriculum specifies how to align curriculum and assessment. As well as providing an assessment of interacting groups of children, it serves as a comprehensive mechanism for overall program review with direction for supporting individual children. The variety and complexity of the documentation allows for a fuller review of what is really happening within the program than most other types of portfolio. Thus armed, educators can make informed decisions about implementing the play-based curriculum, as well as what and where to focus their attention. These educators are prepared to deliver the curriculum and to make assessments founded on refined professional skills.

Digital/electronic portfolios

In the course of Chapter 7's discussion of how technology can support observation and assessment through various media, there was mention of the use of digital portfolios. At the begining of this chapter they were also mentioned. They add a new dimension to how portfolio documentation, assessment, and curriculum planning can work together.

As already pointed out, Finland has a reputation for progressive and successful education practice; that country shares the same reputation regarding digital-portfolio development. Their model offers a great deal to those who live and practise in other parts of the world. Marja Kankaanranta of the University of Jyväskylä has led a recent study, publishing the research as a text, *Developing Digital Portfolios for Childhood Education* (2002). She and her colleagues adopted an ecological model as the philosophical premise for portfolio development. Mindful of Bronfenbrenner's model of **ecological systems** (see Chapters 2 and 6), the ecological model explains the different social systems within which each child functions, and the portfolio ensures that these are represented through both data-collection and assessment processes. The concept here incorporates technology-enriched learning environments that actually shape learning; the information ecology prompts an evolution in the chains of interdependence. (As the technology is adopted it alters the way we communicate and what we communicate.) The project clearly advocates an ethical use of technology because of its potential power.

In practical terms this model of digital portfolio follows the processes by which we learn. Technology heightens that learning for both educators and children. It encourages reflection and metacognition. This raises the portfolio process above basic data collection and storage. The digital portfolio becomes part of the learning process rather than an add-on assessment function. A real challenge for the project lies in the ethical considerations associated with digitizing information—the practicalities of collecting, sifting, and storing information. The ethical issues have become more important regarding limited access to data, excluding identifiable personal material, to what extent the technology should shape the process, who shares responsibility for controlling the contents of the portfolio, and the ongoing concern that, however detailed those contents, they can never adequately reveal the identity of the learner. We can learn from Finland's experience and employ the technology, taking advantage of some preliminary discussion about these issues. But after all this, many educators may consider acquiring the computer skills and accessing the hardware their primary concern!

Observation Sample 8.2

This is an example of the YMCA Playing to Learn *curriculum and assessment documentation.*

Compare and contrast it with the traditional assessment process and typical observation methodologies.

Purses and Bags

The infants were very curious about the large paper bag that I brought in and left in the middle of the playroom floor. Simryn and Claire were the first to venture over to see what was inside the bag. Megan and Conor were not far behind. Claire stuck her head inside the bag and pulled out a blue purse, which she carried over to the climber to investigate. Simryn felt that the black backpack went better with her ensemble. She put the straps around her neck and off she went. Conor could not decide what item to choose and after examining them thoroughly, he selected a white purse that he then draped over his body. Megan chose the black shiny purse and the red gift bag. All of the children moved about the room with their new acquisitions, opening and closing them, filling them with blocks and small toys, dumping them out and repeating the actions. The purses and bags remained in the classroom for two weeks, and the children never grew tired of them. They seemed to find new and different ways of playing with them every day.

Note: This was such a good example of functional, imitative play. They were not exactly role-playing, but they did engage in pretend activities. It was interesting to see how their choices reflected other aspects of their personalities. It was also interesting to see how many other aspects of development came into their investigations. Simryn, for example, discovered that her feet and legs fit inside the big white shopping bag.

The Purpose of the Portfolio

Before starting any kind of portfolio, the educator must have a clear vision or intention. Because there are so many different types, contents, selection processes, and assessment protocols, everyone involved with the portfolio must understand its concept and agree on its focus.

Some of the main reasons for developing portfolios in childcare and education are to

- document a child's development and learning
- store relevant formal documents
- demonstrate a child's abilities
- reveal interactions between children
- collate children's artwork and work samples
- identify children's needs (including any special needs)
- document for purposes of accountability
- record stages of curriculum delivery
- help student teachers understand children's development
- evaluate the achievement of specified learning outcomes
- provide opportunity for teacher reflection
- encourage children's reflection and self-evaluation
- assess a child's overall development in an authentic and culturally sensitive way
- communicate with parents
- design curriculum and guidance strategies
- create a lasting document of the child that is both holistic and contextualized
- evaluate the program's effectiveness at meeting children's needs

Most teachers will incorporate some, but not all, of these potential purposes in their use of portfolios. In any case they need to articulate which of these purposes they are considering. Most teachers will keep their intentions broad, more in keeping with open-ended portfolio assessments, while some will state particular portfolio goals.

Portfolio Entries
Health records

Health information should be updated regularly. A child's health history is an ongoing, changing record that needs additions as new health and growth information becomes available. This type of data will help you know the child better, and also enable you to respond to her needs. Health conditions affect a child's development and are therefore an important part of her portfolio. A child health-information questionnaire is best completed with the parent at an interview. Students should ask only those questions that help them understand the child's development. Use an additional updating sheet to make more entries as needed. Because of the strong correlation among growth, health, and development, it may be a good idea to include measurements as the child grows. (Chapter 6 suggests prepared formats for height, weight, immunization, feeding, and sleeping charts. A sample health questionnaire is given in Observation Sample 8.3.)

TAKING A SPECIAL LOOK: Pre-natal and neonatal conditions

Some babies are born with fetal alcohol syndrome (FAS) or other pre-natal and neonatal conditions caused by the mothers' exposure to alcohol, illegal or prescription drugs, or other chemicals. Teachers and caregivers working directly with such children may observe particular behaviours. Very young babies may be underweight, breathe poorly, and even suffer from withdrawal. More lasting effects may include diminished intelligence, learning disabilities, and problems in social adaptation.

Increasing numbers of children contract HIV from their mothers. Parents may decide to keep this information to themselves, fearing that their children will be excluded from agencies or schools, or cut off socially. While caregivers may observe behavioural or appearance changes that might indicate illness, they cannot diagnose these symptoms or any other diseases themselves. They must always follow "universal precautions" to ensure that infections of any type are not spread.

Contextual information

A working portfolio makes much more sense and is likely to be interpreted more accurately if it contains some **contextual information**. You might make some of the entries according to observation; you will probably have to rely on parental input for a large amount of background information. An initial interview in the child's home can help forge links between home and the agency you represent. There is a fine line between asking for information that is pertinent and asking questions that seem to be none of your business. Conduct these interviews as an informal chat rather than a long question-and-answer-type questionnaire process.

"Why do you want to know that?" is a fairly typical and reasonable question. If you can explain why the information is helpful to you before you ask any questions, the parents' response is more likely to be favourable. Parents can decline to offer information. You must respect this decision.

TAKING A SPECIAL LOOK: Prolonged illness

When children are sick for a long period of time, they may regress to some extent in their development, particularly in the emotional domain. For example, a child with chronic asthma may be hospitalized whenever he has a serious attack. Such children might have great intellectual potential, but they may need special stimulation to encourage their play activity.

The background information form shown in Observation Sample 8.4 may help you know what to ask. Review the questions ahead of time. You may have to modify areas according to legal requirements, your understanding of the need to ask the questions, and the parents' comfort level. The parents are not to complete the questionnaire directly,

Observation Sample 8.3

This health questionnaire was completed by interviewing the child's mother. The information will help the caregivers provide appropriate care, ease the transition from home to daycare, and assess the child's development.

How might you determine the appropriateness of questions? How might you alter some of these questions if you thought the parent might be uncomfortable answering them?

Health Questionnaire

Child's name: _Katie_   Date: _October 29/08_

Age/D.O.B.: _June 2/05_   Recorder: _Tanya_

BIRTH HISTORY

1. At birth, what was your child's length? _52 cm_ and weight? _3.5 kg_

2. What was the length of your pregnancy? _42 weeks_

3. Please describe any complications: _She was not positioned properly; her head was facing the wrong way at delivery._

4. What was the child's state of health at birth (jaundice)? _Born with Trachea Malacia (premature windpipe-closing) of windpipe. The cartilage in her windpipe wasn't formed, very soft. Her airway would close when she cried or fed._

5. Please describe your child's health after birth: _She was ill a lot, breathing complications. In and out of the hospital for her first year. She is much better now._

DEVELOPMENTAL PATTERNS

6. Do you think your child's growth is fairly steady?   (YES)   NO

7. What is your child's approximate weight now? _16 kg_

BEHAVIOURAL PATTERNS

8. Do you consider your child to be outgoing?   (YES)   NO   SOMETIMES

9. Do you consider your child to be shy?   YES   NO   (SOMETIMES)

10. Are there people or objects that comfort your child when s/he's upset? _Mom, Elmo blanket, and her babies (dolls)_

DAILY ROUTINES

11. Does your child generally enjoy mealtime?   (YES)   NO

12. Does your child have any diet restrictions? (cultural, religious, food allergy or sensitivity)   YES   (NO)
    Although I do not allow her to have pop and chocolate (very rare).

13. Please describe an average day on the weekend for your child. Please include when s/he wakes up, feeding, sleeping, and play times until s/he goes to bed in the evening. _8-9 wake up, wash, change diaper, brush hair, teeth. 9:30 breakfast. 10-12 play, watch TV, go outside, on swings, games, neighbours come over. Use potty. 12:30 eat lunch, clean up. 1-5 have snacks, use potty, go visiting at Grandma's, stay home and play, clean together, out for walks. 5:30-6:00 help get dinner prepared. 6:00 dinner_

6:30-7:00 brush teeth, use potty, bedtime story. 7:30 bed.

HEALTH STATUS

14. Do any family members have known allergies or chronic conditions?   YES   NO
    If YES, what: _____ Allergies

15. Has your child had any allergic reactions? (environmental, food, animals, or medications)   YES   NO
    Please explain which allergen and the severity: _____ Grass, hayfever—aggravates asthma

16. Has your child ever been to a medical specialist?   YES   NO
    If YES, what was the ailment? _____ Asthma and premature windpipe

17. Does your child take medication on a regular basis?   YES   NO
    If YES, which medication(s)? _____ Vanceril (for asthma)

18. Please describe your child's general health. (e.g., recurrent ear infections, skin conditions, colds)
    Health has improved over last few months; she does seem to catch colds quite often.

19. Is your child ill on a fairly regular basis?   YES   NO

20. Which infectious diseases has your child had?

Mumps	YES	NO
Whooping cough	YES	NO
Measles	YES	NO
Chicken pox	YES	NO
Meningitis	YES	NO
Pneumonia	YES	NO

IMMUNIZATION RECORD

21. Please list your child's immunization schedule:

IMMUNIZATION TYPE	DATE RECEIVED	ANY REACTIONS
DPT	August 2/05	-
DPT	October 25/05	-
DPT	January 30/06	-
MM Rubella	approx. 12 months old	-
DPT	January 24/07	-

Father and son enjoy time together in a provincial park. This weekend activity was a meaningful experience for the toddler; one that might be shared with his child care educators and included in his portfolio.

although they must be asked for input and allowed access to what has been recorded. It is more useful to use the questions as a basis for discussion. When you record data, gain permission from the parents to do so beforehand. Most jurisdictions have freedom-of-information and privacy provisions of which you should be aware, as your information-gathering processes must comply with such legislation. A full set of contextual information may also include a sociological survey of the child's home neighbourhood.

Observations

Observations are an essential part of the portfolio. They are the core to which you add the other components. You will choose your observational methods on the basis of the developmental information they can reveal. You will have to exercise a variety of styles, repeating some. Refer to the chapters on different methods of observation to help you with your choices.

Unless you focus on what a child can do and observe his behaviour in a natural setting, you will not be able to make adequate evaluations. The central part of the portfolio will be observations from both home and the care agency or school. Those written by the professionals require **objectivity** and detail; parents' contributions should be valued even if they are not written in the format and language of the teacher or in a completely objective fashion.

Not all your written observations will, or could, be included in the portfolio; you will be selecting from that material. Choose the observations that offer the most up-to-date or significant developmental information.

You can make copies of blank observation forms available for parents to complete. Some may be more comfortable with giving you oral anecdotes of what they have seen. Record them on a parent sheet if that works best.

Observation Sample 8.4

These questions were put together by an ECE student to gather contextual information about a child. Rather than ask the parents to fill out a formal questionnaire, the student met with the child's mother to learn about the family through informal conversation.

Background Information

Recorded by: _Simon_   Date: _November 7, 2007_

Method of recording: _Interview with mother_

Child's name: _Robert_   Pet name: _Robbie_

What is the composition of your family? (# of adults/children) _Four adults and one child (Robbie). He lives with mom, dad, uncle, maternal grandma, and grandpa. Grandpa works in the Middle East, and he sometimes lives there._

What links do you have with your extended family? (aunts, grandparents, etc.) _We are all very close. Robbie usually meets with his paternal grandparents, aunts, and uncles every weekend._

Are there any special activities that your family enjoys doing together? _Birthday parties, picnics, Christmas, Thanksgiving dinner, and we usually have a Halloween party at the house._

What kind of home do you have? _We live in a condominium townhouse with a small yard shared with neighbours_

Do you see yourself as belonging to any particular cultural, religious, national, or ethnic background or heritage? _We are a mix: Catholic, Islamic, and Trinidadian. Robbie goes to a Catholic church._

What languages are spoken in your home? _Creole, French, and English._

Is there any special information about your family? (e.g., particular talents, family experiences, interests, special needs, home moves, or stories) _We are all interested in sports. I play soccer in the Ontario Soccer Association. His uncle is a soccer player too._

Do you work outside the home? _No. I used to work at Consumers Gas as a clerk._

What are your current childcare arrangements? _Robbie attends the childcare centre at Centennial College, where I am taking classes._

What were your previous arrangements for childcare? _My grandma used to take care of him – that is, his great-grandma._

Do you have pets in your home? If so, what? _No, we used to have a cat, but when the baby was born we got rid of it._

In your family, do you have special words for things? (e.g., toilet = pee-pee) _In my family, we are used to calling the toilet a "potty."_

What do you hope for your child when s/he grows up? _To have a heart, be able to make good decisions, enjoy life to the fullest and all it has to offer. But most of all, to have an education, so that he will become somebody in the world. It might be hard, but I don't want him to give up ever!_

A parent's spontaneous comments may not always be the best record. A mother may tell you about her child's reaction to catching his parents in an intimate moment or may tell you how exasperated she is about her child's irritating habit of nose-picking. These comments may not be appropriate to keep in a formal record. On the other hand, you might see the validity of including accounts of how the child first slept through the night, rejected breast-feeding, or became more cooperative in play with his cousins. These professional decisions are based on understanding what is significant.

Parental input

We, as educators, can sometimes think that we provide the most significant influences in a child's life. This is not true; parents are the centre of the child's world, and our task is to support them. Parents can help us ensure the children's happy development by providing them with information about their children. They know their children well and are almost always in a better position to decide what is best. We may find it difficult to accept parents' opinions when their values differ from our own, but we must maintain a professional respect for their perspective on their task.

In addition to any forms, questionnaires, and reports filled out during or after communication with parents, it is useful to keep a log of meetings with parents, as a summary of dates, permissions granted, and topics discussed.

If parents have been part of the portfolio process for a while, they might give you information about how a guidance strategy is working, how they are implementing a learning plan, or what they have learned from a health professional or psychologist.

A teacher–parent journal can aid both parties in communication. Some notes may focus on practical requests like "Please drop off more diapers," while a more analytical approach might include thoughtful comments about the child's mood, interests, or development. This record book can be included in the portfolio and would provide an interesting picture of changes in the child's development.

After looking at Observation Sample 8.5, the "Parent Meeting Log for Portfolio," consider how you might use such a documentation process.

Records from previous agencies

You will be fortunate if earlier assessments, health records, and reports have been transferred to your agency. Treat the material with respect while being cautious about believing everything you read. You will be tempted to think that the records are accurate and objective, but without some verification of the findings, avoid making any programming decisions based on them.

Legal requirements govern the transfer of this kind of information, and they vary according to the jurisdiction. Be aware of the legalities and policies that pertain to you, whether they are by-laws, municipal guidelines, board-of-education policies, procedures agreed to by agencies, or local practices.

The contents of the record may prompt useful questions for you to ask the parents; they may wish to see the record themselves and offer opinions on the contents. Their rights may include the option of removing items or including more items or commenting on the information.

Use the records as a base for some informal observations as the child settles into her new environment. Records can be obsolete by the time they are passed on. You may

Observation Sample 8.5

This log is a simple record of all meetings and discussions with a child's parents. Such a record provides a quick summary of which permissions have been requested, which questionnaires have been completed, and what other discussions have taken place.

What other purposes might a parent-meeting log serve? How might you encourage a reluctant parent to become involved in portfolio assessment of his or her child?

Parent Meeting Log for Portfolio

Child's name: Jean-Paul   **Student's name:** Cara

February 6, 2008: First formal approach to Jean-Paul's parents, Mr. and Mrs. Legore, re: observation of their son. Approached with the approval of toddler room supervisor, Christy. Introductions are made and I immediately describe the purpose of my observation. I receive written consent for the event sampling, informing them that further consent forms will be forthcoming for future observations. I now have to start recording.

February 21, 2008: Meet with the parents to discuss Jean-Paul's general routine as recorded in the format of a daily log. At this meeting, I inform Mrs. Legore of Jean-Paul's impressive oral skills and attempts at autonomous activity. We do discuss, however, Jean-Paul's tendency to become very agitated when a child takes his toy or a situation does not coincide with his immediate need for gratification. It is decided that the best way to deal with this typical behaviour is to encourage verbal expression of Jean-Paul's thoughts and feelings, needs and wants. This is not inconceivable given Jean-Paul's strong oral skills.

March 13, 2008: Approach Mr. and Mrs. Legore in the morning to acquire permission to complete remaining elements of the portfolio assignment. I present two permission forms to be checked and validated--one to perform general observation for the purpose of a checklist observation, the second to take photographs of the child as a component of the portfolio. Permission is granted on both counts. Mr. Legore is also informed that a brief meeting will be needed for the purpose of acquiring contextual information. We agree to conduct this meeting the same day--March 13, 2007--at approximately 5:00 p.m., when Mr. Legore arrives back at the childcare centre to pick up Jean-Paul.

Later that day, Mr. Legore arrives back at the childcare centre and we conduct a short 10-15 minute meeting to fill out the contextual questionnaire. The interview is done in a direct, no-nonsense manner in order to keep the meeting short and to the point; both Jean-Paul and his older sister are waiting for Mr. Legore and me to finish in order to return home. At the end of our interview, I inform Mr. Legore that a similar meeting will

---

have to be conducted for the purpose of obtaining information on Jean-Paul's medical history. We agree to set next Friday afternoon--March 21, 2007--as a tentative date for the next meeting to take place. I also receive verbal permission from Mr. Legore to obtain photocopies of Jean-Paul's immunization record from the centre; we agree that this will save time at our future meeting.

March 21, 2008: Mr. Legore arrives at the end of the day to inform me that he cannot meet at this time due to car problems. I ask him if next Thursday afternoon--March 27, 2007--would be an acceptable time for rescheduling. He agrees, and the meeting is temporarily postponed.

March 27, 2008: Mr. Legore arrives shortly after 5:00 p.m., and we immediately sit down in the office to commence the meeting. Once again, we are both motivated to conduct the interview quickly; the children are waiting for their father and it is the beginning of Easter weekend. The questioning is fairly routine and Mr. Legore shows no reservations about answering the questions that I choose to ask. We get into an interesting discussion about blood type and why it is not a required component of childcare health questionnaires, nor a subject even mentioned in the Day Nurseries Act. The interview goes well. I opt to omit certain contextual details from my questioning in order to focus more on the child's health and to keep the meeting moving along at a good pace.

note considerable development and life-experience changes in the time between the child's leaving one agency and starting at another.

Some supervisors limit access to children's histories, because they do not want to colour the attitudes of the teachers directly responsible for the children. Teachers are trained to be objective and professional and to be aware of inappropriate influences. Usually they should evaluate for themselves the content of the records they receive.

Professional reports

Assessment records, reports, suggestions, and plans from professionals contributing to a child's health, education, and well-being may be included in the portfolio. When the caregiving agency requests a report from a specialist, the consent of the parents is usually required. Parents may also seek a specialist's help directly. The report that results from such intervention may be unavailable to you, as caregiver or student, for personal reasons that you may never know. These reasons may have nothing to do with mistrust, although you might feel that you could help the child and the parents better if you had as much information as possible.

In some situations, your input may be crucial to the assessment process. Even if you agree to offer input, you will not necessarily receive feedback.

If assessment results do not reinforce what you have already observed, neither perspective may be "wrong"; you may simply be evaluating the child from a different perspective. Your observations are carried out in a naturalistic setting, so they are more likely to represent what the child can do every day. When test results indicate a level of achievement below that which you have observed, the test was likely inappropriate or presented in a way that induced stress in the child or elicited unexpected responses from him. However, if the results duplicate your findings, you can consider your inferences more likely to be valid. Keep in mind that you could both be wrong! Ideally, the team will work together, the parents will be involved, and you will agree on the outcomes.

TAKING A SPECIAL LOOK: Resource teachers and assistants

Some childcare facilities and schools have access to resource teachers and assistants. **Resource teachers** have specialized training to provide physical assistance, learning activities, emotional and social support, and other aids to children with special needs in mainstream settings. Assistants are sometimes hired specifically to work with one or two particular children with diagnosed special needs; usually, however, they provide general support to the overall program.

Products of learning and experience

Observations may enable you to glimpse the process of a child's learning, and examples of the products confirm achievements. In keeping products such as artwork and writing samples, you still value the process by which they were made. Concrete examples of the

Teachers demonstrate their new learning about portfolios after undertaking the complete portfolio process and focusing on studying one child in depth.

Thanks to University of Delaware

child's end products can help the professional appreciate the particular stage of the child's development.

While you must remain cautious about making invalid, unsupported inferences, representative samples of a child's works can help you evaluate her progress. With knowledge of the sequence of drawing skills and representation of the child's world in art, you can make pertinent comments about the child's feelings, skill level, and perception. You can analyze writing and math work on a similar basis. By looking at what the child can do, you can attempt to appreciate her conceptual understandings and discern her **construction of knowledge**.

Selecting items for the portfolio can be difficult when the child creates a large volume of products. You may be tempted to select "the best" according to your personal responses. More significant is the most typical of the child's work at this time.

Media recordings

Photographs, video- and audio-recordings, and other **media techniques** help you gather information for the portfolio. With them, you can put together a more comprehensive collection of items than you could using only traditional observation techniques.

Video- and audio-recordings of the child supplement the portfolio by adding details about his activity and language that are often superior to a narrative record. Our newest technologies can be better at documenting the processes of thinking involved in creativity and problem-solving. A series of photos or a video sequence can record the actions that indicate the complexity of cognition. However, remember that recordings, of themselves, are not interpretive unless a teacher narrates them or analyzes them in detail after the event. (Review Chapter 7 to help you employ media techniques.)

We are accustomed to using photographs for identification and record-keeping. Keeping a loaded camera near the children's activity area will help you be ready to "snap" the children in action. A variety of action and posed pictures make useful additions to the portfolio and bring it to life for readers.

Inclusions made by the child

A child feels a greater sense of involvement in and ownership of the education process when she has some control over the input to her own record. In choosing pieces for inclusion, the child can identify items of particular significance. If the item is too precious to be stored in the portfolio, perhaps you could photograph it and include the photograph instead.

As the child develops she will be able to take a more active role in selecting samples. She will also reflect on her work, evaluate it, and, with help, be able to plan for future success.

Assembling a Portfolio

Since you are aiming here at building and encouraging a team approach, in which the parents and the childcare practitioners work together, it may be a good idea to decide collectively on the system to be used for record-keeping.

Organizing the contents for storage

Decide how to keep the portfolios according to the space you have available. Box files can be expensive and may not give you the kind of privacy and storage space you need. File folders are most commonly used. However, folders can be too small to accommodate large pieces of artwork. To get around this problem, you might take photographs of the artwork—instead of including flaking paint and unstuck macaroni! Shirt boxes, pizza boxes, or others of that size can work well. You could also put items into ring binders in chronological order for each child and remove them as necessary, or use accordion files, which provide sections for organizing items by type. Whatever method you use, be aware that this kind of record-keeping requires space that is both accessible and secure.

Keep the portfolio in good order. Label it on the outside, and label each item inside clearly and date it. Develop a system to ensure that you remember to make additions.

Choice of contents

What you put into the portfolio will depend on your philosophy and why you are keeping the records. Your team might like to discuss the following considerations to help decide on those contents:

- the purpose of each type of record
- the space available
- who will keep the portfolio up-to-date
- who will have access to the portfolio
- how the data can be analyzed
- the cost of keeping the system

- the philosophy of the agency (child-centred programs may have fewer standardized tests; some may focus on the process of learning and accentuate observations; others may want you to include more products)
- privacy and confidentiality
- the time available to collect and process information
- the attitude of staff and parents

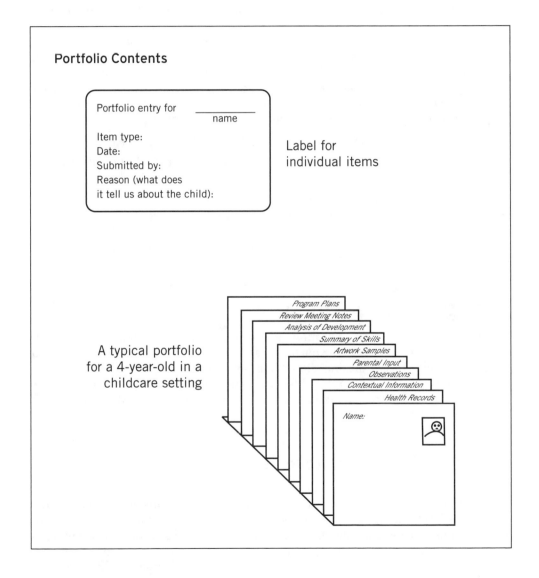

Portfolio Contents

Portfolio entry for _____
              name

Item type:
Date:
Submitted by:
Reason (what does
it tell us about the child):

Label for
individual items

A typical portfolio
for a 4-year-old in a
childcare setting

Program Plans
Review Meeting Notes
Analysis of Development
Summary of Skills
Artwork Samples
Parental Input
Observations
Contextual Information
Health Records
Name:

Rubrics

Rubrics are a set of assessment criteria that specify the learning that constitutes a particular level. Educators frequently use them in authentic assessment instead of grades, or, occasionally, to determine a grade (by adding numerical values to each criterion) when an educational institution demands grades as part of its reporting processes. Rather than being assigned a grade, the learners work to fulfill the criterion set, and know they will be assessed according to the predetermined specifics. Younger children will be unable to understand the criteria unless they are presented in picture form, but you can still use a rubric to measure their performance. Rubrics allow for subtleties in learning and require the assessor to indicate the level of a performance as well as whether the child demonstrated the skill or knowledge. Where rubrics are linked with grades, they can overcome some of the limitations of grading; they can provide clear reasons why the performance merited the grade. In a learning-outcome model you can develop the rubric with the outcomes in mind and so produce a picture, over time, of a child's progress toward achieving specific outcomes.

In portfolio assessment there are several ways to use rubrics:

- to provide a mechanism for evaluating the creation of the portfolio itself
- to offer feedback on any part of the portfolio and to help in the selection of the child's "best work"
- to offer a clear benchmark for what constitutes success
- to assist in developing curriculum or program plans in response to the rubric's evaluation
- to offer a step-by-step sequence of skill development from basic to mastery level

Portfolio Assessment

Although a good collection of portfolio items may seem self-explanatory, the most important part is its analysis—the **portfolio assessment**. To sort, summarize, and then analyze a portfolio takes time and effort, but it is very worthwhile for the child and can help the teacher plan to support the child's needs and emerging skills. Parents are more likely to understand the portfolio's assessment function if they are shown the analysis as well as all the other parts.

New directions in portfolio use

Emerging trends in portfolio documentation parallel advances in technology and developments in thinking about how children learn. Another force is also evident: the move to greater accountability blended with efforts to reform education. Historically, opinions about the form and function of education have changed constantly, and regular patterns emerge over time. The current education models challenge educators, who may have to bridge existing and new practices. This is certainly true regarding portfolio use. Often educators who are child-centred in their approach and who implement developmentally appropriate practice have difficulty documenting children's learning in ways that conform to the reporting requirements of their current administrations.

Some may abandon what they know is good practice and move to a teacher-directed approach to "cover" the curriculum and to satisfy the need to teach to the test. There are better ways of using portfolios to track the children's learning as it occurs and match it to standards, outcomes, and other curriculum requirements. If we trust in appropriate practices rather than rote learning, we must be consistent in aligning our assessment methods with our practice. If standardized testing is demanded, incorporate it along with the authentic assessment that fits with authentic learning. Used this way it may confirm the effectiveness of developmentally appropriate practice. As a consequence of these shifts in education we may see educators using portfolios more and more to

- document the process of learning through display as well as through storage.
- **assess** performance using benchmarks that the education system provides.
- **record** projects undertaken by groups of children.
- reflect on their own learning in a professional portfolio.
- design, implement, and record the group's progress in single curriculum areas as they align with curriculum outcomes.
- monitor the effect of a technological tool, such as digital portfolios, on the process of learning.
- support the developmental needs of individual children who have special needs.
- involve the children more in the portfolio process from an early age—seeing portfolios as a means for learning, as well as a process of assessment.
- document what is happening to the whole group/class of children.

Summary

Portfolio assessment is founded on a philosophy of education, and it is more than a mere collection of observations and other materials. Behind portfolio practice lies a set of beliefs about how learning occurs and how it can be measured. Those who use portfolios tend to focus on a child's individual patterns of development and the importance of child-directed experience, and they see learning and assessment as bound together into a whole. On the one hand, portfolios can provide an alternative to education practices based on content-focused curricula and testing-based assessment. On the other hand, portfolios can offer a holistic and authentic way of documenting an individual's, or group's, learning while monitoring the progress of either or both. Educators need to commit themselves to the philosophy of portfolio assessment so that it can succeed.

Portfolios can take many forms. Even a parent's baby book constitutes a portfolio. Typically the term refers to a systematic documentation of a child's behaviour and learning. Observations and other materials are usually gathered to gain insight into the individual's motivations, interests, stages of development, and other signs of progress. The portfolio would also include some form of analysis of the materials that it contains, and these insights would lead to recommending some course of action, curriculum, or intervention.

Many educators adapt the portfolio process to accommodate their own circumstances and philosophy of practice. While most portfolios would contain a selection of observations, such as running records, anecdotal records, checklists, or rating scales, what each educator seeks—and which child behaviours are to be recorded—usually remains within the educator's control. Some teachers may need to document the children's achievement of specific competencies. This kind of outcome-based education approach offers educators considerable flexibility. With the portfolio method, educators can record children's specific attainments, or document any other interesting activities that might occur.

The portfolio can also include a wide variety of material that offers glimpses into the individual child's context—family information, health data, and items connected with that person's culture and social background. This interesting information affects other parts of the portfolio and helps the educator and other team members get to know the child better and see his behaviour within that context. Samples of the child's work or creativity along with photographs and video-recordings can help round out the portfolio. Thus parents can be actively involved in the child's education through a living document. In time the children themselves can choose to contribute what they consider important; the process becomes a collaborative one. It should be remembered that without some form of analysis the portfolio remains little more than a collection of materials of some sentimental value.

The variety of portfolios has broadened, as has the technology available to educators and parents. Some agencies and schools are successfully creating and using digital or electronic versions. Others combine both an electronic part and a work-sample part in their portfolios. Whatever you eventually choose, consider what resources are available to you before you establish a portfolio process.

Heated debates about approaches to education have tended to produce educators who are either for or against the portfolio approach. Those who have not yet had the opportunity to see a complete and successful portfolio system might try a modified form of portfolio. They may be persuaded to expand the scope of their portfolio process over time.

Key Terms

- accountability
- analysis
- anecdotal record
- authentic assessment
- baby book
- chart
- competency
- construction of knowledge
- contextual information
- developmental checklist
- ecological systems model
- ecomap
- event sampling
- formative

- genogram
- holistic
- learning log
- learning outcome
- life book
- life-experience flow chart
- media technique
- metacognition
- milestones
- objectivity
- observation
- outcomes-based learning (OBL)
- performance assessment
- portfolio

Continued

- portfolio assessment
- professional portfolio
- project
- rating scale
- record of achievement
- reflective practitioner
- Reggio Emilia
- resource teachers

- rubric
- running record
- special need
- specimen record
- standardized test
- summative
- time sampling

Weblinks

http://ceep.crc.uiuc.edu/poptopics/reggio.html
Information and resources related to the approach to early childhood education developed in the preschools of Reggio Emilia, Italy.

www.kidsource.com/kidsource/content3/portfolio.young.pre.3. html#Components
This site offers an article by Cathy Grace, who is an advocate of portfolio use across all ages and stages of development.

http://electronicportfolios.org/portfolios/EPDevProcess.html
Here we have a site that investigates the use of electronic portfolios.

http://depts.washington.edu/cidrweb/portfolio/developmental.html
This is a step-by-step guide to developing a teacher portfolio.

http://families.brighthorizons.com/childportfolio/
This corporation says it wants to use portfolios within their childcare settings. Compare this scrapbook approach with that outlined in this text.

www.ericae.net/
Follow links to an enormous body of resources on portfolios and authentic assessment.

www.learnquebec.ca
Follow pages to "Pedagogy" and "Portfolio" to read an important report on the use of portfolios in Quebec.

www.pampetty.com/assessment.html
A review of terminology in authentic assessment, along with links to many useful resources.

9 Analyzing Observations and Responding to Findings

These educators are discussing observations and other information in their review of the children's portfolios. Analyzing the data is challenging, but provides inferences that guide practice.

With permission of the YMCA of Greater Toronto

Once you have finished the observation, you will have to make some sense of your data. ...
Janet Walters, Capilano College (2005)

Nothing has such power to broaden the mind as the ability to investigate systematically and truly all that comes under thy observation in life.
Marcus Aurelius (A.D. 121–180)

Analysis (from the Greek, "a breaking up") is the process of breaking a complex topic or substance into smaller parts to gain a better understanding of it.
http://enwikipedia.org/wiki/Analysis

In order to keep a clear mind and not become overwhelmed by the sheer amount of data and analytic writings, the analyst [educator/researcher] needs to be organized.
Ann Lewins (2005)

Focus Questions

1. Why does the collection of information, samples, and observations about one child in a portfolio not "speak for itself"?

2. What is the process for analyzing a portfolio?

3. In what way is an observation summary different from an analysis?

Learning Outcomes

By reading this chapter and applying the ideas to practice, learners will

- use a developmental system to summarize observational data.
- review portfolio contents and make appropriate and supported inferences about the subject.
- make analyses of portfolios.
- use observation and portfolio analyses to create responsive curriculum plans.

DEFINITION: Analysis

A process of gaining an understanding of recorded observational data through the study of the component parts of those data, making inferences, and validating them.

KEY FEATURES: Validated inference

- a statement supported by reason
- a statement supported by experience
- a statement supported with the use of a reputable/reliable source
- a statement found agreeable to more than one professional
- a normative statement aligned with an acceptable normative profile
- a statement underscored with reference to an acceptable theory of development
- even when validated, an inference may be incorrect

Analyzing Observations

It is important to review the data you have collected. Even if your data is only a short observation, it needs to be reviewed for several reasons before the analysis is begun. Ask yourself the following questions to check that your collected data is ready to be reviewed:

1. Is it as complete as possible?

2. Has the recorder/observer been identified?

3. Does it include observations using specified methods of recording?

4. Is the context or setting described?

5. Have you recorded any background or contextual information that might influence your analysis?

6. Is it written using conventional spelling and grammar?

7. Have any subjective or biased comments been deleted?

8. Have all ethical and confidentiality issues been addressed?

9. What is your plan to check your findings with a professional person before making your assessment available to others?

10. How do you plan to share the observations and analysis with others—including the parents?

11. Is your intention to use the analysis to plan for the child?

12. How might you follow up your analysis with ongoing observations and data collection?

If you can answer these questions adequately, you are probably ready to move on to the next step of the observation cycle.

If you have gathered a variety of materials including observations, contextual information, photographs, "work samples," recordings, and so on for a portfolio, begin the assessment process.

The observation cycle

Rather than a linear progression, the observation process is a cycle. Almost as soon as we have made observations and recorded them, we need to be ready to observe and record more. We need to learn this cycle and practise it frequently so that we become proficient at making good decisions about the children we care for and educate.

The **observation cycle** is applicable to both a single observation and a complete portfolio. It is also applicable to other forms of observation and documentation—with only a few changes needing to be made by the educator.

The same process applies to analyzing the content of the complete portfolio as for a single observational recording; the difference is only in the size and complexity of the task. Managing all the materials of the portfolio is more challenging, but obviously the outcome will be much richer than from a single observation. Also, the portfolio offers the opportunity for reinforcing and checking inferences when a behaviour or skill is mentioned in more than one piece of data.

First we needed to learn to observe and record; now we need to learn to summarize, reflect, and analyze observations and even whole portfolios. This needs practice, and it also demands different types of thinking:

1. organization, sequencing, **categorization**, and summarization (organizing behavioural information into the categories of developmental domains)
2. convergent thinking (focusing on data)
3. application of theory to observed behaviour (to understand theoretical models and apply them to observed behaviour)
4. questioning (to test ideas and theories)
5. comparing and contrasting (using criteria is a benchmark)
6. **inference-making** (to make statements of assessment based on sound reasoning and theories)
7. **inference-checking** (to check the statements of assessment for their validity)
8. reasoning (deducing ideas)
9. **contextualizing** (considering the subject's home, family, situation, setting, ecosystem, past achievements and experience, belief systems, expectations, etc.)
10. **critical thinking** (to review all elements of the overall assessment)
11. evaluation (determining merit)
12. **reflection** (to think personally and carefully about the process of assessment and its implications)
13. divergent thinking (thinking "outside the box")
14. **analysis** (to think deeply to discern patterns, themes, and reasons for behaviour)

If these aspects of thinking seem new, you might want to research what each means. If you can see how they apply in other situations, you might be better able to adopt the higher-order thinking processes required in analytical thought. At first the process may seem cumbersome, but soon you will become adept at this professional skill. Practice is needed, as has been said, but the step-by-step approach will help you make the leap to professional assessment. (We will consider the response and curriculum plan a bit later.)

Why go through this complicated process?

Things that are worthwhile are rarely easy! The analysis of observational and other data is a case in point. Let's think about the reasons we need to work on the analytic process:

1. An analytical process ensures that authentic experience and authentic assessment are aligned.
2. Analyzing observations helps the student (and other adults) to have a better appreciation of the patterns, idiosyncrasies and complexities of children's development.
3. Good practice in observation requires thorough understanding of learning—and that, in turn, leads to improved curricula and children's environments.

4. By summarizing and making sense of observations we understand each child better, and therefore we can be more effective in individualizing practice and mould who we are in the lives of those particular children.

5. As every educator needs to be a researcher, making and recording child observations— and then analyzing them—must be a part of action research as well as everyday practice.

To be realistic, not all educators are as proficient as they could be at collecting information, observing, and making assessments. In recent years knowledge of good authentic assessment practice has developed considerably; the student may be in a good place to show the seasoned professional. You will need to practise your analytical skills (your observation tools should already be in place). Practice improves those critical-thinking skills.

Using the observation cycle

So far you have learned to make good observations and have the skill to record them using a range of standard methods. You can select observations to get the information you are seeking, record them fairly objectively, and review them to check for their professionalism. You also know how to gain other relevant information that might help you understand the behaviours that you can record. With access to technology you can use a variety of media to assist your observations.

Using the portfolio process, you can also develop a complex portfolio with multiple observations, samples, and other data. These are important foundations for making authentic assessments.

Next we will walk you through the whole observation cycle; you will recognize your current skills and see what your next steps should be.

1. **Look:** Focus on current behaviour.
   Observation is not necessarily an exercise to identify "strengths" and "weaknesses" in children's behaviour. Such value judgments are usually inappropriate in **naturalistic** observation. Observers should look at the skills that are present rather than focus on what a child cannot do. Programs are more positive and more likely to be effective if they are planned to enable the child to build skills from "where he is" rather than from what he has failed to do. A more developmentally appropriate curriculum plan should result from focusing on **emerging skills**.

2. **Record what you see.**
   Document what you see using a format that suits your purpose. Include enough detail according to the method used. Ensure accuracy and **objectivity**. (See Chapters 3 through 8 for methods of recording.)

3. **Summarize information gathered.**
   The observation **summary**, often confused with analysis, is a categorization or organization of the essential parts of the observation. In many open-ended observations, the summary may try to bring together information to identify and list the behaviours seen. It is not an interpretation but a review and organization of

Observation Cycle

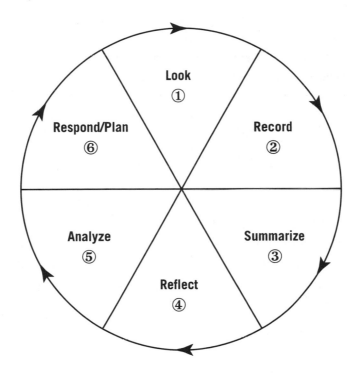

objectively recorded behaviours. Developmental domains might be used as categories in the summary.

In a more structured observation that looks for particular identified behaviours, the summary might contain information such as the number, frequency, **duration**, or triggers of those behaviours. The summary is intended to briefly outline significant observed behaviour.

4. **Reflect on the observation and your summary.**
Review the observation to determine whether you saw and recorded any behaviour or category of behaviour you were seeking. Consider the data in relation to the child's acquisition of new skills, how the context affects the behaviour, and your own feelings, intuition, and expertise. Be aware of your **biases**.

5. **Analyze the content of the observation.**
Here is the opportunity to use your critical thinking skills. Decide on a framework for analysis. Typically this framework might include identifying developmental changes, explaining behaviours, using theoretical models, comparing behaviours to the norm, assessing the achievements of the child with reference to specified standards, and/or identifying challenging behaviours or ones that need to be addressed. Your style of analysis must match your agency's philosophy and practice.

There are a few basic rules of analysis:

1. Focus on what was observed and recorded, not on other, less accurate "bits of information."
2. Always separate the observation from its summary and analysis.
3. Do not make **inferences** unless you can support them; that is,
   a. identify the specific behaviour(s) that lead(s) to such a deduction.
   b. support your inference with reason(s), using inferential language carefully: "It appears that . . . on the basis of . . . I think that . . . demonstrates behaviours in excess of . . . norm for his age."
   c. **validate** each statement with the use of at least one (preferably all) of the following:
      i. observations made by others with similar inferences
      ii. use of theoretical explanations
      iii. comparison with a recognized norm
   d. state the source of the validation (professional input or book reference)
4. Put on paper only what you consider professional and could defend. Avoid judgments, assumptions, and generalizations that cannot be substantiated. For example, do not say, "This occurs because he is an only child" or "He is much smarter than his brother" or "Her English is poor because her parents don't communicate with her."
5. Keep the analysis as well as the observation confidential. Some people may find the word "analysis" quite offputting or coldly scientific.

   "Analysis" is more easily understood as the "making sense of what I saw" section of the observation process. The easiest way to go about an analysis is to ask yourself, and then answer, a series of questions about what was observed. If the observation is set up to seek particular information, then that question needs to be addressed first. Unless you cite the source of "extra" information, it is best to stick to analyzing only what was in the observation just completed.

   Structuring the analysis in a way that considers each of the developmental areas is helpful. Any section where there is no significant information can be left out. In practice, you might find the following developmental analysis plan a good idea. Adapt it to fit your needs. Write it up according to the required style, either as an essay or in notes under organized headings. Of course, the more contextual data you have collected and the greater the number of observations you have recorded, the more valuable the analysis.

6. **Respond to observational data and analysis.** Responses to observed behaviour vary. They might include planning further observation, devising a program to fit a child's needs, making a referral, checking with parents, using appropriate guidance strategies, or developing a different teaching technique.

Observation Sample 9.1

This sample shows how a student uses a prepared form to assist her critical thinking. She makes an inference from her observation and supports it with a quotation from a theory.

How might you use this sequence to clarify and validate your inferences drawn from observations?

Analysis Chart: Observations

Child's name: Zoe

Child's age: 2 years, 8 months

Date: November 4, 2007

Inference # 7

Domain(s) of development *(If possible, state inferences in each developmental area.)*

The following inference concerns this/these area(s) of development:

Social-personal skills; imitative behaviour

Having examined the evidence *(Make a statement that assesses the child's development—is it typical, atypical, or can you explain it using a theoretical model?)*

I infer that Zoe shows some signs of pre-operational thinking. She has internalized a behaviour and imitated it.

The source of my inference *(Which observation or bit of information led you to the inference?)*

Because I recorded that she engaged in deferred imitation, where she imitated how her grandfather had placed a plastic cat-face mask on his face.

My reasoning *(Give your own reasons for stating the inference.)*

I think this because when I babysat a toddler, she held a baby doll in her arms and fed it with a toy bottle, just as her mother had done with her baby brother earlier that day when I had visited.

Quote from norm (if applicable) *(Validate your inference with the use of either a norm, a theory, or both.)*

I found this quote from a normative development profile to support my inference:

N/A

Quote from theory (if applicable) *(Validate your inference with the explanation of a theory.)*

I found a theory that supports my inference. The theory is called pre-operational stage of cognitive development.

This is a quote from the explanation of the theory: "Many children between 24 and 30 months are entering Piaget's preoperational stage of cognitive development. The first sub-stage . . . is preconceptual, which occurs from about 2 to 4 years of age. . . . In deferred imitation the child imitates another person's behavior, even when that person is no longer present."

The name of the theorist is Piaget

Author I found this in a book by LaVisa Cam Wilson

Title The book is called Infants and Toddlers: Curriculum and Teaching (2nd ed.)

Source The book/journal/article is published by Delmar Publishers Inc.

Date of publication: 1990

Page # of quote: 276–277

Observer/assessor/recorder's name: Wanda

Attention deficit, hyperactivity, and attention deficit disorder (ADD) are terms used rather casually by some parents, teachers, and caregivers. These terms are very specific diagnoses and are not for the nonmedically trained to diagnose. Consequently, we should be careful about making inferences using these labels. It is better, without the benefit of a professional diagnosis, to describe behaviours objectively. Use your observation skills and describe exactly what you see!

One of the processes of critical thinking required in analyzing observations is outlined in Observation Sample 9.1. It shows the analysis of an observation; on pages 296–97 Observation Sample 9.2 shows the analysis of a number of behaviours in chart form.

The summary should not contain any inferences; it is a way of restating what was observed in an organized way. You may write it as a series of points under your own headings. The questions above might help create a useful format, but do not hesitate to find your own way of managing the material. Some educators summarize observations and other information according to curriculum area, or according to predetermined learning outcomes.

Plan to Assist the Summary

Use whatever questions are relevant to help you organize your ideas about what can be drawn from the observation(s) or other data.

BACKGROUND

- What was the reason for observing? (Was I seeking specific information?)
- Did the observation occur spontaneously? Was the child aware of being observed?
- What is my role as observer (nonparticipant, etc.)?
- Did I have any preconceived ideas about what I was going to see?
- What contextual information might be helpful?
- Who gave permission for or input into the process?

METHOD

- Why did I choose this method of observing?
- Were there any concerns regarding the procedure?
- Did the method reveal what I wanted? What was it?

CONTENT

Physical development

- What gross motor skills were demonstrated?
- What fine motor or manipulative skills were seen?
- What activity was the child observed doing?
- What responses did the child make to any sensory experience (seeing, hearing, touching, smelling, or tasting)?

Social development

- What evidence was there of the child's sense of self?
- What kinds of connection was the child making

  a. with adults?

  b. with other children?

- What adult interaction did I observe?
- Describe the quality of the interactions.
- What kind of self-help skills were seen?
- Were there any examples of independence or dependence?
- What did I see that indicated understanding of social roles and behaviour?

Emotional development

- What demonstrations of feelings did I observe

  a. in language?

  b. in posture and body language?

  c. in gestures?

  d. in facial expressions?

- Was there indication of control of feelings?
- What attachments were evident?
- What moods did I see?

Play

- Did I see the child in onlooker, solitary, parallel associative, or cooperative activity?
- What type of play (if any) was observed (one or more of imaginative, imitative, pretend, fantasy, sociodramatic, superhero, social constructional, functional, physical, or other)?
- How long and involved were these sequences?
- Was the play self-initiated and self-supported?
- What props were used?

Language and communication

- What utterances were made? In what language?
- What indications of nonverbal communication did I observe?
- What kind of structure did the language have?
- How extensive was the child's vocabulary?
- How effective was the communication?
- What was the child's interpersonal style?

Moral and spiritual development

- Did any of the observed behaviours indicate an understanding of "rights" or "social justice"? If so, how?
- Were any of the behaviours pro-social in nature (empathetic, altruistic, sharing, taking turns, helping others)?
- Was there evidence of beliefs about any philosophical issues, such as the creation of things, in the child's world?
- Did I see the child's curiosity and sense of wonder?
- Did the child demonstrate respect for the dignity of others?
- What indication was there of the child's categorizing himself or herself into a sub-culture (racial, belief system, family make-up, dialect, etc.)?
- What demonstration was there of an understanding of, compliance with, or rejection of any kind of rules or guidelines?

Personality

- Did I observe any behaviours that indicate temperamental type (slow to warm, extroverted, orderly, etc.)?
- What reactions to stimuli did I see?

Cognition

- What drew the child's attention? How long was the span of concentration?
- What behaviours indicated a thought process?
- Did I notice any "mistakes" the child made?
- Did the demonstrated language or behaviour show understanding of any of the basic concepts? If so, what (colour, shape, time, space, classification, relativity, seriation, conservation, etc.)?
- Did the child "experiment" with materials?
- Was there evidence of conditioned responses?
- Did I see any trial-and-error strategies?
- What evidence might there be of an understanding of symbolism in language or behaviour?
- Was there evidence of use of memory?
- Was any of the child's art representational?
- What behaviours indicated to me how the child perceives the world?

continued

- Did the child use concrete objects to help perform tasks? Can the child use any forms of abstraction?
- What humour did the child initiate or respond to?

The whole child
- What outside influences affected what I observed?
- In what ways did I see aspects of the child's development interact?
- What developmental stage did I observe? (What evidence?)

Reflection

The reflective process is about taking a step back from the data and thinking about it in a non-scientific but human way. Frequently the reflection might lead to the educator having a sense of the "essence" of the child. This is a phenomenological approach to the material. You might want to research phenomenological methods to heighten your awareness of the experience of the children, as opposed to your own experience of them.

Other reflections might consider the balance of process and product in the portfolio, focus on the way in which the portfolio process is contributing to the child's own reflection or metacognition (thinking about thinking). The educator might think about how the child can gradually take responsibility for her own learning.

The reflection is an open-ended part of the process without objective parameters. What is recorded about the educator's (and child's) reflections tends to be unpredictable but insightful. It does take time.

The analysis

This is the core of the assessment. Because it takes the place of formal testing and traditional assessments, it needs to be shown to

- present an accurate and real picture of the whole child.
- be thorough.
- offer contextualizing comments that explain individual behaviours.
- contain appropriate supportable inferences.
- be individualized and personalized.
- cover as many developmental domains, curriculum areas, learning outcomes, areas of traditional assessments, or other criteria as possible that fit with the local requirements.
- be carefully considered using a professional approach.
- offer indications of current competence and emerging skills.

- be a reliable document depicting change over time.
- compare favourably to traditional assessments in both the breadth and the depth of its assessment.
- be written in professional language that is also accessible to parents.
- provide opportunity, wherever possible, for the child's own input and self-assessment.

Analysis process

The diagram here depicts the inference-making part of the analysis. This process is repeated as many times as the number of inferences that are made.

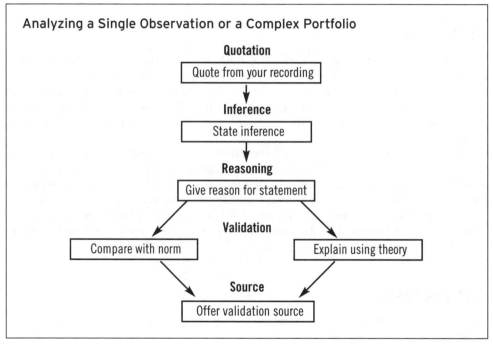

In each of the areas you will explore, ensure that all deductions and inferences can be supported. If such inferences are "checked" using this model, they can be evaluated for their objectivity and the likelihood of their being accurate. If your inferences cannot be validated, they should not be stated.

A *quotation* from your recording might be written like this:

"In the running record #3 and in two of the anecdotal records, #11 & #14, and as highlighted in the photograph of Toby setting the table for six people, I saw Toby several times counting in ways that showed a growing concept of number."

An *inference* is a statement you make might be written like this:

"Toby has an understanding of one-to-one correspondence up to the number 6."

Some *reasoning* for the inference statement might be:

"Toby demonstrated several times that he could count to 6 in sequence, but he could also point to items counting each one, and while setting the table he was able to make 6 place settings (albeit not very straight!)."

A *comparison with norm* might be framed this way:

"Toby's competence with one-to-one correspondence up to 6 is typical of a child of his age [mention age and indicate developmental profile source]."

An *explanation using a theory* might be:

"Piaget described children at Toby's stage as being in the pre-operational stage, in which the child increasingly gains one-to-one correspondence, which is a fuller concept of number than merely reciting the sequence of numbers."

The *validation* might involve using either Piaget's original work or a developmental psychology textbook that will provide support for what you have inferred and explained (offer specific source and page number, preferably with a quote from that source).

Make sure you state your inferences well. Common mistakes include students writing things like: "Piaget says that Toby is counting one-to-one" (Piaget didn't meet Toby!) or "Ellen should be 10 centimetres taller considering her age." (Height is not a moral consideration; "should" must never be part of an analysis!)

CHILD DEVELOPMENT FOCUS: No place for "ought to" in assessments

Students new to making assessments can find the language and concepts of assessment quite challenging. Beginning students often think normative profiles are easier to use than other types of validation, but they soon find the difficult part is in the wording. Many have the tendency to say or imply that a child "ought to" be at a certain skill level, which seems like a moral judgment or a reference to the child's failure. If the child does not yet seem to demonstrate the skill typical for most children her age, the observer should indicate the level of skill as it appears (e.g., "of a three-year-old"). Explaining behaviour may be more authentic than comparing it using a developmental profile.

Review the analysis in Observation Sample 9.2, which is in chart format. Although we may not wholly agree with the observer, he shows how the process works.

Observation Sample 9.2

This excerpt from an analysis chart shows use of a structured approach to critical thinking. Observations are broken down by developmental domain. Explanations of behaviours use recognized theories and norms.

ANALYSIS OF DEVELOPMENT

Child's name: Carolina   Child's age: 18 months

SPEECH AND LANGUAGE DEVELOPMENT

Behaviour observed	Inference	Reasoning
Followed caregiver when caregiver asked her to come	It's typical for children of this age to follow simple requests.	I believe this to be true because I have observed other children following simple requests.
Said hello on toy phone	It's typical for a child almost 12 months to start to use single words.	Children at this age learn through imitation, and the child hears "hello" many times a day.
Would sing before falling asleep	It seemed that the child was soothing herself before falling asleep.	<u>Developmental Profiles</u> states the child will do this as a way of releasing tension.
Would engage in rhythmic singing	It seemed that the repetitive sounds were the beginnings of speech.	David Elkind has noted that babbling and rhythmic sound speed up the acquisition of speech.

PERSONAL-SOCIAL DEVELOPMENT

Behaviour observed	Inference	Reasoning
Watched the delivery man come in and followed him	Child seemed not to have a fear of strangers.	Child felt safe in her environment and does not have the concept of danger yet.
Imitated the adult's action by clapping hands	It's typical behaviour for children of this age to imitate adults.	Child observed what adult was doing and then repeated the action.
Followed caregiver when caregiver asked her to come	It's typical for children of this age to follow simple requests.	I believe this to be true because I have observed other children following simple requests.
Clapped hands and danced to a familiar song	It's typical for children of this age to enjoy rhymed activities.	I have observed other children, and they all seem to like dancing and singing.

BIBLIOGRAPHY
Allen, K.E., & Marotz, L.R. (2006). <u>Developmental profiles: Pre-birth through eight.</u> Albany, NY: Delmar.

Observer's name: Ken   Date: November 6, 2007

Validation by theory	Validation by norm	Source	Bibliographic reference
	Carries out simple directions and requests	K. Eileen Allen & Lynn Marotz	Developmental Profiles, p. 73
	Names everyday objects; imitates sounds	K. Eileen Allen & Lynn Marotz	Developmental Profiles, p. 63
	May sing as a way of winding down	K. Eileen Allen & Lynn Marotz	Developmental Profiles, p. 75
The inability to babble during the early months of life delays language acquisition.		David Elkind	Sympathetic Understanding, p. 21

Validation by theory	Validation by norm	Source	Bibliographic reference
Children will show fear only after they have the concept that they are an object that can be destroyed.		David Elkind	Sympathetic Understanding, p. 12
	Often imitates adult action in play	K. Eileen Allen & Lynn Marotz	Developmental Profiles, p. 74
	Carries out simple directions and requests	K. Eileen Allen & Lynn Marotz	Developmental Profiles, p. 73
	Children enjoy simple songs, dance, and music.	K. Eileen Allen & Lynn Marotz	Developmental Profiles, p. 64

Elkind, D. (1994). A sympathetic understanding of the child: Birth to sixteen (3rd ed.). Boston: Allyn & Bacon.

Portfolio Assessment

After gathering the material for a portfolio, we still have to make sense of it. Some teachers have criticized the use of portfolios for evaluation as glorified **work sampling** rather than real assessment. However, a thorough assessment of a well-kept portfolio leads to a real understanding of the child. The following steps outline the process of careful **portfolio assessment**:

1. *Sort, date, and label all items:* Without a good labelling system, the portfolio will be just a confusing collection of information.

2. *Organize the contents:* Items can be organized by date or by types of data. Add a contents page to show what is included and how it is ordered.

3. *Write an introduction:* Explain the process you have used to create the portfolio. Ensure that you show you are celebrating an individual!

4. *Summarize the material:* Probably the best way to summarize is to scan the current material and categorize skill developments according to developmental domain. A summary can help the assessor determine how well the child is reaching any learning outcomes, expectations, or profile of learning. At this stage, sort objectively; do not explain. (See the sample portfolio summary in Observation Sample 9.3.)

5. *Make inferences about the child's skills:* Using clear statements, write an analysis of the child's development. Your inferences might be based on

   • applying theoretical models to explain a behaviour, skill, or performance

   • matching the child's performance against an acceptable **norm of development** to see where the child is in relation to a specific age or stage (avoiding inappropriate judgments)

   • determining a pattern or cause of behaviour

   Validate or support all your inferences using reasoned arguments and citing reliable sources. Be sure to refer to all sources correctly. (A sample portfolio analysis can be found in Observation Sample 9.4.)

6. *Write a portfolio review report for the parents and for your records:* Restate your inferences in a way that avoids jargon and that helps parents appreciate what you are trying to say. (See a sample report in Observation Sample 9.5.)

7. *Present the parents with the portfolio:* Most parents are anxious to be part of the assessment process. Be prepared to adjust any inferences in your portfolio-review report according to their perceptions. If the child is old enough to appreciate the portfolio collection process, she should be part of the process. At this time, the teachers, parents, child, and other concerned parties (such as social workers or grandparents) can develop an **action plan**.

8. *Design an individual program plan (IPP) or individual education plan (IEP):* Create an IPP or IEP according to the skills that you see emerging. If you have documented the child's learning in all developmental domains, you will be better prepared to design activities that support all domains for him. For children with special needs, you may have to design a plan that contains developmental or incremental stages. (Sample program plans can be found in Observation Samples 9.6 and 9.7.)

9. *Continue the portfolio collection and observations for future in-process assessment.*

Observation Sample 9.3

This summary of skills was prepared as part of a portfolio assessment. The skills are categorized by domain, but they are not explained and no inferences are drawn.

What other developmental criteria or categories might be added to this summary—information that could be drawn from most running records, video-recordings, and time sampling?

SUMMARY OF SKILLS

Child's name: Kirsten
Age/D.O.B.: 19 months

Recorder: Damian
Date: June 4, 2008

Drawn from the following samples: running record, video-recording, time sampling

Appearance
- girl
- dark brown hair
- ears pierced
- fair-skinned
- teeth in upper and lower front
- brown eyes
- small rash behind ears

Posture
- stands erect at water table with legs apart
- sits on carpet with back straight and legs extended in front
- leans forward

Mobility
- walks without assistance
- toddles quickly
- occasionally reverts to crawling

Physical Skills
Gross motor:
- sitting
- walking/toddling

Fine motor:
- palmar grasp (picking up cup)
- pincer grasp (pinching sponges)
- eye-hand coordination (pouring water out of cup into bin)
- uses arm to wave
- points to objects
- uses hands/arms purposefully

Language/Communication
- puts words and sounds together
- squeals (apparently when excited)
- uses one word to signify whole thoughts, e.g. "mine," "frog"
- uses to-and-fro of conversation
- scribbles with crayon (whole-body movement)

-gives a dialogue of sounds and gestures using English
  sound patterns (but without "real word" articulation)
-copies adult words with some success
-says "cup," "sauce," "please," "boo," etc. (20+ words that are recognizable)

Sensory Explorations
-dips hands in water and moves them around
-creates splashes by raising hands in air and forcefully lowering them
  into water
-collects water in cup and then slowly pours it out
-feels sponges with her hands

Demonstration of Cognitive Function
-demonstrates understanding of function of a cup
-fills cup with water and then pours it out
-names objects: "frog"
-responds to experiences with some facial movement (smiling)
-understands physical humour
-appreciates properties of water

Demonstration of Emotions
-periodically squeals and laughs
-smiles while splashing water
-appears satisfied with her accomplishment
-screams and then hits another child
-at this time, apparently unwilling to share or cooperate
-shows attempts to regulate her feelings

Social Interaction
-appears to be quite independent
-engages in solitary play at water table
-engages in associative play with three other children when playing with
  float
-stops splashing when told "No"

Observation Sample 9.4

This portfolio analysis provides a developmental profile of the child. Based on a variety of observations, including narrative recordings, charts, media recordings, and parental input, the student draws inferences about the child's development. The inferences are supported with theories and norms, which are detailed in the list of references.

How might the content of this analysis be shared with parents who have limited English language skills?

PORTFOLIO ANALYSIS

Child's name: Mandy   Observer: Daisy
Age: 25 months   Date: December 2, 2007

The components of Mandy's portfolio were gathered from September 2006 to the present (December 2, 2007). She has reached some significant developmental milestones during this observational period, including the transition from emerging expressive language skills to acquisition of new vocabulary and quickly developing expressive language capabilities. The following analysis gives an overview of Mandy's developmental progress, skills, and behaviours in the following domains: physical, language and communication, emotional, social, cognitive, and temperament/personality.

Physical Development

Mandy's large muscle control appears effective and is at a developmental level expected for a 2-year-old. As the checklist (for 2- and 3-year-olds) indicates, she has mastered the large motor skills typical for a 2-year-old (walks alone, bends over and picks up toy without falling over, seats self in chair, walks up and down stairs with assistance) (Allen & Marotz, 1994, pp. 165–166). In fact, Mandy has shown competence in some physical skills identified as normal for 3-year-olds (runs well in forward direction, jumps in place with two feet together, throws ball, kicks ball forward) (Allen & Marotz, 1994, 165–166). The photographs of Mandy in the playground-- running, walking, climbing into and out of riding toys and on and off tricycles--also offer evidence that she is coordinated and able to use her body competently to participate in chosen physical activities. The running record observation offers many examples of Mandy's large muscle coordination, including use of a variety of riding toys, climbing stairs with ease, and climbing up the slide from the bottom.

Her small muscle control appears typical for most 2-year-olds. The checklist documents that Mandy has mastered use of a spoon; taking off her coat, socks, and shoes; holding and drinking from a cup; turning pages in a book; placing rings on a stick; and placing pegs in a pegboard. One area requiring more practice is the zipping and unzipping of zippers. The only zippers Mandy has experience with are on her coats, and they are

---

smaller than a "large practice zipper." Props in the environment to offer practice would be helpful here.

During the matching game identified in the anecdotal record (October 28), there was evidence that Mandy preferred to use large muscles rather than small muscles. Instead of using her hands and eyes to match the pictures, she chose to stand on the matching picture. This may simply mean that she found the game more fun this way, but may also be an indication that she is more comfortable using her body in this way. While she displays no difficulty with small motor activities undertaken, it may be that, while her visual acuity is maturing, she is more comfortable using larger muscles rather than hand/eye ("How Language Develops").

Language and Communication

Mandy's receptive language skills seem excellent. She appears to understand what is said to her and is beginning to express herself verbally using sentences with correct grammatical structure (e.g., "I want to go outside"). The checklist records that she has mastered the language skills normal for a 2-year-old and has advanced in many areas to a 3-year-old level. During the anecdotal record done November 5, Mandy's mother was able to communicate to her that she had to leave and go to work. Mandy accepted this immediately and responded accordingly by saying goodbye and leaving her mother to join the group .

Evidence of a range of expressive language skills is apparent in the anecdotal record done November 19. Mandy was able to ask the caregiver what she was doing, and responded in a manner that showed understanding ("Can I help?"). She understood the question, "What colour is this?" and responded correctly. Between the ages of 30 and 36 months, it is typical for toddlers to label objects (Wilson, Douville-Watson, & Watson, 1995, p. 348); answer questions appropriately (Allen & Marotz, 1994, p. 93); use pronouns and prepositions (Barrett et al., 1995, p. 235); and say many intelligible words (Sheridan, 1975). Mandy's language skills demonstrate all of these competencies, showing a mastery of language and communication skills beyond expectations for a 2-year-old.

Mandy uses correct words, but sometimes mispronounces them. On the audiotape, she refers to the "sound" on the tape as "tound" and "yellow" as "lellow." As her muscle control matures and Mandy is exposed to appropriate modelling of the proper pronunciation, her next step in development will be to correctly pronounce vowel and consonant sounds. It is normal for children in the age range of 18 to 36 months to simplify the pronunciation of words they find difficult: "All of these implications show that your child is actively learning the sound patterns of language" (Skarakis-Doyle, 1988a).

The contextual questionnaire completed by Mandy's mother identifies language skills as "good for her age." She records that conflicts with Mandy are generally handled via verbal communication, and that this usually works. The same applies when Mandy reacts to new situations. These are also strong indicators that Mandy's language and communication abilities exceed the norm.

Emotional Development

Mandy appears to be well adjusted emotionally to her routine at childcare. The daily log chart indicates that she moves through routines and transitions well, and that she is able to anticipate what is coming next in her day (e.g., she finds her cot after lunch, and knows that after nap she needs to find her shoes and put them on). She displays a cheerful disposition consistently, exploring her environment and engaging caregivers with confidence. This is consistent with the Allen and Marotz (1994) statement that, "the 2-year-old gradually begins to function more ably and amiably" (p. 78). The event sampling based on observations done October 8 and 15 indicates that Mandy displays autonomous behaviours as they relate to her self-help skills. She consistently tries to do things for herself, but does not hesitate to ask for help when she needs it: "Erikson has pointed to the struggle for autonomy as the big issue in the toddler's life. Autonomy means self-determination, independence. It is the ability to decide for oneself what one is going to do. Autonomy means, 'Me do it!' It means, 'no!'" ("Foundations" course). Mandy is often heard saying both of these phrases; however, avoiding direct commands successfully avoids power struggles when caregivers need Mandy to move through a transition (e.g., leaving a play activity to prepare for lunch).

Another issue in toddlerhood that affects Mandy's emotional development is toilet training. Her mother has started leaving Mandy's diaper off at home and has asked for consistency at childcare. The event sampling indicates that Mandy's attempts at toileting are positively supported and that she does not seem to be experiencing any stress in relation to this new routine. She accepts it as part of her day; however, this is a new skill. Sensitive and positive encouragement is very important to keep her from feeling that she is being pressured. Positive reinforcement (big fuss when successful!) results in pride-like behaviour on Mandy's part.

Separation is usually an issue in toddlerhood, but Mandy appears to have successfully achieved the ability to separate from her parents. The anecdotal record done November 5 is evidence that she has formed a positive attachment and trusting relationship with her mother. This enables her to separate, knowing her mother is going to work and will return later. Wilson, Douville-Watson, and Watson (1995) suggest that "becoming a separate psychological being is one of the most complicated tasks a toddler has to face. During the two years starting from birth, the child establishes a very strong attachment to the mother" (p. 302). The more secure this relationship has been prior to 2, the easier the separation process.

Greenspan and Greenspan's(1985)theory of emotional development indicates that, by 24 months of age,children should be encouraged to express their feelings as emotional ideas rather than just act them out. Mandy is very successful at this and often chooses to play in the dramatic play area with dolls,dress-up clothes, toys, and materials from other parts of the room. She is also ableto create images in her mind, pretending to be "mommy" while she cuddles a doll(Greenspan and Greenspan,1985). Her excellent language skills enable her to express her role in play and to use items symbolically.

Mandy's ability to make independent choices throughout the day and her even, cheerful disposition are indicators that her emotional development is healthy for a 2-year-old. She is now entering what Erikson called the stage of initiative versus guilt,reflecting the "beginning of guilt-like behaviour,pride-like behaviour and shame-like behaviour" (Barrett et al., 1995, p. 262).

Social Development

Mandy is happy to play alongside the other children, engaging most often in parallel play, which is typical at this stage (Parten 1932-33). The running record observation andphotographs give evidence that she likes to watch what others are doing, or likes to play alongside them.Her play behaviour in the playground as she walks along with the children playing with the wagon is evidence of onlooker play. The daily log chart identifies pretend and symbolic play activity in which Mandy participates in solitary play or plays parallel to other children. While she may engage other children in play briefly, she prefers to play her own game. Mildred Parten identified six categories of social play. Mandy's play activity best fits Parten's second, third, and fourth levels--solitary, onlooker, and parallel, respectively: "The second level in Parten's hierarchy, solitary play, involves a child playing independently and making no effort to interact with anyone else. The next level, onlooker play, occurs when a child watches other children play. At the fourth level, parallel play, a child plays in similar ways as another child with similar toys but does not interact with the other child" (Barrett et al., 1995, p. 326). The running record observation gives evidence of both solitary and onlooker play. The daily log chart shows that Mandy, while engaged in pretend play,was playing alongside other children in dramatic play, but participating in her own activity.

Mandy likes to play with a variety of materials while in childcare. Her mother identifies her favourite activities at home as "playing with dolls, reading, riding her bike, and helping mom with cleaning or laundry." Likewise, at daycare, Mandy engages in a variety of play activities throughout the day. Her ability to move between different activities contributes to her ability to practise social skills with caregivers and other children in the room: "When toddlers play together, they talk to one another, and this gives them a chance to practice both their language and social skills" (Barrett et al., 1995, p. 238).

The checklist indicates that Mandy imitates adult behaviour in play, as seen in her play behaviours identified in the daily log chart and by her mom in the health report. Although she is egocentric (see the incident in the running record where she is upset that another child is using the slide at the playground), Mandy's language skills contribute greatly to her ability to communicate with caregivers and other children. She is aware of her peers throughout the day; she screams with the other toddlers at the playground in response to their screaming. Still participating in her own play, she does not hesitate to "join the fun" with the others.

Mandy's social development is within the typical range for a 2-year-old. She enjoys dressing up, imitates family activities, likes to be around other children, but tends to observe, sometimes imitating their actions (screaming), and explores everything, including other children. She is independent, but able to approach caregivers when she feels the need (Allen & Marotz, 1999, p. 83). In a photograph of Mandy in the playground, she is motioning that she would like to be picked up; the running record shows that she approached a caregiver for a cuddle.

Cognitive Development

Mandy loves to explore her environment and tries most materials and activities in it. When something new is introduced, she is eager to see what it is and make a decision about her level of participation. She prefers activities that do not involve "getting her hands dirty." As a result, a variety of sensory experiences must be available so that she gets the stimulation she needs as well as opportunities for creative expression through creative art activities.

Mandy's ability to expand symbolic thinking skills contributes greatly to her language development. Her ability to represent things with other things (e.g., she brings a toy car to the dramatic play centre and uses it as a bus to take us to the store; she uses a large box in the room as a slide) indicates that she is moving into the first substage of Piaget's pre-operational stage, called "preconceptual." For example, Mandy is able to keep track of time by understanding what is coming next (e.g., "We are going to eat lunch and then it is time for a nap"; understanding the routine, she knows that she is to go to her cot after lunch). She is beginning to classify and label objects (matching game, mittens and hats) and has some understanding of quantity (more, gone), number (more), space (up, down, behind, under, over), and time (soon, now). Wilson, Douville-Watson, and Watson (1995) identify these concepts as typical for Mandy's age.

Mandy's love of books is an asset and this contributes to her cognitive and language development. She is exposed to a variety of topics and information, facilitating her learning about the world around her. She loves to manipulate linking blocks, and enjoys making things out of them. For example, she makes a hat out of star linking blocks--linking them in a circle and putting them on her head!

Mandy also displays "deferred imitation" in her play activities. For example, during water play in which soap was added to make bubbles, Mandy went to the kitchen centre and brought out some dishes. She identified her activity, "Washing dishes!"--clearly representing imitation of washing dishes at home. The developmental checklist used for this analysis identifies imitation of adult behaviours as within the norm for a 2-year-old.

Mandy's physical development is a factor in her cognitive development: "Toddlers learn with their whole bodies, not just their heads. They learn more through their hands than they do through their ears. They learn by doing, not only by just thinking. They learn by touching, mouthing, and trying out, not by being told" (Gonzalez-Mena, 1986). The use of her whole body rather than just her hands during the matching game is an example of physical development contributing to a cognitive learning experience.

Emotional development also contributes to cognitive learning. Mandy's trust in and comfort with her environment enable her to explore and therefore experience with confidence. This greatly facilitates her learning; she can make choices and find activities that have meaning for her. The major accomplishments of toddlerhood include "growing independence . . . self-help skills such as dressing, feeding, washing and toileting. . . . Learning to use the toilet, like all the other self-help skills, is a physical feat, as well as an intellectual and emotional one" (Gonzalez-Mena, 1986).

Temperament/Personality

The health questionnaire identifies Mandy as "sometimes shy, sometimes outgoing, friendly, cautious, and easygoing." The daily log chart indicates that Mandy is usually cheerful, adapted to routines, and most often in a positive mood. Her activity level is high. She moves easily from one activity to another and is eager to explore new materials in the environment. While Mandy approaches new situations with confidence, it is important to allow her to join the experience at her own pace. She will often watch for a few minutes before joining in.

Transitions pose little problem for Mandy. She listens to instructions and is usually eager to please when asked to do something. Her continuing need for independence needs to be fostered by caregivers. Mandy responds best when given choices that ultimately encourage the desired behaviour, rather than when direct demands are made.

Mandy's cheerful disposition and positive interactions with caregivers and peers can always be depended on. She loves to engage caregivers in her games, especially pretend play, and is able to extend the play experience as it progresses. A dress-up activity turned into a major cleaning out of the dress-up bench--trying on new outfits throughout the activity! Her mother is quite right about Mandy's friendliness. As she matures, pro-social and helping skills are emerging, and her ready smile makes her a positive influence on everyone in the room.

The Whole Child

Mandy's development in all domains meets or exceeds the norms for her age (2 years). While this analysis looks at each domain separately, it is important to note that development becomes more integrated in toddlerhood. Balance is needed to facilitate development: "Overemphasis in one area or limited involvement in another may create unnecessary stress or it may delay development for the child" (Wilson, Douville-Watson, & Watson, 1995, p. 35)

The fact that Mandy was born eight weeks prematurely (see health report) does not seem to have delayed her development in any area. Her physical stature is small (she weighs about 9.5 kg --the average identified in Allen and Marotz (1994) is 12 to 14.5 kg); however, her physical capabilities fall within the norm. Two-year-olds typically weigh about four times their birth weight; this puts Mandy right at the norm (birth weight was 2.3 kg). She is emotionally able to take risks. Her natural curiosity encourages lots of exploration in her environment; this is significantly facilitated by her physical competence, which also contributes greatly to her feelings of confidence.

Mandy's fluent language skills are also critical to her overall development. She can express her needs and desires verbally, understand simple directions and questions posed by caregivers, assert her independence positively, understand the meaning of symbols facilitating symbolic representation and pretend play activities, and expand her knowledge of the world around her via verbal expression and receptive language.

Overall, Mandy is a wonderful, energized toddler, actively exploring her world, eagerly trying new things, all the while asserting her independence. Her egocentricity is beginning to give way as emerging pro-social skills are observed. She is liked by her peers and rarely gets into power struggles with other toddlers. Her sunny disposition makes her a positive influence in the toddler room.

References Used

Allen, K.E., & Marotz, L.R. (1999). *Development profiles: Pre-birth through eight* (2nd ed.). Albany, NY: Delmar.

Barrett, K.C., et al. (1995). *Child development.* Westerville, OH: Glencoe.

Biracree, T.,& Biracree, N. (1999). *The parents' book of facts: Child development from birth to age five.* New York: Facts on File.

Brazelton, T.B. (1994). *Touchpoints: Your child's emotional and behavioral development.* Reading, MA: Addison-Wesley.

Cole, M. et al.(2004). *The Development of children.* New York: W.H. Freeman.

Foundations: Observation and development [Handout, course CY-106]. Toronto: Centennial College.

Gonzalez-Mena, Janet. (1986, November). Toddlers: What to expect. *Young Children.*

Greenspan, S.I., & Greenspan, N.T. (1985). *First feelings: Milestones in the emotional development of your baby and child.* New York: Viking.

How language develops and what you can do [Handout, Toddler Development course]. Toronto: Centennial College.

Intellectual development. (1995). *Readings Package,* 8b iv. Toronto: Centennial College.

McCaie, L. [Supervising teacher, Childcare Centre]. Personal conversations.

Outline of expected ages and stages in the development of spoken language. (1995). *Readings Package,* 8b vii. Toronto: Centennial College.

Parten, M. (1950). *Surveys, Polls, and Samples: Practical Procedures* in *ANNALS of the American Academy of Political and Social Science* 271: pp. 203-204.

Sheridan M.D. (1975). *The developmental progress of infants and young children* (3rd ed.). London: Her Majesty's Stationery Office.

Skarakis-Doyle, Elizabeth. (1988a). Language development. Tuscon, AZ: Communication Skill Builders.

Skarakis-Doyle, Elizabeth. (1988b). Speech development. Tuscon, AZ: Communication Skill Builders.

Weir, M. [Mandy's mother]. Personal interviews.

Wilson, L.C., Douville-Watson, L., & Watson, M.A. (1995). *Infants and toddlers: Curriculum and teaching* (3rd ed.). Albany, NY: Delmar.

Observation Sample 9.5

This report, presented to the parents at the time of a portfolio-review meeting, briefly outlines the contents of the portfolio, the child's developmental profile, and new program plans. It summarizes the inferences made in the portfolio analysis, stating them clearly and concisely for the benefit of the parents.

What curriculum plan could you develop from this report?

PORTFOLIO REVIEW MEETING REPORT

Child's name: Jill   **Date:** November 21, 2007
D.O.B./age: Nov. 22, 2006/1 year old   **Meeting called by:** Art (ECE student)
Those present: Art, Adam and Dulcie (parents), and Tina (teacher)
Intention of meeting: To review portfolio

Review of recent additions to portfolio: Photographs, artwork, and summaries
Changed context, social, or family circumstances: None
Development summary given by: Art

Summary details: Observations (time sampling, checklist, and running record), health report, ecological systems, family tree, videotapes, baby book from parents, daily logs

Cognition: Jill understands the use of many everyday objects. She understands simple directions and has an understanding of object permanence.
Personality: Jill is striving for independence right now and is starting to enjoy doing things on her own, such as eating. She has demonstrated curiosity in new experiences.
Language and communication: Jill babbles typically for a child her age. She also has demonstrated the beginning of her vocabulary by saying "hello." Jill is always able to convey her needs, whether it's by reaching up toward what she wants or by falling down when she does not want to move.
Emotional development: Jill shows no fear of strangers or of being hurt by her actions, which is typical for an infant of her age. She also has demonstrated consistently her wants and needs.
Physical development: Jill's physical development is consistent with a child of her age; however, she does need some encouragement in the area of stair climbing. Her gross motor skills are very advanced and her fine motor skills are also extremely good for her age; she grasps and passes items from one hand to the other.
Social skills: Jill is egocentric, which is quite usual at this age. She seems to enjoy the company of other adults and is not afraid to approach them and ask to be held.

Curriculum implications: Activities are being planned to help Jill in her social skills such as playing beside other children in parallel play. Also there are activities to help her stair-climbing motor skills.
Program plan strategies: Activities involving more pro-social, self-help skills and social interaction will benefit Jill at this time and should be offered to her throughout the day.

Group observations: Analysis

Anecdotal records, checklists, samplings, and a variety of charted observations are suitable methods for gaining observational information about what is happening among groups of children. Though the depth of understanding about individual children must be diminished in **group observations**, we do need them to tell us about the dynamics of the group, their combined interests and motivations as well as their social functioning. Analyzing these observations depends upon the same principles as with other observations, but the focus is typically on the reason why the observation was undertaken— possibly to gain information to help with program planning and curriculum development.

Follow the observational cycle, check your recordings as suggested with individual recordings, summarize the data using a framework that gives you the information you need, reflect upon the information and the experience, analyze everything carefully looking at both individual and collective actions, support all your inferences (as outlined earlier), and then consider how you will manage the findings and what you will do to respond.

The difference between group observations and group portfolios lies only in their complexity; the process for analysis is the same. Usually a **group portfolio** focuses on a project, series of activities or field trips, or an area of curriculum, a particular learning centre, or a domain of development. The educator and children, wherever possible, gather information and observations related to the topic. Both the process and the products of the experience are typically included in the portfolio. Technology may be used to assist the process, as long as it doesn't dominate the learning. Analyzing the portfolio has to centre on the reasons for its creation in the first place. That said, the analysis must include a series of inferences that are suitably supported and validated.

Using Observational Data to Plan

Those who teach teachers often say that students need to learn how to set goals and objectives for children. Such a philosophy makes people believe that achievement is only possible with goal-setting. It disregards the idea that children will progress through the developmental stages, given appropriate support and open-ended experiences that enable them to operate at their own levels. Learning and skills development do not depend only on our overt intervention. There is a difference between making appropriate curriculum provision based on observation of the child's developmental needs and goal-setting that presumes that you know what the child's "next stage" is. However knowledgeable you are about **patterns of development**, it is rarely useful to set specific goals for children who are in the mainstream of our education and care agencies.

Children with **special needs** who are identified and diagnosed may benefit from a more structured goal-setting approach because **objectives** can break down skills into component parts. These objectives can be addressed separately, one at a time.

Interpretation of observational information is essential for all planning and curriculum design. Many inappropriate assessments have resulted in poor provision; the teacher's focus should be on supplying appropriate experiences and guidance to support children in their own efforts to struggle with new skills.

Whether or not you set goals may be inconsequential in shaping how children actually behave. Merely setting goals does not bring about their achievement. However, thoughtful programming must always have some deliberate intention.

Linking observations and portfolios to programming

How the analysis of observations and portfolios will be used depends upon the curriculum model. In the project approach, the children's interests and responses to teacher-initiated ideas might be a starting point. Other curriculum approaches might focus on facilitating the development of each child according to developmental domains and needs. Every program has its own philosophy and practice, so each program needs to use its observational analysis differently. The common element is that the analysis of observations can lead directly to any kind of programming, however structured, emergent, or spontaneous.

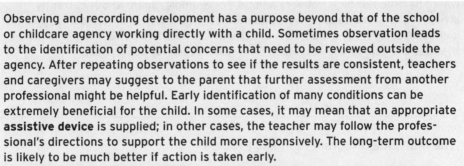

TAKING A SPECIAL LOOK: Early identification and intervention

Observing and recording development has a purpose beyond that of the school or childcare agency working directly with a child. Sometimes observation leads to the identification of potential concerns that need to be reviewed outside the agency. After repeating observations to see if the results are consistent, teachers and caregivers may suggest to the parent that further assessment from another professional might be helpful. Early identification of many conditions can be extremely beneficial for the child. In some cases, it may mean that an appropriate **assistive device** is supplied; in other cases, the teacher may follow the professional's directions to support the child more responsively. The long-term outcome is likely to be much better if action is taken early.

In some situations, a special plan of **early intervention** may be developed to support an infant, toddler, or preschooler. The plan can involve many different strategies to support the child's development and relationships. Psychologists or psychiatrists may try to assist before any potential problem rears its head. In other cases, where a developmental problem already exists, they will work with the child, parent, and caregivers or teachers to find appropriate ways of providing support.

Individual program plans

Individual program plans (IPPs) and **individual education plans (IEPs)** are commonly devised for children with identified special needs. But all children have individual needs that should be met. The IPP helps you in that task, by formalizing the process of converting observational and other assessment information into an action plan.

An IPP requires a team approach to piece together all available information about a child and come up with an appropriate response to the child's individual needs. At its best, it is a dynamic ongoing process that changes and is adapted in the light of new information.

Informal IPPs are devised regularly with parents and teachers working cooperatively to observe, evaluate, and assess needs and respond to them. In this case, it might not be a recorded plan. If there are specific concerns about the child's development, the

IPP can be a much more thorough, written teamwork process with clearly defined intentions and practical suggestions or objectives.

A sample IPP can be found in Observation Sample 9.6, and a sample IEP in Observation Sample 9.7. You might develop these to suit your own needs or use standard IPP/IEP forms used in your education or childcare region or authority.

TAKING A SPECIAL LOOK: IPPs for children who have special needs

The idea of the individual program plan is borrowed from the philosophy of those working with children who have special needs. We should find ways to support emerging skills so that we assist development from the child's current skill level rather than jump ahead to the next stage. Designing activities to get a child to where he "should" be is not very helpful. For example, Juan, who is currently struggling to stand despite having malformed feet, is better assisted if we plan his individual program to include lots of activities to help him perfect this skill rather than set the goal of walking, which he may not reach for some time.

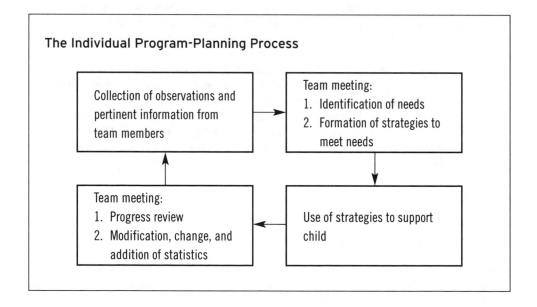

Observation Sample 9.6

This simple IPP is based on behaviours recorded in observations. The child's needs have been determined. Activities are suggested to support skill development.

Individual Program Plan (IPP)

Child's name: Arjumand

Caregiver: Casz

Age/D.O.B.: April 9, 2007/1 year old

Date: April 15, 2008

Area of Development	Needs	Activities
Explores environment using fine motor skills (pincer grasp)	Small objects	Activity pillow with buckle, zipper, shoelace, and Velcro Wind-up toys Putting small blocks in a bucket
Transfer objects from hand to hand	Small objects Chance to explore	Offer toys to Ashley when already has one Passing games (adapted version of "hot potato")
Feed self using a spoon	Opportunity Encouragement Exposure to spoons in a variety of situations	Kitchen play Sensory activities using spoons (e.g., oatmeal play)
Walk alone (began at the end of March)	Open space Encouragement	Gross Motor Room Walks of the centre Nature walks outside Pull toys (e.g., wagons)
Climb on, over, and through objects	Climbing equipment Carpeted/padded areas Sturdy furniture	Slides Cushion ramps, stairs, and blocks Pillows Tunnels
Imitate actions and sounds	Music People Mirrors Toys with sounds	Songs with actions (e.g., "Row Your Boat") Copycat games; if he does something, you repeat it Walks outside so nature sounds can be imitated
Nod for "yes" and shake head for "no"	Opportunity to decide for himself Encouragement Reinforcement	Ask questions and let him tell you when he is done Repeat nods accompanied by you saying "yes"
Follow simple directions	Opportunity Praise Encouragement	Simple "Simon Says" games Head and shoulders, knees and toes Clean-up activities (e.g., put the toy on the shelf) Ask him to do things (e.g., "Please sit down" or "Come here, please")
Openly show affection toward others and his toys (likes to cuddle)	Trust Consistency Soft toys Praise Love	Songs about loving (e.g., Barney song, "I Love You") Pillows Teddy bears (washable) Cuddle Ashley throughout the day

Individual Program Plan

Child's name: _____   Teacher: _____

Age/D.O.B.: _____   Date: _____

Persons participating: _____

Reason for program development: _____

_____

Developmental domain	Observation summary (skills present)	Needs	Intentions	Practical supports	Person responsible

Individual Program Plan Review

Child's name: _____   Teacher: _____

Age/D.O.B.: _____   Date: _____

Persons participating: _____

Reason for program development: _____

_____

Developmental domain	Previous intentions	Observed skills	Progress made	Newly devised supports	Person responsible

Observation Sample 9.7

This thorough IEP was created for Jamilla, who has been identified as needing special support. Jamilla's resource teacher recorded the chart with Jamilla's regular teacher. Note how the link is made between excerpts of observations and what supports and resources Jamilla seems to need.

Individual Education Plan (IEP)

Child's name: Jamilla

Caregivers/Teachers: Ms. Trainor, Ms. Jessop

Age/D.O.B.: 5 years, 7 months

Date: May 7/08

Recorder: Ms. Jessop

Date of last IEP: April 9/07

Comment on success of previous IEP: Jamilla achieved the skills that were needed to perform the activities. There remains some concern about Jamilla's lack of social skills.

Developmental domain	Observation	Support	Response
Physical development: • gross motor	Jamilla watches other children in the playground. Walks around with adult supervisor.	Jamilla needs opportunities to become engaged with other children's activities.	Try parachute games and other noncompetitive games.
• fine motor	Jamilla has started to copy letters and joins in with drawing and "writing." She does some scribble shapes like letters in her name. She notices that other children can write their names.	Opportunities to develop fine motor control (and build self-esteem) are needed.	As Jamilla likes dramatic play, we could introduce a "post office" and writing centre with writing pads, "stamps," envelopes, etc.
Cognition • number	Counting in sequence is no problem 1–20, but Jamilla can only count to 4 or 5 when actually counting objects.	Jamilla needs the chance to have fun with counting experiences.	Sociodramatic play could also have a table (for 6?) to set. Jamilla would enjoy "preparing" a meal for "guests."
• seriation	Jamilla gets confused when putting objects in any kind of sequence. She makes up her own reasons for pictures or objects to be the way she wishes.	Opportunity to seriate in play might add meaning to this.	Provide picture cards of growing seeds, buds opening, etc. (link with spring theme).
• patterning, matching, and sorting	When given assorted items, she can sort them according to colour and kind but not according to two characteristics together. Jamilla likes to play with buttons, shells, and pine cones, making patterns with them. She plays with the materials by herself and rejects involvement with others.	The materials are already available, but these could be extended with other items.	Jamilla can be asked about her patterns--these involve sorting and patterning. She can be encouraged to articulate her reasoning for the patterns.

Developmental domain	Observation	Support	Response
Language • literacy	Jamilla appears to enjoy stories; she wants the same ones re-read. She follows the stories page by page. When sitting alone, she "reads" the story. At other times, Jamilla recognizes word shapes.	Provide other stories and opportunity to talk about the ones she likes. Pick up and reinforce her understanding of words in context.	Offer picture books for Jamilla to create stories. Provide books she likes and reinforce key words. Link words with everyday objects.
• language	Jamilla listens at circle time but only talks confidently one-to-one with an adult. She tends to play alone with a lot of self-talk.	She needs to build confidence.	Avoid forcing Jamilla, but provide opportunity for closeness with an adult.
Social development: • play behaviour	Jamilla tends to play alone. Sometimes she will play alongside others if she is interested in the activity (e.g., cooking).	Jamilla needs confidence to communicate, but her thinking tends to be egocentric. She needs time and play experience.	Encourage parallel play and provide opportunity for some association. Sharing tools may help.
• relationships with adults	Quiet moments alone with the teacher are the happiest times for Jamilla. She jumps up and down with enthusiasm when she starts talking. Soon she is immersed in conversation and she becomes composed again.	She needs one-to-one contact to build trust so that she can become more autonomous.	The new assistant could try to spend extra time so that Jamilla can build trust and begin to "branch out."
Emotions	Jamilla expresses her feelings in quiet communication but does not project her wishes to other children. At times, she is left out of the "girl play" because she can't negotiate.	Jamilla would be happier if she could find her way into the play with her peers.	Role-play situations may help. Strategies to overcome communication problems can come in children's stories.

Note to Jamilla's mom: It would be helpful if Jamilla had opportunity to "help out" with domestic jobs at home and if possible, play with other children. We can discuss ways to helping Jamila to gain social skills at home.

Observation as part of curriculum planning

A child's **curriculum** is his or her whole experience of life. What you may have thought of as "the program" or even "planned activities" forms only a small element of that whole experience. When you take care to observe children in every aspect of their days, from waking through all kinds of family interactions and domestic scenarios as well as more carefully designed daycare or school experiences, you can appreciate the children's styles, individualities, and social contexts, and how these affect their responsiveness and developing skills. As a trained observer, you may make useful inferences from observation in an agency or school setting. Those observations will be much more revealing if you have some previously acquired information about the child's family and background. Observing a child as widely as possible pays off in a picture of the whole rather than unconnected bits of information about some specific area of development.

The great challenge for teachers is to take the time to observe the individual within the group while acknowledging the dynamics of that group and endeavouring to provide for the needs of each child. Teachers need acute observational skills, an understanding of the more **typical patterns of development**, and a philosophy of curriculum that recognizes that everything they provide, including themselves, is part of the curriculum provision. If children are enabled to operate at their own levels, the variation of development within the group can be addressed; if changing environments are provided, children are able to build their own knowledge.

Translating what is observed into plans for meaningful activities and experiences is challenging for many reasons:

1. Observational information can indicate only the child's current **competency** level—this does not, of itself, dictate which skills need enhancing or what new ones could be acquired.

2. Observation and evaluation techniques require detailed analysis of the data if accurate inferences are to be made; analysis requires training and practice.

3. Naturalistic observation puts the emphasis for evaluation on the shoulders of the recorder.

4. The fact that a child is functioning at a particular level does not mean that the child will always develop in a particular sequence within a certain time frame or will always progress and not regress.

5. Programming for groups of children, each of whom is at a different developmental level, can be challenging if the variation is so great that the needs differ.

6. Where teachers believe that programming should focus on developmental needs, they may find that working toward determined learning outcomes or the curriculum of a school board or other authority is not only limiting but impossible.

7. A process needs to be established to move observational information into programming. This is a time-consuming activity that requires observational recording and analytical skills.

These skills are attainable, but teachers have to devote much time and hard work to achieve them. While teachers may struggle against making compromises, they should realize that some compromise is necessary in the most effective curriculum design.

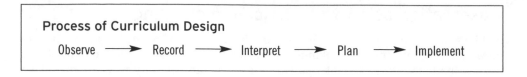

Process of Curriculum Design

Observe ⟶ Record ⟶ Interpret ⟶ Plan ⟶ Implement

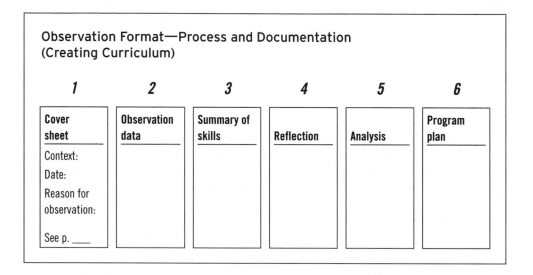

Observation Format—Process and Documentation
(Creating Curriculum)

1	*2*	*3*	*4*	*5*	*6*
Cover sheet Context: Date: Reason for observation: See p. ___	**Observation data**	**Summary of skills**	**Reflection**	**Analysis**	**Program plan**

As part of curriculum design, observation provides ongoing evaluation of each child's environment for development. By observing, teachers can know if their intentions for the children's learning are being fulfilled. How the children respond to experiences helps teachers see how the environment might be changed or modified to facilitate learning.

Teachers and caregivers may use observation as a means of assessing the achievement of previously set goals and objectives. While this may work for some teachers, it may not work for others, particularly if their education philosophy is not one that embraces goal-setting.

Curriculum-planning models

The most effective planning models are rooted in observation and an appropriate evaluation of the child. Such evaluation can be used to indicate current competence in each developmental domain, attempt to predict the sequence of skill acquisition, and provide open-ended experiences from which the child can consolidate or build on skills.

Planning processes should ensure that the needs of the child and the focus of the program are met. Some directions may be set within a developmental context.

Sequential models make assumptions about the stages in which component parts of a competence are acquired. They show little sensitivity to the concepts of learning readiness or levels of **maturation**. Sequential models are more appropriate for children who have special needs and require step-by-step skill building.

Input/outcome planning models factor in both the child's development and adult expectations. Ongoing, well-documented observation of the children may lead the administrator to alter expectations so that unrealistic or inappropriate outcomes are dropped.

Webbing models take into account the child's observed performance and curriculum goals. They try to relate all curriculum areas through a single topic or focus. These plans can generate many good ideas for constructing the learning environment; however, although they are intended to factor in observed information, their structure does not allow for it in any clear manner.

Topic planning may be based on notions of what is appropriate or desirable for the children to learn. This approach does not encourage optimal learning, because it does not grow from the children's needs, interests, and abilities. Children may well get something from the topic, but it is likely to be limiting. Thematic approaches may have similar limitations but do acknowledge, at least, the need for interrelated learning experiences. Where the theme focus lends itself to open-ended activities, the children can operate at their own levels.

Emergent curriculum, demonstrated by many progressive programs, focuses on elaborating on the children's interests, as they are observed by the educator. When these interests and motivations are identified, the educator provides a range of experiences and activities that mesh with and challenge each child. This allows children to operate at their own levels of competence within a group.

High/Scope's **Child Observation Record (COR). High/Scope** is a well-respected philosophy, curriculum, and evaluation system for early childhood designed for centre-based and home childcare. It has a proven success record, in that children in High/Scope programs achieve positive learning outcomes and are particularly conscious of their decision-making, activity, and reflection through guidance to "plan," "do," and "review" their activities.

The **project approach**, which is described in theory and practice by Sylvia Chard (1998 and 2001), involves an in-depth investigation of a real-world topic. It meets the learning needs of a group of children at different stages of development, and provides the opportunity for the individual and social construction of knowledge. Planning for this involves a complex webbing process of connected ideas, starting points for discovery, and a flexible but structured plan of directions and subject areas for learning.

Reggio Emilia uses an emergent curriculum and a project approach for its exemplary practice. Documentation forms an integral part of the reflective process for both adults and children.

Responsive curriculum is a sensitive and caring approach to providing for the immediate and long-term needs of young children. Magda Gerber (1993) exemplifies this approach. Martin (2003) also offers a responsive programming approach based on the observed interests and the emerging developmental competence of babies and toddlers. This approach is most suitable for the youngest children, but its sensitivity is applicable to all children.

What these planning models have in common is the understanding that observation is the key to effective programming, that planning must be based on the realities of the children's development and needs, and that the children's environments are essentially social. Most accept that learning involves an individual social construction (Piaget 1954) as well as a social process (Vygotsky 1978).

Observation Sample 9.8 shows an example of how group interests can result in a complex and dynamic series of experiences and learning.

The gap between what the child can do independently and what she can do with support should be understood when planning experiences. Vygotsky (1978) offers an excellent model for responsive curriculum in the theory of the **zone of proximal development** (see page 67). Sensitive observation of a child's behaviour will indicate when and how to move in to assist learning.

Each of these approaches to planning focuses on observing children and determining their interests. High-quality practice for children involves these kinds of programming rather than approaches using goal-setting, preplanned themes, recipe book activities, or other **teacher-directed** delivery of curriculum content. Because **child-centred** approaches to planning demand detailed observation of each child's needs and interests, observers must pay attention to the methods they select to gain pertinent information, and be able to translate that information into action plans. We address methods in the following chapters, along with how data can be used for planning.

Using planning models

Advantages

- Planning models rely on observing "real" children in "real" settings—rather than imposing unrelated ideas/concepts.
- Visual presentations enable teachers to conceptualize the plan easily.
- These models are based on sound theoretical concepts.
- Teamwork planning can be effective when a common planning model is used.
- A model can be selected to fit the program's philosophy.
- The model may offer planning for developmentally appropriate experiences while meeting program outcomes.
- Most models are circular and ongoing.
- A model may easily build in a component for evaluation of its success.

Disadvantages

- Planning models depend on an understanding of curriculum design.
- The easiest options may be the least developmentally appropriate.
- The plan may be too abstract or not sufficiently flexible.
- If the plan is based on observation, perceptions may vary.
- Models may be used without an understanding of their underlying premise.
- A model may conform to the needs of administrators, rather than children's needs.

Observation Sample 9.8

This web outlines an individual curriculum plan for a child in Grade 1. Moving out from observing the child's interests and abilities, the teacher plans activities to lead to desired achievements or learning.

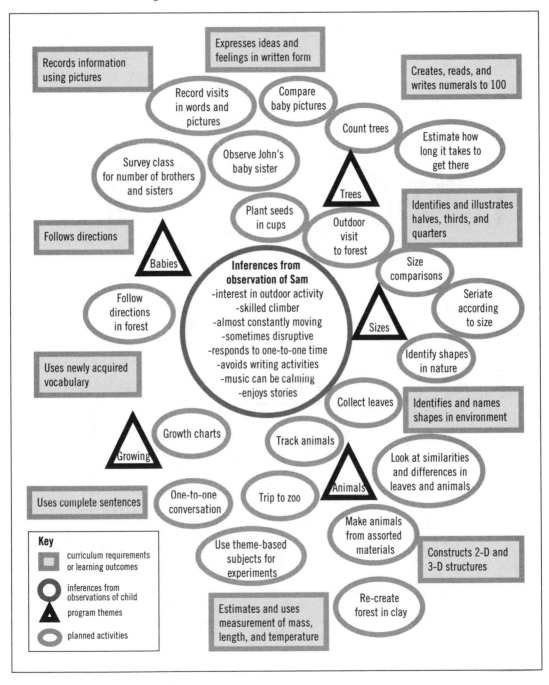

Observation Sample 9.9

This integrative planning model focuses on the whole experience of the child related to a theme rather than on particular curriculum areas. The model leads to planning experiences and environments but does not determine expected outcomes; the open-ended activities allow each child to learn what he or she is developmentally ready to do. Teachers and caregivers can use their observations of the children to help plan motivating experiences and to intervene appropriately to support each child's learning. Observation of the children's responses also leads to modified or new activities.

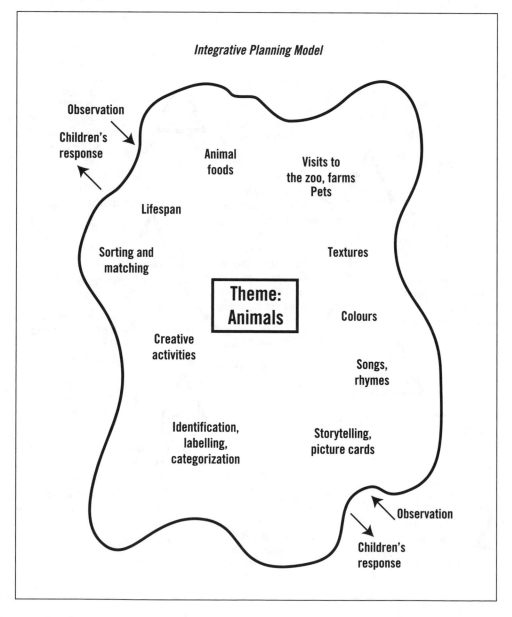

Integrative Planning Model

Observation
Children's response

Animal foods

Visits to the zoo, farms Pets

Lifespan

Sorting and matching

Textures

Theme: Animals

Colours

Creative activities

Songs, rhymes

Identification, labelling, categorization

Storytelling, picture cards

Observation
Children's response

Planning models based on observation

The role of the teacher is as important to the curriculum as the materials and set-up are. These planning models based on observation may help you in your responsibility. More specific samples, showing a curriculum web and an integrative planning model, can be found in Observation Samples 9.8 and 9.9.

Current directions in curriculum design

Some educators who believe in developmental programming have been disheartened by the recent trend toward a standards-based curriculum. A prescribed curriculum may take into account the variations in children's development. However, inappropriate practice demands that young children acquire a particular knowledge base or set of skills; this can produce justifiable concerns. While skills may be acquired according to the curriculum, it is the underlying construction of their meaning that may be out of reach. We know that every child's learning is sequential and developmental, and those programs that facilitate this learning most effectively are holistic, child-centred, and developmental. Teaching skills or trying to impart knowledge outside the child's level of maturation is a waste of time. Take a look at the child's emerging skills and support him with exemplary practice, not formal lessons!

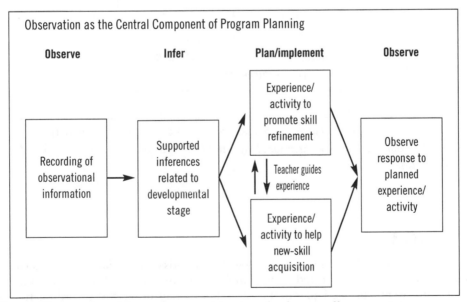

This model is one desired by teachers practising in a developmentally appropriate program, who use naturalistic observation as their primary tool for evaluation. The planning and implementation of learning experiences is supported by the teacher's guidance.

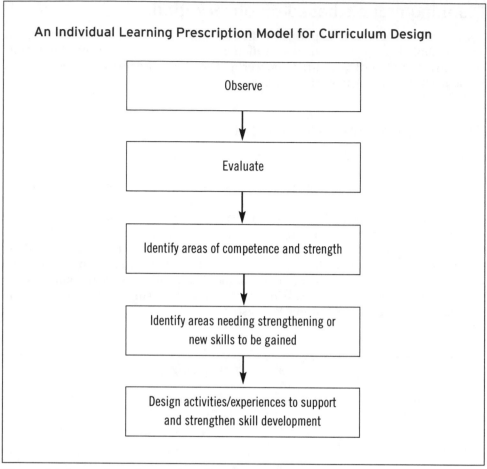

An Individual Learning Prescription Model for Curriculum Design

Observe

↓

Evaluate

↓

Identify areas of competence and strength

↓

Identify areas needing strengthening or
new skills to be gained

↓

Design activities/experiences to support
and strengthen skill development

This model shows a logical progression from observation to the design of an activity. It requires thorough analysis of observational data to identify "areas needing strengthening" or "new skills to be gained."

Summary

The observation cycle is an ongoing process; more observations are sought as earlier observations are being reflected upon, summarized, and analyzed. The student needs to take time to practise each part of the observation cycle: observing, recording, reflecting, summarizing, analyzing, and responding. Readers should already have skill in observing and recording; this chapter requires a number of higher-order thinking skills.

Reflection requires an open-ended thought process, summarizing necessitates organizational and categorizing skills, but the analysis demands the highest level of thinking. Appropriate inferences need to be made about the child that are then supported and validated using norms or theories and good argument. Portfolios that have a large amount of material, simple observations, group observations, and group portfolios all follow the same process that builds toward an authentic assessment. The findings from the analysis are essential for good program planning and curriculum design within almost any philosophical approach.

Key Terms

- action plan
- analysis
- assistive device
- bias
- categorization
- child-centred
- child observation record (COR)
- competency
- contextualizing
- critical thinking
- curriculum
- duration
- early intervention
- emergent curriculum
- emerging skills
- group observations
- group portfolios
- High/Scope
- individual education plans (IEPs)
- individual program plan (IPPs)
- inferences
- inference-checking
- inference-making
- input/outcome-planning model
- maturation
- naturalistic
- norm of development
- objectives
- objectivity
- observation cycle
- patterns of development
- portfolio assessment
- project approach
- reflection
- Reggio Emilia
- responsive curriculum
- sequential models
- special needs
- summary
- teacher-directed
- topic planning
- typical patterns of development
- validate
- webbing models
- work sampling
- zone of proximal development

www.cccf-fcsge.ca/practice/programming/stage_en.html
Information from the Canadian Child Care Federation about emergent curriculum.

www.project-approach.com
The project approach.

www.teachingstrategies.com/pages/page.cfm?pageid=262
This commercial site explains the "creative curriculum" and assessment link.

www.nativechild.com
A look at a Native preschool curriculum.

www.phenomenologyonline.com/inquiry/42.html
Phenomenological reflection.

http://webspace.ship.edu/cgboer/piaget.html
A biography and explanation of Piaget's key theoretical ideas. These may be used to validate inferences made from observational data.

http://www.kolar.org/vygotsky/
A brief biography of Vygotsky. This site has many links to material useful in their application to your observations.

http://kidshealth.org/parent/growth/learning/iep.html
Here you can read about the use of individual education plans as they relate to children who have special needs.

http://www.socialresearchmethods.net/kb/relandval.php
In the context of social research methods this site explains the concepts of validity and reliability in a way that relates to the observation/portfolio analysis process.

www.socialresearchmethods.net/kb/analysis.php
How to manage data, prepare it (summarize), describe it, and test hypotheses and models. The home page lists all the areas that are covered in research areas.

10 Observations That Give Cause for Concern

All activities need to be assessed for their level of risk. Here Jacob climbs although he has already fallen several times while doing the same thing. We need to observe the child's behaviour and make quick decisions about their safety.

As hard as sharing concerns may be, they may make all the difference in the world to a child. The hardest part is getting started.
Stanley Greenspan (2005)

Some sexual behaviours are more concerning than others. Highly inappropriate, intensive, unwanted or aggressive sexual behaviour is a cause for concern.
About Kids Health, The Hospital for Sick Children (2008)

Childcare providers can and should watch for red flags. Where developmental milestones focus on what a child can do by a certain age, red flags usually warn parents, caregivers and health professionals of potential delays and disabilities when a child cannot do something by a certain age, or when a child has significant difficulty doing something that most children can do easily.
Scott G. Allen (2005)

Focus Questions

1. What are the signs or symptoms of health concerns that require documentation and a report to the child's parents?

2. How might an educator document a young child's repeated challenging behaviours?

3. What observed behaviours might lead an educator to infer that a child needs formal assessments that are beyond her scope?

4. How does an educator respond if she suspects from her observations that a child might be being abused?

5. What are the best methods of documentation for each of the following: possible health concerns, challenging behaviours, apparent developmental issues, and possible child abuse?

Learning Outcomes

By reading this chapter and applying the ideas to practice, learners will

- identify a range of causes for concern in the health, well-being, behaviour, development, and protection of young children.

- select appropriate methods and formats for documenting significant signs, symptoms, challenges, behavioural indicators, and other pertinent information about children.

- be prepared to document occurrences of behaviour or other signs of potential abuse and follow policies and procedures appropriate to the situation.

- appreciate both the responsibilities and the limitations of their role when a cause for concern about a child or children has been identified.

Up to this point in the book we have examined a variety of observation and recording methods. Skill needs to be built over time so that these methods are selected wisely to gather the information that the educator seeks. Also, we have spent time thinking about typical patterns of behaviour and the usual demands placed on educators to document children's progress, and documentation that supports children's learning and nurturance. These things form the backbone of the educator's work. However, there are demands on the educator to make sure that she observes a variety of other things—many of which the adult does not want to see.

These **causes for concern** include looking for and recording signs of children's health concerns; this is an ongoing task. From time to time the educator encounters children who exhibit **challenging behaviours**; here, too, she needs to observe closely and find ways of documenting pertinent aspects of the behaviour in order to address it. Although every child's development is different, there will be situations in which the educator has some concerns about a child's developmental progress—this must be observed with careful scrutiny, and appropriate **documentation** is necessary, not only for the child's immediate programming, but also to contribute to formal assessments undertaken by specialists in whatever field is thought necessary. One of the saddest scenarios is a child showing signs of possible abuse or neglect; here objective and precise documentation is essential.

The focus of this chapter, therefore, is to consider the many possible causes for concern that educators might have from their informal observations of a child, or from formal methods of observation and analysis: a change of appearance, behavioural concerns, health issues, changing patterns of development, a range of situational challenges, or even just an intuitive response of "Uh-oh."

Causes for Concern

DEFINITION: Cause for concern

Any sign, symptom, indicator, or intuitive response that leads an adult to think that a problem, concern, or issue might exist that warrants further observation and investigation.

Most causes for concern are relatively minor and can be dealt with easily, but others might need targeted attention but can be solved by the patient educator. But there are also more serious issues that need careful handling and/or help from colleagues and other professionals. The educator has the key role of identifying a potential issue, but in most of these major challenges it is not the educator who makes a formal assessment. Those who have the responsibility for applying specialist knowledge are general practitioners, pediatricians, social workers, psychologists, resource teachers, psychiatrists, child protection officers, early interventionists, counsellors, and those involved in developmental work with children with special needs. The educator usually brings her findings to the attention of the parents (except in the case of potential abuse or neglect), and offers them support, empathy, resources, and suggestions for follow-up; it is not the role of the educator to make a direct referral to a specialist.

Educators need to understand the many observable indicators that constitute cause for concern about a child: health problems, developmental issues, behavioural challenges, abuse or neglect, emergencies, and reactions to trauma. While educators should not make a diagnosis or assessment on the basis of their observations and recordings, these early identifications of potential challenges are important, and may play a key role in protecting and supporting the child's health, development, safety, and well-being.

Categories of causes for concern

Concerns drawn from observations might lead to the need for one or more types of assessment and follow-up:

1. **Signs** *and* **symptoms** *of possible* **health concerns** *or* **failure to thrive**—for example, a child appears to have an untreated condition, seems unwell, is sleepy, has a variety of symptoms, seems to be apathetic.

2. *Apparent developmental concerns*—for example, a child appears to regress rather than progress, seems to be slower than average in gaining specific skills, has some unusual **patterns of development**, has difficulty paying attention.

3. *Challenging behaviours*—for example, a child lacks self-regulatory skills, is disruptive, has difficulty sharing.

4. *Potential abuse or neglect*—for example, a child has unexplained marks on her arms, seems to relate to others with unusual apathy, shows some disturbing behaviour.

5. *Accidents and incidents*—for example, a child falls from a climber, has a seizure, bumps his head, gets a serious cut. (These situations should be dealt with by staff trained in first aid—paramedics should be called if necessary. This type of concern is not fully dealt with in this text. Refer to the Red Cross, St. John's Ambulance, or other first-aid training authority.)

6. *Responses to psychological* **trauma**—for example, a child loses a parent in violent circumstances, experiences a hurricane or tsunami, survives a bomb. (This is a complex and emerging field. At this time we are unable to offer a complete list of indicators of such trauma. In most cases the trauma is known to parents and educators who must monitor the child's behaviour, provide nurturance, and suitable guidance and counselling.)

7. **Emergency preparedness**—for example, knowing what to do if there is an indication that a child is going to be abducted, if terrorists are about to strike, if/when war is imminent, when there is severe weather or there are "acts of God." (While we do mention emergency issues here, we cannot discuss them fully or give sufficient attention to the need for preparedness and established procedures and protocols. Observe, act, and then document when you are able.)

It is the task of this text to offer a variety of behavioural and other indicators that educators might observe. Unfortunately, this does not allow for the kind of discussion that might fully explore the underlying causes of neglect or abuse. In particular, though we offer key points, we focus on documentation rather than the deeper explanations. We recommend that student educators and qualified professionals attend current workshops exploring these issues, read extensively, become acquainted with the policies and protocols that apply to their work, and take steps to be objective and non-judgmental. Each of the types of cause for concern indicates a serious issue; it is essential that everyone understand their role, and not make hasty or rash assessments.

Although we have divided the indicators into four categories, it should be understood that observed behaviours might fall into more than one category. For example, a child who has a developmental challenge might also have a related health concern.

WARNING!

Educators cannot make a diagnosis of a health problem, diagnose a child's disability, or deem abuse or neglect to have occurred; they merely offer evidence in the form of observations so that specialized professionals can make these assessments.

Limitations of This Chapter

Because of the complexity of the issues, this chapter cannot explore all the reasons why causes for concern may have occurred. We advise readers to become acquainted with the medical, social, environmental, and other aspects of the challenges faced by many children. Most early childhood education programs offer courses in health, child abuse, developmental diversity, sociology, etc. that can help you to better understand the issues, offer you tools for supporting any child with a special need, and supply intervention or support after investigations have been conducted, diagnoses made, and support systems put in place. Although most of us would rather not have to deal with emergencies, abductions, war, terrorism, and disasters, we might take a role in managing their effects upon children. Also we need to use our considerable observation and documentation skills to protect children as much as we can; we must make sure that our observation focuses on the whole environment of the child.

There are other causes for concern in a broader context. Although we cannot include much information here about them, we can mention them in passing, and suggest that educators need to become vigilant about safety and security, anticipate problems, practise emergency protocols, and keep an eye out for suspicious people and objects. Such issues are starting to invade the supposedly safe places we provide for children. We cannot leave emergency management up to the government alone. This big picture is as important as, if not more important than, observation within the usual routines of the intimate environment of the children's room. Keep alert and observe!

Strengths of This Chapter

This chapter is about what to look for when you have a **hunch** something is wrong, and how to respond by documenting and reporting such information. In such situations we then see how **policies** and **procedures** are essential. Parents and early childhood educators often know a child's typical behaviour patterns best, and are able to notice when things don't look as expected. Educators provide essential information that leads to otherwise undetected challenges and problems.

In this chapter, you will learn about what to look for, how to respond to hunches about any cause for concern, how important policies and procedures are, and which formats are most useful when observing and documenting. We also remind readers of the heightened need for confidentiality and professional ethics. Most importantly, we look at who needs to be contacted—for although initial responsibility often lies with the educator, there is a need to know one's professional limitations and when to contact specialists. Of course, it is parents who are primarily responsible for seeking professional help for their children; our part is to provide them with good information and assist in problem-solving for the sake of the child. However, in situations in which child abuse may have occurred, the parents must not be questioned or accused by the educator, nor must there be any expression of the educator's concerns to either of them.

Responding to Hunches: Observations and Intuition

Sometimes you may observe things that cannot be ignored; these are straightforward situations to act and follow up on. There may also be policies in place to guide your actions. Other times, you may be less sure, because you lack specific examples of behaviour or signs that lead you to be concerned, but you may have a hunch or feel something isn't quite right. Because you are, or will be, trained and prepared for working with young children, these intuitive thoughts would probably be more reliable than if you lacked that education, so you should pay attention to your hunches. But if you need to report your hunches to others, make sure you do not confuse them with clear, observable evidence. It is appropriate to document your hunches, but they must be identified as such.

In some cases you may be able to wait until your hunch is supported or undermined by what you observe, but some areas of concern cannot wait. If, for example, there is a question of **child abuse** or neglect, your suspicions must be disclosed to a **child protection agency** immediately. Health concerns are similarly urgent and must be documented and shared with the child's parent. The actions that you need to take vary with the type of concern and the need for fast action.

Policies and procedures

Although licensing requirements vary across Canada, childcare centres and schools are typically required to have in place policies covering suspected child abuse, emergencies, health issues, exclusion from the centre (because of infection and/or behaviour), accidents and incidents, behaviour management, privacy and access to information, and child assessment, among others. Usually the regulating ministry outlines the requirements for policies and their content. They need to conform to all levels of legislation, including local regulations.

The policies outline the actions that must be taken in a wide variety of situations. These include to whom situations must be reported, how they are to be documented, and the steps that must be taken. They outline the responsibilities of different members of staff. Policies, when written well, are extremely helpful for all concerned, because they offer an agreed pathway that must be taken, and prevent role confusion. They can help everyone involved to know what to do and to remember all the components of that role. They also signify what is beyond the boundaries of the role—what you shouldn't be involved in or know about.

Become familiar with all the policies that govern your work, and know where they are stored so that you can refer to them if and when a situation arises to which they apply.

As a professional educator you have a higher burden of responsibility than the average "person in the street." In the case of suspected child abuse or neglect, you have a legal responsibility to contact a child protection agency directly if you have cause for concern. However, you are not required to share your observations with any agency staff, including the supervisor or director.

While it is necessary to be vigilant in watching for causes for concern about the health, development, behaviour, or especially abuse or neglect of children, it is possible to be overzealous. It is best to keep an open mind and focus on the positive most of the time. Children need to be seen through a lens of competence: their strengths, newly acquired skills, current interests, sources of inquiry, and other signs of healthy development. Even when we do ask "What is going on here?" we need to remain positive and avoid jumping to conclusions about children, families, or situations, in ways that can be detrimental to the child. The true professional balances her identification, and even **intuition**, of causes for concern that warrant further observation, investigation, or referral to suitable professionals, with her keen observation skills and informed perspective.

How to document concerns Of course, how various causes for concern are documented differ, because of the speed of response each kind might require. But some principles that should be followed are:

1. Select an appropriate method for recording observations (suggestions are offered at the end of each of the four sections here).
2. Determine if there are any relevant policies. If so, follow their requirements for documentation and reporting (avoid unprofessional conduct such as gossiping).
3. Observe and record as much relevant information as possible within the constraints of your work—keep it confidential except in situations that warrant an opinion from another professional.
4. Date, time, and sign every entry.
5. Record information as soon as possible—at the time or soon after your observation.
6. Decide when action/reporting is to occur (many situations require immediate response).
7. Document everything with adequate detail in an objective manner.
8. Review your observations to determine any gaps that need to be addressed, and add further observations if necessary.
9. Record your hunches, but *label them as such.*
10. Share your observations with the parent (except in the case of possible abuse or neglect). Also, seek out the parent's own observations and add them to yours.

1. Signs and Symptoms of Possible Health Issues and Failure to Thrive

When it comes to observing children for possible signs of illness, educators must first acknowledge the importance of daily health observations to identify

Overview of Key Causes for Concern and Appropriate Responses

Type of Concern	Source of Concern	Who to Contact	Resources
Health Signs and symptoms of illness, disease, infection, sleep problems, agitation, alertness, etc. (may result in physical hurt to various degrees, infestations, bacterial or viral infections, sleep difficulties, loss of confidence, emotional difficulties, etc.).	• observation • educator's documentation of signs and symptoms/ health indicators • disclosure by parent • colleague's comments about a child's health or well-being • child's own disclosure of a "problem"	• Mention concern to parents • Share observations with centre supervisor or teacher • Parents have responsibility for seeking medical assistance • Parents need to take the child home if unable to participate in the program • Health department must be contacted if there is an infectious outbreak (notifiable disease) (Advocating for child and her needs may be necessary)	• Share your observations with parents • Agency policies and procedures • GP • Health Department • Social worker • Health fact sheets (Canadian Paediatric Society) • Information from Health Department • *Well Beings*, Canadian Paediatric Society (1992) • *Healthy Foundations*, Pimento and Kernested (2004) • Internet
Development Atypical patterns of development: child does not conform to the norm, particularly talented, individual style not within usual range, communication difficulties, mobility	• parental concern • educator's observation • documented signs/ symptoms/indicators • screening • educator's assessment that the child appears to	• Discuss observations with parents • Share observations with centre supervisor • Assist parents in seeking referrals to specialists via GP	• Parents and families • Agency policies and procedures • Share your documentation with parents • GP

Observation	Indicators	Strategies	Resources
challenges etc. (may determine idiosyncratic developmental patterns, physical disabilities, communicative disorders, cognitive difficulties, delayed development, giftedness).	• have an atypical pattern of skill acquisition • observations from colleagues • child's own concern about "being different"	• Parents typically request developmental assessment • Suggest parents seek referral by GP • Link parents with developmental programs/ early interventionists, etc. • Advocating for the child's funding, accommodations, resource teachers, aides, etc. may be required— approach necessary agencies	• Pediatrician • Assessment (according to possible concern) • Early interventionist • Health, Social Services or Education Ministry • Psychologists/ psychiatrists • Parent support groups • Physiotherapists • Occupational therapists • Resource teachers • Internet sources (check credibility) • Books • Health department • Societies (associated with specific diagnosed conditions)
Challenging behaviour Behaviour that is difficult for the adult to manage, extreme actions, antisocial, nonconformist, disruptive, strong individual style, prolonged egocentricity, social outsider, lacks self-regulation, emotional outbursts, frustrated, etc.	• parental concern • a child's own disclosure • educator's observations • educator's assessment that the child's behaviour is atypical/antisocial • documentation of some indicators of challenging behaviour • complaints by other	• Discuss observations with parents • Develop shared strategies for addressing the concern • Inform and seek expertise of centre supervisor • Suggest parents seek additional help via GP/ referral if strategies are unsuccessful	• Parents and families • GP • Agency policies • Pediatrician • Social worker • Education/social services ministry staff • Developmental specialist • Partnerships between agencies/professionals

(continued)

Type of Concern	Source of Concern	Who to Contact	Resources
(easily observed as the child demanding attention, refusing to cooperate, being antisocial and focused on own wants, will not share or cooperate, onlooker, outsider, acts as "clown," ignores rules, low self-esteem, etc.–as related to expectations for her stage of development).	• children • complaints/concerns expressed by colleagues • concerns expressed by other agencies (religious groups/sports/camp, etc.)	• Follow agency policies and procedures	• and parents • Resource teacher • Psychologist • Psychiatrists • Floor-time (Greenspan) • Early interventionists • Books, e.g., *Challenging Behaviour*, Kaiser and Rasminsky (1999) • Internet sources • Parent support groups
Potential abuse or neglect **Potential abuse:** • Physical • Psychological/emotional • Sexual • Ritual • Institutional (may have been exposed to abuse over a period of time, lacks self-esteem, displays unusual sexualized behaviour, establishes only superficial relationships, lacks boundaries etc.).	• disclosure by parent • disclosure by child • hints/comments from neighbours, family members, etc. • educator observations • documented signs and symptoms • police officers/social workers/child protection agents seeking information	• Inform Child Protection Agency directly–*do not share concerns with others* • Follow Agency policies and procedures	• Follow Child Protection Agency directions/resources/program interventions, etc. • Agency policies • Social workers • National Clearing House on Child Abuse • Toronto Child Abuse Centre • RCMP online • Children's Aid Societies

Potential neglect: • Physical • Medical • Emotional • Educational (may show failure to thrive, attachment disorder, developmental delay, lack of socialization, lack of spontaneous play, miserable, lacks joy, apathetic, etc.).			
Exposure Exposure to toxins, potential infection, predators, extreme weather, radiation, war, terrorism (e.g., exposure to serious SARS-like infection, street drugs, prescription drugs, alcohol, lead, tobacco, environmental toxins). These concerns vary in their severity and need for immediate response (a child's response might vary according to the incident and its severity, and her personality and resilience–behaviours might include psychological difficulties, sleep disorders,	• media information • government warning • disclosure by parent • educator's observations • documented signs, symptoms • observation of accident or incident • behavioural changes • signs on body	• Make a risk assessment • Follow emergency protocols • Act according to perceived risks • Seek accurate up-to-date information • Consider protection/"lockdown"/isolation/(supervisory decisions) • Consider precautionary measures (as necessary) • Follow agency policies • Discuss with parents • Inform Child Protection Agency and/or Health Department directly if concern is ongoing,	• Emergency protocols • Emergency services • First-aid training • Emergency preparedness training • Media • Parents and families • Health Department • GP • Pediatrician • Detoxification/decontamination centres • Environmental protection agencies • Health information online • Advocacy groups • Internet resources • TV weather channel

(continued)

Type of Concern	Source of Concern	Who to Contact	Resources
irrational fears, withdrawal, social interaction problems, drug dependence, clinginess, loss of confidence, compulsive disorders, relationship difficulties, taking responsibility for occurrence, burns, cuts and bruises and other physical hurts, long-term health issues, disabilities and/or developmental problems).		increasing, or potentially damaging (using discretions) • Advise parents to visit physician • Take child to emergency room at nearest hospital • Call all for ambulance • Seek first aid	• Smoking-cessation groups • HIV/AIDS groups • Rehabilitation • Support groups • Assessments by psychological/developmental health departments • Social workers • IPP/IEP • IPRC or other plan • Developmental service worker
Trauma Either involved in or observer of traumatic event–abduction/kidnapping, road accident, violent act, shooting, stabbing, catastrophe, war, plane crash, loss of parent/key figure, home fire, drowning, murder, "act of God," etc.	• media information • government warning • disclosure by parent • information from doctor or counsellor • disclosure by child • educator's observations • documented signs and symptoms	• Talk to parent • Suggest parent seek medical/psychological supports through referral to GP	• Parents and families • Health department • GP • Psychiatrist • Psychologist • Counsellor • Respected Internet journals • Victims of trauma groups

(may be evidenced by challenging behaviour, health issues, post-traumatic stress disorder, psychological problems, flashbacks, sleep disorders, night terrors, or developmental concerns).			• Support groups • Books • Journals • Internet resources
Pornography Exposure to/involvement in pornography (paper-based or online) (may be evidenced by bizarre or sexualized behaviour, unusual play behaviour, disturbing artwork, attachment difficulties, psychological problems, social difficulties, lack of boundaries, onlooker rather than participant behaviour).	• disclosure by parent • observations • signs and symptoms/indicators • disclosure by child • police surveillance of predators • Internet	• Inform Child Protection Agency • Explain issue to Agency supervisor (but not necessarily the details) • Inform the police • Follow Agency policies	• Parents and families • Police resources • Internet sources • Psychologist/psychiatrist • Books • Social workers

ill children. Decisions regarding the care of children are based on the educator's observations, subsequent conversations with the parents, and physician's diagnosis. (Pimento & Kernested 2004, p. 138)

Parents and educators can work collaboratively to identify characteristics of health, and signs and symptoms associated with health issues. Reporting your observations can be helpful for the parent, who might not have noticed something important. *However, it is for the parent to act on the information and seek help from a health professional.*

KEY FEATURES: Documenting health concerns

- uses a daily baseline observation as a key reference point

- identifies signs and symptoms of concern

- avoids diagnosis

- always leads to parent communication

- requires careful and objective documentation

- policies and procedures are to be followed (exclusion, treatment, etc.)

Examples of signs and symptoms of potential health concerns

- delayed/slow growth
- tooth decay/mouth odour
- tooth loss
- skin ulcers/cankers
- warts
- boils
- changes in known conditions
- responses to medication
- itchiness
- muscle weakness
- tripping up
- swollen glands
- nightmares during sleep
- unwillingness to eat and/or drink
- bodily smells/unwashed/urine odour
- sunken fontanel (of baby)
- fever
- flushed cheeks

- crossed eyes/puffy eyes/bloodshot eyes
- nosebleed
- insect bite
- worms (if observed in stool)
- diaper rash
- bruises
- swellings
- changes in activity levels
- dizziness
- unconsciousness
- ill-fitting shoes/blisters
- responses to foods/drink consumed
- swallowing of foreign objects
- foreign objects in nose/ear, etc.
- irritability
- unusually thirsty
- reaction to injection or medical procedure (as explained to educator)

- paleness
- sweating
- spots/whiteheads/blackheads
- loss of voice/croakiness
- runny nose
- blocked-up feeling
- tummy upset/pain
- ear wax (visible)
- holding breath for extended period
- coughing
- clearing throat
- snoring while asleep
- possible sleep apnea
- bleeding
- constipation
- strong urine
- stiff neck
- sleepiness
- balance problems
- disorientation
- falls or bumps
- limping
- sore eyes/styes—rubs eyes
- putting items close to eyes
- headache—holding head/banging head
- earache—holding face
- teething—reddened face, drooling
- swallowing difficulties
- eating challenges (eating disorder?)
- nausea/vomiting/regurgitation of food
- loose stools/constipation/hard/dark stools
- sneezing
- skin colour/tone changes (according to the individual's typical healthy skin)
- inability to pass urine or feces
- tremors
- spinal curvature
- apathy/sleepiness
- deep-coloured/bloody urine
- wheeziness
- parched skin
- rashes associated with infectious diseases
- scalp flakiness/soreness
- body rigidity
- uninterested in environment
- lack of response to stimuli
- low body-fat ratio
- obesity*/rapid weight gain or loss
- irritation/discharge from penis or vagina
- displays little or slow movement
- rashes on any part of the face or body
- shows little stranger anxiety
- seizures
- spastic-type movement
- skin rashes/marks
- skin redness/burn/prickly heat
- apparent allergic response
- sensory deficits:
  i. hearing
  ii. vision
  iii. touch
  iv. taste
  v. smell

*Although obesity and being overweight is not usually an immediate concern, it is an important health issue that is relevant to any child's overall health, well-being, and development. Educators must address this and other body-related issues with tact and sensitivity.

Remember to communicate effectively with the children themselves. For example, if a child appears to hurt, ask him to point to where it hurts. Older children may have gained a vocabulary of words to describe how they feel. These responses are as important as other observable signs and symptoms.

The educator must observe, document, and respond appropriately to any perceived sign/symptom/indicator of a health concern. Even if a sign cannot be labelled, the educator should use her powers of description to good advantage! But remember that, *as an educator, you cannot diagnose an infectious disease*, even if the symptoms are identical to those in other children who have been medically diagnosed. You can tell parents that there are cases of a particular infectious disease, but no names should be mentioned of those who are infected.

When a health concern has been diagnosed by a medical doctor, the educator may have a role in supporting the child's needs according to the doctor's instructions. Obviously the educator promotes health, but he might also need to give medication and perform other functions to support the needs of those children who have a firm diagnosis from a doctor. Follow your policies and protocols for the administration of drugs or helping with devices such as hearing aids or spectacles.

In many childcare centres and schools, there are children who have chronic medical complaints. Typically these will be explained to the educator along with any instructions for the child's management. It is important to be particularly diligent about monitoring the health of medically fragile children; you may wish to create a checklist of signs and symptoms for each child with the particular indicators you need to pay attention to.

Some health issues should be communicated to the supervisor of the centre; where there is any possibility of infecting others, this must be done. *If* a parent indicates that her child is experiencing a **notifiable disease**, the supervisor has a duty to ensure that Health Department protocols are followed. (There is some variation in what is considered notifiable; the local Health Department and Ministry licensing personnel will clarify these.) Useful health resources can be obtained from the Canadian Paediatric Society, the Canadian Child Care Federation, and Health Canada.

A child should be **excluded** from any childcare program if he has a fever, is suffering from a notifiable disease, needs to take doctor-prescribed special medications, is deemed unwell by a doctor, or lacks the health or well-being that would enable him to participate.

Ways to document health concerns

Although many observational formats can be used, health information lends itself to be documented best by using:

A. **Baseline observations**—a quick observation of the child's health condition, alertness, general behaviour, and demeanour at the start of the day (often compared to later observations)

B. Anecdotal records—written when a concern is identified and details the specific signs/symptoms/behaviours

C. Diary accounts—health information documented within regular accounts of the day

D. Time sampling—allows the observer to determine behaviour patterns by looking at the child's behaviour/signs/symptoms at predetermined times

Baseline Observation

This observation should be made each day for every child as they enter the agency. The baseline is not always recorded, and should be undertaken informally.

Name of Child _____   Observer _____

Date _____   Time of Entry to Centre _____

Notable physical characteristics (hair, eyes, mouth, skin, etc.)

_____

_____

Injuries: band-aids, scratches, bruises, etc.

_____

_____

Clothing and cleanliness (diaper?)

_____

_____

Belongings from home

_____

_____

Observable changes (since yesterday/previous attendance)

_____

_____

Separation from parent/greetings/transition into program activities

_____

_____

Emotions: Manner/attitude/disposition/mood/temperament/enthusiasm, etc.

_____

_____

Observations/comments from parent or other adult bringing child into care

_____

_____

E. Documentation of signs/symptoms/indicators when they are identified

F. Physical skills, symptom and behavioural checklists

G. Health/symptom charts

Documenting health concerns relies on a good understanding of what each child is like in her typically healthy state.

2. Indicators of Apparent Developmental Challenges

Early childhood educators are in a unique and important position. They have the opportunity to observe a child within a group context, participating in a variety of activities and routines. As a result, they are often among the first professionals to suspect that a child may be experiencing some developmental difficulties. A dilemma arises from this position, however, as the early childhood educator must then decide what to do with his/her suspicions. (Monaghan 1998)

KEY FEATURES: Documenting developmental concerns

- depends upon professional understanding of what constitutes typical behaviour

- uses regular observational data or portfolio documentation

- requires a variety of observations to be recorded—each chosen to elicit key information in each developmental domain about which there is a concern

- documentation involving naturalistic observation complements further professional assessment

- involves parental perspectives

- agency might facilitate referral or suggest to parents that further assessment is necessary

- leads to program accommodations

Child development: Patterns of behaviour

In Chapter 2 we looked at the domains and explanations for children's development. While we focused on patterns of development, we did not include normative developmental charts. This is because of the concern that any adult reading the book might use such profiles too rigidly and think a particular child had a problem when the child's behaviour was only different in insignificant ways. Instead we examined the developmental domains and gave pointers to help educators to look for certain types of behaviour; this was a much more open-ended approach than a specific checklist. Then in Chapter 5 we examined the uses of checklists; after studying this, educators would be better able to create and use a checklist, while appreciating the limitations of some prepared checklists.

Many checklists are created using normative profiles available on the Internet and elsewhere, but the profiles' validity and reliability should be evaluated. Both Chapters 2 and 5 would make readers familiar with normative profiles, and from them checklists can be created that meet the needs of educators and parents. Remember, though, that normative tools are just that: ways of seeing whether behaviours that are typical for a particular age or stage are present or absent. They don't tell the full story, and if indicators of actual competence are not listed, children may appear to be less able than they actually are.

As you know, children's development usually follows a certain trajectory, skills usually being acquired in similar sequences, but the rate of progress is variable. When an educator senses that a child is performing in an atypical way (according to her knowledge of typical patterns of development), she might want to look more closely at the child's behaviour. Some children exhibit domains of their development that are progressing on target, while others may be lagging in some way. This uneven pattern is quite frequently observed; perhaps the child's development will continue according to that pattern, but this is not always the case. Some patterns are predictable, others not. Some apparent deficits correct themselves. Development may slow down in one domain, yet progress in others. It is for the educator to be thorough about observing and documenting competence, progression, and possible regression.

Some children have special abilities or talents in one or two areas while their development in other areas is fairly typical. Other children might have a **pervasive developmental delay**—delay involving all aspects of development. Some disabilities are interrelated; for example, some cognitive difficulties might involve social interactions, impact the child's self-esteem, and cause them to withdraw. Even children with a similar diagnosis might present themselves very differently and have very different potentials.

Individual children

Every child and every adult is different. While we share many characteristics, the most interesting aspects of human beings are their differences and their individuality. Although educators need to have an understanding of what constitutes the typical patterns of child development, and the range of behaviour observable in most children, their main focus is usually working with individual children with their own temperaments, backgrounds, interests, and experience. From time to time, the educator or the parent notices something of concern. For parents it might be that they see that their child is behaving differently from their older children, or other children they know. Commonly this is more of a question of the children having different personalities and styles of doing things, but sometimes there is real cause for concern.

CHILD DEVELOPMENT FOCUS: Is it just the child's age or what?

Even after we have spent a lifetime working with children at a particular age/stage of life, and we have a good conceptual grasp of typical behaviours, it will not add up to a statistically significant sample from whom a reliable "average" can be determined. Children go through similar stages, but at vastly different rates and with idiosyncratic styles. Sometimes extremes of behaviour make us think there must be a "problem," and we may be right to be concerned. But understanding the wide variations that are possible can prevent us from assuming too readily that this is the case.

Experiencing developmental difficulties

When we describe a child as experiencing developmental difficulties, we mean that, from a professional perspective, that child is not following the typical pathway of progress. It is quite possible that the child has, as yet, little perception of her own difference. Children gain an idea of their categorical self—their individual set of concepts about themselves, their belonging, their attributes, and their abilities over time. Children who have disabilities may have an idea of who they are and what they can do, but these ideas may develop more gradually. It's essential that any perceived challenge or disability is talked about in a positive manner, as this can affect the child's emerging sense of self and self-esteem.

Observing differences: Varied perspectives on disabilities

There are many ways of looking at the issue of identifying and then meeting the needs of children with **special needs**. Some people question whether attention should be paid to the assessment of children's developmental progress, suggesting that every child is unique and that we should focus on abilities rather than deficits. Sometimes these folks view such identification as competitive, stating that development should never be a race. We may agree, but their hands-off approach can lead to a lack of **accommodation** and support for those who need them.

A few hold extreme views about children with **disabilities** and special needs as needing to be removed from the community and dumped in institutions far from "normal" children (an emotive and loaded term). This view was most common some years ago, but shades of it can still be heard today. When people measure the worth of other human beings (adult or child) by their attractiveness, potential, status, ability, or any criteria—other than just being human—they devalue themselves, never mind the individual who is the focus of their attention. Claudia A. Howard expressed this well when she wrote, in an article for the Heartbeat Educational Society, "The Five Laws of Unconditional Human Worth" (1992):

1. All have infinite, internal, eternal, and unconditional worth as persons.
2. All have equal worth as people. Worth is not comparative or competitive.
3. Eternals neither add nor diminish worth. Eternals include money, looks, and achievements.
4. Worth is stable and never in jeopardy.
5. Worth doesn't have to be earned or proved.

The understanding that all children are thinking, feeling human beings (whatever their level of functioning), that they have a contribution to make, that children's competence can flourish under appropriate conditions, that although some children develop more slowly they can often achieve far more than is expected of them, that the full range or variety of human personalities, talents, and competence make for the full and natural spectrum of humanity—might be lost on a few people.

It is important to understand these different points of view, because advocating for children demands that we have a glimpse into the mindset of those we need to persuade or work around.

Indicators

The term "indicators" refers to a particular set of conditions that hint at a cause for concern—in this case about a child's development. Other terms—"red flags," "developmental alerts," or simply "pointers" or "signs"—might also be used synonymously.

Talking about children with special needs

A variety of terms have been used in recent years to describe children who have special needs. Although some appear insensitive, the most important feature is to put the child first—"Doreen has epilepsy" is much better than "the epileptic." Sometimes children are described as being disabled, having a handicap, having a deficit, being exceptional, being differently abled, and so on. If you put the child first in your thinking, you are less likely to go wrong; remember, you are talking about a human being with many more attributes than the one that focuses on what she cannot do. "James" is a lot better than any description of his challenges! Some terms are obviously dehumanizing or insensitive; for example, although "retarded" may be acceptable in some connections because it reflects applicable legislation, it seems offensive to this author. Also, avoid using diagnostic terms in your documentation unless you are sure they apply; description is more useful than labels.

Seeking a diagnosis

One director of a childcare centre argues that having a **diagnosis** serves no purpose other than attracting funding. This is a valid point, but educators hope that they will be able to serve a child and family better if they have an official diagnosis. You might want to think about the advantages and disadvantages of a clinical diagnosis for a particular child, rather than point parents toward assessment as a routine action.

Incidentally, educators are not in a position to offer a diagnosis or prognosis concerning any child. They can and must offer their valuable observations to the assessor. Most developmental screenings and assessments—as discussed in the next chapter—have to be carried out by specialists. Even the pediatricians, early interventionists, psychologists, and others are required to take training to administer many of the developmental assessment tools.

If the child's challenges are not particularly significant, it could be advantageous to avoid formal assessment, but the decision should be made by an informed parent rather than the educator. The educator should share her concerns and specific observations with the parents; at all times the families must be kept up-to-date with the documentation.

Integration and inclusion

"Every child has the right to be included in a program that is developmentally appropriate" (Saskatchewan Education 2008) is a clear statement in favour of inclusion in educational settings. While that principle needs to be a part of every program's philosophy, it also needs to be operationalized: "effective or successful inclusion requires a mix of resources within [childcare] centres and supports to centres" (Irwin, Lero and Brophy 2004, p. 24). Children who have special developmental needs, along with others who exhibit challenging behaviours, or those who are **medically fragile**, are considered to be "included" if the program they are in makes whatever accommodations and offers whatever provisions meet their children's needs. Clearly this requires extra work and makes additional demands on the educators, but with sufficient practical and human resources, an **integrated** or **inclusive** program can be beneficial for all the children in the program.

Cause for concern: when a child's development is atypical

Following is a brief list to help readers to look for general developmental issues. Some items you may notice here are ones involving exceptionalities and special talents; these must be attended to, as well as apparent deficits. For more specific documentation purposes you might want to access **normative profiles** or **red flags** in the domains of development that concern you. When we observe some aspect of a child's development that gives us a cause for concern, that cause is called an **indicator**, that something needs extra special attention. Recordings should be clear and precise—and remember to see behaviour through the lens of age/stage expectations.

- exceptional skills
- early acquisition of language
- special talent
- unusual memory
- deep/prolonged interests
- unusually high cognitive functioning/mental agility
- high level of creative thinking and/or creative functioning
- exceptional problem-solving
- underachievement given apparent competence
- regression in any domain
- mobility difficulties
- dependence
- apparent clumsiness
- limb stiffness or floppiness
- asymmetrical physical skill development
- changes in bowel/bladder control
- non-recognition of danger/consequences
- withdrawal/isolation
- obsessive/compulsive/repetitive
- expressive receptive language extremes

- no development of social play
- attachment/separation issues
- significant resistance to change
- incessant talking/unusual imitation
- gaze aversion
- challenging group skills/cooperation
- oppositional behaviour
- difficulty with "academic" tasks
- failure to show empathy/difficulties with self-control and turn-taking
- speech difficulties
- apparently delayed or erratic skill development (maturational lag) in these areas:

  i. gross motor
  ii. fine motor
  iii. self-help
  iv. language
  v. communication
  vi. social
  vii. cognitive
  viii. self-awareness
  ix. self-regulation and emotion

We do not intend to suggest that educators should be overly focused on a child's difficulties and challenges, but if any should be observable, the educator should respond appropriately. **Early intervention** can make a considerable difference. While an assessment is being undertaken by the appropriate professionals, the educator might be able to assist the process with her developmental observations. Teamwork is usually necessary for the support of children and their families who have diagnosed special needs.

There can be disadvantages to having a developmental diagnosis; labelling and lowering expectations of the child to fit her diagnosis and prognosis can be severely limiting. The good side is that a diagnosis can lead to extra resources being made available and being eligible for increased funding for programs. There can also be an increased understanding of the child's disability and a better ability to access pertinent information that allows educators to work with the child and enjoy her more fully.

Children diagnosed as having a special need (disability or **exceptionality**) can be best accommodated in inclusive programs when the educators know as much as possible about their particular challenges. Observing and recording the skill development and other advances of a child with a special need is very helpful to the team trying to provide an appropriate program for the child. Even small steps forward should be recorded. At times a program with specific goals and objectives might be suitable; these are based on the observations. It may be that the child can integrate into many aspects of the self-directed activity and play of other children, while needing to work on targeted skills for some periods of the day. Depending on parental availability, volunteer help, and human or practical resources available through the agency, the educator will be able to meet the needs of all the children by being a sensitive observer and responsive caregiver and educator:

> Early childhood educators are trained observers and this is perhaps the most critical skill to possess. When concerns are suspected, an educator is able to make observations of the child in a variety of activities throughout the program, taking anecdotal notes whenever possible. Working as a team within the program is also important, with each educator's observations and perspectives noted and discussed. Concrete examples of what the child is doing (both positive achievements and challenges) are useful to have on hand during a discussion with the parents and can assist in confirming for the educator that there is indeed a problem. (Monaghan 1998)

Possible causes of developmental concern

- congenital abnormalities
- birth injuries
- inherited conditions
- accidents, medical emergencies
- poverty, social circumstances
- teratogens and environmental pollutants (pre-natally or after birth)
- deprivation in early life
- emotional distance/lack of engagement of adults

- ingestion of prescription or street drugs
- adult's failure to meet basic needs in early life

Very few developmental concerns can be prevented, but early identification and intervention can alleviate some of the challenges.

Ways to document possible developmental concerns

Observing and documenting causes for concern about health issues might take a variety of forms. With health concerns there should be speedy recording and sharing with parents. In some instances educators should not wait until the end of the day, but might need to call a parent to take a child home via their doctor's office. Emergencies might require an ambulance to be called rather than wait for the parents to arrive. Whenever possible, parental permission should be obtained before any treatment is offered—but if time does not allow this, the educator must take on the task of making decisions based on the child's best interest and with knowledge of the parent's religion or other important issues. After an emergency is over, the educator must record the events as she observed them, and also indicate other adults and children who were present and the exact conditions in which the emergency happened. Serious occurrences are to be recorded in the agency's Emergency/Serious Occurrence Log. Most developmental concerns can be documented using one or more of the following:

A. baseline observations

B. anecdotal records of behaviours, signs, symptoms, or indicators of concern

C. Emergency/Serious Occurrence Log

D. diary accounts

E. developmental checklist

3. Challenging Behaviour

Challenging Behaviour is any behaviour that:

- Interferes with children's learning, development and success at play;
- Is harmful to the child, other children or adults;
- Puts a child at high risk for later social problems and school failure.

(Kaiser & Rasminsky 1999)

Some children are born with **temperaments** that demand greater adult attention. Others enter life in an almost constant irritable mood. Yet others will appear endlessly active, inquisitive, or even destructive. There can be times when a child's challenging temperament meets with a parenting style that increases the challenges rather than works with them. Stanley Greenspan (1995) has suggested that there are five broad categories of temperament or personality behind children's most challenging behaviours:

1. highly sensitive
2. self-absorbed

3. defiant
4. inattentive
5. active/aggressive

Greenspan encourages parents and educators to understand the different temperaments of children and "For a child to reach her potential, she needs her parents to understand her unique traits and also support her progression from one stage of emotional development to the next." That some parents seem to do this more easily than others, and that parents and others in the child's life can be taught how to work with, rather than against, the child's individual style, offers hope to the challenged adult. Being realistic, offering one-on-one personal time (**Floor Time**), being sensitive to the child's physical make-up, working toward a problem-solving orientation, empathizing with the child, taking it step by step, clarifying firm limits, and appreciating the necessity for adult development alongside the child's growth and development are essential.

Diverse environmental factors further increase the stress on family dynamics, which in turn increases the difficulties. Without any fault of the parent, the young child can show many behaviours that are antisocial, inappropriate, and without apparent care as to the consequences. The child may not have learned how to behave appropriately even if taught. In unfortunate situations, the child has not been exposed to appropriate behaviour or had her extreme behaviour corrected inappropriately. Without being socialized, and being attentive to social learning, the child cannot acquire socially appropriate behaviour.

At times the challenging behaviour might be taking on a purpose—getting adult attention, reducing expectations of her, avoiding responsibility, being unwilling to "grow up," or some other function. This should be investigated, because such functions may increase the demonstration of the challenges, and "consequences" such as being excluded from a disliked activity might be counterproductive. The documentation and analysis of the child's behaviour patterns are usually worthwhile, but observation of challenging behaviour should not, itself, offer the child additional attention!

Children who have special developmental or health needs are more likely to exhibit challenging behaviour than those who are growing healthily or developing according to a typical pattern. There are some socioeconomic issues, but challenging behaviour can be observed in children from every ethnic group, culture, and class. Both genders demonstrate challenging behaviours, but those behaviours may differ according to their developmental stage and peer relationships. There are similar proportions of each temperamental type within all social strata, as are ability levels. Challenging behaviour is not directly related to intelligence, although a child of high intelligence might manage to be more manipulative because of her increased cognitive functioning. **Emotional intelligence** involves the ability to understand and control one's own feelings and associated behaviour. For some children this takes a long time!

For other young children, including those already challenged by their own temperaments, there may be situational issues that compound their difficulties. These may include families under stress: perhaps a parent is depressed, disabled, or unwell, or the family is living in poverty and/or unemployment or underemployment; perhaps there are concerns about other family members. Cycles of educational, social, or racial disadvantage may also be made worse by encounters of racism or difficulties because of immigration or the lack of English or French fluency. Each of these exacerbates parental challenges and reduces the energies a parent might have to establish behavioural parameters and develop positive guidance strategies. The child certainly needs positive role models; stressed parents, however well-intentioned, find these difficult to provide.

A number of other issues can also impact the child-rearing available for children in greatest need of solid parenting and consistency between home and caregivers. Lower-priced childcare arrangements might necessitate frequent changes in the adults in the child's life. She may be left with older siblings, family members, or a number of different babysitters. Home childcare providers may also be employed, and the child may then be placed in licensed care. Even if the quality is good in any setting, its lack of consistency may be damaging, especially for the child who is already exhibiting challenging behaviour.

Another hopeful way of looking at challenging and deviant behaviour is to see it as a sign of **resilience**. Although that might seem strange, research (Ungar 2005) suggests that "difficult" behaviours may be a signal that the child is trying to manage her own hurdles, and is on a pathway to health. Ungar states, "Despite our best intentions, we will not be able to influence how seemingly troubled children behave until we appreciate that what we characterize as problem behaviours may well be our children's hidden pathways to resilience." Consequently, though trying to stop challenging behaviours may be desirable for the sake of peace, we must understand its underlying causes so we can work with the child's strength through resilience. Observing a child's challenging behaviour is the surface level of appreciating what is happening for the child; we need to take time to analyze what is going on under the surface to address the real problem.

It may be that the child who shows challenging behaviour in a childcare setting and at home comes from a family with relatively few stressors, and that can provide continuous high-quality care and education. Although it is useful to access a family's contextual information, it should be treated professionally without bias, especially avoiding making assumptions about the child's family circumstances, culture, social standing, or economic status.

Because it is the educator's role to be actively involved in working with children and families, we have mentioned some social and contextual issues. However, these are to provide understanding rather than to attribute blame. Although parents may lack the skills necessary to support their child, their positive intentions for their child and their ability to acquire such skills should not be doubted. The educator needs to

1. gather as much information as is necessary to understand the child's family and how it functions.
2. be a partner with the parents.
3. provide a role model that is helpful to all family members including the child.
4. offer parent education in meaningful, non-condescending ways (if necessary).
5. work with the family to ensure home–agency consistency in how the child's behaviour is supported.
6. help the family to get the child to take ownership of her behaviour (if sufficiently mature)
7. collaborate on sharing observations, documentation, and intra-agency assessment of the child's behaviours—use functional assessment (if appropriate).
8. take preventive measures to improve behaviour (such as changing routines, the environment, or specific triggers).
9. agree to develop, implement, and assess strategies to address the child's behaviour.
10. refer parents to sources for more formal assessments (if necessary).

11. provide the assessor with documentation to support the assessment.

12. work as a team with the parents/family, assessor, colleagues to implement a strategy or IPP/IEP.

13. use Floor Time and other positive behavioural techniques.

14. seek additional supports for the child, and advocate for the family and the child in ways that aim to provide the child with optimal interventions.

15. keep detailed daily records of your observations.

Examples of challenging behaviours

The following behavioural indicators need to be understood within a developmental context (what is typical at the child's age and stage):

- swearing, name-calling, using unacceptable language
- teasing
- shouting and yelling
- "storytelling" and lying
- playing roughly
- disruptiveness
- masturbation in public
- aggression
- physical violence toward others
- tantrums
- slow to warm up
- difficulty sharing
- noncompliance with requests
- bullying behaviour*
- acting out/imitating scenes from violent/ sexual television/ movies
- attachment difficulties
- transitional problems/slow to integrate

- apparent low self-esteem
- emotional outbursts
- eating problem (potential disorder)
- acting as a victim
- difficulty sequencing ideas/events
- withdrawal
- avoidance of particular activities
- separation anxiety
- conflicted personality types
- inattentive
- attention-seeking
- difficulty following game rules
- anxiety
- defiant
- overly sensitive
- overly active or "hyperactive" (not a good descriptor without a diagnosis)
- hitting

- biting
- sad or "depressed" (colloquial—not a diagnosis)
- very messy/ disorganized
- easily frustrated
- hurting animals
- deliberate damage/breaking objects
- passive
- sexually precocious
- lying
- cries frequently, seemingly for little reason
- self-absorbed
- non-acceptance by others
- non-recovery from distress
- flat affect (shows no emotion)
- lives in fantasy world

*Bullying is an extremely challenging problem that is being observed even in early-childhood settings. When it is identified, there needs to be a coherent team approach to the challenging roles of the bullied (victim), bullier (the perpetrator), and the bystanders (the other children).

- talks to invisible people
- does not engage in play
- repetitive behaviour
- gnawing on hands/arms
- observes others for a prolonged period
- unusual risk-taking
- pulling out hair

- lack of eye contact
- difficulty with peer relations
- resistance to coming to the centre/school
- hurting themselves
- toileting issues (smearing feces, etc.)
- shyness

- refusal to eat
- playing with food/throwing food
- head banging
- exceptionally active
- socially unacceptable behaviour
- difficulty dealing with conflict

Most children who show challenging behaviours can be observed and assessed informally by the team of educators. When behaviours are particularly troubling and difficult to manage within the program, or if they are not manageable, further professional help must be found. With professional diagnosis and teamwork, the educator may find that managing the child's challenging behaviour is possible within her group of children. The assessment should lead to developing strategies to assist the child to behave appropriately, as well as addressing the underlying causes for challenging behaviour. As with children who experience other kinds of difficulties, the child who exhibits challenging behaviour should not be labelled; her abilities and appropriate behaviours should be the educator's focus, and she must be called by her name, never referred to by any of her behaviour patterns:

> When caregivers systematically record their observations, they often see a pattern emerge . . . only when caregivers learn to see children as they see themselves, will they be able to discover clues about what is affecting a child's behaviour. The child's inappropriate behaviour should be recorded in the child's file as soon as possible after the event. (Canadian Paediatric Society 1992)

As suggested by the Canadian Paediatric Society, the documentation of challenging behaviour is important:

- Identify the behaviour and describe exactly what it is.
- Measure and record the behaviour (time, day, occurrences, duration, apparent trigger, possible cause)
- Review all the recordings (identify patterns).
- Make a plan for addressing the issue with the parents.
- Suggest the parents seek help from appropriate professionals if the pattern of behaviour warrants further intervention.

Ways to document challenging behaviours

Several documentation methods are particularly useful when recording challenging behaviours:

A. running records—to detail behaviours as they occur
B. event samplings—to determine potential causes, purposes, patterns, and repetitions of specific target behaviours

C. prepared charts—to document specific aspects of behaviours, triggers, and responses

D. anecdotal records—to record significant behaviours soon after they happen

E. diary accounts—to review notable incidents

F. functional assessment—to chart, in detail, the occurrences of targeted behaviours and to identify what functions even inappropriate behaviours have for the child

G. home study/contextual information—to appreciate more about the child's background

See the figure below for an example of a Functional Assessment Observation Form included in Kaiser and Rasminsky's book *Meeting the Challenge: Effective Strategies for Challenging Behaviours in Early Childhood Environments* (1999).

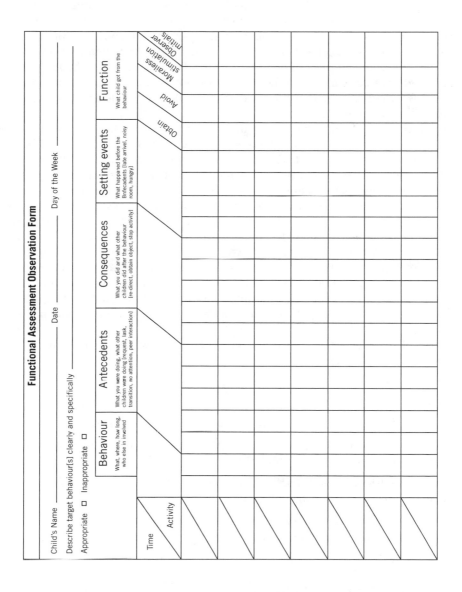

4. Possible Abuse or Neglect

The Department of Justice defines *child abuse* as "the violence, mistreatment or neglect that a child or adolescent may experience while in the care of someone they either trust or depend on, such as a parent, sibling, other relative, caregiver or guardian. Abuse may take place anywhere and may occur, for example, within the child's home or that of someone known to the child" (2005).

Child **abuse** and **neglect** occur in developed countries as much as, if not more than, in underdeveloped countries. They also occur in families of every social standing, economic status, culture, housing type, district, and educational background. The most discernable pattern is that abuse or neglect tends to occur more frequently in families in which a previous victim becomes a perpetrator. And while depression occurs fairly evenly across Canadian society without class or social barriers, though with some familial recurrence, depression in adults may bring about increased incidence of child abuse and neglect. Statistics about abuse and neglect are to some extent unreliable, because such numbers come from reported incidents or criminal convictions and not necessarily the actual number of children affected. Even the statistics themselves point to the number of perpetrators, rather than to the number of victims or of times each victim was abused. Though they are better reported than a decade ago, both abuse and neglect are underreported.

Confusion about who should report abuse, incorrect ideas about a child protection agency revealing its sources to the parents of the victim, and anticipated reprisals prevent some observers from identifying their causes for concern. Additionally, some people feel, albeit wrongly, that they lack evidence to prove a case against a potential abuser, not realizing that they are not the ones to conduct an investigation. Also, people can think that someone else will notice or that another person is somehow better qualified to report a potential situation of abuse. There might be cases in which a person distrusts the protection agency. They might also distrust themselves, or be in denial about what they saw. When an adult sees what they think might be the result of abuse or neglect, if they cannot see who is responsible, they might also fail to report. If there is some possibility that an employer or supervisor abused a child, the person might think that they will not report because of a supposed threat to their employment. All these reasons or excuses for not reporting can have grave effects on the child, and might even lead to the child's death.

Abuse and neglect occur for a broad range of reasons, which are often multiple and interacting. These include

- previous abuse suffered by the perpetrator
- inability to regulate behaviour
- lack of respect for the child/seeing child as an object, not a person
- stressors: financial difficulties, relationship problems, lack of a support system, marital conflict, overwork, unemployment
- lack of social/physical boundaries
- media influences—exposure to violence
- intolerance or irritability
- authoritarian parenting style
- immaturity

- lack of parenting skills
- poor anger management
- depression/loss of hope/anxiety
- poor life skills/lack of self-control
- personality disorder
- lack of attachment to the child
- alcohol, prescription drugs, street drugs, over-the-counter medications
- power and control issues
- un-managed extreme psychiatric disease/psychosis/schizophrenia
- culturally shaped practices
- sexual perversion/sexual play
- heavy use of pornography—especially child pornography
- cults and ritual activities
- unrealistic expectations
- overpowering/feeling superior/ego-boosting/conquests
- temperament mismatch
- the child being unwanted
- poverty coupled with other issues
- frustration
- lack of inhibitions/self-regulation
- opportunity/lack of supervision/lack of interest in the child
- resentments/badly directed anger
- religious extremism

Types of abuse and neglect

Although there are different categories according to the agencies across Canada, most would agree that the following outline covers the majority of abuse and neglect cases:

Abuse

- **Physical:** a component of child abuse that involves being abusive to a child's body; may include direct or indirect damage by shaking, hitting, scarring, or other violent act; can lead to death, disability, long-term medical conditions as well as cuts, bruises, and swellings
- **Psychological/emotional:** child abuse that involves emotional manipulation, teasing, unkind words, a lack of support, diminishes the victim, humiliates, degrades, or otherwise hurts the child's self-esteem, sense of self-worth, emotional well-being, or other aspect of psychological health; witnessing the abuse of either an adult or another child constitutes abuse
- **Sexual:** an extremely damaging form of child abuse that involves touching a child inappropriately, humiliating a child because of their sexual characteristics or sexual

play, penetrating a child orally, anally, or vaginally, exploiting children sexually, having children perform in a sexually explicit fashion, using child pornography, gaining sexual satisfaction from children, sexualizing prepubescent children with inappropriate remarks or clothing, introducing sexual ideas to young children before they are developmentally ready, or any other activity that makes children vulnerable to the sexual deviation of adults

- **Ritual:** a form of child abuse that involves children being involved in or observing various forms of sadistic and psychologically damaging procedures during cult-like ceremonies
- **Institutional:** any abuse or neglect that occurs to children in an institutional setting; the culture of the institution may promote such abuse or deny its existence while taking no steps to prevent it; typically, institutional abuse involves more than one perpetrator and the power dynamics of the institution enable the abuse to continue

Neglect

- **Physical:** a component of neglect that involves failing to meet the child's physical needs such as climate control, protection from harm, failure to provide medical treatment (see medical neglect), failure to provide appropriate and adequate food and drink, failure to provide suitable clothing, ignoring the child's need to receive physical care, changing, kind touch, etc.
- **Medical:** not providing essential medical care that promotes a child's health, and not providing first aid, infection control, medical intervention, medication, or other medical necessity; may include avoiding medical checks, screenings, and/or immunizations
- **Emotional:** not receiving essential attachment to adult(s) nurturance, emotional responsiveness from adults
- **Educational:** not receiving the necessary nurturance, communication, or stimulation necessary for early learning, the lack of preschool, or school programs that hinder educational potential

There are many misconceptions about child abuse and neglect. The facts are as follows:

1. Children rarely lie and cannot offer descriptions of activities or bodies outside their experience.
2. Abuse is rarely an isolated incident.
3. Adults known to the child are more likely than strangers to be the perpetrators of abuse.
4. Abusers do not usually look like perverts or otherwise seem different from others.
5. Addressing addictive behaviours does not necessarily stop the addict's abusive behaviour.
6. Those who abuse or neglect children may also abuse or neglect the disabled or the elderly.
7. Children are often afraid to tell about abuse and may feel shame.
8. Children who are disabled are more likely to be abused.
9. Early childhood educators, teachers, assistants, supervisors, and other professionals cannot and must not investigate or attempt to determine that abuse or neglect has occurred; they must, however, like other adults, observe and record any signs, symptoms, or indicators that might contribute to an investigation by a child protection agency after they have reported their concerns.

10. Trained educators are more likely to observe indicators of potential abuse because they have knowledge of child development, understand what is typical behaviour at every stage of development, are trained observers, have excellent documentation skills, and know what to look for.

Perpetrators of child abuse or neglect

An educator does not need to suspect anybody in particular as the possible **perpetrator**, when they suspect that abuse or neglect has happened. While any objective information might be offered to child protection workers when they inquire into the situation, there is no requirement that an abuser be identified at the initial stage of reporting.

While the key adults in the child's life might be suspected by child protection agency staff, it is the agency's responsibility to look into that along with the police. If there is reason to suspect a member of staff, colleague, or supervisor as the possible perpetrator, that must be reported to the agency. In some instances, this can present difficulties while implementing policies. Seek guidance from the agency about what to do if your childcare centre's policy fails to support you adequately.

Our beliefs about who a perpetrator is may be completely wrong if we imagine men are usually the culprits. Early childhood educators should be aware that "the patterns of abuse are different between genders: females tend to abuse younger children, often infants, while older victims tend to be assaulted by males. Men may be more likely to act suddenly, impulsively, and tend to inflict more hazardous injuries. Sexual abusers are overwhelmingly male" (B. Taylor, Canadian Broadcasting Company, Mar. 26, 2008). However, it became evident in a recent study that the "incidence of substantiated maltreatment was nearly identical for males and females" (Trocmé et al. 2005).

Avoid approaching any possible perpetrator. Make sure you do not impede the protection officer's investigation by questioning people, passing on your observations or hunches to others, putting ideas into the child's mind, or anything else. Such actions run the risk of damaging the investigation and the child.

Indicators of potential child abuse or neglect

It is usual to observe a number of indicators; one alone is less likely to be a cause for concern. (Further indicators can sometimes be observed in the child's physical health status or other aspects of behaviour.)

- noticeable changes in behaviour
- frantic behaviour, particularly that associated with bathing or changing clothes
- regression
- confusion
- expressions of anger
- increased activity or restlessness
- fear of being left alone
- physical symptoms (stomach ache, nausea, etc.)
- isolation from peers
- accident proneness
- clinginess, whining, crying
- performance deterioration
- being unwashed and lacking in personal care
- bite marks
- expressions of guilt and shame
- rope burns/lashings
- toileting problems

- feces smearing
- seeming intimidated
- phobias
- urinary tract infections
- runaway attempts
- fear of going home
- bruises
- welts
- cuts
- burns
- fractures
- poor memory and concentration
- disorganized home life
- cannot recall how injuries happened
- fatigue/sleep problems
- sudden weight change
- difficulty walking or sitting
- torn, stained, or bloody underwear
- injuries to the mouth, genital, or anal areas
- pain in any area of the body
- acting out sexualized scenarios
- atypical changes in personality
- stress
- bizarre, sophisticated, or unusual sexual knowledge
- reverts to bedwetting/soiling
- fearful when startled
- need for constant companionship
- lack of trust
- inability to have fun
- lag in emotional development
- fear of failure

- excessive neatness/compulsive behaviour
- unattended medical/physical needs
- consistent hunger
- nutritional deficiencies
- erratic program/school attendance
- steals food or other items
- takes over adult caring role
- inappropriate dress for the weather
- bald patches on head
- vacant stares/frozen watchfulness
- indiscriminate affection-seeking
- overly compliant or willing to please
- acts out alarming scenes imitating parents/others
- lack of boundaries in physical contact
- unsafe and risky behaviour
- emotional dependence
- unusual inability to communicate
- unexpected/unexplained fears
- atypical attachments
- marks on arms (possible handprints)
- self-abusive behaviours
- sleep and eating difficulties
- excessive masturbation
- inappropriate sexual behaviour
- dramatic mood swings
- outbursts of anger or hostility
- sexually abusiveness toward others
- drawings with sexualized content
- disclosure of abuse

The *Canadian Incidence Study of Reported Child Abuse and Neglect—2003* states that "Neglect was the most common form (30%) of substantiated maltreatment in Canada . . . exposure to domestic violence was the second most common (6.17%) . . . followed closely by physical abuse (5.31%)" (Trocmé et al. 2005).

Ways to document potential abuse or neglect

Use only formats you have become comfortable with, by having used them previously. The focus should be on the information, not the way it is presented. It is particularly important to be as objective as possible and focus on all the details whether or not they seem relevant at the time. What the child tells you (and how), how the child's behaviour changes (if it does), the signs and symptoms of potential abuse or neglect the child has, and what is reflected in the child's play are the important maters in this kind of documentation. Avoid asking direct questions or leading questions, or prompting play to "force" a revelation; doing so may cause a false recollection and confuse a later investigation. Here is a list of useful recording formats, each of which has been explained in earlier chapters:

A. Baseline observations—the quickly observed and recorded behavioural and physical description of the child at the beginning of the day, or start of a particular period of time

B. Running records—to capture random but detailed play behaviours, or to look deeply at the child's behaviour at any time of the day

C. Anecdotal records—to capture particular incidents that give/gave you cause for concern

D. Diary accounts—documentation drawn from your diary that offers pertinent information about the parents or family, or the child's behaviour, demeanour, or physical signs or symptoms

E. Event samplings—may offer behavioural patterns that give experts insight into repeated behaviour

F. Serious occurrence charts—the room/program record of accidents, emergencies, or other serious incidents

G. Lists of signs/symptoms/indicators with descriptions observed

H. Notes of observations undertaken as a result of your own concern—for example, seeing marks on a young child's back while changing her diaper

> Child neglect . . . is the most common form of child maltreatment reported to child protective services. It is defined as a type of maltreatment that refers to the failure to provide needed age-appropriate care, such as shelter, food, clothing, education, supervision, medical care and other basic necessities needed for development of physical, intellectual and emotional capacities. Unlike physical and sexual abuse, neglect is usually typified by an ongoing pattern of inadequate care and is readily observed by individuals in close contact with the child. (Child Abuse Prevention Network 2002)

Remember: *Every observation must be dated, timed, signed, and kept confidentially according to applicable policies.*

The Toronto Child Abuse Centre offers the following advice when documenting indicators of child abuse:

- Record the information as soon as possible, including dates and times.

- Document the facts *without* personal judgments, opinions, conclusions, or medical/emotional diagnosis.

- Give a clear description of the situation, what was *actually* seen or heard, and not what you think *might* be happening.

- Include what you did or said and why.

- Record the words used by a child/parent, even if they are "slang" (especially terms for body parts or sexual behaviour).

- Include anything anyone else has said that might be important.
- Describe the size, colour, and shape of any injury (e.g., bruises, marks, burns).
- Handwrite your own documentation in your own words, using a pen.
- Cross out and initial any mistakes and continue documenting—do not use whiteout.
- Document suspicions of abuse in a separate record.
- Make sure the entry is complete, then sign and date it.
- Start a new entry if, at a later date, there is new information or further suspicions of abuse.

Your first recording of the facts is your documentation:

- do *not* make a rough copy and then write it over in good;
- do *not* go back and change any of your original notes; and
- do *not* shred documentation.

(Toronto Child Abuse Centre 2005)

Summary

This chapter presents a different approach to observation, one that requires the application of some of the skills acquired earlier; you now have to select the method of recording that best suits your purpose. Another aspect of this chapter leads us to be more careful in our observations, and pay close attention to a variety of causes for concern about individual children. We see that there are many signs and symptoms that are indicators of health or other issues. Parents must be involved in every aspect of the child's health and well-being (except if a child is thought to be abused or neglected), and we learn to share our observations with parents. We get to appreciate the range of challenging behaviours exhibited by some children—and we learn to document these behaviours to establish patterns and begin to address some of their underlying issues. Particularly concerning are indicators of developmental problems; what we see, what we record, and what we do with that information is discussed. Educators focus on observing and documenting indicators of developmental concerns, and pass their information on to parents, and ultimately to an assessor who might conduct a formal assessment. One of the hardest tasks when working with young children is acknowledging that they have possibly been abused or neglected; sometimes we do not want to face up to the idea. Recognizing the signs and indicators of potential child abuse or neglect is emotionally challenging. However, the educator may take the key role in reporting what she sees and has documented. The child protection agency will conduct a sensitive investigation when necessary, and the educator needs to keep all information to herself. How we document key information in the areas of health, challenging behaviours, developmental issues, or abuse or neglect is reviewed in this chapter. The use made of the observations and other documentation is particularly important. All observations must lead to improving children's lives.

Key Terms

- abuse
- accommodations
- baseline observation
- cause for concern
- challenging behaviour
- child abuse
- child protection agency
- diagnosis
- disability
- documentation
- early intervention
- educational neglect
- emergency preparedness
- emotional intelligence
- emotional neglect
- exceptionality
- exclusion
- failure to thrive
- Floor Time
- health concerns
- hunch
- inclusion
- indicator
- institutional abuse
- integration
- intuition
- medical neglect
- medically fragile
- neglect
- normative profile
- notifiable disease
- patterns of development
- perpetrator
- pervasive developmental delay
- physical abuse
- physical neglect
- policies
- procedures
- psychological/emotional abuse
- red flag
- resilience
- ritual abuse
- sexual abuse
- signs
- special needs
- symptoms
- temperament
- trauma

Weblinks

www.taca.on.ca/FAQ4.html
The Toronto Child Abuse Centre offers indicators and protocols.

www.cfc-efc.ca/docs/mcca/00000822.htm
Child and Family Canada—coping with abuse.

canada.justice.gc.ca/en/ps/fm/childafs.html
Department of Justice Canada—Child Abuse fact sheet.

continued

www.tcdsb.org/policyregister/S17.html
Detailed policies on child abuse used by a school board.

www.cps.ca/english
Up-to-date health information from the Canadian Paediatric Society.

resilnet.uiuc.edu
Building resilience in children and adults.

www.cccf-fcsge.ca/
Canadian Child Care Federation and also their journal *Interaction.*

www.socialunion.gc.ca/ecd/
The well-being of Canada's children/children with disabilities.

www.aqeta.qc.ca/english/home/who.htm
Web site of the Learning Disabilities Association of Quebec.

www.phac-aspc.gc.ca/ncfv-cnivf/familyviolence/
Child Abuse and Neglect Fact Sheet (National Clearinghouse on Family Violence).

www.ccsd.ca/drip/research
Research into disabilities in children.

www.rightsofchildren.ca
Web site of the Canadian Coalition for the Rights of Children.

www.cybertip.ca
Helpful information for protecting children on-line

www.rcmp.ca/ccaps/child_e.htm
The RCMP's fact sheet on recognizing and responding to child abuse

www.specialinkcanada.org/
National (Canadian) Centre for Child Care Inclusion

www.boostforkids.org
Child abuse prevention and intervention.

11 Screening and Assessment

Assessment of a child's performance in every developmental domain is more authentic if it is done in a naturalistic way.

With permission of the YMCA of Greater Toronto

... [S]creenings are important for early identification of problems and can help eligibility for specialized programs.
E. Wotherspoon & J. Pirie, Calgans Health Region Collaborative Mental Health Care Program (2008)

When unnecessary testing takes time away from teaching, we shortchange children.
W. J. Popham (2008)

Our society has embraced the formal testing mode to an excessive degree.
Howard Gardner (1993)

Observations and assessments ... support the close contact between the two groups responsible for the child's care and education [parents and professionals]. ...
Linda Pound (2003)

Traditional testing ... is one way to measure; however this type of test provides only limited information ... Authentic assessments are more natural. They provide teachers with valuable and practical information to understand and plan for the developmental needs of their children.
High/Scope Child Assessment (2008)

Parents of young children usually have the responsibility for seeking formal assessments. But they are often prompted by an educator who has already observed causes for concern, or identified areas of the child's development that warrant further exploration. Educators who have strong communication skills and take time to meet and talk with parents will often find that they bring up the possibility of assessment almost simultaneously. When professionals and parents are partners, the child and her family are usually much better served.

Educators are often the facilitators of screenings and standardized assessment, but they are not always the administrators of formal assessments. Their involvement may be to offer naturalistic observations to the process, and later assist in developing a plan to support the child's identified needs. Ideally any screening or use of standardized assessment tools should be undertaken in parallel with the educator's authentic assessment. Together these different approaches to assessment are far more meaningful and they offer a context rarely found with formal assessment protocols alone.

Educators have expertise is in the nurturance and education of children, and in the use of observation as their everyday tool for assessment. Other specialists such as psychologists and pediatricians have the expertise to make formal assessments using standardized tools. When educators, parents, and assessment experts work collaboratively, the needs of very young children can be met more effectively. When children enter kindergarten the teacher usually chooses appropriate assessment process, but the teacher may also have to comply with the requirements of the school principal, board of education, government department, legislation, and other regulatory bodies.

Features of Screening and Assessment Tools

Screening

Screening procedures usually involve the use of **standardized tests** in assessing a large population of children in a brief, relatively inexpensive manner. They are usually carried out by medical professionals, psychologists, or diagnosticians. Childcare workers and teachers use informal screening techniques to identify children whose development is in some way atypical.

Early identification of a health concern or developmental challenge can make a significant difference to the child's later progress. **Early intervention** programs may be available either through resource teachers at the school or agency, through the school administration, or through external consultants. The general rule is: the earlier a difficulty is identified, the more likely it can be addressed effectively.

Screenings for young children may focus on identifying any one of the following:

- health or medical issue
- growth concern
- motor skill delay
- learning disability
- language acquisition challenge
- hearing, vision, or other sensory deficit

- autism or other communicative disorder
- other specific developmental concern
- intellectual functioning difficulty

The screening process is intended to identify only those children who need intervention, support, or monitoring. The screening is important because it identifies children who are somehow vulnerable or in need, who might not otherwise be noticed.

The screening involves a kind of test or assessment focused specifically on the one particular behaviour or indicator being looked for. Frequently the screening tool is called an "instrument." This is a professional term; a **screening instrument** is simply the test that is conducted.

KEY FEATURES: Screening tools

- use standardized procedures to evaluate the health or development of a large number of children
- identify children in a special category of need
- are usually applied in a testing environment

TAKING A SPECIAL LOOK: Screening for disabilities

One reason to observe children is to ensure that they are supported in every way possible. Beyond observing children's development, educators use screening to determine whether the children have any specific conditions, syndromes, chronic illnesses, or other exceptionalities. The need for ongoing observation and follow-up assessment continues after a child has been screened. Observations may also reveal other concerns not identified earlier.

Assessment

DEFINITION: Assessment

Assessment is a process of information-gathering, review, analysis, and determining the needs of an individual. The process may target particular health, developmental, or contextual information, or may be more holistic, encompassing a wide variety of facts and opinions.

The assessment process may use many information sourses, including informal observation, standardized tests, teacher appraisal, developmental **checklists**, parental observations, **self-evaluation**, medical diagnosis, or any combination of these or other methods. A variety of professionals such as health professionals, psychologists, social workers, teachers, caregivers, early childhood specialists, and parents may be part of the assessment team.

There are two main types of assessment:

1. **Formative:** Evaluation that is done over time during the process of learning, often considered to be assessment for learning. Formative assessment allows the educator to alter the program during its course to accommodate the findings of evaluations made earlier in the program. Authentic assessments are typically observational, performance-based, and may be documented using portfolios. Sometimes formative assessments include summative assessment results.

2. **Summative:** Evaluation that is done at the end of the process of learning, often considered to be assessment of learning. Summative evaluation is generally the final or total score of an assessment. Summative assessments frequently use standardized assessment tools (meaning the tests themselves).

There are two main philosophies of assessment:

1. **Authentic Assessment** uses naturalistic observations and real-life performances. Data is frequently gathered in a formative way and analyzed frequently so that it informs what the educator does, and how it is done. The main thesis of this book is to explain the methods of collecting observational data, how to make sense of that material, and how to analyze that information about young children bearing in mind each child's family and social context.

2. **Standardized Testing** uses what are thought to be (by educators and test designers) valid, reliable, and appropriate ways of collecting information about individual children.

However, they are not always entirely separate philosophies. Authentic assessment values the information that some tests can offer. Typically, those in the "authentic" school of thought depend largely on naturalistic information and contextualized understandings of that material. Where standardized tests confirm what is already known, or offer results that are consistent with the general vision of the child's development, the test results are gladly included in the child's records and then acted on. If the standardized test offers up rather different results, the authentic assessor will try to confirm the findings using his typical methods of recording. Where the results don't match what is known, they may still be useful but are treated with some level of caution. Those people who think standardized tests are superior tools because they are created by psychologists, or others who are academics and practitioners in various child-related fields, often believe that authentic assessments are "soft," overly intuitive, cumbersome, time-consuming, and lack validity and reliability in the psychometric sense. (**Psychometry** is the science of measuring psychological and other human traits and competencies.)

One concept useful in both assessment paradigms is that of **triangulation**. Triangulation is the process of gathering data from multiple sources and/or multiple professionals and/or using multiple methodologies of data collection. Just like in woodwork, if a table includes a triangle in its construction it will have stability. If there are three (or more) pieces of information that point to the same finding, then it is more likely to be correct. If we use the results of a standardized test as one of those sides of the triangle, then two (or more) other separate recordings may help confirm an aspect of our analysis.

Medical and psychological professionals have developed standardized tests as tools to help them assess particular aspects of children's health, growth, or development. Effective assessments are (1) thorough, (2) contextualized, (3) holistic, (4) multi-sourced, (5) team-oriented, (6) respectful, and (7) tied to curriculum and responsive to needs.

Assessments may focus on one domain or on multiple aspects of a child's performance. Assessments may use one standardized test or several forms of information-gathering. Ultimately all assessments should be carried out to benefit the child, but in practice this does not always happen. Administrators may use assessments to exclude a child from a program, just as they might use the outcome of the test to include a child. Assessment may also be undertaken to provide information for government, independent researchers, or even for competitive purposes.

Here are some of the most frequently used types of assessments of young children that employ standardized tools, or instruments:

- language and communication
- reading/decoding/meaning/comprehension/writing
- kindergarten readiness
- emotional intelligence
- fine and gross motor skills/self-help skills
- social behaviour/self-regulation/cooperative behaviour
- information-processing/intelligence/cognitive/problem-solving/attention
- personality/style indicators
- learning disabilities
- school grade-performance tests/achievement/academics
- psychological
- sensory
- art skills/drawing
- memory
- admissions tests (even for preschool)
- math

"A thorough and comprehensive assessment of a child can greatly enhance his or her educational experience" (Pierangilo and Guliani 2006).

KEY FEATURES: Standardized Assessment tools

- include published tests
- are considered to be valid and reliable (the test is tested)
- demand expensive investment
- state the age/stage the test is designed for
- measure competence, traits, or other specific area of development
- often claim to be predictive
- require training to administer
- use prescribed protocols for administration and analysis
- offer a rating, score, comparison with the norm, and/or reference to specific criteria

Evaluating standardized tests

Even if your early childhood philosophy emphasizes evaluation through naturalistic observation, you will need to recognize the strengths and weaknesses of standardized tests and be able to evaluate the data they provide. The trend has been to use a wide variety of standardized tests to determine **readiness**, **skill acquisition**, developmental stages, learning disabilities, and so on. Acknowledge why some teachers think tests are desirable and useful; you do not have to agree with the approach or follow the trend if you think you can gain the information more easily, naturally, effectively, and cheaply by other means.

Underlying the belief in standardized testing is a philosophy that values some or all of the following ideas:

- A test can measure what it purports to measure.
- A child's behaviour can be evaluated by comparison with an expected norm or stage.
- A test situation can elicit objective information.
- The outcome of a test is a predictor of later development.
- Children evaluated to determine deficits in development can benefit from improved programming.
- Teachers and other professionals can determine behavioural goals on the child's behalf.
- Test data can improve a school or agency's **accountability**.
- Evaluation of published information regarding the **reliability** and **validity** of tests can filter out possible bias or inaccuracies.
- Testing procedures benefit rather than harm curriculum development.
- Teachers, caregivers, and parents can interpret test results accurately and successfully.

Ask yourself what you think about the philosophy, as stated above!

Professionals often use tests to aid their work, in the belief that tests will offer them more **objectivity** than other sources of information. Considering the way in which the data are collected, it is doubtful whether the results can be objective. Children may not perform the same way in a "test" situation that they would in their natural surroundings. Some tests are administered by someone other than the regular educator; in that case the child might be affected by the strangeness of the test or the tester. Without appreciating a child's regularly displayed behavioural patterns, you can tell little about her overall progress. With little understanding of the family background, current issues in her life, or what is normal for this child, you have limited scope for effective evaluation.

Norms derived from a general population may provide unreliable data. Particularly worrisome is the undetected cultural **bias** of many well-used standardized tests. For example, in some cultures, children do not learn self-help skills early in life because they are fed, clothed, and toileted longer. This does not mean that they will not develop normally. Results that reflect acquired skills may not give you more than a quick snapshot of children's current development—in themselves, such comparisons do not help determine appropriate curricula.

One problem with using tests in Canada, or elsewhere, that were designed in the U.S. using American norms, is that those norms may not be applicable. Researchers Frisk and Boychyn have addressed this issue and determined that there is "the need for

Canadian norms for American screening tests, and challenge the idea that screening measures used to identify language impairments are interchangeable" (2008).

If a test has a well-founded theoretical basis, it may suggest the next level of development. When the child will develop particular skills is a matter of **maturation**. Although patterns of development are fairly predictable, we cannot estimate when (or if) a child will gain a skill.

A key issue in evaluating a test is to determine exactly what it does measure. The name of the test or elements of it do not necessarily indicate the test's content. You cannot be assured that it actually tests what it is meant to test. For example, an IQ test may not test intelligence but problem-solving, which is only one component of IQ. Consider the readiness test; it may evaluate a set of skills that the test designer believes are important in determining a child's readiness for, say, kindergarten. In fact, it may reflect skill acquisition in some areas, but not all; these tests commonly leave out social and emotional skills.

Before administering a test, teachers and other professionals should consider the appropriateness of that test for children with varying language and cultural heritages, ages, personalities, interests, motivations, and powers of concentration. There are many biases in assessments. Examples of bias include test items that rely on a child's familiarity with particular domestic items unknown to him because of his culture. Questions may rely too heavily on logical thought, which may be an unfavourable approach for a creative mind! A child's self-esteem may be evaluated as "poor" because the test did not allow for different emotional responses.

Some administrators and teachers wish to test children to prove their own effectiveness. They work on the premise that quality programming can be measured in the short term. Significant data are provided only if the "before" and "after" are measured, and then only if the data are viewed in terms of stages of growth rather than adherence to timeliness. "While it does not provide a complete picture, testing is an important tool, for both its efficiency and ability to measure prescribed bodies of knowledge" (Epstein et al. 2004).

TAKING A SPECIAL LOOK: Referrals

Observing children can lead us to recognize that further assessment of them is necessary. Some situations require professional skills beyond our scope or from a different discipline. While the parents should initiate contact with any specialists, teachers or caregivers may prompt the parents to do so by sharing observations. For example, Kerry's teacher observed that Kerry was not responding to questions, was easily distracted at story time, and would sometimes make comments out of context. She shared her observations with Kerry's mother, who took Kerry to an audiologist. Tests showed that Kerry's hearing was slightly impaired, and she was fitted with a hearing aid.

Not only is it that educators are doubtful about the use of standardized tests with young children. Below we quote from a position statement where psychologists are clear about their direction and the need to contextualize assessments:

> ... standardized assessment procedures should be used with great caution in educational decision-making because such tools are inherently less accurate

and less predictive when used with young children. Multidisciplinary team assessments must include multiple sources of information, multiple approaches to assessment, and multiple settings in order to yield a comprehensive understanding of children's skills and needs. Therefore, assessments should center on the child in the family system and home environment, both substantial influences on the development of young children. Similarly, families' self-identified needs should drive the decision-making process concerning the identification of child and family services. (National Association of School Psychologists 2002)

Making an assessment as successful as possible

While the general thrust of our argument is in favour of authentic assessment over standardized tests, we remain realists and know that the testing culture in North America and Europe is pervasive. What we can do is to select assessment tools and understand what they can do to assist us in understanding children well. Meisels has been an advocate of appropriate and effective assessment for many years. He makes the following statements about assessment in the early years:

Practices to Avoid in Assessment

1. Young children should not be separated from their parents or familiar caregivers during assessment.

2. Young children should not be assessed by a strange examiner.

3. Assessments are incomplete if they are limited to easily measurable areas, such as certain motor or cognitive skills.

4. Normative tests or milestone scales should not be the cornerstone of the assessment of an infant or young child.

(Meisels 2000)

The Association for Childhood Education International has also stated:

In 1976, ACEI called for a moratorium on all standardized testing in the early years of schooling. The association also affirmed the importance of evaluation in classrooms and schools, acknowledging that careful evaluation was the key "to the qualitative improvement of educational practice and the teaming of children." ACEI's position remains similar now with one exception. We now believe firmly that *no standardized testing should occur in the pre-school and K-2 years*. Further, we question seriously the need for testing every child in the remainder of the elementary years. (Perrone 1991)

Standardized tests as part of authentic assessment

If teachers and caregivers use standardized tests instead of employing ongoing naturalistic observation, they will miss much of "who the child is." However, there can be a real place for standardized tests and their results within a child's **portfolio**. A test may confirm what the teachers have observed naturalistically, in which case they can feel sure that their perceptions are correct. Or the assessment might highlight something that they were unable to detect using everyday techniques. In this case, they might respond in a variety of ways, perhaps questioning the test's outcome, checking its findings in other ways, or seeking another professional opinion.

The amount of formal assessment material in an average portfolio is likely to be modest. For some children, there might be a greater need to consult professionals who use standardized testing. Children who might be more likely to need formal assessments include those who

- exhibit behaviours that are difficult to interpret
- have socially disruptive or adaptive difficulties
- suffer chronic health conditions that influence their developmental patterns
- have long-term, serious, or terminal illnesses
- were born prematurely or with low birth weight and continue to have growth or developmental difficulties
- are diagnosed by professionals as having particular conditions or syndromes
- are born into families with genetically inherited conditions
- appear to be developing at a slower rate than expected
- demonstrate particular gifts or talents
- demonstrate discontinuity in their developmental patterns
- regress in their development without obvious reason
- have been brain-injured
- communicate with difficulty or fail to make attachments
- show particular difficulty in paying attention
- experience traumatic events or changes in their lives
- are "at risk"
- have been physically, emotionally, or sexually abused
- show unusual ways of processing information
- have sensory deficits
- face mobility challenges

As you can see from the list above, there are many reasons why a child may not perform as expected. Parents, caregivers, and teachers are the people who frequently advocate for a child and his need to be understood whatever his background, life experience, or potential. When the assessment is conducted without a full appreciation of the whole child within his family and social context, the potential for the assessment to actually harm the child is immense. We need to ensure that every assessment is contextualized.

Look back at the list of causes for concern identified in the previous chapter. Those indicators might prompt useful naturalistic observations that assist assessment.

A commonly used developmental surveillance tool is the Rourke Baby Record, a section of which is reproduced on page 375. The record reviews a number of different issues and bases its developmental screening on normative criteria. Educators and parents can download and even modify the record to suit their needs (**www.cfpc.ca/rourkebaby.htm**).

Drs. Leslie & James Rourke, Goderich Ontario,
Revised September 2000 in collaboration with Dr. D. Leduc, Montreal PQ
Endorsed by The College of Family Physicians of Canada and
The Canadian Paediatric Society
® Copyright *Canadian Family Physician*

Canadian Paediatric Society — Société canadienne de pédiatrie

The Conege of Family Physicians of Canada — Le Conege des Médecins de famille du Canada

Birth remarks:	Risk Factors/ Family History:	**Rourke Baby Record: EVIDENCE BASED INFANT/CHILD HEALTH MAINTENANCE GUIDE II**

NAME _____ Birth Date(d/m/yr)_____ M [ ] F[ ]

Length: _____ cm. Head Circ:_____cm. Birth Wt. _____gms. Discharge Wt. _____gms

DATE/AGE	4 months			6 months			9 months (optional)			12–13 months		
GROWTH	Ht.	Wt.	Hd. Circ	Ht.	Wt. (2 BW)	Hd. Circ	Ht.	Wt.	Hd. Circ	Ht.	Wt. (2 BW)	Hd. Circ (av. 47cm)
PARENTAL CONCERNS												
NUTRITION:	O **Breast feeding*** **Vit.D 10 up = 400IU/day*** O *Formula Feeding (Fe fortified)* O *Iron fortified cereal*			O **Breast feeding*** **Vit.D 10 up = 400IU/day*** O *Formula Feeding Iron fortified follow-up formula* O No bottles in bed O Veg/fruits O No egg white, nuts, or honey O Chocking/safe food*			O **Breast feeding*** **Vit.D 10ug = 400IU/day*** O *Formula Feeding Iron fortified follow-up formula* O No bottles in bed O Meat & alternatives* O Milk products* O No egg white, nuts, or honey O Chocking/safe food*			O Homogenized milk O Encourage cup vs bottle O Appetite reduced		
EDUCATION & ADVICE Safety Behaviour Family Other	O **Car seat (toddler)*** O *Stairs/walker* O *Bath safety*; safe toys** O **Night waking/crying*** O Parent/child interaction O Child care/return to work O Teething			O **Poisons*; PCC#*** O Electric plugs O **Night waking/crying*** O Parent/child interaction O Child care/return to work			O Childproofing O Separation anxiety O **Night waking/crying*** O **Assess day care need*** O **Assess home visit need*** O **Secondhand smoke***			O **Poisons/PCC#*** O *Electrical Plugs* O Carbon monoxide/ Smoke detectors* O *Hot water 54∞C* O **Night waking/crying*** O Parent/child interaction O Teething/dental care*		
DEVELOPMENT (Inquiry & observation of milestones) Tasks are set after the time of normal milestone acquisition. **Absence of any item suggests the need for further assessment of development**	O Turns head toward sounds O Laughs/squeals at parent O Head steady O Grasps/reaches O No parent concerns			O Follow a moving object O Responds to own name O Babbles O Rolls from back to stomach or stomach to back O Sites with support O Brings hands/toys to mouth O No parent concerns			O Looks for hidden toy O Babbles different sounds & to get attention O Sits with support O Stands with support O Opposes thumb & index finger O Reaches to be picked up & held O No parent concerns			O Understands simple requests, e.g. find your shoes O Chatters using 3 different sounds O Crawls or 'burn' shuffles O Pulls to stand/walks holding on O Shows many emotions O No parent concerns		
PHYSICAL EXAMINATION Evidence based screening for specific conditions is highlighted, but an appropriate age-specific focused physical examination is recommended at each visit	O *Eyes (red reflex)* O **Cover/uncover test & inquiry*** O **Hearing inquiry** O Babbling O **Hips**			O Fontanells O *Eyes (red reflex)* O **Cover/uncover test & inquiry*** O **Hearing inquiry** O **Hips**			O *Eyes (red reflex)* O **Cover/uncover test & inquiry*** O **Hearing Inquiry**			O *Eyes (red reflex)* O **Cover/uncover test & inquiry*** O **Hearing inquiry** O **Hips**		
PROBLEMS & PLANS				O Inquire about possible TB exposure			O **Anti-HBs & HbsAG*** (If HbsAg pos mother) O Hgb. (If at risk)*			O *Hgb. (If at risk)** O *Serum lead (If at risk)**		
IMMUNIZATION Guidelines may vary by province	O HIB O aPDT polio			O HIB O aPDT polio If HBsAg-positive parent or sibling: O **Hep.B vaccine***			O TB skin test?*			O **MMR** O Varicella vaccine*		
Signature												

Grade of evidence: (A) **Bold type – Good evidence:**   (B) *Italic – Fair evidence*   (C) Plain – Consensus with no definitive evidence

(*) *see Infant/Child Health Maintenance: Selected Guidelines on reverse of Guide 1*

**Disclaimer: Given the constantly evolving nature of evidence and changing recommendations, the *Rourke Baby Record:* Eb is meant to be used as guide only.   Part #MC0046

Interpreting assessment results

Some medical assessments and psychological evaluations look as if they are written in a foreign language! In a way they are, because they use professional qualitative and quantitative research terms. The most obvious way of understanding what they say is to ask the person who wrote the report to explain them or to ask for a summary of the findings. While it can be helpful to understand some frequently used terms, many reports refer to syndromes, conditions, and assessment results that even those working in the field would have to look up.

Most important for the adults working directly with the child are the recommendations, interventions, and program plans that they will have to implement. These must be very clear; in some cases, parents, caregivers, and teachers will have to acquire certain skills in order to help the child. Ask lots of questions and offer input into the ongoing assessment process by recording plenty of observations of the child while you are involved in the program, and even simultaneously with the more formal assessment process.

Response to assessment results

Educators and parents who have been part of the assessment team from the beginning of the process will understand better the subject of the test or tests. An assessment should lead to a program of action. Educators and families can work as partners to support the child. Ideally, when able and mature enough, the child will be a part of the team as well as being at the centre of attention!

An assessment is usually carried out for a particular reason. This reason should be recalled when interpreting the results. Action should be based primarily on the reason for conducting the assessment in the first place. However, sometimes unexpected results may materialize, and responses may have to be developed accordingly. Some such responses include

- communicating accurate information with parents
- planning special activities at home
- referral to medical specialists
- referral to **psychological services**
- access to **assistive devices**
- referral for targeted **therapy**
- adding assistants and paraprofessionals in school or childcare
- access to early-intervention programs
- development of Individual Program Plans (IPPs) or Individual Education Plans (IEPs) within the childcare or school setting
- referral to special schools or programs
- seeking the assistance of **resource teachers**

Always plan ahead for the **assessment cycle**. Interventions must be evaluated for their own effectiveness. If the intervention proves to be effective, it should be continued. Financial constraints may mean limited access to services. Those in the most need don't always manage to gain access to the necessary services. Local and political advocacy are usually essential to ensure that every child's needs are met.

Psychologists and doctors may be the people trained to conduct a standardized test, though they are not always the only people who can respond to the child's needs as these come to light through the assessment process. Parents, caregivers, and teachers can frequently provide a bridge from the stark assessment to the child's day-to-day life. They are most likely to know what kind of intervention might succeed, once they understand the assessment results. For this reason teamwork is essential, as are honesty and openness.

Individual program plans (IPPs) or **individual education plans (IEPs)** may be developed on the basis of standardized tests. Ensure that the test is only one mode of assessment, as it alone may not offer a broad enough picture. The IPP or IEP will usually focus on particular skills that need support and suggest activities that address these skills; the plans will further indicate how these activities might be designed, who will be responsible for carrying them out, and how their success will be measured.

Assessments should trigger action, review, and further assessment. In this way progress can be monitored effectively. The first assessment establishes a baseline that enables the assessor, parents, and professionals to follow the progression or regression that results. Ideally, the cycle should be regular but not as frequent as monthly; conducting a re-assessment every six months, or yearly, may often be appropriate depending on the age of the child and the nature of the challenge. Developing IPPs or IEPs more regularly can provide a structure to propel the action. When the child achieves the aim of each plan, or when a certain amount of time has elapsed without the child's demonstrating success, the assessment team can develop a new plan.

Using standardized tests as the core of formal assessment in early childhood

Positive aspects of standardized tests

* Psychologists and qualified psychometricians usually design and administer standardized tests.
* Tests provide uniformity of administration.
* Tests give a quantifiable score.
* The tool will have been tested for validity.
* Repeated use may increase reliability.
* Validity and reliability are much higher in later elementary grades.
* A wide choice of tests is available.
* Standardized tests offer specific information to parents, teachers, and psychologists.
* Tests may be administered to an individual or a group.
* Tests identify what the child can do.
* Tests may support informal assessment.
* Tests may identify potential concerns.
* The results may help indicate appropriate curriculum or activity plans.
* The results may be available quickly.
* Test results may improve accountability.

When psychologists or psychometricians are unavailable for testing, there are ways to overcome that. In some cases educators and other professionals may conduct a test legitimately, but there is another option. A "distance model" of consultation and supervision by a psychologist for screening and assessment in early childhood programs is a possibility. Successful in Peel Infant Development (Ontario), the model uses technical support to replace face-to-face communication. Used in remote and inaccessible regions, this supervised test administration and analysis is an innovative solution. The Peel Region initiative has been described by E. Keith and L. Montgomery (2008).

Negative aspects of standardized tests

Standardized tests are often used because of their relative ease of administration, cost effectiveness, and supposed validity and reliability, and because they offer a score or grade, rather than qualitative information. However, standardized tests are not all they may seem to be. Even if educators do not administer tests themselves, they need to be aware of their strengths and challenges, and of the consequences of making decisions on the basis of only standardized testing results.

Not all standardized test are alike, and that makes evaluating them particularly difficult. While some are strong in some areas, those same tests may offer less reliable information in others. When they are used for the wrong purpose, the outcome may be even less useful. For example, some screening tests are sometimes used as diagnostic tests, or even used to decide a child's program needs; so evaluating the test itself is not the only requirement—we need to check that it is used appropriately and its in-built analysis fits our intent. Biases can be hidden, objectivity can be assumed where it is lacking, the test may not have been checked for use on the population of children who are to be tested, the test may be used to predict future performance when it can only assess current performance, and some of the higher-level thinking of the child's competence may be missed because the cognitive attribute the test measures addresses only memory.

Some of the core challenges of using standardized tests with children in their early years can be clustered under six headings:

1. Test Creation
   a. politically motivated testing
   b. test creation for the purposes of teacher accountability and/or cost-saving
   c. government-sponsored grade testing
   d. developing any developmentally or culturally inappropriate testing process
   e. using an assessment paradigm rather than a learning paradigm
   f. creators are sometimes out of touch with real children in real contexts
   g. lack of flexibility
   h. not based on current understandings of child development
   i. false sense of objectivity
   j. does it measure what it claims?
   k. lack of testing higher-order cognition
   l. correlating children's scores with educator competence
   m. evaluation of the test often done by company that creates the test
   n. test cost (who is enriched?)

    o. tests created for only a very narrow purpose

    p. how current tests are

2. Test Administration

    a. failure to use a test for its intended purpose

    b. often requires psychologists or others who need training

    c. child may be removed from familiar situation for testing

    d. administrator may not know young child and may, therefore, not gain the child's best performance

    e. overly reliant on paper-and-pencil requirements

3. Test Analysis

    a. uncertainty whether test measures what it is supposed to measure

    b. contextual information may be lacking or not a factor in assessment

    c. scores open to inappropriate interpretation

    d. the speed of test administration and analysis is often a lure to teachers who feel stressed

    e. focus on what a child cannot yet accomplish (emphasis on failure rather than success)

    f. manipulation of data

4. Use of Test Results

    a. uncertainty whether test has measured what the educator thinks is assessed

    b. labelling children, streaming, and the social, self-esteem, and learning consequences of either or both

    c. inappropriateness of making educational decisions on the basis of the results of one test (the consequences of high-stakes testing)

    d. not predictive of future competence

    e. disadvantage some populations (see Bias below)

5. Problems with Bias

    a. norms may not consider culture or language diversity

    b. lack of inter-cultural reliability

    c. often biased against the poor, those of limited resources (low socio-economic group), children from some cultures, children whose English is not their first language, and children whose experience has been undesirable or lacking in learning opportunity

    d. biased in favour of the prevailing culture

    e. reinforces inequities

    f. may set children up for failure

6. Learning Issues

    a. tests being used for purposes other than helping the child tested

    b. takes away from learning time

    c. tests may fail to address individual needs

d. addressing some developmental domains in favour of others

e. how a child's motivation to learn may be influenced

f. doesn't suit all learning styles and types

g. jeopardizes rounded curriculum content

h. inaccurate links between a group's performance and an educator's competence

i. may result in decreased learning or narrowing its focus

j. teaching to the test (the educator knows what is to be examined and deliberately or not shapes curriculum and delivery to emphasize that)

k. reduces curriculum to rote memory

l. causes programs for young children to be overly academic

m. sometimes drives out good teachers in schools and educators in childcare contexts

n. assessment in more authentic ways, including performance testing and naturalistic observation, as well as the portfolio process, all of which are more likely to gauge true competence in all domains, is neglected

The notes above were created with reference to documents published by Fairtest, the Association for Childhood Education (ACEI), the National Association for the Education of Young Children (NAEYC), the Association for Supervision and Curriculum Development (ASCD), and the Canadian Child Care Federation (CCCF).

No test is good enough to serve as the sole or primary basis for important educational decisions. *Readiness* tests, used to determine if a child is ready for school, are very inaccurate. . . . *Screening* tests for disabilities are often not adequately validated. . . . They also promote a view of children as having deficits to be corrected, rather than having individual differences and strengths on which to build. While screening tests are supposed to be used to refer children for further diagnosis, they often are used to place children in special programs. . . . Test content is a very poor basis for determining curriculum content, and teaching methods based on the test are themselves harmful. (Fairtest 2007)

TAKING A SPECIAL LOOK: Inclusion and testing

Most educators see the need to assess children who appear to have special developmental challenges, and expect standardized tests to be part of that. However, some question exists as to whether it is for the children's good to expose them to assessments held mainly to show how well a school is performing, or how well Canada compares with other countries.

Whatever official information is released, the result is competition. While comparison and trying to do better are admirable, differentiation can have a negative effect on those functioning "below average." Testing has the potential for discouraging exciting and diverse learning communities (at all age levels) and hasten a return to streaming, supporting only the brightest and possibly taking resources away from those children who need them most.

Opposing views regarding standardized tests in childcare and education

Not all standardized tests are used for curriculum planning or to develop strategies to assist those children who are in any category of special need; some standardized tests are conducted so that programs can be compared with others at a local or even national level. Those who oppose these notions of accountability are adamant that "accountability has come to be a code word for more control over what happens in classrooms by people who are not in classrooms, and it has approximately the same effect on learning that a noose has on breathing" (Kohn 2000b). In contrast, Ontario's Expanded Testing Program claims that "a standardized approach to education, including a rigorous new curriculum and regular testing, makes it possible to compare results among schools or among school boards. This helps to identify areas that need improvement and target resources accordingly" (Report to Ontario Taxpayers, Fall 2001). One perspective considers accountability measures essential and considers standardized tests the best way of ensuring clear results and improving standards as the tests proceed. The opposing perspective considers standardized testing an intrusion into the classroom that limits the children's breadth of learning, leads to inappropriate education decisions, and provides little useful data, especially among diverse populations.

The concept of accountability can have hidden costs, claim an increasingly large body of academics and teachers. These include "a weakening of teachers' personal connections with students and the loss of shared learning journeys" (Williamson et al. 2005). They are also seen as compromising child-centredness—a significant issue for all educators, especially those working with the youngest children. "Teaching to the test" may soon be as applicable to preschoolers as to high school and adult education.

By having established **standards** in their own educational institutions, administrators wish to measure which students are reaching those standards and which are not; this trend is increasing across Canada, the United States, and Europe. In practice administrators are not necessarily trying to concentrate attention on children who "fail"; they usually aim to establish a statistical measure of achievement for reasons of program or school accountability. The question of who sets the official standards fuels further debate, as do the content and level of those standards.

The use of standardized tests as assessment methods with individual children is just as controversial. Arguments abound about the relative usefulness of screening populations of children. Some claim that screenings are an expense that society cannot afford, given the low numbers of children who are identified with special needs. Others insist that some screenings are essential because they identify particular children who should receive early interventions. Waiting until those children exhibit more evident signs and symptoms means those children sometimes receive intervention too late to be effective. While some students test well, others are intimidated, overwhelmed, have not had the learning opportunities to succeed, or are being tested in a second language. Assessors should bear this in mind.

Individual assessments of children may also cause concern if those assessments are carried out in ways contrary to authentic assessment principles or are conducted without factoring in adequate contextual information. Various issues come to the fore: cost, bias, appropriateness, focus, fairness, test anxiety, and what is to be done as a result of the assessment. Employing standardized tests, whether evaluated as valid and reliable or not, guarantees heated debate. Rather than considering this a superficial concern, educators must understand the values that are part of differing philosophies, political persuasions lie at the heart of these issues.

Early-years professionals can feel disempowered when dealing with powerful administrators who respond to promotional material claiming the validity and reliability of an assessment tool. Educators need to advocate for rich, thorough authentic assessment—this may incorporate standardized measurements—that is consistent with their philosophical understandings about learning, experience, and curriculum, and undertake such assessments primarily for the benefit of the child.

A major issue in the use of standardized tests with minority populations, immigrant families, and aboriginal people is that of cultural appropriateness. It is not only a bias with test questions that we need to be concerned about, but also the cultural difference between the test giver and the subject. Addressing this issue is Jessica Ball, who believes that monitoring systems must be community-driven. Ball has developed strategies to deal with this cultural challenge, and directs early childhood practitioners to "help reduce the social exclusion and negative stigma experienced by many Aboriginal children" (Ball 2008).

Choosing a Standardized Test or Formal Assessment Portfolio

If you appreciate the concerns regarding testing, you may not wish to use a standardized test at all. But if you do use one, the following criteria will help you choose one that best fits your purpose.

1. **Determine your own role in the assessment procedure.** Will you receive test results as a teacher, supervisor, administrator, parent, or childcare worker? You will want information that is useful to your role and presented in a way you can easily understand and interpret. The role of tester may be appropriate for you if the test you choose fits your qualifications and experience. If you need to find a tester, factor this into your decision-making. Consider the possibility of taking training to administer a test.

2. **Identify your reason for wanting the assessment carried out.** Do you want very specific information about one child, screening for all children in your care, or an assessment system to be used over a period of time? Evaluate the tests available to you to see if they can provide the screening or assessment data you wish. Are you sure a test measures what you want it to measure?

3. **Determine the type of assessment you need.** Are you focusing on health, development, or development of a particular skill? You will have to find a test that contains the criteria for evaluation that fit your needs.

4. **Ensure that the assessment covers the age and developmental stage levels you need.** Are you choosing a test because the title sounds correct, while the span of developmental stages is insufficient? To reuse a test over a period of time, ensure it will include a wide developmental range.

5. **Check that the assessment will produce information in each of the developmental domains or skills you are seeking.** Are you sure that these domains or skill areas are sufficiently detailed to give information about the quality as well as the presence of the behaviours you want to test?

6. **Review the material for objectivity, who uses it, and published critiques.** Have you read only the information produced by the writers and publishers of the test material, or have you checked it out more thoroughly? Look at test validity, reliability, and usefulness.

7. **Find out if the assessment can be obtained easily and how much it costs.** Do you have a budget that allows for the testing you want? Many procedures require updating or the use of duplicate forms that have to be purchased after you obtain the initial kit. Pieces of the testing equipment may also be lost, so check that you can replace them easily. Some have copyright prohibitions that prevent your copying the evaluation forms. A few tests may require computer access for scoring; ensure that your hardware and software are compatible. We discussed this usage of the computer in Chapter 7. Most of the recognized tests and inventories require verification of your professional qualifications before you can buy the materials.

8. **Evaluate the items for possible bias (cultural, sexual, or language).** Will the assessment be appropriate for the particular children you have? Consider test items to ensure that they are not faulty in their expectation of Eurocentric responses or a strong dependence on English-language skills. If there are such items as a doll in the assessment kit, could you change the type of doll to match the ethnicity of the child to be tested? Check for any built-in biases that might be relevant in tasks such as sequencing a storyline or identifying similarities or differences that children from various cultural backgrounds might perceive differently.

9. **Consider the assessment's ability to give you results that are easily understood.** Can you interpret the statistical information and understand the terminology of the test's results? You will waste money in buying testing procedures that are probably quite valid in themselves yet produce scores or outcomes that the teacher cannot use. This type of information may lead to impressive record-keeping, but be of very little help in program planning.

10. **Think about how you will use the test results.** Will you use them for screening or across the group for evaluation? What will you do when you identify a child in need of further assessment or an individual program plan? Work out whether you can make the necessary responses. What will you do with the information on the progress of each child?

If you use a test with caution and understand its limitations, it can help you be more sensitive to a child's needs and modify the learning or social environment for her benefit. If it enables you to work with your colleagues and the child's parents more effectively, you may have chosen an ideal method of testing. You might also have collated better information through informal observation and achieved your intentions more effectively and inexpensively by using a parent-involved naturalistic assessment.

The most effective assessments are **portfolio assessments** that involve a variety of information-gathering techniques. This ideal form of evaluation includes a careful selection of observations of the child's spontaneous play and social learning activities, some interpretive checklists of skill development, any necessary screening or test results, examples of the child's art, evidence of academic skills in the child's products, photographs of the child's activities or constructions, video-recordings of play, audio-recordings of language and music, and any other samples that reflect the child's processes and products of learning. These elements can produce a more accurate, broader contextual picture of the whole child. The perceptive teacher can select the methods most pertinent to her own skills, time, budget, and team of colleagues, as well as to the context, the degree of parental involvement, and the child's stage of development.

The next illustration shows a developmental screen based on a sample from the Nine-Month Nipissing District Developmental Screen. Although it is called a developmental screen, and is a useful tool to identify a child in need of developmental support, in practice it serves as a parent-directed assessment. Note the checklist observation

The following is a sample of the Nine-Month **Nipissing District Developmental Screen**™:

Nipissing District
Developmental Screen™

Child's Name _____

Birth Date _____   Today's Date _____

The Nipissing District Developmental Screen is a trademark of the Nipissing District Development Screen Inc.
©First published in 1963 and revised in 2002. Nippissing District Developmental Screen Inc. All Rights Reserved.

The Nipissing District Developmental Screen is a checklist designed to help monitor your child's development.

✓   ✓
Yes No   *By **Nine Months**, does your baby. . .*

☐ ☐   1. Look for a hidden toy?
☐ ☐   2. Imitate facial expressions?
☐ ☐   3. Turn to look for a source of sound?
☐ ☐   4. Understand short instructions (e.g. "Where is the ball?" "Wave bye-bye")?
☐ ☐   5. Babble a series of different sounds? (e.g. ha. da. tongue clicks, dugu-dugu)?
☐ ☐   6. Make sounds to get attention?
☐ ☐   7. Sit without support for a few minutes?
☐ ☐   8. Attempt to move by crawling, "burn" shuffling or pivoting on tummy?
☐ ☐   9. Stand with support?
☐ ☐   10. Pass an object from one hand to the other?
☐ ☐   11. Pick up small items using thumb and first finger (e.g. crumbs, Cheerios, rice)?
☐ ☐   12. Bang two objects together?
☐ ☐   13. Have a special smile for familiar adults?
☐ ☐   14. Fuss or cry if familiar caregiver looks behaves differently?
☐ ☐   15. Reach to be picked up and held?

Always talk to your health care or child care
professional it you have any questions about your
child's development or well being. See reverse side for
Instructions, limitation of liability, and product license.

ACTIVITIES FOR YOUR BABY. . .

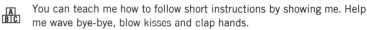

♡ Emotional ♥ Fine Muscle ✗ Large Muscle ⌂ Learning Thinking
⌛ Self Help ♔ Social ⊚ Speech, Language

The Nipissing District Developmental Screen is a trademark of the Nipissing District Development Screen Inc.
©First published in 1963 and revised in 2002. Nipissing District Developmental Screen Inc. All Rights Reserved.

The following activities will help you play your part in your child's development.

[ABC] You can teach me how to follow short instructions by showing me. Help me wave bye-bye, blow kisses and clap hands.

⊚ Let me imitate your actions and facial expressions. Play with me face to face and wait for me to respond. Repeat actions several times. Once I can do it let me lead and you imitate me.

⊚ I like books with short sentences and simple pictures. Let me hold the book and turn the pages. Name the pictures. Don't be afraid to read the same book over and over again. I like the repetition. Read animal books and make the animal sounds tool Cut out pictures from magazines and use photos to make me a book of my own.

✗ When I am on the floor I can move in many different ways. Put toys out of my reach and encourage me to move towards them.

✗ Let's climb. Place pillows and cushions on the floor, put one of my favorite toys on top of the pillow and I may try to get it. When you are lying on the floor. let me climb over you too.

✗ When I am in my crib or near the couch. I like to try to pull myself to stand. Remember I am not too steady so stay close by.

♥ When I am sitting. alone, encourage me to reach up and to the side for toys. I like to practise getting in and out of sitting position by myself.

♥ I like things that I can hold and bang together, such as plastic bottles, pots, pans and blocks. Give me a spoon or toy hammer and show me how to top the pot lid, plastic container, block or floor.

♥ Help me practise using my fingers. Give me chances to feed myself with finger foods like crackers and dry cereal. Place them in a small bowl and encourage me to pick them out. I could choke. Stay close by.

[ABC] Encourage me to drop my toys into large containers such as dishpans. shoeboxes or plastic buckets. Show me how to dump them out and put them back in again.

♡ Hug and cuddle me often throughout the day. Tell me how wonderful I am.

♡ Continue to talk to me about my world. Make me feel safe and secure by holding me, singing, and having quiet time with me. It is very common for me to make strange with new people and even with people I already Know.

♔ I would like to join you for dinner. Let me sit with you for family meals.

I'm getting into everything. Time to child proof my home.

Always talk to your health care or child car professional if you have any questions about your child's development or well being. See reverse side for instructions, limitation of liability, and product license.

and sample activity suggestions, and the structure for developmental assessment of infants through to six years. Combining the normative profile with activities is helpful and appropriate, and can identify potential problems.

Detailed listings and descriptions of frequently used standardized tests can be found in the Instructor's Manual that goes along with this book. It is impossible to review every test; the test administrator is responsible for its selection and use, and for explaining its purpose, implications, and results to educators and parents.

Summary

The more educators know about standardized tests, the better. Some significant issues surround the use of assessment methods—specifically that, although considered valid and reliable, these tests may not provide a holistic picture of the child tested. The mere mention of standardized tests can inflame some informed adults with passion. Some believe that they offer accountability and raise education standards. Others think that they absorb precious learning time and are drenched in biases that lead to inappropriate and unfair educational decision-making.

Screening instruments can help identify children who are particularly vulnerable or in need of some kind of intervention. Screenings are quick and efficient tools that do not provide a whole understanding of the child or indicate what should be done to respond to any identified need. While assessments can be broad-based and thorough, use of a standardized test rarely provides adequate information for educators or parents to act on. When standardized assessment tools are used the educator is wise to collect other data as well, including naturalistic observations, to offer a rounder understanding of the child who is the subject of the assessment. Augmenting the standardized test with authentic assessment processes will provide a more useful set of information. These observations and other documentation can confirm or contradict the findings of the standardized test.

Responding to the outcome of assessments is necessary; otherwise, the whole process is a waste of time. Parents and educators who, it is hoped, have been part of the assessment team, can ensure an assessment cycle that evaluates any intervention for its effectiveness, develops individual program plans (IPPs), observes and documents progression or regression, devises alternative or additional strategies to support the child, and ensures the conducting of further assessments at appropriate intervals.

Key Terms

- accountability
- assessment
- assessment cycle
- assistive devices
- bias
- checklist
- early intervention
- individual education plan (IEP)
- individual program plan (IPP)
- maturation
- objectivity
- portfolio
- portfolio assessment
- psychological services

continued

- psychometry
- readiness test
- reliability
- resource teacher
- screening
- screening instrument
- self-evaluation

- skill acquisition
- standardized test
- standards
- therapy
- triangulation
- validity

Weblinks

www.naeyc.org/about/positions.asp
This National Association for the Education of Young Children (NAEYC) site features position papers relating to standardized testing of young children. See also their journal *Young Children*.

www.ldac-taac.ca
This Learning Disabilities Association of Canada (LDAC) site outlines in-depth assessment strategies for children with suspected learning disabilities.

www.acel.org
Association for Childhood Education International. See also their journal *Childhood Education*.

www.ascd.org
Association for Supervision and Curriculum Development Resources on all educational topics including assessment. See also their journal *Educational Leadership*.

www.fairtest.org
The National (U.S.) Center for Fair and Open Testing.

www.zerotothree.org
Zero to Three. Follow links to many topics, including screening, assessment and diagnosis. See also Zero to Three journal and publications.

www.cospecialneeds.ca
A large chart and information about assessment tools.

12 Observing and Evaluating Children's Environments

In quality ECD [Early Childhood Development] environments, caregivers with education in child development use their skills of observation to plan appropriate experiences.
Karen Chandler (2003)

A well-planned environment will be safe and healthful, will meet the needs of both children and adults, will facilitate classroom management, will enhance the process of learning through play, and will support the implementation of program goals and objectives.
Carol E. Catron and Jan Allen (1993)

To understand a specific institution, one must observe its environments and teacher-child interactions, read its documents, interview staff, and talk to past and present parents and children.
Carolyn Pope Edwards (2002)

You come back impressed, once you've been up there, with how thin our little atmosphere is that supports all life here on Earth. So if we foul it up, there's no coming back from something like that.
John Glenn (1962)

The Child's Environment

What is an environment?

The child's **environment** includes every aspect of her surroundings. These include her family, housing, geographic location, economic status, social relationships, space, resources, and other relatively concrete circumstances. In an educational or care giving context, the environment includes the children's indoor rooms, outdoor play spaces, bathrooms, and other places where the children spend time. There are other aspects of her context that are less easily observed. These environmental factors include the values, attitudes, and beliefs of those around her, her culture, religion, perceptions of safety, and other less easily documented experiences and exposures. In this chapter we consider the individual child's environment as well as the environment of groups of children.

Do we have control over the environment?

Educators, parents, and caregivers can control some of the elements of the environment. Others are the responsibility of community agencies or constitute elements of the natural environment about which adults have a less direct responsibility. It could be argued that some environmental conditions fall outside everyone's control. We need to think about what is within our control. As educators we have some control over the environments we create for children: classrooms, childcare rooms, and outdoor spaces.

What environments are good for children?

What specifics you consider most important in an environment depend on your own values and priorities. For example, some people think the qualities of the learning environment are most important. If you ask many parents what they look for in a good environment, their first priority will likely be safety. So the criteria for a good environment depend on what adults value most highly—social competence, independence, intellectual functioning, or other aspects of human development. At the most basic level, the environmental conditions necessary for survival include:

- clean drinking water
- an adequate food supply
- appropriate shelter and housing
- good air quality
- safety and protection from harm
- sufficient space
- access to social services
- a positive standard of living (absence of poverty)
- a health service that meets individual and community health needs
- access to appropriate education

All of the things mentioned above serve to meet children's **basic needs**. As informed adults we need to be aware of children's needs and advocate for the high-quality provision of these elements for all children. While we know, of course, that meeting these needs is essential, meeting them alone is not enough for healthy child development. It is essential to provide for individual **psychological needs**, which support a child's sense of self and allow the child to become a fully functioning human being. The adult's responsibility is to provide for

- physical contact
- **nurturance**
- consistency of relationships
- encouragement and the conditions for experiencing success
- conditions for individuation (enabling the child to become a separate person)
- facilitating the emergence of the child's sense of "self" and his "categorical self" (the child knows who he is and his individual characteristics)
- support to become independent
- opportunity to acquire social skills and to function within a group
- validation of the child's experience of emotions
- support to recover from difficult situations
- the development of social emotions (empathy, altruism, etc.)
- self-respect and respect for others
- building resilience to imperfect relationships and environments

These conditions for psychological health and well-being can be met only through human relationships. As these constitute a core part of the child's experience, we will consider them as parts of the child's environment, even more significant than other, more tangible elements.

> Young children experience their world as an environment of relationships, and these relationships affect virtually all aspects of their development— intellectual, social, emotional, physical, behavioural and moral. (National Council on the Developing Child 2004)

Why observe environments?

Behaviour cannot be understood outside its context. We must observe the elements of a child's environment in order to attempt to understand the behaviour we observe. Environmental conditions influence children's functioning, learning, and well-being, so we need to observe them in relation to how children behave.

What is the adult's responsibility?

The challenge for the adult who takes responsibility for children's environments is to

1. seek out information that leads to designing and implementing exemplary environments for young children.
2. function as though she or he is part of the child's environment.
3. recognize that the child experiences environments over time (past, current, and future)—not only in one snapshot moment.
4. educate community partners about relevant environmental concerns (if necessary) and build a common vision for improving the children's environment with colleagues, parents, and other stakeholders.
5. observe the environment critically and improve elements of it that are within our control or influence.
6. advocate for the environmental conditions necessary for healthy children's development.
7. consider the influences of both the physical environment and the psychological environment on the behaviour of individual children and groups of children.
8. determine possible links between children's behaviour and their environments, individually and collectively.
9. regularly document relevant information relating to aspects of the environment, having conducted an **environmental scan** (an environmental evaluation based on specified criteria).
10. implement an **action plan** aimed at improving that environment.

Although observation is only one of a number of responsibilities for the adult, without it there can be no useful program evaluation or improvement.

What is the difference between the environment and the curriculum?

In early childhood practice the two terms are closely associated. The **curriculum** is the planned part of the child's experience. It usually involves the content—of what is to be learned and how it is to be learned (or taught)—and the outcomes, or end product of the learning process. The curriculum is usually written in a document that directs educators. All curriculum documents are based on beliefs about how children develop and learn; some state these beliefs, others do not. The curriculum is delivered within an environment—one that is shaped, in part, by any curriculum being delivered. But the child's experience is much larger than the curriculum. Much of this experience is other than what the curriculum or what the teacher intended. The **hidden curriculum** includes the values and beliefs underlying the practice.

So the environment is everything that happens to the child, what is demonstrated by adult actions, and the concrete surroundings that she experiences. The curriculum is the part of that experience that is planned.

Are we aiming to be objective when we observe environments?

Earlier in this text we discussed the idea of objectivity and subjectivity, and concluded that objectivity is typically valuable but in observation and assessment there can never be absolute objectivity. Clearly there is a lens that we look through when we observe, and that lens is shaped by knowledge and experience. When we observe, we are doing it while holding on to what we know, so that what we see is to some extent, if not completely, subjective.

Whatever we learn is **value-laden**, not value-free; the way we construct knowledge is through a subjective framework, and so what we know cannot be entirely objective or without personal perspective. Even when we are not conscious of our perspective or philosophy, it influences what we do and what we create. Engelhart was succinct when he said, "Knowledge is always value-laden" (1992). Every institution is value-laden, as is every aspect of every created environment. Our actions within the environment are also driven by values. This presents a particular challenge for educators; not only do we have to observe the environment, we need also to determine the values that are the foundations of its existence, and the framework of values that lead us to evaluate it.

While we make time to evaluate the environments that we provide for young children, we should also evaluate the values that underlie them. What might seem to be an ideal environment for preschoolers according to one philosophy or practice may be totally inappropriate to another. There are many sets of program standards that reflect commonly recognized principles—but even these can be critiqued. For example, providing a wide range of clean manufactured books and toys (considered by many people to be developmentally appropriate) and offering them in brightly lit spaces decorated in primary colours (a frequently chosen environment for children) may satisfy a program standard indicator. However, educators who have different philosophical ideas may prefer to offer home-made books, child-made toys, and open-ended activities in a quiet, peaceful, pastel environment. As a consequence we need to ensure that our practice is not only in accordance with current research about children and their spaces, but a true reflection of our philosophy.

> The objects of mass and popular culture—the Fisher-Price kitchens, Little Tikes table toys, wagons and Disney icons—so familiar in North American pre-school settings, are virtually invisible in the Reggio schools; mass produced toys, board games, and climbing centres are replaced by hand-made objects, specially designed for the space and the projects. It is as though the cultural static—the white noise of mass and popular cultures—has been reduced, filtered out of the learning environment, creating a place for careful attention to original expression." (Garrett-Petts 2008)

Following are questions to get you* thinking about elements of your philosophy before deciding on what criteria you choose to evaluate an environment (as well as set it up in the first place):

1. Merely offering a program environment for children sends a message; how is it political? What is the program designed to accomplish?
2. How important are children? How can that level of importance be reflected in the environment? How should relationships be supported through the environment?
3. What aspects of the "real" world do you wish to emulate in the microcosm of the children's environment?
4. What values and morals do you wish reflected in the program's environment?
5. Do you think that the process or products of learning/development are more important?
6. What is your perspective on how children learn and how their development can be supported?
7. What role does the environment have in supporting health, hygiene, safety, taking risks?
8. In your ideal environment, what is your position on the place for the following: child-directed play, games, computers, creativity, direct instruction, display, documentation, manners, aesthetics, media, personal space?
9. How does "going green" figure in your thinking? How does the broader environment link with the children's environment?
10. How you plan to guide/discipline children's behaviour, and how might the environment support that guidance approach?

As an example of how both research and philosophical perspective shape the way environments are designed and evaluated, read the following quote about the Reggio Emilia approach to early learning:

> As researchers into children's skills and abilities, teachers create learning environments that encourage both reflection and examination of their own personal beliefs about what children can and should be doing within educational settings. (University of British Columbia Faculty of Education 2008)

Is there a difference between programs and environments? The terms are often used together.

The program often focuses on the delivery of the curriculum itself, and it includes other unintended experiences. The environment is the place and culture of the program and includes every aspect of the child's experience. There is a big overlap between the terms. **Program evaluation** and **environmental evaluation** mean different things. Evaluation

*We use the word "you" to mean you as an individual and/or you as a group.

of the program is a broad process that looks at how the curriculum is delivered and how effective it is at reaching its goals. An evaluation of the environment can include these things and usually focuses on

- contextual data, and how effectively the overall environment meets the needs of its targeted group of children and families
- how well the environment helps meet the program's intentions (goals)
- to what extent the physical environment supports activity and learning
- how well the environment allows for the development of morals and values
- measurement of environmental indicators (which promote the program's philosophy), such as:
  - quality
  - developmental appropriateness
  - inclusiveness
  - how well it promotes physical well-being
  - the effectiveness of the learning environment
  - how effectively the environment promotes health and well-being

Later in the chapter we look at each of the areas mentioned above and identify specific criteria for observation. That said, evaluating the children's environment can easily include other criteria, such as

- measuring the environment's ability to accommodate children who have mobility challenges
- how "green" the environment is
- how the environment's aesthetics influence the children's behaviour
- if the environment promotes social relationships
- the quality of play that the environment supports
- the long-term social implications of providing a quality environment
- to what extent the environment facilitates the achievement of Developmental Assets (Search Institute 2008)
- how well the environment promotes family involvement
- whether the environment is safe and how risks are managed

> Theory and research on children's relationship to the physical environment is necessary for the planning and design of children's spaces that are challenging and supportive learning environments. (Children's Environments Research Group 2006)

How do I develop a rationale for observing?

We need to be focused when we are gathering data about a program. Before we start to observe we need to know why we have decided to observe the environment. There are many reasons for **environmental observation**. Knowing what to look for is important. Some of your reasons for observing the children's environment might include:

- ensuring suitability for the needs of the children's ages/stages, and the needs of families
- maximizing social interactions
- designing new experiences and activities
- facilitating better routines, rituals, and transitions
- improving the aesthetics (colour, lighting, comfort, textures, visual and auditory stimuli, temperature, air movement, use of spaces, inclusion of natural materials) and checking on how children and adults are affected by these elements
- ensuring safety
- promoting health
- including space for individual and group activities
- ensuring multiple usages (flexibility to change to accommodate differing interests and activities)
- facilitating language and communication
- maximizing the space and making accommodations to improve the inclusion of all children
- promoting emotional development, well-being, and nurturance
- reducing potential conflict or congestion
- supporting physical development (use of space and range of activities)
- supporting learning, including discovery, science, math, literacy (as appropriate for the children's ages, stages, interests, and needs)
- challenging preconceived ideas about what the environment should look like
- carrying out regular program evaluation

Do these reasons for observing indoor spaces extend to other environments?

Beyond the indoor environment we may also want to observe outdoor spaces. Our outdoor environments may be evaluated for many of the same purposes as those given above, but additionally we may want to include the following (remember that this is not a complete list):

- checking surfaces and structures for safety
- ensuring the space is appropriate for the children who will use it
- facilitating exploration and discovery learning
- maximizing natural elements (shade, plants, trees, wood, sand, water, soil)
- gauging risk-taking
- checking on access
- enabling sports, games, and spontaneous activities to occur

How is it possible to understand children's home environments?

One of the ways to have a better appreciation of a child's home is to conduct a home visit. This is often done before the child starts a new program. The information collected may be as a result of responses to a prepared questionnaire, but the visit usually elicits a broader understanding of the child and family through informal observation and spontaneous dialogue. The questions you ask depend on the situation and kind of program the child will enter. The criteria mentioned on page 406 associated with the Home and Family section of what to look for in the child's environment may be a start. Also, the Child Contextual Questionnaire on page 407–408 may assist the conversation and note-taking necessary in a home visit. Educators conduct home visits, but they may also be undertaken in a more methodical way for research purposes, such as in the NICHD study of *Child Care and Youth Development* (2005).

A well-known home-environment-measuring tool that focuses on mother-child interactions and the child's environment is Caldwell and Bradley's (1984) *Home Observation of the Measurement of the Environment* (HOME). It offers an inventory to look at the quality and quantity of stimulation and support available in the home environment. It was originally developed to help researchers move away from looking only at social class and socio-metric status of the family, a way that led researchers down a biased path of judgments. The HOME is a standardized test available in several formats appropriate for differing ages, and may be conducted by educators as well as psycho-metricians.

Looking beyond the indoor and outdoor spaces for children are the broader community and social environments where families live. To have a better understanding of the children and families you serve, observing these environments is essential. Here we should remind you to be both professional and unobtrusive when approaching and observing a community.

Writing up your notes rather than relying on a question-and-answer format will help you to reflect and make meaning and apply it to your role. Expecting answers to speak for themselves is a mistake. Adding a sociogram (see page 184–85) is helpful, but the narrative report is essential.

If we try to understand the child's home, should we try to understand the child's community?

Of course we can do a better job working with children (in any capacity) if we have a good understanding of where they come from. We can do this at many levels, but if we go beyond casual observation of their community, we will gain a broader appreciation of the things that shape the child's early experience.

If you were to do a thorough study and produce a **cultural portrait** that is "an overview of an entire cultural scene by pulling together all aspects learned about the group and showing its complexity" (Creswell 1998, p. 61), it might be considered **sociological fieldwork** or **ethnography**. Sociological fieldwork is the act of gathering information about a social group or area using observations as the main tool, and supplementing them with interviews of key people (informants) and obtaining significant artifacts (documents) that help explain the culture. It is a process that uses participant observation (see Chapter 3); you are the observer, but you are also immersed in the context. An ethnography is "a description and interpretation of a cultural or social group or system" (p. 58). What is so useful for educators is that ethnography enables us to understand what seems obvious and may be the everyday experience of our children. Wolcott explains this when he says, "Our fieldwork excursions ordinarily take us among ordinary people likely neither to have been subjects of research nor to have encountered researchers in action" (Wolcott 1995, p. 228). While physical aspects of the environment are relatively easy to observe, getting to the relationships within the social community may present challenges that must be overcome. "'Relational community' refers to the people, adults and children, who help form a child's social identity: tribal, ethnic, religious, language/cultural. Often, this is not a geographically clustered community" (Siddiqi & Hertzman 2007, p. 7).

Here are some of the things you might want to look for, or at least some starting points:

- whether you see an urban, rural, suburban, or combined area, and its state of upkeep
- events both spontaneous and planned, large-scale and small
- maps, land-usage plans, population-density images, climate, topography, archival resources, local newspapers and flyers, advertising, posted notices
- federal or state, provincial, municipal, or other levels of law, administration, regulation, how it is upheld, consequences, law and order, policing, security guards, security measures, freedom of movement, democracy/freedoms and limitations
- how homes are constructed (number of storeys?), density, age, condition, aesthetics, number of living rooms and bedrooms, design, use, common spaces, quality and amount of space, yards, gardens, passages, home insurance, play spaces, safety, presence of books, CDs, toys
- family composition (nuclear and extended), patterns, marriages, partnerships , age of giving birth, number of children, proximity to each other, styles of communicating, wants and needs, family trees, life insurance
- art, craft, everyday objects, prized possessions, emotionally linked articles, knick-knacks, prizes, trophies, medals, cultural or religious artifacts
- material goods, including cars, equipped kitchens, bathrooms, home decor, sound equipment, television, jewellery, computers and games, bikes, play materials, phones, artwork, and ephemera
- the **relational community**; not just the geographic area, but the people to whom and with whom the child gains an identity
- life-styles, standard of living, moral codes, evidence of bias, hierarchy, democracy, dependence, rules outside the law
- old and new photographs and video recordings of people, events, places
- purchasing power, what people buy, shops, on-line purchasing, gas stations, malls, independent/nationally owned stores, drive-through facilities, banking, spending and saving, coupons, dollar stores, budget purchasing, high-end stores, consignment stores, businesses closed/liquidating assets, financial demands and inducements to buy, yard sales, bartering
- meals, what is eaten, when its eaten, how food is shared, lunches, snacks, their cost

- routines, rituals, shared occasions, celebrations, feasts, fasts, family-together time, time alone
- what is in the garbage, recycling, social responsibility
- evidence of languages spoken and range of cultures
- types, sizes, and signs of wealth of industry, natural resources, retail, restaurants, businesses, and other economic activity
- political opinions, economic well-being, levels of employment
- public offices, public spaces, play spaces, recreation centres, swimming pools (user fees)
- schools, childcare facilities, home childcare (including public, private, for-profit, independent, not-for-profit), resources, space, how they serve the community, licensing, standards, curricular, qualifications of educators, parental involvement, safety
- religious buildings and practices, services, programs, and membership
- where the children are: schools, childcare, home, outdoors, hanging out, after-school programs, sports, extracurricular activities, malls, supervision, baby-sitting
- social activities for parents and families: eating out, games, sports, pubs, things to do, religious celebrations, inclusion of children
- health promotion, hospitals, clinics, water quality, fire service, birthing choices, emergency planning, paramedics, early-years health provision, immunization, health checks, access to GP, cost of services
- how the disabled and elderly are treated, housed, respected, accommodated, and the cost
- social services/programs: public, religious, and independent
- social statistics: population, crime, income, employment, immigration
- structural needs, social needs

Writing up the information you have sought adds to the process of understanding. Using a narrative form, you may want to tell the story of the information you gathered.

Fieldwork can obviously help our understanding, but what about talking to people within the community?

Approaching people may be difficult, so you could start with the contacts made through a home visit. You do need to be bold and be ready for rejection by some, but many folks like to be asked about their points of view. If you are able to get to know people in the community, you may want to find out more about the community and get to understand individual perspectives about some of the following:

- how they feel about living in the community
- life histories and personal life-styles
- how their experience has shaped their world view
- values, beliefs, attitudes, codes of behaviour, consequences of poor behaviour
- education level, attitudes to education, credentials, certificates, nonaccredited learning, life-long learning

- travels, perspectives, exposure to diverse cultures, attitudes
- the strengths of the community, and its weaknesses or challenges
- perceptions of today's young people and the elderly
- what they want for the community's children—and if it is achievable
- how the current economy affects them
- feelings about the future

Remember that the way you ask questions is very important, so ensure you use appropriate ways of asking questions, be sensitive to responses, and avoid leading interview subjects in ways that give you replies they think you are seeking rather than what represents their truth! However, we need to be respectful to those who assist us. "One way we show appreciation for what informants tell us is the serious respect accorded to the information they provide," suggests Wolcott (p. 107). Observing, listening, a tolerance for ambiguity, filtering the large amounts of printed material gathered, being skeptical of everything you hear and read, and writing up your extensive notes are the art, craft, and graft of fieldwork!

Ethnography is a challenging process, but done well, it can be most informative. What we must not do, though, is imagine that our findings hold true for everyone, including those we have not even met! Aligning information from several different sources helps to strengthen any statement we make about our fieldwork. In qualitative research, which is the category of research that includes ethnography, the term **triangulation** is used to describe this process of verifying corroborating evidence. It is a way to crystallize themes that emerge from your evidence (observations, artifacts, and questionnaires) and to feel comfortable that your claims are reasonably reliable. That said, be careful to avoid generalizing on the basis of your evidence, even if you think it is crystallized and triangulated. Typically, qualitative research cannot be thought to be **generalizable**; that is, your findings cannot be considered applicable to other contexts, people, or communities. But the understanding you will have gained is immeasurably important for understanding the lives and contexts of the children for whom you are responsible.

Knowledge of the child's context is going to enable you to create better programs for children and facilitate improved communications between you and each child. Let's go back to the environments that we have some control over.

What constitutes good-quality programming? What am I looking for?

1. **A global view**

   We can find the conditions for quality in many diverse programs. Rather than stipulate exactly what a quality program should look like, we can use well-researched indicators of quality. Audrey Curtis, the former president of OMEP (Organisation Mondiale pour l'Éducation Préscolaire, the international organization for Early Childhood Education), suggests that some educators are concerned about suggesting that there is any one way of providing quality care and education. She says that there should not be a "universal decontextualized child" and that "good practice does not exist in a vacuum, it is part of a complex situation in which cultural values and assumptions also play a part as well as an understanding of child development" (2000).

In her speech to OMEP in 2000, Curtis suggests four ways of determining quality, each of which must "acknowledge a diversity of circumstances and a diversity of perspectives and values." Quality services for children include indicators that relate

1. directly to the children and curriculum content
2. to the staff
3. to the family and community
4. to cost analysis and program quality

The values underlying delivery of the service for children will shape the way a program is delivered. Following the same curriculum, or even a similar philosophy statement, does not ensure the same program delivery. Also, each child's experiences within a program will differ, and what the educators and parents think about the program will also vary. Experience is always individual.

2. **Dimensions of quality**

There are several useful ways of looking at quality environments. In her *Five Perspectives on Quality in Early Childhood Programs*, Lillian Katz (1993) suggests several ways of looking at quality early childhood programs:

1. the top-down perspective (which includes setting characteristics and measurable features of the program)
2. the bottom-up perspective (considering the child's experience of the program)
3. the outside-inside perspective (parent–teacher relationships)
4. the inside perspective (colleague relationships, staff–parent relationships, and relationships with a sponsoring agency)

All but perspective 2 are environmental issues.

3. **Climate**

We can look at the quality of a program by measuring the **climate** of the place. This measure is usually found in school practice rather than childcare, but it has something to offer both settings. The climate is a more subjective measure of experience. It concerns what people think about the service that institution provides, how they feel about it, whether or not they feel comfortable or safe within it, and how they value it. To describe this measure as subjective does not mean this perspective is unimportant; the way people feel about an institution or service affects how it will be used and how well participants will benefit from it.

Measuring a climate usually means conducting interviews and **focus groups**, sending out questionnaires, and compiling observations of those participating in the program. The challenge comes in analyzing the data that are produced. Determining the climate of a program delivered to young children is very difficult because it involves asking the children directly what they think. Asking parents about their children's responses to the program and observing the children as they are involved in it can be most helpful.

Deciding what constitutes quality care can be challenge enough for most of us; the question of why society should be concerned and support such care is another issue entirely. More than educators and parents are concerned about quality childcare; it can have benefits for society. According to *The Benefits and Costs of Good Child Care: The Economic Rationale for Public Investment in Young Children* (Cleveland & Krashinsky

1998), quality care has long-lasting effects: "The future of our society absolutely requires good care for young children. Can we afford to spend the money for good child care? If we want an equitable and economically effective society, we cannot afford not to."

4. **Indicators of quality**

An **indicator** is something that is observable and is to be looked for. It guides us to seek evidence for something we think important—in this case a sign that the environment stands up to our idea of what constitutes quality. Because there are many indicators of quality, we need a way of measuring the environment that is manageable, so we use checklists and rating scales.

Checklists are very popular ways of measuring, but they can only attempt to look at what is on the list, not other things that may be present. You may recall that when we discussed checklists in Chapter 5, we looked at the strengths and weakness of the checklist method when observing individual children and groups of children; the same issues apply in observing the environment. Lists of **quality indicators** are, essentially, the criteria for checklists. Similarly they are the criteria measured when we rate the degree to which they apply; this is a rating scale. Rating scales were described in Chapter 6.

The quality indicators themselves have usually been developed as a result of research findings into quality in childcare (or whatever type of environment is to be evaluated). Additionally they are shaped by prevailing beliefs about what the indicator should include; for example, in recent years we have been increasingly interested in ensuring that we create and evaluate our programs for their inclusion of children who have special needs, accommodation of children who have learning differences, and sensitivity and inclusion of children and families whose culture, language, and knowledge differ from the prevailing culture, language, and ways of knowing. What we are seeking is to "create a society in which all children and their families are welcomed and valued" (Sapon-Shevin 2008, p. 49)

CHILD DEVELOPMENT FOCUS

Environmental observation and evaluation may

- lead to physically or emotionally safer environments

- allow better use of space for all activities

- maximize learning opportunities

- increase inclusion of all children

- improve adult–child relationships

- bring about a better experience for each child

Are observing the environment and measuring the environment the same thing?

Observation can contribute to evaluation, but observation and evaluation are not the same thing. Just as we observe children in ways that contribute to our assessment of their behaviour, so we observe programs that offer data for a program-evaluation process. Multiple observations, as well as other ways of gathering information, add to our collection of adequate data to evaluate a program's effectiveness.

Are there different levels of quality in early-childhood environments?

Yes, there are many different levels of quality, whatever yardstick you are using for measurement. We would like to think that the majority of programs for children demonstrate an acceptable standard, but not all do. Some offer environments that satisfy some children's needs, and others offer environments that meet the needs of the children's families. Each program has its own strengths and weaknesses. As you recall, rating scales aid the measurement of environments, but the presence or absence of quality indicators in a checklist provides a good overview.

Many researchers take a global view of quality programming based on the goal of ensuring that the child's basic and psychological needs are met. Some environments may meet these needs while other environments surpass them. By observing different environments, the learner sees how very different programs can appear to be successful, even according to the same criteria.

Are indicators of quality the same for childcare, schools, and other children's programs?

Educators in all settings share some ideas about what constitutes quality. That said, the bodies of research tend to look at the broad environmental needs of all children or the specific environmental needs of children in either childcare or education settings. Both sectors may learn something from each other's research. Clearly teachers emphasize the learning environment, although they differ in their articulation of what that actually means. The childcare environment provides both childcare and education (within a differing philosophy, some may say), so their emphasis is different.

Here are some examples

1. If a kindergarten-aged child is in a half-day program at school and he spends the other half day at a childcare centre, should the environments be the same? Should they offer the same indicators of quality? Maybe they should be observed using the same quality criteria, because the child's needs may remain the same. However, the programs' goals differ, and what constitutes a quality environment therefore changes with them. This is a challenging issue that has not been resolved!

2. We may also think that a set of quality indicators will tell us what constitutes a good school. The OSSTF/FEESO (Ontario Secondary School Teachers' Federation/La Fédération des enseignantes-enseignats des écoles secondaires de l'Ontario) lays out a broad view of what makes a "Good School" in public education in their AMPA House Paper (2001):

   1. universality—access for all
   2. comprehensiveness—opportunity for all
   3. proficiency—achievement for all
   4. accountability—value for all

   Although focused on secondary schools, these principles are applicable at the primary levels and, perhaps, to all levels of childcare.

3. Those involved in early and later childhood education have conducted research that influences today's thinking about quality environments for children. Lawrence Lezotte (1991) has been particularly influential. His "Seven Correlates of Effective Schools" are central to his work:

   1. safe and orderly environment
   2. clear and focused mission
   3. climate of high expectations of success
   4. opportunity to learn and student time on task
   5. frequent monitoring of student progress
   6. positive home–school relations
   7. strong instructional leadership

   No one is likely to take immediate offence at Lezotte's leading indicators for effective schools. At the same time it should be pointed out that these indicators, too, imply certain beliefs about the goals of education. Together they denote a "reform" perspective and exclude other indicators that some educators might value just as highly. In applying any yardstick, educators need to consider some indicators and eliminate others. So selecting the criteria is of enormous importance. Lezotte's criteria are not necessarily "wrong"; however, they are value-laden. Criteria for evaluation typically include some idea of the transformatory value of experience. That being so, the environmental backdrop has great significance.

4. The Vista School District, Newfoundland and Labrador, has developed a school-evaluation tool that others can adopt. It studies 40 criteria statements built around five dimensions of school life:

   1. the learning experience
   2. school leadership
   3. school climate and culture
   4. school/community relationships
   5. the teaching environment

   To ensure that each of these dimensions is measurable, the district has developed a criteria statement linking each of their goals to one of the five dimensions. In the form of a chart to be completed using questionnaires, focus groups, personal interviews, observation, and group discussion, the internal team documents what has been done, how well it has been achieved, and then evaluates what these results tell them. The process is logical and detailed and produces the data each school needs. The evaluation also contributes to the province's efforts to make its childcare and education system accountable. (For details, go to **www.K12.nf.ca/vista/schooldevelopment/internalcriteriaas.html.**)

   These notions of "good schools" and effective learning environments have some application to childcare settings. But close examination points up the fact that early childhood educators working in childcare and teachers working in schools may have different philosophies or may think that they are offering entirely different services. This distinction is of considerable importance because it highlights the differing emphases possible in measuring the environment. North American early childhood practice may, at times, separate the functions of nurturance and education to the possible detriment of the children. Agreement about what is good practice, how children's needs are best met, what constitutes an optimal environment to support healthy child development, and what services families need may be a long way off.

Who or what should decide what is a quality early-childhood environment?

All the stakeholders in programs for young children should participate in determining the specific criteria for developing positive early-childhood environments, for evaluating those environments, and for making changes as necessary. These people include

- parents
- community members
- educators and paraprofessionals
- directors, supervisors, and principals
- the children (when they are able to participate)
- the program's administration, owners, and government departments
- key informants (such as university faculty and community experts)
- the communities' philosophy and beliefs about each other
- solid research that is valid, reliable, and applicable

Only when these people share a common vision can they also share an understanding of how those environments should be funded, supported, evaluated, and explained, and how the parents and educators will work together to improve the children's overall experience.

So where do I begin observing the environment?

At first it may seem simple to observe the environment, but you may find it more complicated than it looks! You will need to

1. determine your reason for observing and recording.
2. develop criteria that demonstrate the characteristics you are seeking.
3. create a format to document the information.
4. observe and document what you see in relation to each criterion.

If you have taken these four steps you will be able to document useful data that you can analyze in keeping with your reason for observing the environment in the first place.

How do I use the observational material to evaluate the environment?

When you have collected your data, you may want to sort the information, especially if it has become overwhelming. Themes may emerge when you review the information, or even as you collect it. You may find the following steps useful in moving toward a plan of action:

1. Sort data according to themes.
2. Present main themes—paper, charts, and diagrams can be helpful.
3. Review data for strengths and themes.
4. Suggest strategies to build on those strengths.
5. Review data for weaknesses or gaps.
6. Develop strategies to address these negative aspects.
7. Create an overall plan for change.
8. Formulate a timeline for implementation of plan.
9. Communicate plan to all stakeholders.
10. Ensure a regular cycle for environmental evaluation.

Environments: Details of the Children's Contexts

KEY FEATURES: Environmental observation

- involves observing and recording data on how items in the environment are being used

- identifies all components of the child's environment, including the hidden curriculum

- includes observing children's behaviours related to any of these components

- is usually naturalistic

What to look for in the child's environment

Anytime and anywhere are the times and places to observe a child's environment. If you observed a child's context only in formal times of organized learning in a planned environment, you would miss most of the child's experiences.

You might gather much of the information regarding that context directly from the parents. Some parents might, quite reasonably, resent your request for this information. Some initial interviews for childcare are held in the child's home—if this is the case, avoid the clipboard-checking-off approach, as this can seem clinical and off-putting to parents. Seek the information through more natural conversation about the child's home situation, while being open about recording some of the bits of information that the parents reveal. Be sure to record the sources of the information.

Here are some things you might look for that constitute the "environment" in a broad sense:

Home and family

- **nuclear family**—composition and size
- siblings, birth order
- health, abilities, and disabilities of family members
- location of extended family
- changes in family composition, moves
- nonfamily adults or children in the child's home
- religious or cultural heritage and practices
- mother's role and guidance
- father's role and guidance
- siblings' or others' roles in caregiving and guidance
- daycare or school enrolment and attendance
- memberships
- play space, play materials
- books and toys available

- TV, VCR, video games
- employment of parent(s), hours of work
- finances
- accommodation (rent or own)
- number of rooms (private or shared)
- clothing availability
- laundry facilities
- kitchen, food-preparation equipment
- temperature, indoor climate
- practical needs met or not met
- safety of environment
- outdoor space
- transportation, access, mobility
- need for social work, therapy, or other support
- family concerns

Sociological and geographic context

- nation and city of residence
- urban, suburban, or rural location
- accommodations (rent or own)
- type of neighbourhood
- population density
- building types, age, and history
- transportation, mobility
- shopping amenities
- local industry
- community services and buildings
- banks, finances, economy, taxation, benefits
- cultural mix of local population
- play spaces

- schools
- provision of childcare
- community concerns
- religious buildings and practices
- health services
- restaurants, cafés, fast-food outlets
- social organizations
- communications
- climate
- prevalence of disease
- demographic changes
- employment
- social services

Childcare agency/school

- type of establishment
- number and organization of staff, full-time or part-time schedules, supply staff
- funding and budget
- age ranges, hours open, size of group or classes, ratios
- catchment area
- staff qualifications, union membership, sex of staff, representation of ethnic groups
- indoor space and organization
- interior design of space
- philosophy as reflected in design
- stated philosophy
- variety of activities (name them)
- washrooms—access, independence level for child
- routines—meals, sleep, etc.
- food preparation and snacks
- policies, procedures, meetings, communications
- guidance strategies
- exterior space and equipment
- emergency plans
- safety precautions indoors and outdoors, first aid
- transportation
- availability of parking
- resources, space, and access
- involvement by parents, available parent education
- involvement with community—trips, within centre
- relationships between staff and children
- types of programs offered
- expendable resources—paint, paper, soap, etc.
- temperature and humidity
- hygienic practices
- provision when child is sick
- staff liaison with child's home
- entry or acclimatizing plan for new children
- accommodation for children with special needs
- cultural or ethnic mix of those enrolled
- referrals to other services if and when required
- personal belongings, storage
- structure, flexibility, expectations

Recording information about the child's environment

Looking at the world with the eyes of a child is one of the most effective ways to really see a child's environment. Recording the **context** involves much more than checking off the presence or absence of an element of that environment on a list. Compare the checklist and the narrative in the following excerpt from a family context.

Family Context

A. Checklist	Yes	No
Child has own room		✓
Child has personal storage space in bedroom	✓	
Child has appropriate toys	✓	
Child owns books	✓	

B. Narrative

Sian lives in a downtown third-floor apartment with her mother and two older sisters, with whom she shares a small bedroom. The apartment offers space for Sian to play between the kitchen and living room where Mom can watch over her. The three girls go to the library with their father alternate Saturday mornings when he has custody. The shared arrangement with the father is amicable, according to Mom, who said she liked to have a little time to herself when the girls are out. When they returned to sleep at home on Saturday night, I observed Mom playing with Sian. Her toys are not all new but seem to challenge Sian without causing her much frustration. . . .

As you can see, the **narrative observation** offers much more detail and background than the Yes/No approach of a **checklist**. While open to greater interpretation, the narrative description also provides pertinent information that explains the content of the checklist. Neither is incorrect, but each presents a different version of the situation. Checklists can be handy when you want to record lots of information quickly, and they serve as a reminder to look for particular criteria. The narrative takes much longer and is more open-ended, so it can include what the observer thinks pertinent.

Rating scales can also be helpful in recording the degree to which an attribute or characteristic is present. Both checklists and rating scales require that the observer make inferences while collecting that data.

Open-Ended Checklist

14. small wheel toys, cars, trucks   yes/no/not applicable

  comment/description _____

  _____

15. carpentry/sewing/cooking equipment   yes/no/not applicable

  comment/description _____

  _____

16. child-sized furniture   yes/no/not applicable

  comment/description _____

  _____

17. outdoor play equipment   yes/no/not applicable

  comment/description _____

  _____

You can make visual representations of the environment using photographs, video-recordings, and **mappings**. Any of these can add usefully to checklists or narratives, and they offer a record of the context that may be quicker, more detailed, and longer-lasting. Recording the environment in one of these ways enables you as observer or evaluator to consider the depiction away from the site or after the context has changed.

You can also use acetates designed for overhead projection for floor plans and overlay them to compare the use of space. Alternatively, you can draw a blank floor plan and photocopy it so that you can plan room arrangements.

Features of Environmental Evaluation

DEFINITION: Environmental evaluation

Environmental evaluation involves consideration of all the planned and unplanned aspects of a child's surroundings to ascertain their appropriateness or quality.

KEY FEATURES: Environmental evaluation

- evaluates any or all components of the environment against the stated philosophy of care and education

- determines the effectiveness of any or all components of the environment for safety, inclusion, nurturance, learning potential, or other criteria

- develops plans to improve environmental conditions in line with program goals

- is usually naturalistic

Examples of environmental measurement

Base a **qualitative evaluation** of any environment on a clear understanding of the philosophy underlying the construction and use of that environment. For example, you would find it difficult to assess a curriculum for **anti-bias** if you did not subscribe to the concept of anti-bias education.

1. The simplest evaluation format is the checklist. The items must be clear, focused, and as complete as the writer can make them. A more open-ended checklist may have space for including "add-on" items. You can attach a rating scale to the list of environmental criteria, allowing for a more qualitative response than simply a presence or absence or a "good" or "bad" answer.

A section of an environmental checklist

Checklist for Quality Inclusive Education

	F	O	S
I.1.c Visual displays reflect equity in representation.			

I.1.c.16. Do I display photographs and pictures of children involved in a variety of activities? e.g.,

	F	O	S
• girls in nontraditional activities	☐	☐	☐
• boys in nontraditional activities	☐	☐	☐
• children with varying abilities engaged in active play	☐	☐	☐

Examples:

I.1.c.17. Do I balance displays of children in special, traditional clothes in appropriate situations (e.g., celebrations) with displays of children in their everyday clothes?   ☐ ☐ ☐

Examples:

I.1.c.18. Do I use visual displays that represent diversity?

	F	O	S
• varying physical, visual, and sensory abilities	☐	☐	☐
• varying ages	☐	☐	☐
• varying appearances	☐	☐	☐
• different beliefs	☐	☐	☐
• multicultural backgrounds	☐	☐	☐
• different family compositions	☐	☐	☐
• females and males	☐	☐	☐
• multiracial backgrounds	☐	☐	☐

Examples:

F = frequently   O = occasionally   S = seldom

Source: Early Childhood Resource Teacher Network of Ontario.

2. Standardized checklists prepared by a recognized authority are checked for **validity** and **reliability** and reflect a particular philosophy. The best-known, most reliable, and most user-friendly environment rating scales are Harms and Clifford's *Early Childhood Environment Rating Scale* (1998) and Harms, Cryer, and Clifford's *Infant/Toddler Environment Rating Scale* (1990). You can use another rating scale Harms and Clifford have developed, the *Family Day Care Rating Scale* (1989), for evaluating home-based childcare. A wide variety of professionals, including teachers and assistants, can administer them. Each rates an item on a scale of 1 to 7 and allows space for comments. Each of the major categories is divided into several components, with clearly identified criteria for grading. Completing them is straightforward, but good results depend on general early-childhood training and familiarity with some terminology. You can gather checklist and rating scale results from both parents and professionals. If the criteria are clear, the perspectives of both parties may offer insight; frequently the outcomes will be similar. An example from the *Family Day Care Rating Scale* follows:

Name of lead caregiver _Roberta Poole_

No. of caregivers present _1_

Most children attending at one time _5_

Number of children present today _5_

Ages of children enrolled (youngest to oldest in months) _9 mos._ to _40 mos._

Name of rater _Pam Eckerd_

Position of rater _Resource and referral trainer_

Date _June 29, 2006_

SPACE AND FURNISHINGS FOR CARE AND LEARNING

1. Furnishings for routine care and learning

   1 2 3 ④ 5 6 7

   Children kneel on chairs—not adapted for their size.

2. Furnishings for relaxation and comfort

   1 2 3 4 ⑤ 6 7

3. Child-related display

   1 2 ③ 4 5 6 7

4. Indoor space arrangement

   1 2 ③ 4 5 6 7

   Space safe and adequate.

5. Active physical play

   1 2 3 4 ⑤ 6 7

   Fenced outdoor area. Uses activity records indoors on rainy days.

6. Space to be alone

   a. infants/toddlers

   1 ② 3 4 5 6 7

   Doesn't interact frequently enough.

   b. 2 years and older

   1 2 3 4 ⑤ 6 7

   Private space used for older children's games.

Total Space and Furnishings (Items 1–6)

27

BASIC CARE

7. Arriving/leaving

   1 2 3 4 5 6 ⑦

8. Meals/snacks

   1 2 3 4 ⑤ 6 7

9. Nap/rest

   1 2 3 4 ⑤ 6 7

10. Diapering/toileting

    ① 2 3 4 5 6 7

    Doesn't wash hands after each child.

11. Personal grooming

    1 ② 3 4 5 6 7

    Children's hands not washed before eating.

12. Health

    1 2 3 ④ 5 6 7

    Not careful about preventing spread of germs; no set rules for giving medicines to children.

13. Safety

    1 2 ③ 4 5 6 7

Total Basic Care (Items 7–13)

27

FAMILY DAY CARE RATING SCALE

Teachers College Press

Source: **Thelma Harms and Richard M. Clifford, 1989.**

3. *Quality Control: A Manual for Self-Evaluation of a Day Care Agency* (Campbell 1987) offers a format for assessment covering almost all the functions of a childcare centre. Supervisors and daycare operators may find this a useful overview of a centre's general effectiveness. It may not offer enough detail to help educators examine the learning environment in a specific area. The steps for program evaluation, however, are clear and can be applied even when used with other evaluation systems. Another strength of the evaluation is that it incorporates parental input. Based on a rating scale attached to "Standards of Performance Statements," parents score components such as administration, facilities, staffing, admissions, and the program.

4. Measurement of the home and family environment has long intrigued many researchers. Caldwell and Bradley (1984) devised a measure of the environment called the HOME inventory—*Home Observation for Measurement of the Environment*. We looked at this briefly when we discussed home visits. The evaluator scores a series of Yes/No questions, makes observations, and interviews the parent about a typical day in the family, interactions with the child, and the material environment. The original intention was to see whether the HOME inventory scores and the children's IQs were correlated, which they were. Replication of these studies has highlighted the importance of some of the components of the inventory, while we do not understand all the reasons for the correlations. The studies agree that features of children's home environments do have an impact on their performance, competence, or IQs. While the inventory was designed for research purposes, it could be used for evaluation of individual families. What to do with the results is less certain; only a relevant professional's identification of a clear dysfunction can justify any intervention in a family's lifestyle and interaction.

5. In 2000 the University of Guelph's Centre for Families, Work and Well-Being in Ontario published *You Bet I Care—Caring and Learning Environments: Quality in Child Care Centres Across Canada* (Goelman et al.). This important project links quality care with program characteristics, teaching-staff wages and working conditions, and teaching-staff characteristics and attitudes. The low levels of provision of care cited—in more than 7 percent of the programs investigated—and the poor levels of care found for infants and toddlers are of particular note. The findings present a powerful argument for delivering quality programs and for early childhood educators' pushing for better work conditions:

> The Canada-wide studies examine the wages, working conditions and best practices in child-care centres, and the overall quality of care in child-care centres and in family child-care homes. Findings from the first study detail the human resource challenges of a workforce that is chronically underpaid and undervalued. The latter two quality of care studies found that it is the norm for children to be cared for by warm and responsive adults in settings that protect their health and safety, but that there is significant room to improve on the third dimension of quality—the provision of activities that support and stimulate children's development. (2000)

The *You Bet I Care* study applied a variety of measures of quality, including the Early Childhood Environment Rating Scale—Revised (ECERS-R).

6. We frequently run into difficulties when we compare quality by using different indicators. The United Nations Special Session on Children (UNICEF) (2000) suggested a model for making such comparisons in education: "A new way forward in defining the issue of quality education is to view it through a broader lens, involving at least five dimensions: what learners bring, content, processes, environments, and outcomes." Experts agree on the "critical importance of education quality to genuine learning and human development and reviewed best practices." Representatives of a wide group of countries have developed a plan for the World Declaration on the Survival, Protection and Development of Children as part of the World Summit for Children. It calls for each country to establish appropriate mechanisms for the regular and timely collection, analysis, and publication of data to monitor relevant social indicators relating to children's well-being. Over the last ten years, UNICEF and its partners have helped establish international agreement on a common set of indicators by which to measure progress.

   Not all countries have signed the Convention on the Rights of the Child and, unfortunately nonparticipating countries can lack support for their children's needs and the power to advocate for change with other countries outside the Convention.

7. The Canadian Child Care Federation's *Research Connections Canada 2: Supporting Children and Families* underscores the link between the environment and health from a protective stance (Schwartz & Chance 1999), rather than from the usual educator's perspective—an approach that highlights exposure to dangerous chemicals, climate change, and the need for air and water quality assessment. The 1998 Declaration of the Environment Leaders of the Eight (the G8) on Children's Environmental Health discusses associated health problems and provides a framework for domestic, bilateral, and international efforts to improve protections of children's environmental health. We must keep these broad-based environmental issues in mind as we work to ensure the quality of our own programs and environments. Global and local views of the environment are equally important.

8. "Appropriate practice" is a phrase commonly used in childcare circles, though its meaning varies. The National Association for the Education of Young Children (NAEYC), the American organization that has identified the components of **developmentally appropriate** practice, endorses a holistic and child-centred approach as its philosophy. Based on research into the determinants of quality programs, the NAEYC publication *Developmentally Appropriate Practice in Early Childhood Programs Serving Children from Birth Through Age 8* (Bredekamp 1997) serves as a manual of good practice. You can use it to evaluate an existing program or to help develop provisions from scratch. The age-stage integrated components of appropriate and inappropriate practice cover goals, ratios, and teacher qualifications as well as specific developmental practice. If you use each item with a rating scale, putting appropriate practice at one end and inappropriate practice at the other, the charts become an evaluative tool. The items can be used to focus discussions with parents or staff and to support a more structured environmental evaluation. Your instructor can assist you in explaining the appropriate/inappropriate paradigm with some useful examples.

9. "The EDI (Early Development Instrument) is a validated survey instrument used to gauge the 'developmental readiness' of populations of 5-year-olds as they enter kindergarten" (**www.help.ubc.ca** accessed September 12, 2008). Development of the

EDI came under the auspices of the Human Early Learning Partnership (HELP) and the Offord Centre for Child Studies. "The instrument provides information for groups of children in order to

1. report on areas of strength and deficit for populations of children

2. monitor populations of children over time

3. predict how children will do in elementary school"

(Fact sheet from the Offord Centre for Child Studies web site, accessed September 12, 2008 **www.offordcentre.com**)

The EDI may not seem like an environmental evaluation measure, but it is in the way it is used. Children are assessed from different geographic areas, and their "developmental readiness" is assessed. However, the outcome of these studies is not focused on assisting particular children; the community's achievement level is the focus. The five measures of development (physical health and well-being, social competence, emotional maturity, language and cognitive development, communication skills and general knowledge), in combination "provide a good picture of the developmental status of populations of children." Those surveyed constitute an efficient sampling of the population, including children of First Nations heritage. The instrument and the resulting EDI maps are available to download, as are further resources related to the EDI. Originally the EDI was developed to compare areas within British Columbia, but today it is used much more widely across Canada. The identification of areas with children who are particularly vulnerable allows these areas can be targeted with specialized programming and resources.

Whether or not the competence of a child before entering school is a predictor of later performance is debatable, although we can assume some correlation between the two. Although tested for its validity and reliability, the EDI may ask young children questions that are dependent on having particular social and other experiences; indeed the framework of the EDI, however useful as a survey measure, may contain some cultural and linguistic biases. That said, the EDI is a well-respected tool and is being used in many locations in a way that contributes to a better understanding of children's "developmental readiness" across Canada. For example, in Manitoba EDI results are given to the schools, childcare centres, community partners, health agencies, and others who, together, under the banner of "Healthy Child Manitoba" work to improve early learning.

10. Linked to the previous example of environmental evaluation is the Total Environment Assessment Model for Early Childhood Development (Siddiqi & Hertzman 2007). The link is due to the development of the model under the HELP at University of British Columbia, but this evidence report was undertaken for the World Health Organization's Commission on the Social Determinants of Health. "The principal strategic insight of this document," claim the authors, "is that the nurturant qualities of the environments where children grow up, live, and learn matter the most for their development, yet parents cannot provide strong nurturant environments without help from local, regional, national and international agencies" (p. 7). The essence of the work is equity, and the scope of the report includes demonstration of which environments matter most for children, aspects of environments that are economic, social, and physical, determining the "contingency relationships" that link the big community to the intimate social environments that are needed, and to highlight opportunities that can foster nurturant communities. The idea of the bio-ecology

of social communities can be found in Bronfenbrenner's work, as displayed by interacting concentric circles—we discussed this in Chapter 6. In this tool the focus becomes the primacy of the family for nurturance, and the place of increasingly wider environments and communities is explored. Each level of community shapes and supports the child's development within their family. The authors hope that their work will continue, the research agenda on early development will be continued, and the "grass roots to global" (p. 90) efforts to disseminate information in order to generate action and further the goal of a child-centred social investment strategy will be reinforced.

11. At a national level, Environment Canada takes a leadership role in measuring elements of the environment for change and concern. Their particular concern is the country's natural resources and protection from natural disasters. Although this may seem a far reach from measuring our immediate environments, determining what we can change and what we cannot, the principle is the same, and the criteria on a broader scale. Their environmental evaluations are undertaken through the Environmental Protection Agency. Environment Canada's web site can be found at **www.ec.gc.ca/**. A little later we mention matters related to global issues that are within the hands of adults and children: greening.

12. Health Canada, along with its many other activities, conducts evaluations that concern the interaction between health and the environment. See its evaluation reports, such as The Action Plan on the Environment and Health (1996) and The Evaluation of Environmental Hazards (1996). The methods for these studies can be researched and their findings explored at the Health Canada web site **www.hc-sc.gc.ca/**.

13. Returning to the smaller-scale environment, we should be aware of Special Link at the University of Manitoba. They have a "Measuring Inclusion Progress project, funded by Social Development Canada, [that] has helped us to develop, refine and test ways of 'Measuring Inclusion Progress' in child care centres" (**www.specialinkcanada.org** accessed September 10, 2008). Workshops are available to those interested in using the Inclusion evaluations, including practitioners, parents, and volunteers. **Inclusion**, in this context, is about ensuring that children who have special needs are welcomed, fully accommodated, made to feel part of the group, and engage in experiences alongside children who are developing along typical trajectories in an equitable way.

14. Evaluating a program through the educator's eyes is usual. Adding perspectives from parents and community members is highly desirable, but enabling children to evaluate their own environments is often unheard of! Young participants in YMCA programs in the Greater Toronto area, as well as in other programs, are sometimes asked for feedback in ways that convey their thoughts. Younger children are seldom asked. Taking a lesson from phenomenology and common sense, several projects have been initiated that seek the young child's perspective of their environments (physical and social). Clearly they are not expected to complete a questionnaire, but observed behaviours give insight into the child's responses to the environment. Barclay and Benelli wrote an article entitled "Program Evaluation through the Eyes of a Child" (1995) in which they pose a number of questions based on Katz's work on the bottom-up perspective, evaluation that considers the child's perspective. Earlier, Driscoll, Peterson, Browning and Stevens (1990) reported positive results in eliciting responses to the environment from four-year-olds, and Peterson (2000) is serious about including student evaluations of their environments by even quite young children. The conclusion of the Barclay and Benelli report was similar in

that they "demonstrated the feasibility of including the children's perceptions of their experiences within a program and, therefore, their perceptions of its quality" (p. 5).

15. We have mentioned developmental assets earlier (Chapter 2). In the 1990s the Search Institute created a list of Internal and External Assets. They are building blocks to healthy development; conditions in which each child or young person needs to thrive. Many institutions (schools, clubs, sports programs, after-school programs, and social agencies, including childcare, faith-based organizations) across Canada, the U.S., and the world have adopted these assets as a framework for understanding what children need in their immediate and community environments. The focus is resilience-building in each child and the community. **Resilience** is the ability to manage difficulties that arise in life without their damaging the individual.

    "Grounded in extensive research in youth development, resiliency, and prevention, the Developmental Assets represent the relationships, opportunities, and personal qualities that young people need to avoid risks and to thrive" (**www.search-institute.org** accessed September 10, 2008). Look for the Developmental Assets on the Search Institute's site, as well as those of reputable organizations that have adopted the Assets. Anyone can access the Assets in various forms suited to differing age groups in 13 or more languages. They can be used as criteria for evaluating the current environment, as well as a set of intentions (or goals) for improving the environment.

Devising Your Own Environmental Observation or Evaluation Tool

Informal methods

A list of environmental components may suit your own observation purposes. Serving as a reminder of things to look for, it may help refine your perceptions. As you form the list, you will probably become aware of the philosophy behind the criteria; the fact that you include an item means that it is important to your belief system. You might want to explore your philosophy and how it can be evidenced. To ensure that the listing is complete and organized in another task. As you work, you may decide to limit your task and narrow your focus more precisely. You might also want to structure it under separate headings to make the parts more manageable. As the list evolves, you might phrase the items throughout more consistently as questions with a Yes/No reply or as statements to be graded. Trial use of the checklist or rating scale will probably reveal some gaps and items that need to be restated. This kind of tool can be useful as it fits the setting well; remember that it may not be as inclusive or objective as other tested tools, or it may not be valid or reliable if applied elsewhere.

Structured methods

An effective tool records or measures what it intends to measure. To devise such a tool for environmental observation or evaluation, work through the following process:

1. Identify the need for evaluation.
2. Specify the area(s) to be observed or evaluated.

3. State the goals or intentions of the project and the philosophy underpinning the tool.

4. Seek team or committee support.

5. Assign the roles and responsibilities of team members.

6. Clarify the process through which the tool is to be devised.

7. Agree on a timeline.

8. Arrange for a trial of the tool.

9. Evaluate its effectiveness.

10. Make changes as necessary.

The methods for devising a tool may include any or all of the following activities, separately or simultaneously and in any sequence:

- Researching quality issues (or your focus for evaluation)
- researching existing tools
- reviewing stated philosophies and articulating your own
- evaluating the environment by using different tools
- brainstorming ideas
- surveying parents, professionals, and/or the community to determine opinions and needs
- revising tools used previously
- identifying component parts of "environment"—that is, stating your criteria
- editing
- conducting trial runs with items used as checklists, rating scales, or open-ended criteria
- clarifying grading criteria

Working through a structured method in devising a tool makes that tool more likely to fit the need, to reflect a common philosophy, and to be more detailed and inclusive than a checklist informally put together. It will probably find wider acceptance and be more reliable in its use.

As fashions in education come and go and research constantly supplies us with new information, you will probably find your existing observation and evaluation tools less effective than you would wish. You must continue to update, change, and recreate your tools. You will also find that the qualitative methods most likely need modification because the purely observational approaches make fewer inferences and are more open.

Caregivers, parents, and educators most frequently review the health and safety, quality, appropriateness, and effectiveness of the children's environment. You do not have to keep these categories if other concepts are more suitable. Each major category can have many component parts that you will need to identify.

Indicators of appropriate environments for young children

The following lists feature broad components that warrant consideration when observing, evaluating, or planning group-care environments. You may have to itemize specific criteria according to your own needs and settings. When you have defined these components, you can then use them in the form of a checklist, as the criteria for a rating scale, as the basis for a narrative description, as the focus of group discussion, or as a starting point for plans to create or modify an agency. The items are set out in no particular order of priority.

Environmental Evaluation

Rating scale:

5 = exemplary performance: maintains high standard
4 = good performance: exceeds minimum standard
3 = adequate performance: meets minimum standard
2 = below adequate performance: falls short of minimum standard
1 = poor performance: fails to meet minimum standard

Indicator	Observation	Identification of need	Rating

This chart can be used to evaluate environmental indicators. Depending on the school or agency, the standard against which performance is measured may be determined by the province or state, by a local board, or by the agency or school itself.

Seeing a teepee outside a child care centre tells us that this is not a typical setting. The Mahmowenchike Family Development Centre has a philosophy and curriculum that incorporates the Anishnawbe language, traditions, and culture.

With thanks Mahmowenchike Family Development Centre

In general use, the quality indicators chart allows the recording of greater amounts of evidence and observation than space allows on these pages.

General indicators of a quality environment	Evidence
❏ clearly stated philosophy based on researched indicators of quality	____
❏ small group size	____
❏ low ratios	____
❏ demonstration that individual children's needs are being met	____
❏ appropriate and stimulating learning environment	____
❏ developmental appropriateness of design, activity, and guidance	____
❏ high degree of staff training	____
❏ high level of parental involvement and partnership	____
❏ positive quality of interactions with children	____
❏ effective teamwork with parents and professionals	____
❏ low staff turnover	____
❏ positive communications among staff	____
❏ optimal safety, health, and nutrition	____
❏ regular program evaluation	____

Inclusion: Quality indicators

	Evidence
❏ clearly stated anti-bias policy and practice	____
❏ welcome and **inclusion** of all children whatever their race, appearance, class, ethnicity, ability, sex, origin, religion, or beliefs	____
❏ high level of staff training in cultural **diversity**, anti-bias education, and acceptance of diverse lifestyles	____
❏ demonstration of avoidance of superficiality, **tokenism**, **stereotypes**, and **touristic approaches**	____
❏ presentation of cultural and ethnic variety of music, images, scripts, artifacts, food	____
❏ sensitivity to and accommodation of range of family backgrounds, cultures, and experiences	____
❏ accommodations made for children's differing needs and abilities	____
❏ effective conflict resolution strategies	____
❏ resources available for children with **special needs**	____
❏ support of first languages and cultural heritages	____
❏ developmentally and individually appropriate activities and experience	____
❏ activities in which children of all abilities can participate and cooperate	____
❏ process for sharing intentions for children as a parent–professional partnership	____
❏ large-group and small-group activities that allow children to participate at their own levels	____
❏ range of activities and playthings to allow independence while also providing challenges to children of varying abilities	____
❏ active encouragement of community involvement in program	____
❏ effective communication and partnership with parents	____
❏ knowledgeable and sensitive communication with all children, demonstration of respect to all	____
❏ strategies that support the children's growth of empathy and altruism	____
❏ avoidance of labelling	____
❏ access to resources to aid inclusion	____
❏ ongoing evaluation of all books, images, toys, playthings, and materials for the appropriateness of their images and messages	____
❏ policies and practices that address racism, prejudice, judgmental behaviours, and exclusion	____
❏ effective communication with parents and involvement of families	____
❏ accommodation of a wide variety of parenting styles and child-rearing practices	____

The "evidence" required to fulfill each quality indicator can include observations, documents, photographs, diagrams, video recordings, or specific examples.

Educators or other professionals may select some of these quality indicators or use the complete list. It may be better to look at one main category, such as physical well-being, rather than seek to evaluate several at once.

Physical well-being: Quality indicators	*Evidence*
❐ good **hygienic practices** that control the spread of infection	_____
❐ policies, practices, and protective measures for physical and emotional safety	_____
❐ reduction of inappropriate stressors	_____
❐ clearly stated policies and procedures for health, safety, and nutrition, and reporting potential child abuse and neglect	_____
❐ access to first aid	_____
❐ demonstration that children's physical and emotional needs are being met	_____
❐ adequate kitchen equipment, food storage, preparation, and serving of food	_____
❐ nutritious and healthy snacks and meals	_____
❐ adequate space and opportunity for physical play and exercise	_____
❐ positive **role models**	_____
❐ resources and support available to parents on health-related issues	_____
❐ provision for sick children	_____
❐ adequacy of toileting and washroom	_____
❐ protection from extreme weather conditions	_____
❐ health education for children	_____
❐ regular program evaluations and review	_____
❐ challenging but safe outdoor play space	_____
❐ environment constructed for children's safe use and healthy development	_____
❐ routine safety checks	_____
❐ supervision adequate for children's well-being	_____
❐ maintenance of a safe environment	_____
❐ children encouraged to take risks within safe boundaries	_____
❐ provision for rest, sleep, and quiet	_____
❐ opportunity to experience nature first-hand	_____
❐ high level of cleaning, sanitizing, and sterilizing appropriate to building, furniture, and materials	_____
❐ monitoring pollution	_____
❐ appropriate waste management	_____
❐ reporting to parents of changes in behaviour, health conditions, and general development	_____
❐ effective communication with parents	_____
❐ maintenance of appropriate temperature, humidity, and air quality	_____
❐ confidential and complete health records	_____
❐ adequate clean-water supply	_____
❐ community health resources accessible	_____
❐ adequate training and professional development of all staff in matters of health, safety, nutrition, first aid, and child abuse	_____
❐ compliance with local, provincial or state, and federal legislation and regulations	
❐ sensitive consideration of parental wishes	_____
❐ accident and serious-occurrence records	_____
❐ documentation and sensitive handling of allergies and medical conditions	_____
❐ regular and ongoing observations of children's health and behaviour	_____
❐ early identification of behavioural changes and indicators of concern	_____
❐ children's positive attitudes to well-being demonstrated	_____
❐ appropriate storage of materials	_____
❐ accommodations for specific abilities and disabilities	_____
❐ separation of areas for different purposes	_____
❐ maintenance of caregivers' health and management of stress	_____

If an indicator is not present or if its evidence is poor, there is a need for it to be addressed.

Nurturance: Quality indicators	Evidence
◻ small group size	_____
◻ caregiver/educator continuity	_____
◻ low child-to-adult ratio	_____
◻ staff retention	_____
◻ personal space for belongings	_____
◻ space for relationships to develop	_____
◻ acceptance of individual styles and behavioural patterns	_____
◻ reading of children's cues	_____
◻ opportunities for personal attachment	_____
◻ children demonstrating enjoyment, fun, and enthusiasm	_____
◻ positive role models that demonstrate the range of human feelings	_____
◻ support of self-regulation, empathy, and altruism	_____
◻ sensitivity, responsiveness, and attunement to individual children	_____
◻ opportunity for play activity with peers	_____
◻ consistency of caregivers and caregiving	_____
◻ flexibility of routines and patterns to meet individual needs	_____
◻ stability of family and home circumstances	_____
◻ positive communications between parents and caregivers/educators	_____
◻ maintenance of a stable, consistent program	_____
◻ opportunity for family involvement in the program	_____
◻ home/centre continuity	_____
◻ design of agency for contrasts to suit children's moods and temperaments	_____
◻ encouragement of both cooperative and solitary activity	_____
◻ play encouraged as therapeutic activity	_____
◻ providing a safe place to go when hurt or needing quiet	_____
◻ observation and monitoring of the program's emotional climate	_____
◻ demonstration that feelings are acknowledged and allowed	_____
◻ appropriate interest in caring for and providing comfort and encouragement to individual children	_____
◻ encouragement of emotional expression	_____
◻ open exploration of reality and fantasy	_____
◻ positive communication with children about feelings, changes, crises	_____
◻ encouragement and modelling of empathy	_____
◻ encouragement of objects that link home and agency	_____
◻ support to develop children's strategies to cope with strong feelings	_____
◻ acceptance of diversity in action and voice	_____
◻ practical indications of support for children's self-identity	_____
◻ support for positive body-image awareness	_____
◻ fostering of creative thinking and success	_____
◻ opportunity for children's self-categorization and self-discovery	_____
◻ demonstration of support regarding separations and reunions	_____
◻ meeting needs for privacy and quiet	_____
◻ clear indications of the parameters of behaviour and the consequences for noncompliance	_____
◻ opportunity for the children to make choices	_____
◻ open-ended activities that avoid correct or incorrect responses or winners and losers	_____
◻ engaging with children at their physical level	_____
◻ process-focused activity	_____
◻ authentic praise and encouragement	_____
◻ use of positive guidance strategies	_____
◻ support of adults for each other	_____
◻ nurturing philosophy agreed upon among caregivers and educators	_____

Some indicators may not be present; these gaps can lead to the development of an environmental improvement plan. The learning indicators can be adapted or extended to meet the particular developmental needs of the children.

Learning: Quality indicators	Evidence
❐ physical design meets children's learning needs	_____
❐ child-sized furniture and materials	_____
❐ opportunity for children to make choices	_____
❐ self-direction supported	_____
❐ **spontaneous play** valued	_____
❐ curiosity allowed to flourish	_____
❐ focus on process of activities	_____
❐ freedom of movement	_____
❐ developmentally appropriate programming	_____
❐ observation of children to help determine their needs and programs	_____
❐ opportunity for experimentation and discovery	_____
❐ sensitivity to the child's stage of understanding and experience	_____
❐ space organized for movement flow and optimal usage	_____
❐ children's leads followed	_____
❐ adult enthusiasm demonstrated and positive, inquiring role model	_____
❐ curriculum evolved from children's interests	_____
❐ activity extended (but not directed) by adults	_____
❐ activities allow for success and minimize failures	_____
❐ fun repetition of learning	_____
❐ communication of ideas encouraged	_____
❐ open-ended and evolving activities	_____
❐ stimulation of children in all developmental areas	_____
❐ cooperative activities supplied	_____
❐ focus on hands-on activity and participatory learning	_____
❐ a routine without structure and rigid timetabling	_____
❐ family contribution and participation encouraged	_____
❐ children's experimentation encouraged	_____
❐ imitative, fantasy, and sociodramatic play opportunities provided	_____
❐ language offered to help children classify and conceptualize new experiences	_____
❐ adults help by scaffolding experience	_____
❐ adult interactions that help children focus on learning	_____
❐ knowledge extended from the base of the child's current understanding	_____
❐ language, print, symbols, literature, and storytelling supported	_____
❐ sensory exploration promoted	_____
❐ strategies to overcome challenges offered	_____
❐ role models and support of moral understanding provided	_____
❐ clear direction regarding expectations and behaviour	_____
❐ ecological awareness supported	_____
❐ program changes made at differing pace according to needs	_____

- ❏ wide range of traditional and nontraditional curriculum components   _____
- ❏ use of the Zone of Proximal Development principle   _____
- ❏ links supported between home and children/school   _____
- ❏ opportunities for encoding and decoding offered   _____
- ❏ construction, science, inquiry and mathematical concepts are each supported with materials, starting points, and encouragement   _____
- ❏ child-centred learning supported with some direct instruction   _____
- ❏ problem-solving skills taught in situations as they occur   _____
- ❏ connectedness of experience supported across the curriculum   _____
- ❏ assisting each child to plan and review her own activities   _____
- ❏ use of natural world a key element of program   _____
- ❏ children's range of feelings accepted   _____
- ❏ interactive learning and construction of knowledge   _____
- ❏ memory skills supported   _____
- ❏ children's understanding of similarities and differences encouraged   _____
- ❏ sensitivity to different needs of members of the group demonstrated   _____
- ❏ different ways of "being smart" supported (theory of multiple intelligences)   _____
- ❏ plans for individual and collective needs   _____
- ❏ therapeutic or compensatory care provided if/when needed   _____
- ❏ programming responsive to changing needs   _____
- ❏ well-trained staff share a philosophy of how children learn   _____
- ❏ encouragement of self-evaluation processes   _____
- ❏ cooperation and communication with parents   _____
- ❏ regular evaluation of program   _____
- ❏ regular observation of children and documentation of their learning   _____
- ❏ learning planned from what is known to what is unknown   _____
- ❏ open-ended activities and materials that encourage creativity   _____
- ❏ curriculum that sets appropriate and achievable challenges   _____
- ❏ higher-order thinking promoted   _____
- ❏ success encouraged and errors treated as learning experiences   _____
- ❏ skills development monitored   _____
- ❏ program justified in measurable ways   _____
- ❏ community resources used and dialogue maintained with community representative   _____
- ❏ learning outcomes/objectives/standards achieved by individuals and groups documented appropriately   _____
- ❏ compliance with all regulatory bodies   _____
- ❏ curriculum content knowledge in subject areas documented appropriately   _____

Observation Sample 12.1

This environmental observation provides comments on various health issues. These observations could be used to evaluate the environment and to suggest changes and improvements.

What could this type of recording tell the educator about its centre's health programs? What other criteria might be added? Identify the strengths and weaknesses of this documentation.

Environmental Observation: Health

Observer's name: *James*   Date: *December 9-12, 2006*

Setting: *Unionville Child Care Centre (a centre for 60 children, birth to school age)*

Number of children: *19*   Number of adults: *2*

Ages: *3 years, 3 months, to 5 years, 7 months*

Space available: *L-shaped room. One end used for gross motor activities, sleep, and meals.*

Purpose of observation: *To evaluate the environment for its part in supporting the children's healthy development.*

Criteria	Observations
1. Good hygienic practices	*regular hand washing, disinfecting using a bleach solution*
2. Positive role model	*teachers follow proper practice*
3. Nutritious snacks/meals	*bananas, oranges, apples for snack; meal plans appear appropriate*
4. Protection for extreme weather	*2 sets of clothes are stored (spring/winter)*
5. Effective communication with parents	*parent board, reports, and communication logs*
6. Health education	*posters, art supplies, talking*
7. Toileting/washroom adequate	*2 washrooms (1 large, 1 small)*
8. Parent reports	*separate reports for everyone*
9. First-aid provision	*box/kit in each room, large in office*
10. Parental wishes adhered to	*notes taken in communication log and passed on if necessary*
11. Separation of areas for different purposes	*reading area, blocks, floor toys, table toys*
12. Appropriate storage	*large cupboard in each room labelled and cleaned regularly*
13. Accommodations for abilities and disabilities	*minimal stairs, lots of space for gross motor, etc.*
14. Accident and serious occurrence records kept	*each child has a file, book of "serious occurrences" shown to parents*
15. Maintenance and stress for caregivers	*separate/comfortable room for breaks and quiet time*
16. Demonstrated positive attitudes to well-being	*talk about vitamins in oranges, milk, etc., hand washing*
17. Documentation and sensitive handling of allergies and medical conditions	*lists in every room for every child and separate larger one in individual rooms*

TAKING A SPECIAL LOOK: Inclusion and integration

In recent years, the **integration** of children with special needs into mainstream care and education has become an important trend. This practice produces a more natural environment for all children and a better acceptance of diversity. However, child-care agencies and schools that advocate integration face challenges in terms of time, equipment, support, and expertise. These issues need to be resolved before inclusion and integration become feasible in many mainstream settings. Evaluating aspects of the environment should include its accommodation of children with diverse abilities and backgrounds as well as its design, furniture, and materials.

Responding to an Environmental Evaluation

Earlier in this chapter we reviewed the stages of environmental evaluation. Here we discuss issues arising out of that process.

We move toward better planning and programming by carrying out an environmental evaluation. Before we attempt to change things, however, we need general agreement among the team members that change is necessary. Change can be unsettling and can make people feel that they have failed at their jobs; team members may need some time and encouragement before they are ready to adapt their program or ways of doing things. In some circumstances, administrators or even legislated requirements drive change, and it may be necessary to move forward without complete agreement. Working out an efficient and effective process of change is most likely to produce a successful outcome. If the team agrees on the process at the start, and all the parties have an opportunity to participate, people are more likely to "buy into" the need to make changes. Take a look at observation sample 12.1 and consider what response strategy is advisable.

An excellent resource for educators who wish to design exemplary environments for children is Rebecca Isbell and Betty Exelby's book *Early Learning Environments That Work*, published by Gryphon House (2001). It offers well-illustrated and practical ideas on how to create the type and quality of environment that fits your values, philosophy, and resources.

Greening our environments

Before completing this section about environments, it behooves us to mention another aspect of the environment—**greening**. As you may imagine, greening involves reducing our use of nonrenewable resources, supporting the growth of trees, plants, and food, limiting our carbon footprint, reusing or repurposing materials, buying products that do the least environmental damage, eliminating toxic substances, keeping water clean, saving resources, preserving animal species, being kind to the earth, giving back what we take from the earth, reducing climate damage, recycling as much as possible, and doing what we can to make the world a good place for future generations.

Children, as well as adults, are actively engaged in learning about their environments, most especially on a global level. Canadian Environmental Awards 2008 mentioned several schools across the country that achieved significant results in their efforts. Teacher Natalie Schneider at the winning school, Dunrankin Drive Public School, Mississuaga, said, "They're learning about having a common goal and being global citizens. Plus it's really helping to build a sense of community in our school." For the full report go to the Canadian Geographic web site **www.canadiangeographic.ca/**.

Making our schools and childcare environments "green" and ecologically responsible is another task for educators. *Growing Up Green: Bay and Child Care* (Imus 2007) is a book focused on the parental aspect of the job. The author asks, "But what does it mean today, to 'keep our children safe'? In recent years, the job of raising—and protecting—our children seems to have become a lot more complicated." Ecosource from the Region of Peel, Ontario, offers resources for parents, teachers, and volunteers to help the process of "Growing a Green community." They offer a variety of pointers that might contribute to a green environment checklist **www.ecosource.ca/**. Greening Canada's play spaces is another related issue that influences children today, as well as tomorrow. The web site **www.treecanada.ca** can assist with this effort, and small grants are available for that purpose. Green Communities Canada is promoted through the resources found at its web site **www.gca.ca**.

A remarkable design effort at the Charles Dickens Elementary School, which was highlighted in an article by Fiona Morrow of the *Globe and Mail* (May 2, 2008), has made it Vancouver's first "green" school. Opened in May 2008, the school provides a template for building schools (and other institutions). Geothermal heating, motion-sensor lights, low carbon emissions, environmentally friendly materials, electric car and bike storage, recycling station, drought resistant, and rainwater flushing toilets. They followed the LEED (Leadership in Energy and Environmental Design), which has 69 areas and several levels of achievement. As well as the school being green, children are surrounded by an environment that challenges them to think about living a green life.

In the *Wall Street Journal* on April 14, 2008, is an article about preschoolers in Germany whose childcare and learning experience is entirely natural and outdoors. The Waldkindergarten, or "forest kindergarten," is the ultimate green experience. The programs echo the work of Friedrich Froebel, who invented the term "kindergarten," meaning child's garden. However, the Waldkindergarten elaborates the Froebelian premise and centres on the world of discovery and exploration in a natural setting. Similar programs are offered in Denmark, where they first started, and Scandinavia, Switzerland, and Austria. There is trust in children's own ability to learn. Use of the children's imagination, real-world skill acquisition, the social relationships that occur through natural activity, and the opportunity for play are each extensive. Typically the children thrive and are healthier than their indoor peers. This green school provides a model for environmental learning.

What to change

Like any other kind of evaluation, evaluating the environment may tell us what the problem is, but will not usually tell us how to fix it. Review your evaluation and do some collective problem-solving with your colleagues to determine how to address each issue. Some issues may be related, so one solution may address several problems.

Remember that not everything is within your power or scope to change. You may be unable to improve your budget or change the staffing situation overnight! You might want to prioritize your results according to what you all consider possible. As a group, you might choose to be undaunted by some obvious limitations. The bigger issues, those concerning philosophical perspectives or values, are harder to address. If you need to look at these big issues, do so, but accept that they demand effort and heart-searching.

List the things that need to be changed, with or without reference to the relative difficulty of achieving those changes. Examine the list to see if the items are superficial and cosmetic or if they signal a more profound problem. Your evaluation may show several unconnected items, or they may be clustered in a particular area. Scattered items are more likely to be bits and pieces that can be "fixed" quickly. A group of related things can highlight a need for philosophical reflection or a deeper evaluation of the program's achievement or direction. Of course, your bits and pieces may actually relate to deeper issues, too; check for any connection.

You may need to set priorities in your activities according to the time, money, and professional-development opportunities available.

Taking action

After reviewing and discussing the data comes action, preferably with a timeline and specific responsibilities assigned. Keep timelines realistic; bear in mind that a transition period might be harder to deal with than the actual change will be when fully implemented. The scale of the change also makes a difference to how the change should be accomplished. If you need to move some furniture, few people may resist the change. On the other hand, if the change requires a review of policies regarding inclusion, equity, and anti-bias, you might need to plan for a lengthy discussion of those topics.

Depending on the urgency of the issue, the possibility of making changes speedily, and the need for complex negotiation, you will want to create an action plan. Here using a prepared format can be helpful.

The process of evaluation and change needs to be a cycle rather than a one-time experience. If you evaluate your environment regularly, you will find the process of change becomes easier. Individual responsibility for evaluation is commendable, yet programs for young children are usually of higher quality if regular evaluation is a mandated requirement. This process requires a budget, encouragement, time, and staff training.

Environmental evaluations; some programs to review and evaluate

The following short descriptions, along with web sites and other resources, will enable you to have an extensive look at some different programs. Each of these has at least one important innovation. Each one offers an exemplary program of a different type. You may view these programs from different perspectives, but notice that each is based on a different philosophy.

Children appreciate some structure to their day and most enjoy a story before going home. Here the teacher is very aware of the need to support children to become literate. Fran reads a story to her class; their engagement and the lack of behavioural difficulties attests to her skill and the children's interest.

With thanks to The Royal Mile Primary School

1. **The Forbes Nursery, Edinburgh, Scotland**

   This nursery for babies, toddlers, and preschoolers offers a wonderful natural environment where children learn self-confidence through discovery learning. "The mature secluded garden allows space to run, climb and explore. A range of equipment and surfaces encourages individual initiatives and games under supervision," says their web site. Therese Duriez, the director of the private nursery, is a calm but enthusiastic individual who is passionate about offering children authentic experiences. She and the carefully selected staff members offer love, as well as stimulation; relationships are at the core of the program. The program complies with the Scottish legislative requirements and conducts regular program evaluation using "The Children at the Centre, Self-Evaluation in the Early Years," a document produced by Her Majesty's (Scottish) Inspectorate of Education (2007). In this unusual setting children have the benefit of being assessed using a continuum of outcomes that measures competence in children from childcare contexts seamlessly through into the years of school. Detailed reports about individual children at preschools are avidly read by teachers in the school system.

   www.forbesnursery.com The Forbes Nursery
   www.hmie.gov.uk/ Scottish educational resources
   www.carecommision.com Scottish Commission for the Regulation of Care

2. **Sensory Garden Child Development Centre, near Bolton, Ontario**

   Fabi Tempio-Hillier runs this delightful independent preschool according to her deep-felt beliefs about how children learn and what environments they need. Recently the program won a Governor General's Award. The preschool uses its own Curriculum for Life© (1998) document that "focuses on meeting the developmental needs of each child," according to their philosophy statement. Fabi is a mother and a qualified Early Childhood Educator, and has years of experience meeting the needs of children and their families. Her assets lie in a personality that inspires confidence and a passion that drives her to work hard. She surrounds herself with like-minded staff members who offer a caring program that facilitates play in an environment that is positive, constructive, and conducive to learning. The program's central concept is an updating of Froebel's notion of the **kindergarten**, the child's garden. The children are viewed as growing individuals who are different and need respect. Teachers are facilitators of learning within the "garden"; natural environments support the children's discovery using sensory exploration. Learning is first-hand rather than taught, but adults assist with language support and scaffolding sensory experience to solidify learning. The environment is partly created by nature and partly by the Early Childhood Educators; together the place indoors and out is stimulating and fun. Children are seen as competent young people who are high achievers within their individual developmental progression. Parents are considered partners.

Your instructor will be able to offer you some information about this program, its philosophy, and the quality indicators used for its regular program evaluation. This program meets or exceeds the licensing standards of the Ontario Day Nurseries Act (RSO 1990), and the regulations specified by Peel Region.

www.e-laws.gov.on.ca/ Ontario Day Nursery Act (1990)

www.froebel.org.uk/ Froebel Education Institute (history, principles, and resources)

Sensory Garden has no current web site.

3. **Reggio Emilia school and child care, Reggio Emilia, Italy**

The Reggio Emilia children's programs of the 1990's were hailed as being the best in the world by *Newsweek* magazine; the impact of these programs continues to grow. Reggio Emilia is a place in northern Italy that has also become the name of internationally recognized programs for children. Responding to the devastation after the Second World War and seeing that communities needed support in a variety of ways, Loris Malaguzzi (1920–1994) founded the Reggio Emilia approach for children within a community context. The environments of Reggio Emilia programs are carefully thought out but remain flexible to accommodate various uses for children under six. In this approach the environment is thought of as the "third teacher." Observing the environment, you will notice that aesthetics and beauty are important; much consideration has been given to how the children will perceive what is around them.

The approach sees children as competent, curious, resourceful, imaginative, inventive, and possessing a desire to interact with others. The curriculum is **child-centred**, but the program is **family-centred**; complex long-term projects guide the content of what is learned, but how the children explore the project ideas is largely directed by them. Both the individual and community as a whole have an identity. The documentation and portfolios processes allow children to show what they know. This part of the learning process also provides information for assessment and further programming. "Observation is an important skill for most early childhood teachers but the educators in Reggio Emilia have taken observation a step further. Observation, for them, is only the first step in collecting the data that are used to develop pedagogical documentation that captures the story of the children's experiences in the classroom as well as the progression of the teachers' own developing understandings. Documentation becomes a tool for teacher research, reflection, collaboration, and decision-making" (Institute for Early Childhood Education and Research 2008). Teachers are co-learners with the whole community, as well as the children, and they act as everyday researchers. Reggio Emilia's provision for children is run by education authorities at the municipal level—even the childcare part. Education is considered a right and is highly valued.

We might observe and describe the Reggio Emilia program according to our North American understandings of children and their environments, but what needs to be appreciated is that what occurs is framed according to a different way of knowing, one that is deeply culturally shaped. The backdrop to Reggio Emilia is almost mono-cultural, rural, closely community-focused, in part religious, and has a collective identity. For that reason using some Reggio Emilia program ideas in a different cultural context needs very careful consideration and adaptation.

www.reggioalliance.org/ North American Reggio Emilia Alliance

www.glebereggiocentre.ca/ a Canadian childcare centre that follows the Reggio philosophy

www.ericdigests.org/2001/ research papers, including one about Reggio Emilia, by Rebecca New, with links to further resources

4. **Te Kohanga Reo, Wellington, New Zealand**

New Zealand is an English-speaking country, but the aboriginal peoples have their own languages, which are under threat of extinction as their people become more integrated into the majority culture. Te Kohanga Reo is a language program for preschool children in New Zealand and offers a strikingly different model of preschool education. Their idea is to immerse the children in the language and culture of the Maori people. This "promotes learning in an appropriate cultural context by drawing on Maori styles of learning and teaching" (Martin & Corson 2007, p. 243). The program was created about twenty-five years ago as a response to the challenge of keeping the Maori language alive. The agency is run as a home rather than an institution, with the centre being a community hub. The environment may be seen as less organized than a typical North American preschool program, with spontaneity as important as relationship-building. Children start in infancy and continue their care and education in **Kohanga Reo** language nests. There is a routine, although the day is relatively unstructured. Some rituals associated with the Maori culture are integral to the program; these are to do with prayers, welcoming ceremonies, and meal-times. The program is delivered according to a set of principles, **Te Wharki** (Maori word for "woven mat"), a nationwide concept that provides the framework for all early-childhood programs in New Zealand. It includes the idea that learning occurs in a spiral rather than ladder progression. The principles of this program also centre on empowering children to learn, holistic development, and reciprocal relationships. There are usually many adults available to the children, and they support language learning through songs, rhymes, helping children focus on their play, storytelling, and conversation. The program conforms to the New Zealand required curriculum. While in the program children gain some Maori language proficiency and at the same time they acquire English in the outside world. When they enter school, they have the language foundations to be fluent in Maori. Te Kohanga Reo "work[s] towards the ultimate goal of a bilingual and bicultural nation" (Te Kohanga Reo web site accessed September 11, 2008).

www.kohanga.ac.nz/ Te Kohanga Reo

www.tpk.govt.nz/ Te Punti Kokiri, Raising Maori Potential

www.mdrc.co.nz/ The Maori Development Research Community

www.ece.govt.nz/ information and resources for early-childhood education, including the curriculum

5. **Mahmowenchike Family Development Centre, Thunder Bay, Ontario**

Janet Owens is the current director of the Mahmowenchike Family Development Centre, which is run on two sites. Some subsidies are available for children whose parents cannot afford the fees of this municipally run not-for-profit agency. The centre allows both First Nations and non–First Nations children to mix in an urban setting in ways that allow them to experience the heritage, language, and culture of the Anishnawbe people. They do this while attending to every element of care and education that supports all areas of child development. Their program includes a smudging ceremony on Mondays and Fridays to open and close the week. "The daily curriculum is based on and incorporates the Anishnawabe language, traditions and culture (arts/crafts, traditions, folklore, ceremonies, storytelling etc.)," states a promotional flyer. The environment is immersed in the culture of the Anishnawbe people, with pictures, images, artifacts, musical instruments, and a variety of well-displayed symbols. The Ontario Early Years program is offered at one site. The shape and design of the main building—a renovated fire hall—reflects similar images and highlights the conical tepee shape and other symbolic designs. Indoors is a special space for song, prayer, story, or other circles. It is decorated in Anishnawbe images and echoes in a surreal way. Traditional crafts are taught, the children wear indoor moccasins, and stories and legends are told. Oral history is important, as is music and the spiritual dimensions of life. All the staff members are willing to share their knowledge and expertise with others (but they are not all Anishnawbe people). They welcome high school co-op students and college students to the centre, and mentor early childhood education professionals. Recently they won a certificate of achievement in the Prime Minister's Awards for Excellence in Early Childhood Education. The program meets and surpasses the Ontario program standards.

> **http://josephsutherland.myknet.org/** description of the Anishnawbe culture
> **www.gov.on.ca/children/oeyc** Ontario Early Years Programs
> **www.aeceo.ca/** Association for Early Childhood Educators, Ontario
> **www.collegeofece.on.ca** new College of Early Childhood Educators

6. **The Magic Ladybug Learning Centre, Halifax, Nova Scotia**

What is special about this program for children aged 18 months to five years is that it emphasizes both Chinese and Canadian cultures. Children gain exposure to both cultures within a developmentally appropriate program of activity and exploration. Two English-speaking educators work with the children in English and two Mandarin-speaking educators work with children in Mandarin (Chinese). "This ensures that the children are hearing both languages within the context of daily interactions and routines . . . ," claims their web site. Mandarin is also taught through storytelling, music, singing, games, poems, and discussions. Part of the children's learning experience is to understand something of the culture of the Chinese people, along with their traditions and ways of life. The Magic Ladybug offers an innovative program according to a clearly articulated philosophy. The curriculum is what might be expected in a high-quality childcare environment, but its philosophy differs from the norm. There is plenty of evidence that acquiring languages early in life is highly beneficial; it allows more complex brain structures to be developed. But the beginning stages can be a challenge, and children may suffer some temporary vocabulary confusion. Grammatical forms take longer to acquire, but the sooner the child gains them, the better off she will be. Keeping up the usage of Mandarin is necessary for later fluency. The Magic Ladybug offers parental support, resources, and explanations about their program. Patricia Monaghan is the current director.

www.magicladybug.com Magic Ladybug web site and links

www.cccns.org/NSCCA/home.html Nova Scotia Child Care Association

7. **Nightingale Preschool/Junior Kindergarten, Victoria, British Columbia**
"The school provides an exceptional high-quality programme that combines education, learning through play and active learning in the early years. The School curriculum planning is within the framework of the Early Learning Goals in Britain and The Foundation Stage that blends the Montessori/Reggio Emilia/High Scope philosophies," says the Nightingale Preschool/Junior Kindergarten program's web site. Their philosophy is somewhat eclectic, drawing from several historical perspectives, as well as current research into early-development. Independence, industry, continuity, and progression appear to be common themes within the curriculum. The teachers are well travelled and have gained various pertinent qualifications. Their experience clearly adds to what is offered to the children. The program has recently been recognized within British Columbia for its excellence.

www.nightingalepreschool.com/ web site of the Nightingale Preschool

8. **Montessori Learning Centre, Winnipeg, Manitoba**
The centre advocates for Montessori programs for young children can be passionate about the philosophy and practice of Montessori, especially for preschool children. Here at the Montessori Learning Centre, which is an independent not-for-profit agency, the semiformal way of teaching and learning meets with parents' approval. The program has been in Winnipeg for twenty-five years and has many devoted families that hold it in high regard. Current Montessori programs have evolved since the days of Maria Montessori (1870–1952), and she may not have been entirely happy with the programs that flourish under her banner today! Montessori was a physician with a strong interest in psychiatry. She was also schooled in both psychology and philosophy and had an ardent desire to better the lives of children who were considered uneducable. In 1907, she set up her school, the Casa dei Bambini, in a poor district of Rome. The school was for children who were disabled or had challenges for various reasons, possibly autism, developmental difficulties, and other unnamed syndromes. With these children she had remarkable results. She used homemade materials that encouraged the acquisition of specific life-skills. Her success led to reform in provision for disabled children, who were thought then to be "idiots." Her work spread around Europe and was particularly well received in North America. Her writings, in which she articulated her beliefs about children, were also successful. She focused on children's work rather than play, thinking that this was children's true preference. Before she died—in Holland, her chosen country—she made a significant impact on the understanding of young children.

The Montessori Learning Centre explains the link between Montessori's philosophy and practice: "She designed unique materials that are manipulative, didactic, and sequential. Through exploration and manipulation of the specialized Montessori apparatus, children develop such skills as co-ordination of movement, sensorial awareness, concentration, language and number concepts" (Montessori Learning Centre's web site, accessed September 12, 2008). Montessori teachers have special training to work with young children—this is in addition to the province's requirements. The kindergarten program has a Montessori teacher with the credentials to work in Manitoba schools. In the Montessori preparation, adults learn how to offer a prepared environment and encourage children's development in each developmental domain. Being noncompetitive, acquiring good work habits and organizational skills, building confidence, learning to make decisions and experiencing their consequences, learning through the senses, cultural learning, exposure to French, physical exercise, and the Carl Orff music program are all elements of the centre's program. It is hoped that the children stay for the full three years of the program in order for them to be inculcated with Montessori values and benefit from cumulative learning.

www.mlcwinnipeg.ca/ Montessori Learning Centre

www.oise.utoronto.ca/research/ Ontario Institute for Studies in Education, an overview of Montessori's work

www.montessori-ami.org/ Association Montessori Internationale

Summary

The environment is something we can easily take for granted, although it shapes the experiences that we offer children and our interactions with everyone. For very young children the environment is an integral part of their curriculum; it is their experience. What we can afford financially is only part of what determines the quality of that environment. As parents and educators we hold values that determine how that environment is shaped. While there are many aspects of any environment, for purposes of improvement the details are as important as the general overview. Adults bear the responsibility for monitoring every aspect of the child's environment and for taking steps to bring every element to the highest level. We must do everything we can to make every aspect of the child's experience the best possible.

At the global level we face ecological issues that need to be addressed to ensure that current and future generations have good-quality air, water, and a generally good living environment. This chapter also looks at the environment at the micro level, the level within the control of the adults in the lives of the children under their care.

We offer a number of examples of tools for environmental evaluation at the global and local levels.

In appreciating a child's basic needs, educators have a baseline of what is considered vital within the childcare centre or classroom. Safety measures are essential; we need to evaluate these regularly while the details will vary according to the particular setting, materials, and objects being used. Psychological needs may be more difficult to determine, but also must be met. How adults behave within that environment is just as important as the walls, physical amenities, and objects.

Several bodies of research help inform us about environmental observation and evaluation. Some base their findings on notions of what constitutes quality environments. We can agree on common elements within most environments for children. From such research, environmental rating scales have been developed for use in childcare. Other studies highlight characteristics of environments in which children are found to be successful. Some of these measures are both valid and reliable. We must take care in selecting a tool that conforms to the philosophy of the school or centre where it is to be used.

In designing an evaluation tool to monitor and improve a particular environment, we are wise to base it on research that focuses on high "quality." This will mean including such aspects of the programs as adult–child ratios, space, safety, and health issues. We must consider translating what each element of quality means in a particular setting. Consider adding or eliminating indicators that do not fit your goals or the philosophy of the program. Well-being, nurturance, the learning environment, and the program's inclusion are elements of quality environments that we need to evaluate, but new criteria are evolving as we have a better understanding of what children's environments need to be.

Key Terms

- action plan
- anti-bias
- basic needs
- checklist
- child-centred
- climate
- context
- cultural portrait
- curriculum
- developmentally appropriate
- diversity
- environment
- environmental evaluation
- environmental observation
- environmental scan
- ethnography
- family-centred
- focus groups
- generalizable
- greening
- hidden curriculum
- hygienic practices
- inclusion
- indicator
- integration
- kindergarten
- Kohanga Reo
- mapping
- narrative observation
- nuclear family
- nurturance
- program evaluation
- psychological needs
- qualitative evaluation
- quality indicators
- rating scale
- relational community
- reliability
- resilience
- role model
- sociological fieldwork
- special needs
- spontaneous play
- stereotype
- Te Wharki
- tokenism
- touristic approach
- triangulation
- validity
- value-laden

www.healthychild.org
Healthy Child Healthy World.

www.cafcc.on.ca/
The Co-ordinated Access for Child Care (CAFCC) site provides families with information and tools that will help them choose appropriate quality childcare.

www.safety-council.org
The Canada Safety Council serves as a credible, reliable resource for safety information, education, and awareness in all aspects of Canadian life.

www.wstcoast.org
The West Coast Child Care Resource Centre site is "committed to contributing to healthy communities by supporting families, promoting equality for children, and strengthening and enhancing quality child care."

www.ccsd.ca/perception/2712/yes.htm
Canadian Council on Social Development—inclusion issues and other topics.

www.childcareadvocacy.ca/index.shtml
Quality childcare and how to advocate for better childcare.

http://philosophyofeducation.org
Philosophy of Education Society.

www.childenvironment.org/
Children's Environmental Health Center.

www.michaelolat.net/
The Montessori method.

www.waldorfanswers.org/waldorf.htm
A description of Waldorf education and philosophy.

www.cehn.org/
Children's Environmental Health Network.

www.ecdgroup.com/download/cc118bdi.pdf
Definitions of quality in early childhood programs.

www.childcarequality.ca/
Elements of a system for high-quality early learning and childcare. A project of the Childcare Resource and Research Unit.

www.childcarecanada.org
Follow pages to get to "What does the research tell us about quality childcare?"

www.specialinkcanada.org/
The National Centre for Child Care Inclusion is a Canadian organization devoted to inclusion. The site includes a major document on quality and inclusion.

continued

www.ccl-cca.ca/ccl
The Canadian Council on Learning offers background papers that contribute to the improvement of environments for young children.

www.highscope.org
This is the main HIGH/SCOPE web site. Follow links to the "Classroom" and "Characteristics of the learning environment."

www.allianceforchildhood.net
An organization that promotes play and its importance. Persuasive articles can be downloaded.

www.froebelfoundation.org/philosophy.html
Froebel's ideas of the perfect child's garden (kindergarten), an environment where children can play, explore, discover, and learn.

www.cape.ca/children
Children's Environmental Health Project, with definitions and explanations.

Glossary of Key Terms

abuse (in relation to babies and children) any act, failure to act, or permission to act, that results in physical harm, developmental harm or regression, sexual interference or exploitation, emotional humiliation, shaming, frightening, or other damage to the child's self-worth and self-esteem, or any mal-treatment that results in death. Any act, omission, or failure to act that presents an imminent risk of serious harm. Any form of neglect that constitutes failure to meet a child's physical, developmental, emotional, or other basic or significant needs. Any use of corporal punishment (physical punishment), or rejection, isolation, exploitation, corruption, or terrorizing a child. Any failure to supply basic needs including food or drink, or acts that lead to sleep deprivation, or lack of nurturing; whether or not the intention was to guide or discipline the child. A lack of respect, or denial of any of a child's rights (refer to the Office of the High Commission for Human Rights and the Convention on the Rights of the Child). Definitions of abuse vary in different jurisdictions. Most schools and other agencies use short definitions that might be open to interpretation; their task is not to prosecute the offender, but to protect the children and take steps to prevent abuse from occurring

accommodation practical or program changes that enable an individual with a disability or challenge to function as well as she is able; in child psychology, one element (along with assimilation) of the two-part learning process that involves altering existing schemes (ideas/concepts) to fit new knowledge

accountability the process of demonstrating the success, and usually the financial effectiveness, of a program or intervention

action plan a plan for change developed as the result of an assessment

action research a branch of qualitative research involving observation, documentation, and analysis conducted while maintaining responsibility for a group or class of children

analysis The process of reviewing all available observational records and other information to make inferences about a child's development or needs; often the summary (see **summary**) is used to structure the analysis; each inference must be sup-portable and valid. Normative profiles, theoretical explanations for behaviour, lists of indicators (such as challenging behaviour) and other tools may be used.

anecdotal record a short narrative account of a child's activity

antecedent event the event that occurred just before the example of the sample behaviour

anti-bias active opposition to negative or inappro-priate attitudes towards or prejudgment of groups of people, practices, or things

assessment measurement of an individual's performance or development, which may be based on observations, tests, or the person's products

assessment cycle the sequence of observation, data collection, analysis, and planning that is an ongoing part of assessment

assimilation one element (along with accommo-dation) of the two-part learning process that involves taking in new knowledge

assistive devices mechanical or supportive aids that enable an individual to function better

assumption accepting as true an approach that has not been considered objectively or analytically

attachment the process of making an affectional bond or emotional connection with another individual

atypical not what is usual, typical, or average (in relation to a norm, atypical might refer to above-average performance or below-average performance)

authentic assessment assessment of learning that focuses on performance of skill or knowledge in a manner within an appropriate context; naturalistic, developmentally appropriate, and culturally sensitive evaluation of children using observation and other informal methods of data collection

baby book a book or album used for recording information about a child, often used by parents

bar chart a graph that represents observational material as bars of varying heights along an axis

baseline observation an observation of a child that provides an overall picture of what the child is like in her typical state of health, or an observation of a child made at the start of the day or beginning of a program that provides a reference against which later observations can be made and compared

basic needs   conditions that allow a human being to survive

behaviour   the actions and reactions of an individual; anything a person does, whether deliberate or not

behaviourists   the school of psychology that studies what it considers to be the objective, observable, measurable, and quantifiable aspects of behaviour and excludes subjective aspects of behaviour such as motives, drives, and emotions

behaviour modification   a technique that attempts to change, stop, or modify a demonstrated behaviour

bias   known or unknown personal or philosophical values, attitudes, or beliefs that influence objectivity

bioecological systems model   the diagrammatic representation of an individual's complex biological and ecological social systems, and the connections between elements of several sub-systems, using a series of concentric circles to show each of the systems (microsystem: immediate environments; mesosystem: connections between elements of the immediate environments; exosystem: external factors that affect development; macrosystem: the larger social context; chronosystem: the pattern of experience, especially the events and traditions over the course of life). This systems model is a development of the work of Urie Bronfenbrenner (1979)

biological clock   the force of an individual's program of maturing determined by the nature of the individual or organism and by genetic inheritance; one of three forces that drive human development through the life cycle

categorization   grouping observational information in terms of types or domains, the process by which ideas and objects are recognized and understood (categorization is fundamental in decision-making)

cause for concern   any sign, symptom, indicator, or intuitive feeling that leads an adult to think that a problem, concern, or issue might exist, and that warrants further observation and investigation

cause   the reason why something occurs, or what motivates an individual to behave the way they do. This is not necessarily the same as the trigger—the trigger may only be the superficial event that brings about a certain behavioural response; the root cause may require much further analysis

cephalo-caudal principle   a principle of development that states that bodily control typically starts with the head and proceeds down

challenging behaviour   actions or language that present a challenge for adults to manage, or behaviour that is anti-social, dangerous, delinquent, disordered, socially unacceptable, or otherwise inappropriate or presents difficulties within families, peer groups, childcare programs, schools, the community, or broader society

chart   a prepared format or map on which observed information is recorded according to specified criteria

checklist   a listing of skills or other behaviours used as a guide for recording the presence or absence of each behaviour

checkmarks   the ticks or correct marks √ used to signify the presence of a behaviour or trait on a prepared checklist

check sheet   a structured, prepared form for collecting and analyzing data. A generic tool, it can be adapted to various needs; observations can be managed more easily if the check sheet structures the observational information using specified categories.

child abuse   any damaging, violent, hurtful, neglectful, or other behaviour, or lack of it, that infringes upon a child's right to dignity, respect, nurturance, medical care, appropriate freedom, or the lack of the provision of a child's basic needs, or an extreme lack of appropriate guidance or protection

child-centred   a philosophy of childcare and education that emphasizes the importance of the child's need to direct his or her own activity, to make play choices spontaneously, and to learn at a self-determined level

child development   the dynamic process of change and progression that enables each child to become increasingly independent, knowledgeable, skilled, and self-sufficient

Child Observation Record (COR)   "The Preschool Child Observation Record (COR) is an observation-based instrument providing systematic assessment of young children's knowledge and abilities in all areas of development." It is part of the High/Scope approach to early learning, although it can be used in other programs. "The COR is organized into six broad categories of child development. Within each category is a list of observation items. These items are based on key developmental indicators—KDIs (formerly known as key experiences) " (www.highscope.org)

child protection agency   a professionally run organization that has authority to investigate families, environments, programs, and individuals for possible abuse or neglect, and that offers support, supervision, alternative care, and/or programs for children who need temporary protection from possible or further abuse or neglect. The agency typically has a coordinated relationship with the police and refers children and family members to other professionals for medical or psychological assistance.

chronological age   an individual's actual age

climate (school)   the way both internal and external stakeholders think about, feel, and experience an educational institution, or an aspect of that institution

cognition   the process of knowing, thinking, and understanding

competency   what an individual is able to do or perform; the component part of a learning outcome that is measurable and observable

concept map   a prepared presentation of ideas and the relationship between those ideas. A concept is a cluster of abstract ideas that, in its entirety, generates a novel construction of ideas; concept maps are consistent with constructivist theories.

confidentiality   the principle of privacy behind the practice of storing information securely so that it is disclosed only to those considered appropriate

consequent event   the event that occurred immediately after the example of the sampled behaviour

construction of knowledge   the creation of meaning through personal experience; children construct knowledge by experimenting and building "schemes" of understanding

constructivist theory   a theory of developmental psychology and learning theory that regards individuals as active learners who create (construct) their own knowledge (Piaget and Vygotsky were constructivists)

contemplative observer   an observer who is reflective, thoughtful, and engaged

context   the circumstances, situations, or background in which an observation is recorded

contextualizing   giving pertinent background information that may alter the perspective of an observer

contextual information   family, social, cultural, medical, geographic, economic, or other information about the child's background that enables a teacher or another stakeholder in the child's life some insight into factors affecting the child's health, growth, or development

continuum   a representation of two opposite words, ideas, or concepts, with a continuous line between them, with one concept at each end. This allows an individual to place their perspective or position somewhere between the opposites. For example, the terms objective and subjective can be considered opposites. When asked how objective or subjective observers have been, an answer could be shown at a place between the two conditions. The use of a continuum does not necessarily mean that an idea is "right" or "wrong", or even "desirable" or "undesirable"

critical thinking   a mental process of analyzing or evaluating information gathered from observation, experience, reasoning, or communication, that has its basis in intellectual values that include clarity, accuracy, precision, evidence, thoroughness, and fairness (**www.enwikipedia.org/wiki/ Critical_thinking/**)

cue   conscious or unconscious indication or communication given by a child that an adult "reads"; may include facial expressions, gestures, or changes in posture

cultural diversity   individuals from varying linguistic, ethnic, or religious backgrounds within the same group

cultural portrait   a narrative description, overview of the whole cultural scene, and a sociological analysis of a culture that includes the people and what they say, their behaviour and life-ways, along with artifacts associated with their lives

curriculum   the child's whole experience; usually refers to the teacher's or caregiver's provision for the child's developmental needs

data   factual information, often used to refer to pieces of information that are gathered and managed by electronic means

Developmental Assets   a set of conditions—the 40 Development Assets—determined by the Search Institute, necessary for optimal health and development. They include (external) experiences gained from the environment and (internal) conditions (values, strengths, commitments). Many institutions have framed their programs and services around creating or improving children's Developmental Assets.

developmental checklist   a list of behaviours typical of a specified age and domain of development, formulated as a checklist to guide the observer's attention

developmental diversity   varying levels of ability within the same group

developmentally appropriate   a program or procedure that suits an individual's stage of progress and personal needs

diagnosis   the process of identifying and assessing the nature and cause of a disease, injury, condition, or disability through observation, evaluation, and analysis

diary record   a record made on a regular, usually daily, basis

digital camera   a camera that uses digital technology rather than traditional film (analog); the term digital relates to a numerical computer system

disability   not having the full abilities of a typically functioning child, or having a disadvantage or deficiency, especially a physical, cognitive, or social challenge, that interferes with or prevents typical levels of achievement in a particular area, or something that hinders or incapacitates (a term that some think focuses too much on what a child cannot accomplish, rather than what she can do)

diversity   a wide range of various abilities, appearance, ethnicity, sex, culture, belief, religion, or place of origin

documentation   written observations and other recorded information about a child, a group of children, or a whole program

duration   the length of time a behaviour is observed

early intervention   a program for infants and young children designed to address developmental concerns, vulnerability, and the need for family support, and to provide other resources to enable a child to develop as well as possible

ecological systems model   a model that explains the components of the environment that influence an individual's life and development (e.g., Bronfenbrenner's model)

ecomap   a diagram representing an individual's environment and his or her relation to the elements of that environment, including people, activities, and organizations

educational neglect   not providing to the child the nurturance, communication, or stimulation necessary for early learning, or the lack of preschool or school programs, which hinders educational potential

emergency preparedness   a state of being ready for possible war, violence, "Acts of God," extreme weather, terrorism, abduction, accidents, or other serious events; includes readiness of government, organizations, families, and programs

emergent curriculum   a child-centred approach to a childcare or educational program that tends to be spontaneous and is based on the interests, skills, motivation, and learning styles of the children; children are seen as competent and effective researchers

of their own play-based inquiry; educators act as facilitators and co-learners

emerging skill   a learned behaviour at a starting or incipient stage

emotion   a feeling or, in observable terms, a change in arousal patterns

emotional intelligence   a term coined by Goleman to describe an ability to understand and use an individual pattern of responses to personal advancement

emotional neglect   not providing essential attachment to adult(s), nurturance, or emotional responsiveness from adults

environment   an individual's surroundings, including places, objects, and people

environmental evaluation   a consideration of all the planned and unplanned aspects of a child's surroundings to ascertain their appropriateness or quality

environmental observation   observation of the use of a child's surroundings, including those elements that are designed and implemented deliberately and those parts that occur without planning

environmental scan   a review of a program, setting, or aspect of that setting using predetermined criteria

equilibration   the state of balance between assimilation and accommodation (i.e., applying previous knowledge and changing behaviour to account for new knowledge), part of Piaget's explanation of how children are able to move from one stage of thought to the next

ethical issues   concerns relating to moral beliefs and professional conduct

ethnography   a narrative process and product requiring writing extensive field notes; it involves participant observation, interviews, conversations, case studies, data collection, document analysis, and other processes depending on the purpose and context for the research. Deeper meanings are sought through reflection and analysis

event   an example of a selected category of behaviour

event sampling   a method of observation in which occurrences of a preselected category of behaviour are recorded

exceptionality   having a talent, skill, or competence that exceeds the level of performance of other children of a similar age

exceptional child   a child whose development is not typical (**atypical**) of those of a similar age; the child's development may be less advanced, uneven, or gifted

exclusion   designing or implementing a program for children that, unintentionally or deliberately, keeps some children from participating. Within the philosophy of diversity and inclusion, exclusion is the condition that is most feared for its damaging effects

failure to thrive   a grave situation in which emotional or other neglect leads to a child's reduced capacity to be healthy, play, gain self-help skills, make relationships, or develop along typical developmental trajectories

family assessment   a process aimed at understanding how a family functions, why its members behave the way they do, and how the family itself can take responsibility for its improvement. May include various forms of data collection, including observations, interviews and questionnaires, documents, genograms, and sociograms

family-centred   an approach or a program that seeks to understand the functioning and needs of the whole family, not only the child for whom a service is being provided. Being family-centred is an ongoing pursuit of being responsive to the priorities and choices of families

family tree   a visual depiction of the individuals within a family and their relationship to one other. Some family trees are presented in the shape of an actual tree, but professional family trees are usually multi-generational, include dates, and use recognized symbols to denote particular relationships

fine motor skills   learned behaviours involving the small muscles of the body

five Ws of communication   a visual device to assist in analyzing observations or conversations, and other communications (five Ws: who, says what, in what way, to whom, with what effect)

Floor Time   is a technique developed in a multidisciplinary non-profit organization that supports child development. "It is a treatment method as well as a philosophy for interacting with children (and adults as well). Floor Time involves meeting a child at his current developmental level, and building upon his particular set of strengths" (www.icdl/dirfloortime) "The Developmental, Individual Difference, Relationship-based (DIR/Floortime) Model is a framework that helps clinicians, parents, and educators conduct a comprehensive assessment and develop an intervention program tailored to the unique challenges and strengths of children with Autism Spectrum Disorders (ASD) and other developmental challenges" (www.icdl.com/dirFloortime/overview). Floor Time practices have been adopted by many child care and home environments because they support relationship-building, understanding the child's perspective, play partnership, and the child's socio-emotional development

focus groups   gathering information from a group of informed people using an open and fair hearing of all participants. Informed consent is necessary even when the risks seem very low

forced-choice scale   a rating scale that requires the observer to judge the degree to which a characteristic or quality is evident

formative   individual assessment that involves tracking and measuring learning over time; it focuses on the process of learning and enables the teacher to assist the learner throughout the learning process. This is an example of assessment *for* learning

frequency   the pattern or number of occurrences of a specified behaviour

functional assessment   behavioural observation and analysis that seek to identify a challenging or "problem" behaviour, determine its purpose, and develop alternative ways of behaving that are more acceptable

generalizable   research results or findings that can reliably be applied to multiple or all applicable contexts

genogram   a diagram representing a family structure, which may include historical and observational information about its style and functioning

graphic scale   a rating scale designed to record judgments of characteristics or qualities on a continuum according to predetermined word categories

greening   aligning oneself or a program with the "green" movement that seeks to protect the earth's resources, reduces wastage, uses organic food, composts vegetable matter, saves threatened animal species, re-uses materials, eliminates garbage, encourages gardening for food, is energy-efficient and uses non-fossil energy, uses less-damaging cleaning and personal products, addresses climate change, encourages responsible manufacturing, sustainable organic farming and foresting

gross motor skills   learned behaviours involving the large muscles of the body

group checklist   a checklist formatted to determine if specified behaviours are present or absent in each child within a group

group level measure   a way of quantifying or otherwise measuring information about a large number of children, the group level measure may attempt to assess different criteria than would be possible with an individual child or a small group of children. For example, the Early Development Instrument (EDI) is designed to measure the development of groups of children in particular locations to ascertain the number of developmentally vulnerable children in a particular place

group observations   observations of children interacting in play, learning, or activity; an observation format that allows specific behaviours to be recorded

group portfolios   a collection of information, observations, reflections, and samples that represents the work, interests, and progress of a group of children; a portfolio based on group achievement of a set curriculum

Guttman scale   a series of rank-ordered questions, given in an interview or questionnaire, requiring yes or no responses. The sequence is such that if the responder agrees or disagrees with an item, then all the questions before or after will also be a yes or no

health concerns   any signs, symptoms, indicators, or other pointers to the possibility that a child's health or well-being is compromised—not necessarily a child who has a disease or is infectious

hidden curriculum   elements of the child's experience that are affected by the unstated attitudes and beliefs of the responsible adult

hierarchy diagram   a visual representation of a ranking or ordering, or the categorization of a group of people according to ability, authority, or status

high/scope   an independent and non-profit approach to meeting the developmental needs of infants and young children. High/Scope incorporates a curriculum based on active participatory learning that can be facilitated in multiple contexts, authentic individualized formative assessment—using The Child Observation Record (COR)—specially prepared teachers, and multi-strategy research

histogram   a bar chart or diagram that uses lines or blocks to indicate the relationship between two broad types of information (e.g., could represent the number of children who have particular personality styles or preferences) or to graphically summarize and display the distribution of a set of data usually drawn from observation

holistic   a way of perceiving an individual that assumes the person is more than the sum of her parts; a way of considering the whole human being that disregards domains, the separation of mind, body, and spirit, or other characteristics in favour of seeing people as complex human beings; or emphasizing the importance of the whole (person, object, situation, etc.) and the interdependence of its parts

human subjects   people who are the focus of a study, and who have agreed to be part of the study and have any potential risks explained to them.

Ethical and professional conduct is essential throughout the study

hunch   An intuitive feeling, a premonition, or an idea that is based on only a little information

hygienic practices   behaviours that promote cleanliness, sanitary conditions, or the sterilization of bodies, materials, furniture, buildings, or other aspects of the environment

inclusion   the practice of ensuring that all children are treated equally and given equitable support in their development, regardless of their ability, ethnicity, sex, or beliefs

indicators   behaviours, situations, outcomes, or other evidence that point to something significant, such as child abuse or a child's successful achievement of a specified learning

individual education plan (IEP)   a plan of goals and objectives, tailored to a child's needs

individual program plan (IPP)   a curriculum, activity, task, or education plan designed for an individual child

inference   a deduction made from observational data

inference-checking   taking steps to make sure that a stated inference is credible, logical, applicable, and validated

inference-making   stating a conclusion from premises known or assumed to be true (about observed or reliably documented information); reasoning from factual knowledge or evidence; a part of the process of analyzing observations and portfolios

input/outcome-planning model   curriculum-planning based on observed information as well as designated requirements, such as competencies

institutional abuse   any abuse or neglect that occurs to children in an institutional setting; the culture of the institution may promote such abuse or deny its existence while taking no steps to prevent it; typically institutional abuse involves more than one perpetrator and the power dynamics of the institution enable the abuse to continue

integration   a philosophy of care and education, similar to inclusion, where children are enabled to move into a program and function as well as they are able amongst a diverse group of children (diverse in their backgrounds, cultures, ethnicities, gender, and abilities)

interpretive graphic representation   visual presentation of information analyzed from data previously collected

intuition The act of knowing or sensing without the use of rational processes; a sense of something not evident or deducible; an impression

irreducible needs a term used by Brazelton and Greenspan, and others, to refer to the physical, social, and emotional needs of every individual, without which he or she cannot develop adequately

Ishikawa representation a fishbone-style diagram of causes and effects used as a problem-solving tool and originally designed for quality improvement in business settings, but now used in many fields

kindergarten the child's garden—a concept created by Friedrich Froebel (in *The Education of Man*, 1826) who believed that there should be a special environment in which children should grow and learn and have their emotional and intellectual development nurtured through play and discovery. A kindergarten was intended to be a place for young children to play and explore. In this environment the adult acted as a play facilitator who closely observed the developing children. Today kindergartens are not all child-directed programs for children to play and learn from experience; many are structured programs focused on premature academics

Kohanga Reo Te Kōhanga Reo (language nest) is a Maori total immersion family program for young children from birth to six years of age

language a tool of communication that facilitates the exchange of ideas, thoughts, and meanings using a complex rule-regulated system of sounds (typically supported by gestures and other body signs—and with a corresponding set of written symbols). Language develops in stages that are driven by social and other experiences along with increased meaning-making, understanding of rules, and not merely imitation

learning log a record-keeping device used to document the objective description of experiences and the child's response to the experiences

learning outcome a broad statement of learning or achievement that must be observable, measurable, and attainable. Typically each learning outcome (LO) is framed around a skill that requires certain knowledge, and the skill must be performed in a certain way (these are the KSA: Knowledge, Skills and Dispositions or attitudes that are integral parts of all LOs). Learning Outcomes are part of the Outcome-Based Education philosophy. (Ask your instructor about reviewing this text's additional chapter on Measuring Outcomes that is in the Instructor's Manual)

life book a book used to record significant people and experiences in a child's life over a period of time; often used by social workers and adoption-agency workers

life-experience flow chart a diagram representing the series of key experiences in an individual's life

Likert scale a visual representation of responses to questions posed as warranting one of three, five, seven, or nine responses, usually from "strongly agree" to "strongly disagree" with a central neutral option. Each question is a Likert item, the resulting score the scale

map or **mapping** a diagram of an area where children are observed, used to record their movements or evaluate the program

maturation the innate aspects of human growth and development, or the observable and measurable characteristics of stages of growth and development

media in this context media refers to any means of communicating, managing, processing, and storing information—particularly observation, portfolio, and assessment information. The media for recording and playing back data include cameras, video, and audio equipment. Computer functions including a computer's hard drive, removable drives, USB drives, and software programs are further examples

media technique any method of recording or storing observational data that is achieved by mechanical, electronic, or technical means

medically fragile children who have a serious, ongoing illness or chronic condition, require prolonged hospitalization and ongoing medical treatments and monitoring, and may require devices to compensate for the loss of bodily function

medical neglect not providing essential medical care that promotes a child's health, and not providing first aid, infection control, medical intervention, medication, or other medical necessity; may include avoiding medical checks, screenings, and/or immunizations

megabytes units of information or computer storage—often called MB. Large computer files are usually measured in megabytes

memory cards or flash memory cards are reusable electronic data storage devices for digital cameras, handheld and mobile computers, and other electronics

metacognition the process of thinking about thinking; being aware of one's own thinking processes

milestones observable steps or stages during the process of human development

morality an intellectual understanding of right and wrong and a social understanding of the consequent social responsibilities; may be rooted in religious or cultural beliefs

multiple intelligences the theory, developed by Gardner, that people have different ways of being "smart" or different forms of intelligence, including spatial, logical/mathematical, linguistic, bodily/kinesthetic, musical, interpersonal, and intrapersonal

narrative observation   a sequentially written, detailed description of a child's actions

naturalistic   without interference, or as nature would determine

naturalness   the behaviour of individuals without interference or influence

negative behaviour   a behaviour judged to be undesirable, inappropriate, or socially unacceptable

neglect   failure to provide for a child's basic needs: food, shelter, nurturance, physical contact, protection, an appropriate environment, adequate supervision, and/or medical care

neural plasticity   the brain's ability to "sculpt," adapt, or "wire itself" in response to experience, injury, or maturation

neuroscience   the discovery of the structure and functions of the brain and central nervous system

nonparticipant observation   the observation of an individual or a group by a person who is not interacting with that individual or group

norm   an average level of demonstrated behaviours, skills, results, or measurements determined from statistically significant populations

norm of development   what is deemed, by experts, on the basis of valid and reliable research, to be the characteristics of the "average" child's skills and competence

norm-referenced assessment   the process of interpreting data according to an accepted range of performance (usually age-related)

notifiable disease   a disease that must be reported to public health authorities at the time it is diagnosed because it is potentially dangerous to humans, sometimes called a *reportable disease* (what constitutes a notifiable disease varies across different jurisdictions)

nuclear family   immediately related individuals who reside together

numerical scale   a rating scale that requires the observer to quantify the degree to which a characteristic or quality is evident

nurturance   the whole care and experience of the child that fosters development

objectives   the behaviours considered necessary to achieve a set goal or aim

objectivity   the quality of an approach that is undistorted, impartial, unbiased, analytical, and reliable

observation   the informal or formal perception of behaviour of an individual or group of people, or the perceptions gained from looking at an environment or object

observation chart   a prepared chart with sections used for categorizing and recording behaviour at the time it is observed or soon after

observation cycle   the circular process of observing, recording, summarizing, analyzing, and planning central to effective program planning in any curriculum approach

observation scale   a measurement showing the degree to which a characteristic is present

operational definition   a working, usable description of the behaviour to be sampled

outcome-based learning (OBL)   a philosophy of learning that structures curriculum and assessment on learning outcomes

Pareto chart   a bar graph that arranges information in such a way that priorities for process improvement may be established. Chart appears much the same as a histogram or bar chart, but bars are arranged in decreasing order from left to right

participant observation   the observation of an individual or a group by a person who is interacting with that individual or group at the same time

pattern of development   the sequence of skill acquisition in each developmental area or domain

perception   receiving information through any one of, or any combination of, the senses and processing it to deduce meaning

performance assessment   a form of authentic assessment that requires a demonstration or performance of specified knowledge or skills

perpetrator   the individual responsible for something (such as child abuse)

personality   an individual's personal characteristics including **temperament**, patterns of behaviour, awareness of self, and ability to meet challenges

pervasive developmental delay   a child's development that is perceived to be, or diagnosed as being, behind expected or typical development in ways that involve most if not all, domains of her development

phenomenology   a philosophy that studies personal experiences from the point of view of the subject rather than that of the "objective" world;

also, the systematic study of conscious experience, the study of the experience of a person re-created as a new experience by another person

physical abuse   a component of **child abuse** that involves being abusive to a child's body; may include direct or indirect damage by shaking, hitting, scarring, or other violent act; can lead to death, disability, and long-term medical conditions, as well as cuts, bruises, and swelling

physical development   an individual's growth and acquisition of gross and fine motor skills and sensory acuity

physical neglect   a component of **neglect** that involves failing to meet the child's physical needs such as climate control, protection from harm, medical treatment (see **medical neglect**), appropriate and adequate food and drink, suitable clothing, as well as ignoring the child's need to receive physical care, changing, kind touch, etc.

pictorial representation   any form of recording or interpretation that displays collected data in visual form

pie chart   a circular diagram that represents "slices" of a circle to depict proportions or percentages

play   activity that emanates from the child and underpins every domain of their development. Its process is almost always more important than its product. Play is an experience of childhood that involves one or more of the following: sensory exploration, learning the properties of materials, discovery, finding out about the natural and man-made world, creativity and making things, scientific understanding, gaining a vast range of concepts, learning about roles and relationships, exploring a full range of emotions, using imagination and pretending, extending gross and fine motor skills, progressing through several social stages from onlooker, through solitary activity, then through parallel and associative stages to that of full cooperation and finding a place in group functioning. Engaging in activity with rules, or developing rules can also be play; it may be supported by adults but true play needs to be child-centred and as child-directed as possible. Adults need to be play partners and play facilitators and be led by the child(ren). The history of play theories goes from early times when the belief was that it was merely a way of filling time or using up energy, to the idea, supported by Pestalozzi, Froebel, and today's theorists, that play is the essential activity for learning and living. Play must never be hurried, suggests Elkind, and it needs to be allowed to be spontaneous and fun, says Frost

play patterns   observable recurring behaviours seen in a child's play activity. For example we might see a child repeatedly engaged in parallel play—playing alongside but without involvement with another child's activity, or we might observe a child encountering similar challenges each time she attempts to make a sandcastle. The adult sees the play pattern and decides whether to intervene, and if so, decides to use a particular technique

policies   formal documents that outline the actions required in given circumstances; offer guidelines for identifying particular scenarios, clarifying roles and responsibilities, indicating what documentation is required; often required by government/ministry/licensing bodies

portfolio   a collection of information about a child's development gathered over time, used by teachers for assessment and record-keeping

portfolio assessment   the process of observing, recording, and gathering contextual information about a child in order to evaluate his or her performance, support development, and create an appropriate curriculum

positive behaviour   a behaviour judged desirable, appropriate, or socially acceptable

pre-reading skills   early literacy learning involving knowledge and skills such as identifying letters and their sounds, looking at picture books from left to right, or recognizing the link between words and meaning

procedures   the steps or protocols required in a given scenario

product   the object that is evidence of a process of learning; products may become work samples that demonstrate learning and progress

professional portfolio   a collection of materials, reflections, and evaluations of performance that represent the personal and/or professional development of an educator or other professional

professionalism   the way of behaving that is appropriate and ethical for trained, skilled, and practising workers as they perform their roles

professional responsibility   behaving in a manner that is consistent with a moral code, ethical principles, and the requirements of a particular profession. Professional responsibilities include what is to be done, when it is to be done, and how it must be undertaken

program evaluation   the collection of information, review, and analysis of data regarding each aspect of an educational or caregiving environment, using predetermined criteria, conducted to improve service delivery

progress or **progression**   improvement in learning or development

project an approach to curriculum that links different aspects of learning through an investigation of a particular topic or theme. This may be teacher-directed or child-centred activity, or an in-depth investigation of a real world topic worthy of children's attention and effort.

pro-social skills performance of behaviours that are considered positive that supports a desired morality

proximo-distal principle a principle of development that states that bodily control typically starts at the centre of the body and proceeds to the extremities

psychoanalytic (theory) the set of ideas developed by Freud that make up a psychology leading to treatment or understanding of human development

psychological/emotional abuse **child abuse** that involves emotional manipulation, teasing, unkind words, and a lack of support; diminishes the victim; and humiliates, degrades, or otherwise hurts the child's self esteem, sense of self worth, emotional well-being, or other aspect of psychological health

psychological clock the force of an individual's quest to meet his or her own needs; one of the three forces that drive human development through the life cycle

psychological needs the conditions and relationships required for social and emotional development

psychological service any support system, either privately or publicly funded, that assesses individuals and provides them with therapy or other interventions for their emotional and social health, well-being, and development

psychometry a branch of psychology concerned with theory-making and research into the quantitative measurement of mental processes and functions. Commonly used in education, psychometric processes demand standardized design, administration, and analysis of tests used for the measurement of psychological variables such as personality, intelligence, abilities, personal traits, or preferences. Whether or not such tests measure what they purport to is open to debate

qualitative "Qualitative research is an inquiry process of understanding based on distinct methodological traditions of inquiry that explore a social or human problem" (Cresswell 1998, p.15). Qualitative research approaches are situated within five theory-driven traditions (Biography, Phenomenology, Grounded Theory, Ethnography, and Case Study). Typically they use a variety of data-collection methods including participant observation, open-ended questionnaires, action research, case studies, and/or unstructured interviews. Data is coded, managed,

and analyzed in a variety of ways. Qualitative research challenges positivistic researchers who believe that what cannot be measured is not amenable to scientific research

qualitative evaluation measurement that involves the kind and degree of developmental change

quality indicators norms, standards, and criteria that are qualitative and quantitative assessment measures used in determining the quality of care and education. Typically quality indicators are used to assess one or more of the following program areas: environmental design, aesthetics, climate, space and conditions, equipment and materials, how well a program meets the needs of children and families, the child's experience and engagement, observation and assessment processes, the curriculum, ratios, staffing, training, professional development and remuneration, policies and practices, any "hidden" curriculum, health and hygiene, community involvement and decision-making, program outcomes, nurturing, caring and adult engagement, learning activities and experiences, and parent, researcher, staff, and the child's perceptions

quantitative measuring data using numerical or other values. The process of measurement is central to quantitative research because it provides the fundamental connection between empirical observation and mathematical expression of quantitative relationships. Quantitative research data management demands that objectivity, validity, reliability, generalizability and standardization are rigorous. Quantitative research is inclined to be deductive, it tests theory

rating scale a predetermined list of behavioural characteristics that is accompanied by a numerical, semantic, or other grading system

readiness test a test designed to evaluate the individual's cognitive functioning in order to determine his or her potential success in a program at a "higher" level

record of achievement a record kept by the teacher or learner (child) that logs anecdotal notes regarding the learner's skill development and achievements

recording (technological) mechanical, electronic, or technical methods of recording information

red flag an observable **indicator** that something is wrong or needs attention

reflection an act of thinking involving calm meditative contemplation; an open-ended process of thinking divergently

reflective practitioner an approach to the role of educator (or other professional) that involves frequent sensitive evaluation, review of practice, personal qualities, and effectiveness

Reggio Emilia a region in Italy; in early childhood education an Italian approach to education that involves the whole community, is driven by the children, recognizes the different channels (or voices) of the children, and documents the process and products of learning to "make learning visible"

regression the loss of skills or learning

reinforcement supporting a behaviour by offering an inducement or encouragement

relational communities socially bonded communities based upon commonalities such as religion, race, or ethnicity. These communities offer social, emotional, and practical supports to children and their caregivers that support their well-being

reliability the degree to which a method can be consistent; the degree to which scores for a test or measurement tool remain constant, consistent, or reliable

representational a presentation (often visual) that shows data collection, sorting of information, or theoretical ideas

research discovery with the aim to find an answer to a specific question; any gathering of data that furthers knowledge. Informal research is conducted at any time without rigorous methodologies. Formal research, following the principles of scientific method, demands that a hypothesis is stated, objective observations of the phenomenon are collected, data are gathered and processed, and a conclusion is drawn. Scholarly investigation may involve qualitative and/or quantitative approaches

research methods the methods of inquiry, including qualitative and quantitative approaches, used to answer a question, prove a hypothesis, or explore a topic; a scientific method of research requires that standard methods of inquiry be used, that questions be formed appropriately, and that the process of data management and analysis be documented

resilience human capacity and ability to face, overcome, and be strengthened and even transformed by experiences of adversity

resource teacher a specially prepared teacher who works with children diagnosed with medical, developmental, or learning needs

responsive curriculum an approach to childcare or educational programming that is respectful of the child, and sees the child as full of interests that the educator can promote; typically the approach to children is nurturing and responsive to their needs. Educators read the child's cues, support the child's

independent learning, and enables the child to become responsive to her environment and the adults in her life; attachment forms the basis of all social, emotional, communicative, and cognitive elements of learning.

ritual abuse a form of **child abuse** that involves children being involved in or observing various forms of sadistic and psychologically damaging procedures during cult-like ceremonies

role model a demonstration of the behaviours associated with a particular task, employment, or responsibility

rubric a set of criteria used to measure the level of performance indicating learning; an assessment tool (most often used instead of grading) that specifies the requirements of a performance, presentation, or product that demonstrates that learning has taken place

running record a sequential written account of a child's behaviour that employs rich description and detail

running record (reading) the process of observing and recording a child's skill at reading, often used by schools from kindergarten to grade 3. The record includes an ongoing analysis of the important elements of reading, such as the child's ability to decode words and whether this is done phonetically, visually, or contextually. The number of correctly read words is documented, and the speed of reading observed.

sampling an observation in which examples of behaviour are recorded as they occur or behaviours are recorded as they are demonstrated at previously decided intervals

scaffolding a term coined by Bruner to describe the adult's role in assisting the child in learning

scale a way of measuring information that uses lists of behaviours or other items and rates them according to predetermined values

scientific method a method of research designed to further knowledge in a specific area (usually in response to an identified problem) in which a hypothesis (a theory or explanation) is stated and then data gathered through observation and experiment to prove or disprove the hypothesis. Rooted in the idea that subjectivity must be removed and objective truth found

screening a process of reviewing and evaluating specific behaviours or individuals' characteristics across a population or group to identify those who need a more thorough assessment or specific support

screening instrument any assessment process that is used with a large population to identify a small number of cases. For example, the PKU screening (heel prick test) taken soon after birth is designed to identify any children who have phenylketonuria, a treatable condition that could cause severe brain damage if left undetected

self-evaluation   the process of evaluating one's own performance or creation of a product, involving comparison with a norm, measurement against specified criteria, or a general reflection on one's own process of learning

semantic differential scale   a rating scale designed to record judgments of characteristics or qualities on a continuum, listing pairs of opposites

sensitive period   a time in the developmental process when an individual is susceptible to particular kinds of influence

sensory acuity   the degree to which the senses perceive information accurately or in detail

sequential model   a diagram representing a curriculum plan to design learning based on the breakdown of a competency into a series of stages

sexual abuse   a extremely damaging form of **child abuse** that involves touching a child inappropriately, humiliating a child because of his or her sexual characteristics or sexual play, penetrating a child orally, anally, or vaginally, exploiting a child sexually, having a child perform in a sexually explicit fashion, using child pornography, gaining sexual satisfaction from children, sexualizing pre-pubescent children with inappropriate remarks or clothing, introducing sexual ideas to young children before they are developmentally ready, or any other activity that makes children vulnerable to the sexual deviance of adults

sexual development   the domain of development concerned with identification by sexes and roles, physical growth and maturation, emotional and social competence, and reproductive capability

sign language   a language that uses hand, face, and body movements to convey thoughts and ideas. Often used by people who are deaf, or who wish to communicate with those who are deaf. American Sign Language (ASL) is most frequently used in North America. Baby signing systems based on ASL are available for use with hearing and deaf infants and young children, to aid early communication

signs   observable behaviours or physical indications that something needs attention

skill acquisition   the process of gaining new behaviours or of modifying or refining existing skills

social clock   the force of society's and the family's expectations; one of the three forces that drive human development through the life cycle

social emotions   the feelings, expressions, and body language associated with learned emotions (ones acquired through social interactions) rather than primary emotions that emanate from the child automatically or reflexively

social intelligence   the ability to demonstrate skills of successful communication, sharing, being part of a group, or any other social behaviour. One of the many ways of being smart

social interaction   the process of communicating, sharing, playing, or otherwise interacting with another individual

social map   a representation of social relationships by means of a diagram

social play   play activity involving others, whether seen or unseen

sociogram   a diagram representing the social relationships of those within a peer group

sociological fieldwork   being out in the site of cultural interest, and gathering observational material, asking questions, interviewing key informants, gathering facts, taking photographs, looking at adult–child relationships, seeing children at play, identifying artifacts and their symbolic function, recording material, identifying rites and rituals, participating in the experience, noticing patterns of behaviour, and recording thoughts and interpretations

sociomatrix   a chart that represents data similar to that of the sociogram, but is shown in a table with several lines and columns

sociometry   the study of social interactions using pictorial representations to record data

special needs   the necessities required to support the health and development of a child whose development is **atypical** in one domain or more

specimen record   an extremely detailed, sequential narrative recording of an observation of one child made as the behaviours are observed; frequently uses coding devices to ensure that the particulars are accurate and complete

spirituality   an approach to experience that may involve personal reflections, a connection with a power outside the self, or an appreciation of the significance of people and things; may relate directly to religious or philosophical beliefs about our existence

spontaneous play   the naturally occurring, unstructured activity of the child

standard   a broad statement of achievement that is accepted as a requirement at a specified level

standardized test   a valid and reliable tool for evaluation that specifies the method of administration, content, and scoring

stereotype   a description or image of individuals or groups that depicts them according to clichés, or exaggerated or erroneous criteria, without regard for actual characteristics or individual differences

subjective   distorted, partial, biased, lacking in analysis, or unreliable

subjectivity   usually means the opposite of objectivity. Subjectivity refers to a conditioned perspective, bias, judgment, or lens through which an individual sees something from their own viewpoint. While objectivity is typically thought desirable in the scientific method, there can be a place for carefully considered responses to observations that use intuition, experience, and the identification of patterns of behaviour that are not objective, yet still have usefulness

summary   the process of organizing, prioritizing, and categorizing observational information; might review documentation and list all skills in each developmental domain and/or determine behaviours giving cause for concern

summative   assessment that focuses on what has been learned at a specified end-point of time. Typically summative assessments give teachers information about the success of learners; summative measurement may be a means of checking that standards (such as learning outcomes) have been achieved by a group. Summative assessment is an example of the assessment of learning (see formative assessment)

symptoms   physical conditions that show that a child may have a particular illness or disorder

tally   a system of marks used to count instances of the observed behaviour

teacher-directed   an activity, program, curriculum, or other organized learning environment that is led by the adult, that guides the children to "keep on track," and is directed toward an identifiable teaching goal

temperament   the relatively enduring characteristics of an individual often present soon after birth; although each individual is different in her style, interests, and demeanour, there are possibly a limited number of temperamental characteristics that show themselves in different permutations

Te Wharki: Te Whāriki is New Zealand's Ministry of Education policy on early childhood teaching and learning. Their approach is to see early learning within a socio-cultural context; emphasizing empowerment, holistic development, family and community, and relationships

theory-bound   said of a process that rests on implicit beliefs

therapy   any support or intervention that provides the individual with the resources to manage more effectively

time sampling   an observation method in which random or previously chosen behaviours are recorded at pre-set time periods

timeline   a linear visual display of a specified time frame with indications of key events

tokenism   the practice of exceptional favour, based on negative prejudice, to "prove" one's fairness

topic planning   planning for children based on predesignated areas of learning

touristic approach   the practice of presenting cultural differences and places of origin in a superficial holiday, festival, or vacation style

tracking   recording a child's movement on a diagram or map of an area where a child is to be observed; may be used to identify interests, mobility, concentration span, or interactions

transactional analysis   an approach to psychology and psychiatry, developed by Canadian Eric Berne, that is drawn from several traditions, including psychoanalysis. It attempts to understand personality, communication, and behaviour, and enables an individual to change what doesn't "work" for him.

trauma   an event, incident, or response to an event that is extreme in nature

triangulation   a process used in qualitative research to increase the validity and credibility of findings. There are several ways of using triangulation: having three or more researchers, obtaining three or more data sources, using several theoretical models, or using three or more different methods of data collection

typical patterns of development   the trajectory of development expected and associated with the norm (average)

validate   to ensure that the inferences made from observational data are supported or confirmed by one or more reliable authorities

validity   the degree to which a test or observation tool measures what it purports to measure

value-laden   any word, image, program, or other entity, that conveys a subjective meaning, judgment, or perspective. For example, a school's design might convey the idea that learning is important and that its use of natural materials and light upholds the idea that beauty is important. Wearing old, dirty, casual clothes to a job interview could convey the idea that that the applicant doesn't think highly of themselves or the job, and has not prepared themselves for the interview. There are few value-free institutions, situations, or programs, even if an attempt is made to be value-free

Venn diagram   A depiction of two or more data sets (usually different but related) represented by circles, and their overlap, the overlap being the segment(s) of data common to both or all. For example, observational data might warrant a Venn diagram showing children's influenza symptoms.

webbing model   a planning model that relates all curriculum areas through a single topic or focus

whole child   a concept of the child that sees all domains of development as interacting, the child being more than the sum of the domains

work sample   any product of a child's art, creativity, work, or other evidence of learning

work sampling   a teacher's, parent's, or child's choice of work intended to demonstrate a particular competency

XY scatter graph   a diagrammatic representation of the range (or scattering) of findings that are plotted on two numerical (vertical and horizontal) axes

zone of proximal development   a phrase coined by L.S. Vygotsky that refers to the supposed gap between what the child can do in an independent manner now and what the child can do in a supported way

Bibliography

Adamson, L.B. (1996). *Communication development during infancy.* Boulder, CO: Westview.

Ainsworth, M.D. (1972). Individual differences in the development of attachment behaviors. *Merrill Palmer Quarterly* 18, 2, 123–5.

Allen, K.E., & L.R. Marotz. (1994). *Developmental profiles: Pre-birth through eight* (2nd ed.). Albany, NY: Delmar.

———. (2003). *Developmental profiles: Pre-birth through twelve* (4th ed.). Albany, NY: Delmar.

Allen, K.E., et al. (1998). *Exceptional children: Inclusion in early childhood programs.* Scarborough, ON: ITP Nelson.

Arena, J. (1989). *How to write an I.E.P.* Novato, CA: Academic Therapy Publications.

ASPIRE Assessment System. Alexandria, VA: ASCD.

Ball, J. (2008). Cultural safety for aboriginal families involved in screening, assessment, and early intervention. Presented at the Early Years Conference 2008, Vancouver, BC.

Bandura, A. (1977). *Social learning theory.* Englewood Cliffs, NJ: Prentice Hall.

Barclay, K., & C. Benelli. (1995). Program evaluation through the eyes of a child. *Childhood Education,* Winter, 72(2), 91–96.

Barna, Ed. (2002, Winter). High noon for high stakes: Alfie Kohn at Middlebury College. *Paths of Learning.* Retrieved on January 23, 2009 at **www.pathsoflearning.net/Paths11-Barna.pdf.**

Barrett, K.C., et al. (1995). *Child development.* Westerville, OH: Glencoe.

Beaty, J.J. (1996). *Preschool appropriate practices* (2nd ed.). Fort Worth, TX: Harcourt Brace Jovanovich.

———. (1998). *Observing development of the young child* (4th ed.). Upper Saddle River, NJ: Prentice Hall.

Bentzen, W. (1993). *Seeing young children: A guide to observing and recording behavior* (2nd ed.). Albany, NY: Delmar.

Bergen, D. (1994). Authentic performance assessments. *Childhood Education,* 70(2), 99–102.

———. (ed.). (1998). *Play as a medium for learning and development.* Olney, MD:

Bergen, D., & J. Coscia. (2001). *Brain research and childhood education: Implications for educators.* Olney, MD: Association for Childhood Education International.

Berger, J. (1972). *Ways of seeing.* London: Penguin.

Berk, L.E. (1994). *Infants, children, and adolescents.* Needham Heights, MA: Allyn & Bacon.

Berne, E. (1961). *Transactional analysis in psychotherapy: A systematic individual and social psychiatry.* New York: Ballantine Books.

Berne, E. (1964). Games people play: The psychology of human relations. New York: Grove Press.

Bertrand, J. (2001). *Summary of research findings on children's developmental health.* Ottawa, ON: Canadian Child Care Federation.

Best, J.W., & J.V. Kahn. (1989). *Research in Education* (6th ed.). Englewood Cliffs, NJ: Prentice Hall.

Biracree, T., & N. Biracree. (1989). *The parents' book of facts: Child development from birth to age five.* New York: Facts on File.

Bloom, B. (1956). *Taxonomy of educational objectives: The classification of educational goals. Handbook 1: The cognitive domain.* New York: Longmans Green.

Boehm, A.E., & R.A. Weinberg. (1987). *The classroom observer: Developing observation skills in early childhood settings.* New York: Teachers College Press.

Bowen, M. (1978). *Family therapy in clinical practice.* New York: Aronson.

Bowlby, J. (1965). *Child care and the growth of love.* Harmondsworth, England: Penguin.

Bracken, B. (2006). Bracken Basic Concept Scale, 3rd ed.: Receptive. Toronto, ON: Harcourt Assessment.

Brazelton, T.B. (1992). *Touchpoints: Your child's emotional and behavioural development.* Reading, MA: Addison-Wesley.

Brazelton, T.B., & S.I. Greenspan. (2000). *The irreducible needs of children: What every child must have to grow, learn and flourish.* Cambridge, MA: Perseus Publishing.

Bredekamp, S. (ed.). (1997). *Developmentally appropriate practice in early childhood programs serving children from birth through age 8* (rev. ed.). Washington, DC: National Association for the Education of Young Children.

Bredekamp, S., & T. Rosegrant. (eds.). (1992). *Reaching potentials: Appropriate curriculum and assessment for young children* (Vol. 1). Washington, DC: National Association for the Education of Young Children.

———. (eds.). (1995). *Reaching potentials: Transforming early childhood curriculum and assessment* (Vol. 2). Washington, DC: National Association for the Education of Young Children.

Brian, J., & M. Martin. (1986). *Child care and health for nursery nurses.* Chester Springs, PA: Dufour.

Bronfenbrenner, U. (1979). *The ecology of human development: Experiments by nature and design.* Cambridge, MA: Harvard University Press.

Brown, J.L. (1995). *Observing dimensions of learning in classrooms and schools.* Alexandria, VA: Association for Supervision and Curriculum Development.

Brown, Richard. (1998). The teacher as contemplative observer. *Educational Leadership,* December/January.

Bruner, J.S. (1966). *Toward a theory of instruction.* Cambridge, MA: Harvard University Press.

Burke, K. (1994). *How to assess authentic learning.* Palatine, IL: IRI/Skylight Training.

Burke, K., R. Fogarty, & S. Belgrad. (1994). *The mindful school: The portfolio connection.* Arlington Heights, IL: IRI/Skylight Training.

Bushweller, K. (1995). The high-tech portfolio. *The Executive Educator* 17(1), 19–22.

Caldwell, B.M., & R.H. Bradley. (1984). *Home observation for measurement of the environment.* Little Rock, AR: University of Arkansas Press.

Campbell, S.D. (1987). *Quality control: A manual for self-evaluation of a day care agency.* Ottawa: Health and Welfare Canada.

Canadian Centre for Knowledge Mobilisation. (2008). Measures of children's development. Retrieved on November 3, 2008 from **www.cckm.ca**.

Canadian Child Care Federation. (1995). *Towards excellence in ECCE training programs: A self-assessment guide*. Ottawa: Canadian Child Care Federation.

Canadian Day Care Advocacy Association. (1992). *Caregiver behaviours and program characteristics associated with quality care*. Ottawa: Canadian Day Care Advocacy Association.

Canadian Institute of Child Health. (2000). *The health of Canada's children: A CICH profile* (3rd ed.). Ottawa.

Canadian Paediatric Society. (1992). *Well beings: A guide to promote the physical health, safety and emotional well-being of children in child care centres and family day care homes*. Ottawa: Canadian Paediatric Society.

Carney, S. (2007). Pre-reading skills for toddlers. Retrieved on January 23, 2009 at **parentingmethods. suite101. com/article.cfm/raising_a_reader**

Children's Environments Research Group (2006). Retrieved on January 18, 2009 at **http://web.gc.cuny.edu/ che/cerg.**

Catron, C.E., & J. Allen. (eds.). (1993). *Early childhood curriculum*. New York: Merrill Publishing.

Centennial College Early Childhood Education Programs and Child Care Centres. (1998). *Philosophy check-in*. Toronto: Centennial College.

Center for Effective Collaboration and Practice. *Functional Behavioral Assessment*. CECP "mini-web" at **cecp.air.org/fba/default.asp**.

Chandler, K. (2003). *Administering for quality*. Toronto: Pearson Education Canada.

Chard, S. C. (1998). *The project approach: Making curriculum come alive*. New York: Scholastic.

————. (1999, Spring). From themes to projects. *Early Childhood Research & Practice* 1 (1), **ecrp.uiuc. edu/v1n1/chard.html**.

————. (2001). *The project approach: Taking a closer look* [CD]. Prospect CDs, ISBN 0-9732165-0-6.

————. (2005). Definition. The Project Approach, accessed October 8, 2005, at **www.project-approach .com/definition.htm**.

Chess, S., & A. Thomas. (1996). *Temperament: Theory and practice*. New York: Brunner/Mazel.

Child at the centre: Self-evaluation in the early years. (2007). HM Inspectorate of Education for Scotland: Livingston, Scotland.

Choate, J.S., et al. (1995). *Curriculum-based assessment and programming* (3rd ed.). Needham Heights, MA: Allyn & Bacon.

Chomsky, N. (1979). *Language and responsibility*. New York: Knopf.

Chud, G., & R. Fahlman. (1985). *Early childhood education for a multicultural society*. Vancouver, BC: Western Education Development Group.

Clemmons, J., D. Cooper, & L. Lasse. (1996). *Portfolios in the classroom*. Jefferson City, MO: Scholastic.

Cleveland, G., & M. Krashinsky. (1998). *The benefits and costs of good child care: The economic rationale for public investment in young children*. Toronto: Childcare Resource and Research Unit, University of Toronto.

Cohen, D., & V. Stern. (1978). *Observing and recording the behavior of young children*. New York: Teachers College Press.

Consumer Reports: Electronics Buying Guide, Fall 2008

Creswell, J.W. (1998). *Qualitative inquiry and research design: Choosing among five traditions*. Thousand Oaks, CA: Sage.

Curtis, A. (2000). *Indicators of quality in early childhood education and care programmes*. Speech by World President, OMEP, **www.worldbank. org/children/nino/basico/ Curtis.htm**.

Department of Health, Great Britain. (1988). *Protecting children: A guide for social workers undertaking a comprehensive assessment*. London: Her Majesty's Stationery Office.

Department of Justice Canada (2003). Family violence: Child abuse fact sheet. Department of Justice site, accessed October 9, 2005 at **http:// canada.justice.gc.ca/en/ps/ fm/childafs.html**.

Dewey, J. (1963; orig. ed. 1938). *Education and experience*. New York: Collier.

Dodge, D.T., C. Heroman, & L.J. Colker. (2001). *The Creative Curriculum® Developmental Continuum Assessment Toolkit for Ages 3–5*. Washington, DC: Teaching Strategies.

Doherty-Derkowski, G. (1994). *Quality matters: Excellence in early childhood programs*. Don Mills, ON: Addison-Wesley.

Driscoll, A., K. Peterson, M., Browning, & D. Stevens. (1990). Teacher evaluation in early childhood education: What information can young children provide? *Child Study Journal* 20(2), 67–79.

Dudiy, S. (2005). Management Fortress Newsletter, retrieved on January 17, 2009 from **www. time-management-guide.com.**

Durkheim, E. (1982). *The rules of sociological method, and selected texts on sociology and its method*. Ed. S. Lukes, trans. W.D. Halls. New York: Free Press.

Early Childhood Resource Teacher Network. (2008). Checklist for quality inclusive education. Retrieved on November 6, 2008 from **www.ecrtno.ca**.

Early Childhood Resource Teachers Network Ontario. (1997). Checklist for quality inclusive education: A self-assessment tool and manual for early childhood settings. Barrie, ON: ECRTNO.

Edwards, S., D. Buckland, & M. McCoy-Powlen. (2002). *Developmental and functional hand grasps*. Thorofare, NJ: Slack Books.

Elkind, D. (1988). *The hurried child: growing up too fast too soon* (rev.). Reading, MA: Addison-Wesley.

————. (1994). *A sympathetic understanding of the child: Birth to sixteen* (3rd ed.). Boston: Allyn & Bacon.

Elliott, B. (1995). *Measure of success*. Toronto: Association for Early Childhood Educators.

Ely, M., et al. (1991). *Doing qualitative research: Circles within circles*. London: Falmer Press.

Engel, B.S. (1990). *An approach to assessment in early literacy*. In C. Kamii (ed.), *Achievement testing in the early grades: The games grown-ups play*. Washington, DC: National Association for the Education of Young Children.

Epstein, A. et al. (2004). Preschool assessment: A guide to developing a balanced approach. *NIEER Preschool Policy Matters*, Issue 7.

Erikson, E.H. (1963). *Childhood and society* (2nd ed.). New York: Norton.

————. (1994). *Identity and the life cycle*. New York: Norton.

Esterl, M. (2008). German tots learn to answer call of nature. *Wall Street Journal*, April 14, 2008; retrieved on September 15, 2008 at **http:// online.wsj.com**.

Fairtest. How Standardized Testing Damages Education. Retrieved on January 17, 2009 at **www.fairtest.org.**

Farr, R., & B. Tone. (1994). *Portfolio and performance assessment: Helping students evaluate their progress as readers and writers.* Fort Worth, TX: Harcourt Brace.

Ford, L., C. Merkel, & M. Kozey. (2005). A primer of tools commonly used in the cognitive and academic assessment skills of young children. UBC Assessing School Readiness Conference, May 26, 2005.

Fox, H. (2004). Involving parents in using the infant/toddler COR. *High/Scope ReSource* 23(7), 14.

Franklin, J. (2002, Spring). Assessing assessment: Are alternative methods making the grade? *ASCD Curriculum Update.*

Freeman, N., & M. Brown. (2008). An authentic approach to assessing pre-kindergarten programs. *Childhood Education* 85(5), 267–273.

Friendly, M. (1994). *Child care policy in Canada: Putting the pieces together.* Don Mills, ON: Addison-Wesley.

———. (2001). Social inclusion through early childhood and care. Conference presentation—A new way of thinking: Towards a vision of social inclusion. November 2001, Ottawa, ON.

Frisk, V., & E. Boychyn. (2008). Screening Canadian preschoolers for language weaknesses is more difficult than it seems. Presented at the Early Years Conference 2008, Vancouver, BC.

Froebel, F. (1974; orig. ed. 1826). *The education of man.* Clifton, NJ: A.M. Kelley.

Gardner, H. (1993). *Multiple intelligences: The theory in practice.* New York: Basic Books.

Gardner, H., et al. (2001). *Making learning visible: Children as individual and group learners.* Reggio Children/USA.

Garmezy, N., & M. Rutter (eds.). (1983). *Stress, coping and development in children.* New York: McGraw-Hill.

Garrett-Petts, W. (2008). The Project Approach, Historical Fairs, and documentation as visible listening. Retrieved on October 10, 2008 from **www.heritagefair.sd73. bc.ca.**

Gesell, A. (1940). The first five years of life. New York: Harper.

Glaser, R. (1963). Instructional technology and the measurement of learning outcomes: Some questions. *American Psychologist* 18, 519–21.

Gerber, M. (2003). *Dear parent: Caring for infants with respect* (2nd ed.). Los Angeles: Resources for Infant Educarers.

Goleman, D. (2006). Social intelligence: The new science of social relationships. New York, Bantam Books.

Goelman, H., et al. (2000). *You bet I care! Caring and learning environments: Quality in child care centres across Canada.* Guelph, ON: Centre for Families, Work and Well-Being, University of Guelph.

Goleman, D. (1997). *Emotional intelligence.* New York: Bantam.

Gonzalez-Mena, Janet. (1986, November). Toddlers: What to expect. *Young children.* Washington, DC: NAEYC.

Goodrich, H. (1996/97). Understanding rubrics. *Educational Leadership* 54(4), 14–17.

Goodwin, W.L., & L.A. Driscoll. (1980). *Handbook for measurement and evaluation in early childhood education.* San Francisco: Jossey-Bass.

Grant, J.M., B. Heffler, & K. Mereweather. (1995). *Student-led conferences: Using portfolios to share learning with parents.* Markham, ON: Pembroke Publishers.

Greenspan, S. (1995). *The challenging child: Understanding, raising and enjoying the five "difficult" types of children.* Reading, MA: Perseus Books.

Greenspan, S.I., & N.T. Greenspan. (1985). *First feelings: Milestones in the emotional development of your baby and child.* New York: Viking.

———. (1985). *First feelings: Milestones in the emotional development of your baby and child from birth to age 4.* New York: Viking.

Greenspan, S. & Wieder, S. (2005). Infant and early childhood mental health. Arlington, VA: American Psychiatric Publishing.

Hall, G.S. (1891). The contents of children's minds on entering school. *Pedagogical Seminary* 1, 139–173.

Harms, T., & R.M. Clifford. (1989). *Family day care rating scale.* New York: Teachers College Press.

———. (1998). *Early childhood environment rating scale.* New York: Teachers College Press.

Harms, T., D. Cryer, & R.M. Clifford. (1990). *Infant/toddler environment*

rating scale. New York: Teachers College Press.

Harrington, H.L., et al. (1997). *Observing, documenting, and assessing learning: The Work Sampling System for teacher educators.* Ann Arbor, MI: Rebus.

Harris, T. (1969). *I'm OK – you're OK.* New York, NY: HarperCollins.

Harrow, A.J. (1972). *A taxonomy of the psychomotor domain: A guide for developing behavioral objectives.* New York: D. McKay.

Havard, L.A. (1995). *Outcome based education through the school system.* New York: Norton.

Health and Welfare Canada. (1980). *Children with special needs in daycare.* Ottawa: Health and Welfare Canada.

Hedgecoe, J. (1992). *Complete guide to video: The ultimate manual of video techniques and equipment.* Toronto: Stoddart.

Herman, J.L., et al. (1992). *A practical guide to alternative assessment.* Alexandria, VA: Association for Supervision and Curriculum Development.

Hews, J., C. Massing, & L. Singh. (1995). *Many ways to grow: Responding to cultural diversity in early childhood settings.* Edmonton, AB: Alberta Association for Young Children.

Hills, T.W. (1992). *Reaching potentials through appropriate assessment.* In Bredekamp & Rosegrant 1992, pp. 43–63.

Hlady, J. (2004). Child neglect: Evaluation and management. *BC Medical Journal* 46(2), 77–81.

Hobart, C. & J. Frankel. (2004). *A practical guide to child observation and assessment* (3rd ed.). Cheltenham: Nelson Thornes.

Hornby, G. (1977). *Photographing baby and child.* New York: Crown Publishers.

Howard, C. (1992). The five laws of unconditional human worth. Retrieved on January 23, 2009 at **www.heartbeatvancouver.ca.**

Hughes, F.P. (1999). *Children, play and development* (3rd ed.). Boston, MA: Allyn & Bacon.

Illingworth, R.S. (1990). *Basic developmental screening, 0–5 years* (5th ed.). Oxford: Blackwell Scientific Publications.

Imus, D. (2007). *Growing up green: Baby and child care,* vol. 2. New York, NY: Simon & Schuster.

Institute for Early Childhood Education & Research. (2008). Research in Reggio Emilia. *Research into Practice*, vol. 4. Retrieved September 15, 2008 from **www.earlychildhood.educ.ubc.ca**.

Ioannou-Georgiou, S. & Pavlou, P. (2003). *Assessing young learners: Directed reading and thinking activities for second language students.* New York, NY: Oxford University Press.

Ireton, H. (1995). *Teacher's observation guide.* Minneapolis, MN: Behavioral Science Systems.

———. (1997). *Assessment: Appreciating children's development using parents' and teachers' observations.* Earlychildhood NEWS. Retrieved on January 23, 2009 at **www.earlychildhoodnews.com/ earlychildhood/article_view.aspx ?ArticleID=10.**

Irwin, D.M., & M.M. Bushnell. (1980). *Observational strategies for child study.* New York: Holt, Rinehart, and Winston.

Irwin, S.H. (ed.). (1999). *Challenging the challenging behaviours: A sourcebook based on the SpeciaLink Institute on Challenging Behaviours in Child Care.* Wreck Cove, NS: Breton Books.

———. (2005). *Inclusion voices: Canadian child care directors talk about including children with special needs.* Wreck Cove, NS: Breton Books.

Irwin, S., D. Lero, & K. Brophy. (2004). *Inclusion: The next generation in child care in Canada.* Wreck Cove, NS: Breton Books.

Isbell, R., & B. Exelby. (2001). *Early learning environments that work.* Beltsville, MD: Gryphon House.

Jablon, J., et al. (1994a). *Work Sampling System omnibus guidelines: Kindergarten through fifth grade* (Vol. 2, 3rd ed.). Ann Arbor, MI: Rebus.

———. (1994b). *Work Sampling System omnibus guidelines: Preschool through third grade* (Vol. 1, 3rd ed.). Ann Arbor, MI: Rebus.

Jackson, W. (1988). *Research methods: Rules for survey design and analysis.* Toronto, ON: Prentice-Hall.

Kaiser, B., & J.S. Rasminsky. (1999). *Meeting the challenge: Effective strategies for challenging behaviours in early childhood environments.* Ottawa, ON: Canadian Child Care Federation.

Kankaanranta, M. (2002). *Developing digital portfolios for childhood education.* Jyväskylä, Finland: University of Jyväskylä Institute for Educational Research.

———. (1989). *Engaging children's minds.* Norwood, NJ: Ablex Publishing.

Katz, L.G. (1993a). *Five perspectives on quality in early childhood programs.* CEEP, archive of ERIC/EECE, Digests, at **http://ceep.crc.uiuc.edu/ eecearchive /books/fivepers.html**.

———. (1993b). *Multiple perspectives on the quality of early childhood programs.* CEEP, archive of ERIC/EECE Digests, **http://ceep.crc.uiuc.edu/ eecearchive/digests/1993/ lk-mul93.html**.

Katz, L.G., & B. Cesarone (eds). (1994). *Reflections on the Reggio Emilia approach.* Urbana, IL: ERIC/EECE.

Katz, L.G., & S.C. Chard. (1996). *The contribution of documentation to the quality of early childhood education.* CEEP, archive of ERIC/EECE Digests at **http://ceep.crc.uiuc.edu/ eecearchive/digests/1996/ lkchar96.html**.

Keith, E. & Montgomery, L. (2008). A distance model of consultation and supervision by a psychologist for screening and assessment in early years programs. Presented at the Early Years Conference 2008, Vancouver, BC.

King, J.A., & K.M. Evans. (1991, October). Can we achieve outcome-based education? *Educational Leadership*, 49(2), 73–75.

Klaus, M.H., J.H. Kennell, & P.H. Klaus (1995). *Bonding: Building the foundations of secure attachment and independence.* Reading, MA: Addison-Wesley.

Kohn, A. (2000a). *Beyond the standards movement: Defending quality education in an age of test scores.* National Professional Resources (Video; ISBN 1-887943-43-9).

———. (2000b). The deadly effects of tougher standards. *Harvard Education Letter*, March/April.

Krathwohl, M.B. (1964). *Taxonomy of educational objectives: The classification of educational goals. Handbook 2: The affective domain.* New York: McKay.

Kraus, K. (1909). *Die Fackel*, no. 288 (Vienna, October 11, 1909). Quoted in T. Szasz. (1976). *Anti-Freud: Karl Kraus's criticism of psychoanalysis and psychiatry*, ch. 8. New York: Syracuse University Press.

Krishnamurti, J. (1981). *Education and the significance of life.* San Francisco: Harper & Row.

Langford, R. (1997). *Checklist for quality inclusive education: A

self-assessment tool and manual for early childhood settings.* Barrie, ON: Early Childhood Resource Teacher Network of Ontario.

Leavitt, R.L., & B.K. Eheart. (1991, July). Assessment in early childhood programs. *Young Children*, 46(5), 4–9.

Lewington, J., & G. Orpwood. (1993). *Overdue assignment: Taking responsibility for Canada's schools.* Toronto: John Wiley.

Lewis, R. (1993). *Learn to make videos in a weekend.* New York: Alfred A. Knopf.

Lezotte, L.W. (1991). *Correlates of effective schools: The first and second generation.* Okemos, MI: Effective School Products Ltd.

Linder, T.W. (1990). *Transdisciplinary play-based assessment: A functional approach to working with young children.* Baltimore, MD: P.H. Brookes.

Locke, J. (1989; orig. ed. 1963). *Some thoughts concerning education.* New York: Oxford University Press.

Lorenz, K. (1937). Imprinting. *The Auk* 54, 245–73.

McCain, M.N., & J.F. Mustard. (1999). *Early years study: Reversing the real brain drain. Final report.* Toronto: Canadian Institute for Advanced Research.

McCain, M., J.F. Mustard, & S. Shanker. (2007). *Early Years Study 2: Putting science into action.* Toronto: Council for Early Child Development.

McCormick, K., et al. (2008). Using eco-mapping to understand family strengths and resources. *Young Exceptional Children* 11(2), 17–28.

McCormick, K. et al. (2008). Using Eco-Mapping to Understand Family Strengths and Resources. *Young Exceptional Children*, Vol. 11, No. 2, 17–28 (2008).

McCullough, V.E. (1992). *Testing and your child: What you should know about 150 of the most common educational and psychological tests.* New York: Plume.

McGoldrick, M., & R. Gerson. (1985). *Genograms in family assessment.* New York: Norton.

Mager, R.F. (1962). *Preparing instructional objectives.* Belmont, CA: Lake Publishing.

Malaguzzi, L. (1993). History, ideas, and basic philosophy. In C. Edwards, L. Gandini, and G. Forman, *The hundred languages of children: The Reggio Emilia approach to early childhood education.* Norwood, NJ: Ablex.

Martin, S. (1988). Your child study: A new approach. *Nursery World*.

———. (1996). DAE-DAP: Making sensitive assessments of infants and toddlers. *Interaction*, Spring. Also available at **www.cfc-efc.ca/docs/ cccf/ 00000083.htm.**

———. (2003). *See how they grow: Infants and toddlers*. Toronto: Thomson Nelson.

Martin, S., & P. Corson. (1995). *Learning to look* [14 videos and workbook]. Toronto: TVO.

———. (2007). *Intentional and rela-tionship-based guidance*. Toronto, ON: Thomson Nelson.

Meisels, S.J. (1992). *Early screening inventory revised*. Ann Arbor, MI: Rebus.

———. (1993). Remaking classroom assessment with the Work Sampling System. *Young Children*.

Meisels, S., et al. (1996–97). Using work sampling in authentic assess-ments. *Educational Leadership* 54(4).

———. (1998a). Rebus Inc. Pearson Early Learning site, accessed October 9, 2005, at **www.pearsone-arlylearning.com/index2.html**.

———. (1998b). *The work sampling system*. Toronto: Pearson Early Learning.

———. (2002). *Performance assessment*. Teacher Resource Center, Scholastic Inc., at **teacher.scholastic.com/ professional/assessment/ perfassess.htm**.

Meisels, S.J., & D. Steele. (1991). *The early childhood portfolio collection process*. Ann Arbor, MI: Center for Human Growth and Development, University of Michigan.

Mindes, G., H. Ireton, & C. Mardell-Czudnowski. (1996). *Assessing young children*. Albany, NY: Delmar.

Mitra, Hodges and *Learning Together Every Step of the Way*. Retrieved on January 19, 2009 from **www.connectability.ca**.

Monaghan, P. (1998). I'm Worried About this Child: Referring Young Children with Developmental Difficulties to Special Services. Connections, vol. 2.2 Retrieved on January 23, 2009 at **www.cccns. org/pdf/journal_nov98.pdf**.

Montessori, M. (1963; orig. ed. 1913). *Montessori training course*. Ann Arbor, MI: Ann Arbor Press.

Moreno, J. (1934). Who shall sur-vive? Washington, DC: Nervous & Mental Disorders Publishing Co.

Moreno, J. (1960). The sociometry reader. Glencoe, IL: The Free Press.

Morris, D. (1995). *Illustrated baby-watching*. London: Ebury Press.

Morrow, F. (2008). The ABC's of building a green school. *Globe & Mail*, May 2, 2008.

National Association of School Psychologists (2002). Retrieved on January 18, 2009 at **www. nasponline.org**.

National Association for the Education of Young Children. (1988). *Healthy young children: A manual for programs*. Washington, DC: National Association for the Education of Young Children.

National Council on the Developing Child (2004). Retrieved on January 18, 2009 at **www.developingchild.net**.

National Science Teachers Association 2003, NSTA Position Statement. (2003). Retrieved on January 17, 2009 from **www.nsta.org**.

Newborg, J. (2004). *Battelle develop-mental inventory. (2nd Ed.)*. Toronto: Nelson.

Neill, P. (2004). A better way to do preschool assessment: Announcing the revised preschool COR. *High/ Scope ReSource* 23(1). Retrieved on January 23, 2009 at **www.highscope .org/file/Newsandinformation/ ReSource/Reprints/CORarticle.pdf**.

NICHD Early Child Care Research Network. (2005). *Child care and child development: Results from the NICHD study of early child care and youth development*. New York: Guilford Press.

Nicolson, S., & S.G. Shipstead. (1998). *Through the looking glass: Observations in the early childhood classroom* (2nd ed.). Upper Saddle River, NJ: Prentice Hall.

Niguidula, D. (1997). Picturing per-formance with digital portfolios. *Educational Leadership* 55(3).

Nipissing District Developmental Screen. (2007). Retrieved on November 3, 2008 from **www.ndds.ca**.

North Central Regional Educational Laboratory 2006, retrieved on January 18, 2008 at **www.ncrel.org**.

North Central Regional Educational Laboratory 2008 retrieved on January 18, 2008 at **www.ncrel.org**.

North York Board of Education. (1992). *Beginnings: The early years*. North York, ON.

Nova Scotia NDP Caucus. (2001). *Public education: Limitations and successes of the past, visions for the future*. Halifax, NS: Nova Scotia NDP Caucus, at **www.ndpcaucus.ns.ca**.

NSTA Position Statement. (2003). Retrieved on January 17, 2009 from **www.nsta.org parentingmethods. suite101.com/article.cfm/raising_ a_reader**.

O'Neil, J. (1995). Future of OBE is up in the air. *Education Update* 37.

Ontario. (2001). *Report to Ontario's taxpayers, fall 2001*. Toronto.

Ontario Day Nurseries Act, RSO 1990.

Ontario Ministry of Education and Training. (1998). *The arts: The Ontario curriculum, grades 1–8*. Toronto: Publications Ontario.

Ontario Secondary School Teachers Federation. (2001). *What makes a good school?* AMPA 2001 House Paper, at **www.osstf.on.ca/www/ abosstf/ampa01/goodschools/ whatmakesgoodschool.html**.

PACER Center. (1994). *What is a functional assessment?* Parent Advocacy Coalition for Educational Rights, at **www.pacer.org/ parent/function.htm**.

Parten, M.B. (1932–33). Social partic-ipation among pre-school children. *Journal of Abnormal and Social Psychology*, 27, 243–269.

Pastor, E., & E. Kerns. (1997). A digital snapshot of an early childhood class-room. *Educational Leadership* 55(3).

Pavlov, I. (1927). *Conditioned Reflexes: An Investigation of the Physiological Activity of the Cerebral Cortex*. Translated and Edited by G. V. Anrep. London: Oxford University Press.

Perrone, V. (1991). *ACEI Position Paper on Standardized Testing: A position paper of the Association for Childhood Education International*. Olney, MD: ACEI. Retrieved on November 3, 2008 from **www.acei.org**.

Peset, J. & Gracia, D. (eds). (1992). *The ethics of diagnosis*. Norwell, MA: Springer-Verlag.

Pestalozzi, J.H. (1894). *How Gertrude teaches her children*. (L.E. Holland & F.C. Turner, trs.). London: Swan Sonnenschein.

———. (1906). *A father's diary*. New York: Appleton.

Phillips, D.A. (ed). (1991). *Quality in child care: What does research tell us?* Washington, DC: National Association for the Education of Young Children.

Piaget, J. (1929). *The child's concep-tion of the world*. (J. & A. Tomlinson, trs.). New York: Harcourt Brace.

———. (1954). *The child's construc-tion of reality*. (M. Cook, tr.). London: Routledge & Kegan Paul.

———. (1976). *The language and thought of the child* (3rd ed.). London: Routledge.

Picciotto, L.P. (1996). *Student-led parent conferences*. New York: Scholastic Professional.

Pierangelo, R., & G. Giuliani. (2006). *The special educator's comprehensive guide to 301 diagnostic tests*. San Francisco, CA: Jossey-Bass.

Pimento, B., & D. Kernested. (1996). *Healthy foundations in child care*. Toronto: Nelson.

———. (2004). *Healthy foundations in early childhood settings* (3rd. ed.). Toronto: Thomson Nelson.

Pinder, R. (1987, September). Not so modern methods. *Nursery World*.

Popham, W.J. (1998). *Classroom assessment: What teachers need to know* (2nd ed.). Boston, MA: Allyn & Bacon.

———. (2001). *The truth about testing: An educator's call to action*. Alexandria, VA: Association for Supervision and Curriculum Development.

———. (2008a). How to play the appraisal game. *Educational Leadership* 65(4), 88–89.

———. (2008b). *Transformative assessment*. Alexandria, VA: Association for Supervision and Curriculum Development.

Popular Photography, July 2008.

Preyer, W. (1973; orig. ed. 1888). *Mind of the child*. New York: Arno Press.

Puckett, M.B. (1994). *Authentic assessment of the young child: Celebrating development and learning*. New York: Macmillan.

Purcell, J.H., & J.S. Renzulli. (1998). *Total talent portfolio: A systematic plan to identify and nurture gifts and talents*. Mansfield, CT: Creative Learning Press Inc.

Purkey, W.W. (1999). *Creating safe schools through invitational education*. ERIC Clearinghouse and at **www.ericdigests.org/2000-3/safe.htm**.

Put Children First (2004). Referred to in Toronto Regional Plan: Children & Youth Mental Health Fund, retrieved on January 17, 2009 at **www.ontchild.ca.**

Quilliam, S. (1994). *Child watching: A parent's guide to children's body language*. London: Ward Lock.

Radler, D. (2001). Quoted in Unisci.com, retrieved January 19, 2009 at **www.unisci.com.**

Rathvon, N. (2004). Early reading assessment: A practitioner's handbook. New York: Guilford Press.

Rimer, P., & B. Prager. (1998). *Reaching out: Working together to identify child victims of abuse*. Toronto: ITP Nelson.

Robertson, J., & J. Robertson. (1967–71). *Young children in brief separation* (videocassette series). London: Tavistock Institute of Human Relations.

Rose, V. (1985, November). Detecting problems with growth development charts. *Nursery World*.

Rothchild, I. (2007). Induction, deduction, and the scientific method: An eclectic overview of the practice of science. Retrieved on January 19, 2009 at **www.ssr.org.**

Rourke, L., D. Leduc, & J. Rourke. (2001). Rourke Baby Record 2000. *Canadian Family Physician* 47, 333–334.

Sacks, P. (2000). *Standardized minds: The high price of America's testing culture and what we can do to change it*. Cambridge, MA: Perseus Books.

Sapon-Shevin, M. (2008). Learning in an inclusive community. *Educational Leadership* 66, 49–53.

Sax, G. (1997). *Principles of educational and psychological measurement and evaluation* (4th ed.). Belmont, CA: Wadsworth.

Schermann, Ada. (1990). Learning. In I. Doxey (ed.), *Child care and education: Canadian dimensions*. Scarborough, ON: Nelson.

Schlank, C.H., & B. Metzger. (1989). *A room full of children: How to observe and evaluate a preschool program*. New York: Rochester Association for Young Children.

Schwartz, S. & G. Chance. (1999). Why focus on children? Environmental contaminants and the special susceptibility of children. In *Research Connections Canada 2: Supporting children and families*. Ottawa: Canadian Child Care Federation.

Search Institute. (2007). Why are the 40 developmental assets important? Retrieved October 7, 2007 from **www.search-institute.org**.

Search Institute (2008). Retrieved on January 18, 2009 at **www.search-institute.org.**

Shea, M. (2000). Taking running records. Toronto: Scholastic.

Shepard, L.A. (1994). The challenges of assessing young children appropriately. *Phi Delta Kappan* 76(3), 206–12.

Sheridan, M. (1992). Spontaneous play in early childhood. London: Spon Press.

Sheridan, M.D. (1975). *The developmental progress of infants and young children* (3rd ed.). London: Her Majesty's Stationery Office.

———. (rev. and updated by M. Frost & A. Sharma). (1997). *From birth to five years: Children's developmental progress*. London: Routledge.

Shinn, M.W. (1975; orig. ed. 1900). *The biography of a baby*. New York: Arno Press.

Shipley, D. (1994). Learning outcomes: Another bandwagon or a strategic instrument of reform? *Educational Strategies* 1(4), 3.

———. (1997, Spring). Play—for development and for achieving learning outcomes. *Interaction*. Ottawa: Canadian Child Care Federation.

Shore, R. (1997). *Rethinking the brain: New insights into early development*. New York: Families and Work Institute.

Siddiqi, A., Irwin, L. & C. Hertzman. (2007). *Total environment assessment model for early child development*. Geneva: World Health Organization.

Simpson, E. (1972). *The classification of educational objectives in the psychomotor domain*. Washington, DC: Prentice Hall.

Solley, Bobbie. (2007). On Standardized Testing: An ACEI Position Paper. *Childhood Education*, Fall, 31–37.

Southern Early Childhood Association. (n.d.) *Early childhood assessment* (special series of reprints from *Dimensions of Early Childhood*). Little Rock, AR: SECA.

Spady, W. (1977). Competency-based education: A bandwagon in search of a definition. *Educational Researcher* 6 (1), 9–14.

Spitz, R.A. (1965). *The first year of life: A psychoanalytic study of normal and deviant development of object relations*. New York: International Universities Press.

Standardized Testing of Young Children: 3 Through 8 Years of Age (1987). National Association for the Education of Young Children: retrieved on November 3, 2008 from **www.naeyc.org/resources/position_statements/pstest98.pdf**.

Steiner, R. (1982; orig. ed. 1924). *The roots of education*. London: Rudolf Steiner Press.

Steinhauer, P.D. (1996). *The primary needs of children: A blueprint for effective health promotion at the community level*. Working paper for the Promotion/Prevention Task Force, Sparrow Lake Alliance, Toronto.

Sternberg, R. (2008). Assessing what matters. *Educational Leadership* 65(4), 20–26.

Sunseri, R. (1994). *Outcome-based education: Understanding the truth about education reform*. Sisters, OR: Multnomah Books.

Tindal, G.A., & D.B. Marston. (1990). *Classroom-based assessment: evaluating instructional outcomes*. Columbus, OH: Merrill Publishing.

Toronto Observation Project. (1980). *Observing children through their formative years*. Toronto: Board of Education for the City of Toronto.

Trocmé, N., et al. (2005). *Canadian incidence study of reported child abuse and neglect 2003*. Ottawa, ON: National Clearinghouse on Family Violence.

Trocme, N., B. MacLaurin, et al. (2000). *Canadian incidence study of reported child abuse and neglect*. Ottawa: Public Health Agency of Canada.

Tufte, E. (2001). *The visual display of quantitative information* (2nd ed.). Cheshire, CT: Graphics Press.

Tyler, L.E. (1965). *The psychology of human differences* (3rd ed.). New York: Appleton-Century-Crofts.

Ungar, Michael. (2005, August). Delinquent or simply resilient? How "problem" behaviour can be a child's hidden path to resilience. Voices for Children at **www.voicesforchildren. ca/report-Aug2005-1.htm#four**.

UNICEF. (2002, May). Special Session on Children. UNICEF site, accessed October 9, 2005 at **www.unicef.org/specialsession/acti vities/education-qual-report.htm**.

Vallavik, M. et al. (2006). *Observation: A focus on evaluation, planning and growth for the kinder-garten learner*. Toronto: Elementary Teachers' Federation of Ontario.

Van Manen, M. (1990). *Researching lived experience: Human science for an action sensitive pedagogy*. London, ON: Althouse Press.

Vista School District. (2002). Critical Assessment Worksheet. Vista School District, Newfoundland & Labrador, at **www.k12.nf.ca/ vista/ schooldevelopment/ internalcriteriaas.html**.

Von Baeyer, C., S. Baskerville, & P. McGrath. (1998). Everyday pain in three- to five-year-old children in day care. *Pain Research & Management* 3(2), 111–116.

Vygotsky, L.S. (1978). *Mind in society: The development of psychological processes*. Cambridge, MA: Harvard University Press.

———. (1986). *Thought and language* (revised edition). Cambridge, MA: MIT Press.

Waterloo County Board of Education. (1993). *Invitations to literacy learning*. Waterloo, ON.

Watson, J.B. (1930). *Behaviorism*. Chicago: University of Chicago Press.

Weitzman, E. (1992). *Learning language and loving it: A guide to promoting children's social and language development in early childhood settings*. Toronto: Hanen Centre.

Whitbread, N. (1972). *The evolution of the nursery-infant school: A history of infant and nursery education in Britain, 1800–1970*. London: Routledge & Kegan Paul.

Wiggins, G. (1996/97). Practice what we preach in designing authentic assessments. *Educational Leadership* 54(4), 18–25.

Williamson, P., et al. (2005, Summer). Meeting the challenge of high stakes testing while remaining child-centred. *Childhood education* 81(4), 190–95.

Wilson, L.C., L. Douville-Watson, & M.A. Watson. (1995). *Infants and toddlers: Curriculum and teaching* (3rd ed.). Albany, NY: Delmar.

Wolcott, H.F. (1990). *Writing up qualitative research*. Newbury Park, CA: Sage.

———. (1995). *The art of fieldwork*. Walnut Creek, CA: Sage.

Wortham, S.C. (1992). *Childhood, 1892–1992*. Wheaton, MD: Association for Childhood Education International.

Wotherspoon, E., & J. Pirie. (1996). *The integrated classroom: The assessment–curriculum link in early childhood education*. Englewood Cliffs, NJ: Merrill Publishing.

———. (2008). Infant mental health and family law: Questions every lawyer should ask about infants in child protection hearings. Presented at the Early Years Conference 2008, Vancouver, BC.

———, A. Barbour, & B. Desjean-Perrotta. (1998). *Portfolio assessment: A handbook for preschool and elementary educators*. Olney, MD: Association for Childhood Education International.

YMCA. (Susanne T. Eden and Lorrie Huggins). (2001). *YMCA Playing to Learn: A guide to quality care and education of young children: A YMCA guide to quality care and education of young children*. Toronto: YMCA of Greater Toronto.

Young children develop in an environment of relationships. (2004). *National Scientific Council on the Developing Child*, Working Paper No. 1.

Zitterkopf, R. (1994). A fundamental-ist's defense of OBE. *Educational Leadership* 51(6), 76–78.

Index

Credits

Canadian Childcare Federation; Carol H. Schlank and Barbara Metzger, *A Room Full of Children* (1989); Department of Health, Great Britain (HMSO). *Protecting Children: A Guide for Social Workers Undertaking Comprehensive Assessment* (p. 85); Janice Beaty, *Observing Development of the Young Child*, 4th ed. © 1994. Adapted by permission of Prentice-Hall, Inc., Upper Saddle River, NJ; K.E. Allen, C. Paasche, and A. Cornell, *Exceptional Children: Inclusion in Early Childhood Education*, 2nd ed. © 1998. Reprinted with permission of Nelson Thomson Learning: A division of Thomson Learning. Fax 800-730-2215; Laura E. Berk, *Infants, Children, and Adolescents*. Published by Allyn and Bacon, Boston, MA. © 1993 by Pearson Education. Reprinted by permission of the publisher; Monica McGoldrick and Randy Gerson, *Genograms in Family Assessment.* © 1985 by Monica McGoldrick and Randy Gerson. Used by permission of W.W. Norton & Company, Inc.; National Association for the Education of Young Children. Reprinted with permission; Thelma Hams and Richard M. Clifford, 1989; Urie Bronfenbrenner, *The Ecology of Human Development: Experiments by Nature and Design* (Cambridge, MA: Harvard University Press, 1979); YMCA of Greater Metropolitan Toronto, 2005; Early Childhood Resource Teacher Network of Ontario (*Checklist for Quality Inclusive Education: A Self-Assessment Tool and Manual for Early Childhood Settings,* 1997) Reprinted with permission.